Studies in Evangelicalism

Edited by Donald W. Dayton, Northern Baptist Theological Seminary, and Kenneth E. Rowe, Drew University Theological School

More Than Opium

*An Anthropological Approach
to Latin American and Caribbean
Pentecostal Praxis*

Edited by
Barbara Boudewijnse, André Droogers,
and Frans Kamsteeg

Studies in Evangelicalism, No. 14

The Scarecrow Press, Inc.
Lanham, Md., & London
1998

SCARECROW PRESS, INC.

Published in the United States of America
by Scarecrow Press, Inc.
4720 Boston Way
Lanham, Maryland 20706

4 Pleydell Gardens
Kent CT20 2DN, England

British Library Cataloguing in Publication Information Available

Library of Congress Cataloging-in-Publication Data

Algo más que opio. English
More than opium : an anthropological approach to Latin American and
Caribbean Pentecostal praxis / [edited by] Barbara Boudewijnse, André
Droogers, and Frans Kamsteeg.
p. cm. — (Studies in evangelicalism ; no. 14)
Rev., updated, and enl. translation of: Algo más que opio.
Includes bibliographical references and index.
ISBN 0-8108-3390-5 (hardcover : alk. paper)
1. Pentecostalism—Latin America. 2. Pentecostalism—Caribbean Area.
3. Latin America—Church history—20th century. 4. Caribbean Area—
Church history—20th century. I. Boudewijnse, Barbara. II. Droogers, A. F.
III. Kamsteeg, Frans. IV. Title. V. Series.
BR1644.5.L29A4413   1998   97-30704
278'.082—dc21   CIP

BR
1644.5
.L29
A4413
1998

⊖™ The paper used in this publication meets the minimum requirements of
American National Standard for Information Sciences—Permanence of
Paper for Printed Library Materials, ANSI Z39.48–1984.
Manufactured in the United States of America.

Contents

Editors' Introduction

This collection of articles is based on an earlier and similar book in Spanish, entitled *Algo más que opio; una lectura antropológica del pentecostalismo latinoamericano y caribeño*, which was published in 1991 by DEI in Costa Rica. As the title indicated, it was conceived as an anthropological contribution to the study of Pentecostalism in Latin America and the Caribbean. Almost all the chapters were based on anthropological, local-level fieldwork by Dutch anthropologists who have been working together since 1986 in the Pentecostalism Study Group at the Vrije Universiteit of Amsterdam. The book's aim was to go beyond an oversimplistic explanation of Pentecostal expansion, which it is why it was called *More Than Opium*.

Its publication was well received and the book has been acclaimed for its case studies. But this was not the only reason to publish an English version. In recent years, the region's Pentecostalism has continued to expand at an accelerated rate. Two influential and widely publicized macrostudies (Martin 1991 and Stoll 1991) stimulated interest in the issue.

The present edition is not just a translation of the Spanish collection. Five chapters were especially written for this edition, three chapters were revised, and only two were translated without modification. The bibliography was updated. Three of the new contributions were written by Latin American anthropologists. In view of the almost

proverbial and often puzzling variety of forms of Latin American and
Caribbean Pentecostalism, it seemed advisable to add case studies on
local groups and specific themes. They complement the more general—and often hypothetical—studies on the growth of the continent's
Pentecostalism. Our aim it is not so much to shed light on Pentecostalism as to illustrate the Pentecostals' praxis. The global trend of Pentecostal expansion—like all processes of globalization—should be studied in its local manifestations. Research was conducted in five different
countries.

This local focus does not mean the present collection fails to contribute to the theoretical debate. The first chapter discusses the paradoxical nature of Pentecostalism as well as the social science theoretical perspectives on Pentecostal expansion. Most of the other chapters,
while literally locating Pentecostalism, contain indirect theoretical
considerations of a more general nature, especially referring to the
idea that human beings, both the researched and the researcher, make
sense of their experiences. In other words, the contributions illustrate
the dialectics between actors–whether academic or ecclesial—and
structures—whether social or symbolic. The actor/structure dichotomy has haunted social science theoretical debate. Praxis theories
offer a convincing solution to this quandary.

In this sense, the Pentecostals' praxis is the prime focus of this
collection, and praxis theories, used in an eclectic manner, offer a
promising theoretical and heuristical framework. This group of theories indicates the importance of how people make sense of their experiences by referring to structures. They are either being influenced by
these structures or directly seek to change or replace them. Conversion is, of course, the most striking example of a structural change in
an actor's life, just as the rise of Pentecostalism was a dramatic transformation of ecclesial social and symbolic structures. Yet, the radical-
ness of the changes does not eliminate all continuity, as becomes clear
in more than one contribution to this book. A praxis approach makes
it clear how discontinuity and continuity are related.

Another possible application of praxis theories involves the
recurring tension between Pentecostal discourse and practice. But
praxis theories have other advantages. They invite scholars to reflect
upon their own role as constructors of knowledge. Moreover, with
dynamism as a focus, historical changes inevitably receive attention.

Power is an important aspect of this dynamism. Asymmetrical relations should be taken into account, especially in such a seemingly symmetrical and leveling religion as Pentecostalism, and because the societies it is part of have a distinct power constellation in the religious as well as the secular field. Praxis theories suggest contextual studies of everyday life and therefore advocate localized research.

In the editors' view, the eclectic perspective of most of the authors should be appreciated as a necessary tool in the study of such a rich field. Eclecticism suggests moreover that scholars have reflected upon their theoretical framework, and therefore bears witness to the double hermeneutic (Giddens 1984) of the researched and the researchers.

This approach has been applied to a series of themes. Not only does the expansion of Pentecostalism receive attention (Droogers, Hoekstra, Míguez, Slootweg, Willemier Westra), so do the gender dimension (Boudewijnse, De Theije, Kamsteeg, Mariz, Slootweg), the analysis of discourse and practice (Kamsteeg, Míguez in the most explicit manner, but a recurring theme in the whole collection), the power dimension, within Pentecostal groups (Kamsteeg), between Pentecostal and Charismatic groups (Boudewijnse), between Pentecostals and non-Pentecostal groups (De Theije, Willemier Westra), and between Pentecostals and society, the comparison with similar, competing groups (Machado, De Theije, Willemier Westra), the urban/rural comparison (Hoekstra), and the contribution to the resolution of social problems (Machado, Mariz).

The diversity of the contributions and the fact that they refer to more than one theme appear to suggest more than one way of organizing the book. The editors opted for the rather arbitrary solution of a geographical subdivision, starting with the Spanish-speaking countries Argentina, Chile, and Peru, continuing with the chapter on Curacao, and ending with the five on Brazil. Droogers' article on the paradoxical nature of phenomenon and theory opens the collection.

1

Paradoxical Views on a Paradoxical Religion

Models for the Explanation of Pentecostal Expansion in Brazil and Chile

André Droogers

The only way to an accurate view and confident knowledge of the world is through a sophisticated epistemology that takes full account of intractable contradiction, paradox, irony, and uncertainty in the explanation of human activities (Marcus and Fischer 1986, 14-15).

Introduction

Pentecostal churches and Charismatic movements, brought together here in the concept of Pentecostalism, are expanding spectacularly in various parts of the world, including Latin America and the Caribbean. Social scientists studying Pentecostalism have mainly paid attention to the striking growth of this form of Protestantism and to its position in the religious market, rather than to Pentecostalism itself. In this article, I will discuss some of the explanations that have been given for this surprising growth. I will limit myself to the Brazilian and Chilean cases, because various authors have written about these particular situations, and their work can be seen as an illustration of a debate that has repercussions beyond these two countries. This does not mean that an exhaustive summary will be given of what has been written so far about Pentecostalism in these countries: my primary purpose is to reflect on the explanatory process.

Pentecostalism came to Brazil for the first time in 1910 when through the efforts of two Swedish-American lay missionaries the foundation was laid of what was later to become the Assembly of God in Brazil. In 1911, Italian-American Pentecostals working among Italian immigrants founded the Christian Congregation. In the fifties a new wave of expansion occurred, partly inspired from the United States, with several churches emerging that are now in action nationwide. The most recent significant addition has been the Universal Church of the Kingdom of God, founded in the eighties from a purely Brazilian initiative, nowadays seeking expansion in several countries of the world. Today around 10 percent of the Brazilian population is estimated to be Pentecostal.

In Chile, Pentecostalism had a different origin, much more—but not exclusively—from within the country. Though there were some previous manifestations, it really started in 1909, as a consequence of a revival in the Methodist church, in which an American missionary, Hoover, played a central role. He and his followers founded the Pentecostal Methodist Church, today still the largest of the Chilean Pentecostal churches. In 1932 this church went through a phase of schism, leading to the birth of another Pentecostal church, still active and thriving today. In the course of time several other churches were founded, bringing the number of Pentecostals to a 1992 census percentage of 13.2 percent (Kamsteeg 1995, 63).

Usually social scientists look primarily for external social conditions that can be identified as causes for a form of religious change such as the expansion of a religion. Yet this does not exclude keeping an eye open to the relative autonomy of factors that belong to the internal characteristics of a religion. In fact, the question regarding the relation between religious and societal processes is one of the most fascinating in the debate about the Pentecostal growth. As we will see shortly, the question has given rise to a variety of answers.

Generally speaking, the authors of the explanatory models have paid little attention to the Charismatic movements. The Pentecostal churches have been the main object of investigation. Yet implicitly much of what has been said about Pentecostal churches makes sense when applied to Charismatic movements. This justifies the use of Pentecostalism as a general term.

Many authors pay attention to certain contradictory characteristics of Pentecostalism. Interestingly the models advanced for the explanation of Pentecostal growth, when compared, themselves contain contradictory elements. Scientific logic would demand that contradictions should be avoided. If inconsistencies are persistent they are experienced as problematic. I will suggest that when we take our point of departure in an eclectic position (Droogers 1985; cf. Marcus and Fischer 1986, x, 7-16; Tennekes 1985, 61-62, 64, 86), combining a variety of explanatory models, contradiction need not be treated as problematic, but as an enrichment of the discussion. Independently of our models, reality contains more contradiction and is more complex than we usually dare to admit.

Most of the persistent contradictions in Pentecostalism can also be identified as paradoxes, as seemingly contradictory, because related to different moments and places. Pentecostal believers would not worry about them. Similarly some of the contradictions between explanatory models can positively be understood by reference to the rather one-sided choices authors, at a certain moment and a particular place, make from a spectrum of possibilities. Once this is understood, the contradictions become less problematic. Accordingly, this chapter is double focused. Not only will the Pentecostal expansion be discussed, but also the social science craft of explaining.

As is the case for about half of the articles in this collection, this contribution is an English version of a text that was first published in Spanish (Boudewijnse et al. 1991, 17-42). I considered fundamentally rewriting the text, but decided to reproduce the argument of the Spanish version, albeit with minor modifications, and to add an epilogue on recent insights. I am aware of the fact that some of the debates described in the original version have lost their edge to anthropologists, and that a polyparadigmatic approach has become more normal since I wrote the previous version.

Yet it is my impression that many of the ideas that were discussed then are still current in other circles, for example in some missiological studies of Pentecostalism. Besides, it seems useful to have an overview of the history of at least some debates regarding the growth of Pentecostalism, especially in view of its current global growth. It is a fascinating question how far the interpretations developed over time in Latin America can be applied elsewhere (cf. Poewe 1994).

Much of the Spanish version has therefore been retained in the current text. An epilogue is added, as a programmatic statement on directions that might presently be followed, and are in fact already being followed. Interestingly they represent approaches that, more than their predecessors, do justice to the paradoxical nature of the phenomenon of Pentecostalism. Social science theorizing seems to have left behind the phase of the production of exclusive paradigms.

The article opens with a discussion of the variety in theoretical approaches. The contradictions—real or supposed—in Pentecostalism are discussed. In the following sections, different modes of explanation, based on anomie, class, and failed modernization respectively, will be summarized. Each time it will be asked what the model clarifies, but also what remains problematic in its application. In the conclusion the double focus will be discussed again. In the epilogue I suggest what contribution current theoretical perspectives in the social sciences might make to the study of Pentecostal growth.

Theoretical Diversity

Though the theme of Pentecostal expansion in two Latin American countries is a relatively limited issue, a series of approaches and models exists, nourished by the theoretical diversity in the social sciences and by the variety of the phenomenon studied. An inventory of the basic options will help us to get a grip on the often contradictory suggestions that the literature contains. Such an inventory may include each author's formulation of the central problem, because it will be based on a particular selection from the characteristics of the phenomenon of Pentecostal differentiation and growth.

A number of examples of conflicting trends may be given:

- The selection of characteristics may, for example, be influenced by the option for either consensus or conflict as basic to social processes. The issue almost always has ideological connotations.
- Another option refers to the choice of either a mechanistic or a subjectivistic approach, the first emphasizing, roughly stated, what structures do to actors, the other what actors do to structures (cf. Alexander 1990).
- Authors differ in their appreciation of the role of religion: as a response to social change, or as a cause of social change.
- Similarly there may be much attention given to factors external to religion, or to internal religious factors with external results.
- To some the essential quality of religion is what it *does*, what it brings about in society and in the lives of its adherents, whereas to others the crucial question is what religion *is*, and they then ask primarily what it means when it is said that religion refers to an invisible dimension in reality.
- It also makes a difference whether the focus is on the rise of a religious phenomenon, or on its persistence. Similarly either the rupture with the past is emphasized, or the continuity, or both.

It follows that if the point of departure in the search for explanation shows such different positions, the construction of a theory, indicating causal connections, is an arbitrary enterprise. I take it then that the models currently on the market, if taken alone, are of a limited value. They show their usefulness much more when the map of the field under study—including its particular causal relations—is to be drawn, than as conclusive and exclusive explanations. In the eclectic view adopted here, models do not exclude one another in advance, but stand a good chance of being complementary. Their purpose is to open the researcher's eyes to possible causal relationships. Exclusivism would reduce the scope of one's observations. Understood in this manner, the contradictions in models mentioned above are much more a blessing in disguise than a curse. They enrich the heuristic instrumentation at one's disposal and draw attention to the most diverse characteristics and relationships.

To give an example, when I discuss below the role of Pentecostalism in a situation of rapid societal change, some models will draw my attention to tendencies in society towards a new consensus, others will point to continuous conflict. Consequently in studying the role of Pentecostal churches and Charismatic movements, I will look at their role in promoting consensus as well as in provoking conflict.

Thus the contributions different authors have made are to be fitted together like stones in a mosaic. Only together will they produce a faithful though never complete image of Pentecostal reality (cf. Lalive d'Epinay 1977, 9). This does not mean that ideological disputes must be ignored; on the contrary, ideological options may prove instrumental in the formulation of the central research question, or in the choice of research methods, or in the selection of a form for the final report. As long as the goal is to understand social reality, every hint, whether one-sided and biased or not, is useful. It will be difficult indeed to find models that are free from ideological influence, ideology understood in the sense of a constellation of ideas that legitimate a certain type of society, either realized or wished for.

This does not mean that all that has appeared in print is by definition of importance. It is also good to warn against exaggerated expectations concerning the social science contribution to the understanding of Pentecostalism. Even though an eclectic approach seems to guarantee better results than a mono-paradigmatic method, modesty remains advisable.

An Ambivalent Religion

So even before the theme of Pentecostal growth is discussed, a theoretical diversity that is both confusing and enriching makes itself felt in the social science study of religion. If we turn to Brazilian and Chilean Pentecostalism, we are confronted with even more contradiction, paradox, and variation. Let us take a closer look at the paradoxes that can be perceived in what has been written about the growth of Pentecostalism in these countries. The following list contains those I came across:

- Because of its emphasis on the Holy Spirit, Pentecostal belief rehabilitates the lay person. Nevertheless there are strongly hierarchical churches in which the pastors have much power. As a consequence egalitarian and hierarchical tendencies occur simultaneously.

- Liberty of expression, especially of emotions, is a common characteristic. At the same time church services are masterfully controlled and discourse is in certain cases fundamentalistic. Sermons and church discipline can be legalistic.
- Pentecostal believers treat the surrounding society with a dualistic, antithetical attitude. The "world" is depicted as lost and corrupt. In this connection terms such as "protest" and "social strike" have been used. Pentecostal believers have taken leave from the world and have started a radically new life (Tennekes 1985). Yet, they have also established a reputation for being exemplary citizens and employees, excellent participants in a world they are supposed to detest.
- Generally Pentecostal believers avoid politics, but precisely because of this abstention they can be a factor of importance. Moreover, some authors speak of a symbolic protest by Pentecostals, which indirectly criticizes the dominant system. One may also find churches that adopt a political role, either to defend their members' interests, or to attack the devil identified as communism or immoralism, or both.
- Pentecostals emphasize the apocalypse and Jesus' return, but give equal attention to practical short-term solutions for problems here and now.
- Women are often more numerous than in other churches, but in positions of leadership only rarely. With a justifying appeal to the Bible, leadership is often exclusively reserved to male members.
- In the case of Charismatic movements, a paradoxical tendency is that their members remain faithful to their church, but seek to be as autonomous as possible. Another characteristic, closely related, is that clergy play an important role, yet laity have often been able to create their own space, especially in the prayer groups.

As a consequence, not all characteristics that authors have mentioned as typical of Pentecostalism are to be found in all churches and movements. Though everywhere the gifts of the Holy Spirit (healing, glossolalia, prophecy) are the center of attention, practice differs in intensity, from strictly controlled emotion to seemingly unlimited ecstasy. Exorcism can be either common practice or exceptional. Healing may have a central as well as a marginal role. Though most

Pentecostal churches combat or ignore ideas from the theology of liberation, to some these are a source of inspiration (see e.g. Bonilla 1985; Kamsteeg 1995).

Speaking of variation, one distinction has been alluded to already: that between Charismatic movements, seeking Pentecostal renewal within the established churches, both Protestant and Roman Catholic, and autonomous Pentecostal churches. Between the latter, various types of churches can be distinguished (cf. also Souza 1969; Yinger 1970, 251-281). First there is a difference in historical depth. The oldest churches were founded at the beginning of this century and are presenting characteristics of denominations: more hierarchy, more compromising with secular values, sometimes ecumenical relations. More recently, in the forties and fifties, a new wave of church founding occurred, not infrequently initiated by a mass campaign under foreign leadership. In the sixties, mass campaigns more often came to have a political agenda and the call for conversion was meant to influence a decision against leftist ideology. As a consequence new churches, though not always Pentecostal in nature, were founded (Dominguez and Huntington 1984; Valderrey 1985). Pentecostal churches may also appear as a one-person initiative and grow to become nationwide. Historically speaking the Charismatic movement is a special case: it came about at the end of the sixties and soon spread, to Catholic parishes, but also to the established "mainstream" Protestant churches. In Brazil the Igreja Universal do Reino de Deus (Universal Church of the Kingdom of God) represents both a recent wave of growth and a very idiosyncratic form of Pentecostalism.

Second, a difference in the method and practice of churches, and therewith often in their size, can lead to a distinction between types of churches. One type is formed by the healing halls, with three services a day and often located near hospitals or polyclinics. Another type is that of the neighborhood livingroom community, brought together at the home of its leader and founder. Then there are the churches that operate nationwide. They often started as urban churches but are now present all over the countryside. These national churches sometimes have a huge church building as a token of their success and as the seat from where their leader(s) operate(s). Some of them use mass media and have been referred to as the electronic church, others abhor electronic media. As far as practice is concerned, Charismatic movements must be distinguished again because they seek to renew established churches from within. They operate within existing parishes, often though not exclusively with the local clergy as leaders. Prayer groups are important at the grass roots level.

A third distinction can be made according to the social position of believers. Usually the lower-class position of Pentecostal believers is referred to as a generalized characteristic. Yet a more refined typology would include churches that specifically address the poorest people in society, but also churches that have begun in that manner but were gradually more populated by middle-class persons. One explanation often found in the literature is that Pentecostalism promotes upward social mobility. There are, moreover, churches that seek to attract people from middle and upper classes. It goes without saying that for the success of these different churches in each case different explanations can be given.

Such a variety of criteria and subsequent typologies indicates that it will be difficult to come to generally applicable explanations and conclusions. If one adds the circumstance that contradictory characteristics may occur within seemingly homogeneous types, it will be clear that generalization is almost impossible. As a matter of fact, the diversity and contradiction encountered have stimulated theorizing work on Pentecostalism. Interestingly, they have hardly been noticed by Pentecostal believers themselves. It is from the side of researchers that attention has been drawn to the variety in characteristics. Sometimes a social science frame of reference, ideologically colored or not, sometimes a more ecclesiastical view, Catholic or Protestant, generated interest in Pentecostalism. Whether from an academic or an ecclesiastical point of view, Pentecostal deviation from models that were familiar to them struck the observers.

One more circumstance contributed to the complex picture emerging. If the growth of Pentecostalism must be linked to profound changes in society, then the coexistence of the old and the new will give extra impetus to contradiction and the sensation of paradox. Total rupture is impossible. The transition from the old to the new, even when dramatic, does not happen in a single moment. For some time old and new elements will coexist. Contradictions will abound. As I will now show, these paradoxical characteristics have all represented a challenge to authors who have sought to explain the growth of Pentecostalism. In the following sections anomie, class, and modernization will successively be discussed as explanatory themes.

Anomie and Pentecostal Growth

The anomie approach can be summarized as follows. In the social science jargon, anomie stands for a situation in which absence of norms is the cause of uncertainty about appropriate behavior. As a consequence relations between people come under pressure. Rights and duties are no longer clearly defined. Within social relationships the sense of security is lost. Words and gestures no longer carry the same meaning to different people.

In societies that are subject to rapid and drastic changes and to strong contrasts of interests, anomie seems to be inevitable. Yet, according to the authors who work with this model, mechanisms are set in motion which will lead to a new definition of norms, adapted to new circumstances. A total absence of norms would mean the end of society. From their basic needs people start the quest for a new community. Thus a new consensus gradually emerges—until the cycle repeats itself after some time. Anomie is considered a temporary deviation from consensus, which is considered to be normal.

Applying this model to the case of the growth of Pentecostal churches in Latin America, authors have suggested that these churches are successful because they offer new norms in a situation of anomie. Anomie came about because of migration to the urban centers. For a variety of reasons people leave the rural areas. In the cities the system of norms has not been able to keep up with the rapid urbanization and industrialization. Rural norms are no longer applicable, urban norms have not yet been invented. The personal relationship, characteristic of life in the countryside, has lost its meaning in the impersonal city with its anonymous inhabitants. Because in the city survival is problematic, norms run the risk of being eroded. According to some prominent authors, Pentecostalism fills this social and ethical vacuum. Therefore there is a positive functional relationship between sociocultural change and Pentecostal church growth (Lalive 1970, 60; Willems 1964, 96; 1966, 209, 231).

The work by Emilio Willems (e.g. 1964; 1966; 1967) is my first example of the application of the anomie model, primarily to the

Brazilian situation, although he has also studied Chilean Pentecostalism. Willems sees anomie not only in the city but also in rural areas, since the feudal structure has increasingly lost its significance. Writing before Vaticanum II and the impact of the theologies of liberation, he saw the Roman Catholic church as the symbol of a backward structure. In Willems' view the Pentecostal church is so successful because, much more than the other Protestant churches, it is far removed from the ailing traditional social structure. He speaks of a symbolic rebellion (1964, 103; 1966, 226; 1967, 140), not only against tradition but also against Catholicism. Pentecostals are able to organize themselves without the help of an elite and thus show that paternalistic relationships have lost their meaning. The equality of believers denies feudal and class society. The Catholic clergy's monopoly on the distribution of salvation is replaced by the ministry of all believers who are inspired by the Holy Spirit. The gifts of the Holy Spirit transform the powerlessness of the humble into strength. Those who have been ignored by the world, in their turn ignore the world.

It is clear that the strictness of Pentecostal morals is very effective in an anomic context. New converts start a new and radically different life because conversion puts an end to the absence of clear norms. The Pentecostal community provides the socially uprooted with a new framework, a "personal community" (Willems 1966, 224-225). They find a new home, including new brothers and sisters who replace the relatives left behind in the countryside. From a marginal position, people move to prestige within the community, according to the task given to them and their performance in their roles. From losers they become heroes of faith, blessed with the gifts of the spirit. Anonymous people become "sister" or "brother so-and-so." All the money that was formerly spent on alcohol, lottery, women etc., now considered sins, can be used for upward social mobility. Thus, in Willems' approach, Pentecostalism is not only a response to an anomic situation, but at the same time it stimulates the growth of the middle class and therefore contributes to modernization.

Another author using the anomie concept, though sometimes and especially in his later work mixed with Marxian insights, is Christian Lalive d'Epinay (1970, 60, 80). He too links Pentecostal growth in Chile with urbanization (1970, 78-79). Yet his interpretation differs from Willems', even though he claims to follow Willems (1970, 88; see also Fernandes 1977; Tennekes 1985, 61-87). The main difference is that Lalive does not emphasize the failure of the rural feudal structure, but sees it continued in the urban Pentecostal church. The role of the landowner, who as a patron determines to a large extent the life of his clients, is taken over by the Pentecostal pastor (1970, 88, 126-127). The symbolic protest against modern society is a return to the past. To Willems, the Pentecostal church was a stimulus to democracy and liberalism, to Lalive authoritarian relationships and political confor-mism abound, even though he admits the possibility, new for Chilean society, for commoners to rise to leadership within the church (1970, 147). Whereas Willems thought highly of the modern rational nature of Pentecostal faith, Lalive is struck by its irrationality. While Willems saw a connection with the values of modern society, Lalive interprets conversion as a breach with those values.

As a consequence Lalive does not hail progressive, modernizing, and democratizing tendencies, but discovers conservatism, feudal continuity, and therefore support for the political and economic sta-tus quo. Modernization and liberalism are out of the question. The answer to anomie is largely a reconstruction of the past, though not a one-to-one copy but a reinterpretation. The reconquered past is reli-giously legitimated. Lalive speaks explicitly in terms of paradoxes and dialectics (1970, 14, 88-89, 101, 121, 344), e.g. between continuity and rupture, authoritarian relationships and equality. Alienation is com-bated through integration in a community, while at the same time people are screened off from society (cf. Tennekes 1985, 64-69).

There is another point of difference, where positions are reversed, with Willems stressing continuity and Lalive pointing to breach. Ac-cording to Willems Pentecostalism is a continuation of popular Ca-tholicism and of Brazilian millenarianism, whereas Chilean Pente-costalism is pictured by Lalive as a cultural island, even though it serves social adaptation (1970, 344).

So it can be seen that similarity in model does not necessarily lead to common conclusions. Admittedly, Willems had Brazil in mind when he wrote, though he was acquainted with the Chilean situation, whereas Lalive restricted his analysis to the Chilean case.

The differing results of the studies done by Willems and Lalive inspired Judith Hoffnagel to do fieldwork in a local Pentecostal church, a branch of the *Assembléia de Deus* in Recife, Northeastern

Brazil. In her Ph.D. thesis (1978) she reaches the conclusion that Pentecostalism stimulates individual change but is an obstacle to the transformation of society (1978, 5). One striking result of Hoffnagel's study (1978, 254-255) is that in the church she researched, more than half of the migrants among the members had already been Pentecostal believers before leaving their rural home area. Also, the majority of the members who had joined the church while living in Recife had done so after having lived there for a long period. This particular church does not attract the poorest but what Hoffnagel calls "the successful poor" (1978, 256). The members' upward social mobility is not as striking as Willems had predicted, though still present.

What Hoffnagel did in the Brazilian case can be compared to Hans Tennekes' study (1985) of Chilean Pentecostals. He too studied local churches, this time in Santiago, with the objective of verifying the theories Willems and Lalive had formulated. His approach was inspired by the work of Poblete (1969; O'Dea and Poblete 1970), who had applied the anomie model to the case of Puerto Rican Pentecostals in New York. What is new in Tennekes' approach is that he does not contrast anomie with community, but with an integrated social structure. A community is only one type of social structure and therefore not the inevitable result of the reduction of anomie. In addition he suggests that one should distinguish between individual anomie and social anomie and that the two do not necessarily occur together.

When trying to verify the anomie model, Tennekes found that it was difficult to translate the general hypotheses into research questions. Nevertheless he was able to draw some interesting conclusions. He suggests, for example, that the social characteristics of Pentecostal believers do not really differ from those of the popular classes: the poorest migrants and the recently arrived are not overrepresented in Pentecostal churches. He depicts Pentecostalism as an important asset in people's quest for meaning and therefore as a form of popular religiosity.

He criticizes the interpretation of Pentecostalism as a millenarian movement, directed passively towards the future. Instead he emphasizes the importance of the radically new life, here and now, that a convert actively begins to lead. He warns against underestimating the protest value of Pentecostalism, even though its nature is much more moral than structural, let alone political. With regard to political options, Pentecostals do not differ from other members of the popular classes, even though, mainly for practical reasons, Pentecostals do participate less in political organizations. Compared to progressive political parties, Pentecostal churches are much more attractive: popular culture is valued, the leaders come from popular classes, an alternative community is offered and short-term solutions are readily available. These advantages, visible to all in democratic times, become obvious under repressive political regimes. Then Pentecostal churches grow even more rapidly.

Rubem César Fernandes has also commented on the anomie model (1977). The point he makes is that anomie does not refer to a transition phase in a regular cycle, to be corrected by inbuilt mechanisms of society, but that it is part of a capitalist economy. He suggests that in the application of the anomie model to Pentecostal believers, an evolutionist approach to religion becomes manifest, as if in future, more secularized, conditions the people who have now turned to a Pentecostal church, would become members of a political party or a trade union. Whereas authors like Willems suggested that Pentecostalism contributed to modernization, the same process is supposed to ultimately put an end to religion, and so Pentecostalism seems to be digging its own grave. In the meantime, it is useful as a remedy for temporary afflictions, but in the long run life will become so well off that Pentecostalism will loose its function.

Like Hoffnagel, Fernandes points to the fact that both second generation city dwellers and people in rural areas convert to Pentecostalism. Further, anomie and social vacuum do not occur as dramatically as the models had predicted, even though the city cannot be said to be a smoothly integrated whole (cf. Fry and Howe 1975, 85). Slums do not lack clear moral codes, power networks and social stratification. Those in search of a "personal community" can find it there. So when Pentecostalism is studied, it would be wise to pay attention to networks and the exchange of favors (see also Brown 1974, 300-301; 1994, 167-169).

A final point Fernandes makes is that the boundaries of religious groups and social categories only rarely coincide. Easy and simple explanations are, therefore, excluded. Likewise a reference to class society is not very helpful, since Pentecostal believers belong to a variety of social strata. Besides, people of the same stratum do not necessarily have the same religious preferences. I will return to this point when Howe's work will be discussed (cf. also Fry and Howe 1975).

At the end of this section a provisional conclusion can be formulated. The insights of the authors who worked with the anomie model can be said to be applicable to certain forms of Pentecostalism and to specific categories of believers. That some people find a "personal community" in the Pentecostal church and succeed in moving upwards on the social ladder can be stated without hesitation. There are, however, many cases of ingression in a Pentecostal church that cannot be explained by an appeal to the anomie model. The explanation that model offers is, therefore, partial.

Yet even if the anomie model is applicable in a number of cases, critical questions cannot be avoided. One such question inquires after the implicit views and metaphors of society and modernization. Society figures as an organism that recovers from an illness. It is represented as if it were acting like a person, seeking a new equilibrium. Modernization seems to be viewed as an inevitable and natural process. But is it really irreversible? To many people in countries like Brazil and Chile modernization seems like the horizon: the closer you come, the more it retreats. Population growth and unfair distribution of wealth reduce the effects of economic expansion. Another point of the critique refers to the presupposed normality of consensus and order. Do conflicts only occur as a symptom of anomie, and disappear when anomie is over? Are urban areas really lacking in order? Or is it possible that neighborhoods take on village-like characteristics? A question that can also be raised refers to the value of symbolic protest if the actors are not conscious of it. Can the effect of this protest be verified in research? Or is the scholar performing as a ventriloquist?

Finally, in this approach explanation is looked for in factors that are external to religion. The specific contents of that religion are hardly taken into account. Religion, in this case Pentecostalism, is only important for its contribution to the maintenance of order and values in society, not as a phenomenon as such. It is not explained how people choose between religions with similar functions. The same type of explanation as advanced for Pentecostalism can be found in the literature on another urban Brazilian religion, the Afro-Brazilian spirit-medium religion Umbanda. Admittedly, one exception is Willems

(1966) who, in a comparison of Pentecostalism, Spiritism, and Umbanda, presents Pentecostal churches as more attractive than other Protestant churches. Yet, in this case too the main question is what religion *does*, not what it *is*.

Class and Pentecostal Expansion

Many of the objections just mentioned have also been raised by an author whose work will now be discussed: Francisco Cartaxo Rolim. Taking his point of departure in a Marxist model with Weberian addenda, he inevitably finds different answers to the questions that were raised by the authors working with the anomie model. In all fairness it must be said that the latter were not totally blind to conflicts between interests, these conflicts being viewed as a cause of anomie. But Rolim's approach leads to an essentially different interpretation of social conflicts, taking the criticisms against the anomie model seriously.

Social conflicts are not identified as caused by confusion about norms and values, but as a consequence of class differences. The so-called stable social relationships considered normal in the anomie model are qualified as asymmetrical and pregnant with conflict. As long as access to the means of production is not open to all, conflict is the norm and not cohesion. The lack of consensus is not temporary but permanent and structural.

In this type of approach, and faithful to Marx, religion generally appears in two ways: first and foremost as an appeaser—an opiate—and therefore as a cause of alienation; second and less frequently as a channel for protest. As in the anomie approach, religion is understood functionally, and not for its specific contents. Such an approach can, therefore, be as partial as the anomie approach. The choices that oppressed individuals make between religious alternatives cannot be explained.

Rolim, though taking class society as his point of departure, goes beyond this partiality by combining Marx with Weber (Rolim 1973a; 1973b; 1977; 1979; 1980; 1981; 1982; 1985; 1987; 1991; 1995). Interests open up the path, but religious vision directs human action along that path (1991, 127). Rolim affirms a dialectical relationship between capitalist society and the Pentecostal vision of the world (1991, 128).

As a consequence, he is not only interested in what religion *does*, but also in what it *is*. Not only external but also internal factors are taken into account. From his first publications onward Rolim is critical of the anomie approach: When it is shown that Pentecostalism reduces anomie, nothing is said about the contents of that religion. Beliefs and rituals should be integrated into the explanation. The essential point is that Pentecostalism is a *religious* reaction (1977, 13).

Like Hoffnagel, Rolim did fieldwork on Pentecostalism. His research was done in the seventies, in Nova Iguaçu, a suburban town near Rio de Janeiro. Two-thirds of his respondents had been Catholics before converting to Pentecostalism. Popular Catholicism is a good preparation for Pentecostalism (Rolim 1973b; 1980, 178-180; cf. Tennekes 1985, 77-86). In both, salvation is directly accessible, dispensing with clergy. It is obtained through vows (*promessas*). Free expression is normal in both types of religiosity. In both cases, solutions to practical problems are reached through thaumaturgical means. Faith is a personal affair.

Yet there are also differences. According to Rolim, in the Pentecostal church the Bible takes the place of the popular saint. The cult of the saints is even combated with an appeal to the Bible: all the faithful are saints in principle. Those stories in the Bible where God's power becomes evident are favorites. Conversion stories, especially when based on a miracle, are seen in the same context. The Bible also provides the legitimation for the command to preach the gospel, which is done on individual initiative and at any occasion that may present itself. Every new believer is the start of a group of at least two. This continuing partition of cells (Tennekes 1972, 151; 1985, 21) contributes to the success of Pentecostalism.

Rolim, like the anomie authors, seeks a connection between social change and Pentecostal growth, and he too refers to migration and urbanization—yet in a Marxist version (1985, 119). Urban society is characterized by capitalist production relationships that are decisive for the type of communication between classes (Rolim 1977, 14; 1980, 163). Pentecostalism must be viewed within that context, though not in a deterministic manner. To Rolim religion is not a mere reflection of class relations. This does not alter the fact that in his view they influence religion (1977, 15).

Thus Rolim, like Tennekes (1985, 114-121), sees a close relationship
between the growth of Pentecostalism and the limitation of political
freedom. In a phase of democracy when dissatisfaction with capitalist
society can be expressed through political channels, the growth of
Pentecostalism will stagnate (Rolim 1980, 184). In Brazil this happened between 1960 and 1964. When from 1964 onwards for economic reasons political freedom was restricted, Pentecostal churches
resumed their growth (Rolim 1995, 172, 186).

In his own fieldwork Rolim found that the majority of the Pentecostals he studied were employed in the tertiary sector, the fastest
growing in the urban labor structure of Brazil. In terms of class these
people belong to what Rolim considers an improper—because intermediate class; in Poulantzas' terms the new small bourgeoisie (Rolim
1985, 139n), neither workers nor middle class (1977, 15), but in between. In other publications Rolim speaks of lower middle class (1980,
169; 1985, 139-140). Why is Pentecostalism so attractive to exactly this
category of people? Rolim's answer is that these people do not occupy
a clear position in the class struggle. Therefore, they are susceptible to
the prospect of social progress. The ideal and example of the middle
class raise expectations. Yet these are not always fulfilled (Rolim 1980,
159). Pentecostalism offers compensation through its moral reformism and its status-elevating tasks. The same mechanism is active in
middle-class circles and consequently here too Pentecostalism recruits
members.

This explanation with reference to class structure does not prevent
Rolim from looking at the question of why the compensation is *religious* in nature. Maintaining the class perspective, an explanation is
sought in terms of the free access to religious production that is
characteristic of Pentecostalism. Rolim thus returns to a problem already raised by Weber and reformulated by Bourdieu (1974, 27-98;
Rolim 1985, 130-135). In doing so he avoids and criticizes a simple
mirror approach (religion reflects the social situation). Besides, living
people of flesh and blood appear from behind the social structures and
mechanisms. The question is who has a right to be a religion's spokes-
man. Who is allowed to introduce changes into a religion? Who is
actually in control? Bourdieu refers to this problem, borrowing Marxian economic terms, as the problem of the access to the religious
means of production.

In the case of Pentecostalism the, admittedly ideal, answer is that with the exception of baptism and holy communion, every member enjoys access (Rolim 1977, 17; 1980, 150-160). For everybody can be baptized with the Holy Spirit and act from and with that authority. The Pentecostal churches rediscovered the ministry of all believers. Those who in the mainstream Christian churches were objects of evangelization by a monopolizing and remunerated clergy, in the Pentecostal church become themselves autonomous subjects of that evangelization.

This inversion—instead of reflection—is, according to Rolim, the essence of the symbolic protest by the Pentecostal believers against society. The division of labor current in society is denied in Pentecostalism. In these churches, those who in society are excluded from access to the economic means of production, are transformed into subjects with free access to the religious means of production (1980, 171, 173). The reaction to class society is religious because religion allows for this inversion. Glossolalia illustrates this symbolically, because its nonverbality denies the verbality of the erudite higher class (1977, 20).

In this manner, Rolim (1980, 155-160) emphasizes that the criticized world is represented symbolically. Other examples are the tone of the sermons, which expresses an "outmoded academicism" (1980, 155), and the bourgeois suits worn by the men in the churches Rolim studied. The outside world thus made present is subsequently subjected to inversion and denial by means of the nonverbal forms of expression and the church/world dualism that are typical of a Pentecostal church service (1980, 157).

An already familiar paradox presents itself. On the one hand a basic structure in society is symbolically reversed and thereby repudiated. On the other hand, the Pentecostal church avails itself of values that are at a premium in class society: moral reformism and careerism. Thus, despite all the criticism of a sinful world, Pentecostal believers, led by a particular reading of Romans 13, happen to be good citizens and good workers in that selfsame world. The capitalist relations of production are thereby accepted. Rolim (1977, 20) refers to this as ideological dependency. Despite this there have been examples of protest actions, led by Pentecostal believers, that were more than symbolic (Kamsteeg 1995; Novaes 1985; Rolim 1985, 85-89, 244-251;

1987, 70-90; 1995, 66ff; Tennekes 1985, 116-120; see also Hoekstra, this volume).

Summarizing Rolim's contribution, it can be said that his approach meets some of the objections that were raised when the anomie approach was discussed. He makes a serious attempt to integrate the specific contents of Pentecostal belief and practice in his mode of explanation. It is clear that he considers Pentecostalism to be a religious phenomenon and that in doing so he does not restrict himself to what religion *does*. He offers clarifying analyses of the production of religion in Pentecostalism and of the continuity with the popular Catholic past.

Some questions can nevertheless be raised. When Rolim characterizes the Pentecostal believers he studied as belonging to an improper intermediate sort of class, it seems that he sticks to a two-layer model of society. If that is the case, one may raise doubts as to the validity of such a model. Whereas the anomie model was determined by the metaphor of the organism, here social reality is reduced to a metaphor of layers and to dualism. What is the explanatory value of the fact that one belongs to a certain class? Rolim explicitly says that he wants to avoid determinism. If moreover he labels the tertiary sector workers an improper class, one may ask what the pretense of this approach is.

Another question concerns the fact that Rolim's research and perspective are urban. Of the type of relations his class model identifies, the best examples are urban. If the setting for Pentecostal growth is nonurban, the question about the value of the class model becomes even more pertinent. A further problem is that what Rolim describes in terms of inversion and protest remains difficult to operationalize. Proof is therefore difficult. Respondents' statements can hardly be used to confirm or falsify these affirmations.

Failed Modernization and Pentecostal Growth

Another illustration, both of the paradoxical nature of Pentecostalism and of the models used to explain its growth, can be found in two articles by Gary Howe (1977; 1980). Howe was mentioned when I referred to an article he wrote together with Peter Fry (1975) which can be read as a prelude to the other two. Like Rolim, Howe endeavors to include the religious contents of Pentecostalism in his explanation.

In his 1977 article, Howe puts Brazilian Pentecostalism in its economic, political, and social context. In his view the fundamental relationships are those between capital and labor, and between state and citizen. Economically speaking commodities are produced, for export and for the national market, through a capitalist mode of production. Industrialization is supposed to be a substitute for the agricultural export economy that was based on monocultures. Simultaneously, on the political level, a strong bureaucratic state is formed, its purpose being to monitor the economic process. Socially, the tendency is towards individualization, with an emphasis on the responsibility as well as the submission of the person. In sum, the new situation is characterized by concentration of economical and political power, strict rules in the production process and in the state, and individual submission.

These three features Howe finds reflected in Pentecostalism. This religion, therefore, perfectly suits the new situation. There is a parallel between societal developments and the contents of Pentecostal faith. In the believers' view, power is concentrated in the hands of an almighty God. They submit themselves to this God and to a strict moral code. The paradox is that they deviate from society, and yet adapt themselves (1977, 42).

Howe admits that this is an "ideal type" picture and a simplification of reality (1977, 46). In his 1980 article, he shows the other side of the picture and therewith the ambiguity of the situation and its interpretation. Combining the modernization approach with the so-called dependency theory, Howe's thesis is that Brazil, though changing, is not modernizing. This also implies a criticism of Willems' model as discussed above. To Howe the Third World constitutes, almost by definition, the periphery of the First World. Having this role it will never be able to modernize fully. The history of the First World cannot be repeated in the Third. The latter lacks a periphery of its own, unless this is to be found within the country itself: the poor areas. Anyhow, the process called modernization is in fact absorption into a capitalist economy, as dominated by the First World (cf. Rolim 1980, 178).

Howe also draws attention to the fact that there are various and widely different religions in Brazil. Even if it were accepted that they all reflect modernizing society, then the differences still have to be explained. Thus the two religions that have expanded most in this century and in an almost parallel way, Pentecostalism and Umbanda, may have similar functions, but in beliefs and practices are each other's opposites.

This is clear from the vehemence with which Pentecostal preachers condemn Umbanda as diabolical. In this respect the relationship is asymmetrical: The Umbandists are much more tolerant. Like Pentecostals, Umbandists accept God as the supreme being, but the many divinities and spirits of different origins that manifest themselves through the mediums' trance are much more important. There is no strict ethical system. Instead improvising negotiations with sacred powers are emphasized. The type of power and the way it is approached depends on the problem to be solved. This may involve the intention of doing harm to persons considered the cause of the problem. Since problem-solving takes such a central place, a person seeking relief generally only takes part in the rituals as long as the problem is not satisfactorily solved. Only a few enter mediumship as a consequence of the treatment they receive. The mediums form the hard core of the Umbanda temples. The audience is characterized by a large turnover. In sharp contrast with the Pentecostal preachers, Umbanda mediums do not seek to bind their clients in an exclusive, total, "eternal," committed relationship. The visitors to the Umbanda temple make a strategic, manipulative use of the network it offers, and disappear after being helped.

The comparison of the two contrasting religions raises the question whether all religions reflect modernization to the same degree. The model of a deterministic reflection with a single-track causality, therefore, hangs in the balance. A way out of this deadlock Howe finds by abandoning the idea that modernization is a coherent process. The three features of modernization—concentration of economic and political power, strict rules in the production process and in the state, and individual submission—have their reverse in nepotism, patronage, regionalism, corruption, favoritism, personal networks, and improvisation, on a scale that has never occurred before. Ultimately the opposition is between favors and rights (and duties!), between manipulation and law. Howe (1980) links this dichotomy to the one put forward in his earlier article, between traditional rural oligarchies, the manipulators, and the new industrial bourgeoisie, the bureaucrats. Howe is inspired in this type of assertion by the work of the Brazilian anthropologist Roberto DaMatta who has written extensively about what he calls "the Brazilian dilemma" (1973; 1979; 1985; 1986a; 1986b; 1991).

Howe and his colleague Peter Fry had used DaMatta's interpretation in an article (1975) in which they raised the question why some urban migrants opt for Umbanda and others for Pentecostalism. If, according to the anomie model, the two religions have the same functions (Willems 1966, 208; Camargo 1973, 184), what motivates the preference a person has for one of the two? Pentecostalism stands for rules, law, and duties, whereas Umbanda represents the manipulative, improvising pole. Pentecostals are loyal to the church, the group, Umbandist clients to the individual medium. The Pentecostal symbolic system is orderly and fixed, that of Umbanda malleable and open to manipulation. Using an economic metaphor: It depends on the migrant's biography and personal strategy where he or she will choose to invest, and what the balance is between expenses and results (Fry and Howe 1975, 83-85). The two religions meet the same demand, but with a different supply. Recognizing that this does not contribute much to an explanation of the beliefs and rituals of the two religions (Fry and Howe 1975, 89), the two authors point out that the effectiveness of the symbols used depends on the personal biography and social experience of the migrant. These will influence the meaning people attach to symbols (see e.g. Burdick 1993; Ireland 1991; Mariz 1994). It is as if God and divinities, the Spirit and spirits become part of the people's networks and are used in the same manner: respecting the rules and laws (Pentecostalism), or manipulating and improvising (Umbanda).

So hypothetically people with a "bureaucratic" social experience will prefer Pentecostalism whereas "manipulative" persons will opt for Umbanda (Fry and Howe 1975, 90-91). Pentecostalism represents successful, Umbanda failing modernization. In a similar manner Howe (1980), in comparing Pentecostalism and Umbanda, makes a virtue of need and opts for a double reflection of society in religion, representing the two sides of the Brazilian dilemma and thus of the failing modernization process. Historically speaking, the new industrial bourgeoisie had to give in to the demands of the traditional oligarchy. Although modernization had been adopted as official policy since the thirties, in practice it was made harmless by all the concessions to the traditional elite. In Howe's view (1980, 135) the failure of modernization implies that Umbanda is more the rule and Pentecostalism the exception. The Pentecostals are too modern for Brazilian society. They refuse to play the manipulative game and are, therefore, prone to abuse especially in their relationships with employers and the state.

Ingenious as this solution may be, some critical questions can be asked. Does this hypothesis really take religious contents into account, or is it a mere variation of the anomie and reflection model? Are religious attitudes not represented as social attitudes in disguise? Is the whole argument not an example of the chicken-and-egg problem? Where does the reasoning start: on the side of the demand as influenced by biography and social experience, or on the side of supply as advanced by Pentecostal preachers and Umbandist mediums? Are Pentecostals successful participants in the modernization process, while Umbandists are losers? As in the case of Rolim, the hypothetical connections between religious and societal processes are difficult to operationalize. The parallels depend on theoretical presuppositions. Why is the industrial bourgeoisie not entirely Pentecostal, and the traditional oligarchy Umbandist? Again the question is the weight of economic modernity or dependency as factors for the explanation of religion. Howe's approach does not escape determinism and reductionism. Finally, Pentecostals have their manipulative experiences as is shown by the internal politics, scandals, and schisms of their churches. Equally Umbandists have bureaucratic inclinations as shown by the formation of regional and even national federations.

Conclusion

In this chapter two tracks have been followed simultaneously: that of the expansion of Pentecostalism, and that of social science explanation of this phenomenon. Special attention was given to contradiction and paradox as encountered on both tracks. By way of a start, an inventory was made of the alternatives and contradictions. In the course of the chapter it became clear how authors developed their own preferences with regard to the options available, rarely in an extreme manner but always selectively. Researchers, like the researched, try to make sense, produce meaning. This process of signification establishes identity. In science as well as in religion identity often seems to be based on the one-sided selection of characteristics.

The two inventories, of researchers and researched, proved to be connected. A scholar's choice of one particular characteristic in a theoretical model of society often leads to an emphasis on a certain aspect of Pentecostalism. Thus if Lalive (1970, 14) opts for the element of continuity, even though recognizing fault lines in the religious landscape, he cannot but emphasize the hierarchical tendency in Pentecostalism. Similarly Rolim's starting point lies with conflict and protest and so he discusses emotional freedom, the inversion of the relations of production, and glossolalia's symbolic protest as deserving our particular attention. The other authors and their views may also be situated somewhere within the two inventories.

It might be suggested that the diversity of models has contributed to a focus on contradictions in Pentecostalism. He who seeks regularity—and that is what scientific work is about—dislikes contradictions. The latter are a complication in explanatory work. Logical consistency is the rule, contradiction the deviation. Being called contradictory is a pejorative appellation. When a scholar's model puts hierarchy as the norm, he will experience egalitarian tendencies as contradictory. When the emphasis is on order and consensus, he will find emotional freedom puzzling. Only when an eclectical attitude is adopted are paradoxes no longer problematic, because these are then viewed as the consequences of explaining only partially and unilaterally.

This partiality is not only based on scientific preferences, but may also have ideological connotations and may reflect a particular worldview. Scholars, despite being trained to produce objective knowledge, are marked by their context. The study of culture is itself a cultural phenomenon. A surprised reaction to the discovery that Pentecostal believers are not *of* but yet *in* the world, may be based on a personal option for socially engaged Christianity. Similarly astonishment at the paradox of apolitical Pentecostal pastors' support for military dictatorship may reveal the author's opinion that a church should always resist dictators or that Romans 13's advice on respect for authorities should not be read in the literal sense. So it seems that the overexposure of paradoxical traits in Pentecostalism can at least partially be traced to the views of the researchers.

This does not mean that the approaches described above can be consigned to the dustbin. Though I saw fit to raise critical questions about each of the models, each also was shown to have its positive aspects. Each author contributed an essential element to the—still incomplete—mosaic. So what image does that mosaic give of the growth of Pentecostalism in Latin America and the Caribbean? This collection of articles presents the beginning of an answer.

Epilogue 1996

The three models just discussed represent approaches that belong to a particular phase in the history of the social sciences. This does not mean that they have had their time; on the contrary, they are part of the eclectic approach advocated in this article. Yet, they should be complemented by some rapid observations on the programmatic relevance of some recent theoretical perspectives for the study of Pentecostalism and its growth, particularly because these approaches are more eclectical and as a consequence seem to take the paradoxical into greater account. This section will contain short references to praxis theory, cognitive anthropology, globalization, gender approaches, and postmodernism.

In concrete cases, the degree to which these perspectives can be applied and be integrated into a theoretical framework that fits the specificity of the case under research must be considered. If a synthesis is reached this might suggest a monoparadigmatic approach, yet it may in itself be the start of a new eclectic cycle. Theoretical perspectives like those presented below are primarily of heuristic value, drawing attention to aspects that seem promising for further research. In proceeding in this manner, some approaches may prove of little value, whereas others will be most helpful, all depending on the particular case and the specific researcher. It goes without saying that each perspective has its own concepts and metaphors and, therefore, seems unique as a way of constructing scientific knowledge. It may thus not be easy to integrate perspectives into a single framework. Yet, in a dialectical movement between induction and deduction, scientific syncretism can be reached to a certain degree. The eclecticism advocated here is of a practical nature, leading to a temporary synthesis, but always of a provisional nature.

The first of the perspectives to be mentioned, praxis theory, exists in such a variety of forms, that it hardly can be considered a paradigm or school. Yet some common characteristics can be distinguished as a kind of family resemblance between them. The central question is how actors and structures are related. In answering this question a one-sided stance is avoided. Praxis theorists seek to go beyond the familiar dichotomies and paradoxes that, as we saw, have also troubled the social science study of Pentecostalism. So they look for the delicate and complex link between actors and structures, trying to show how actors are influenced by social and symbolic structures and at the same time change these structures. In this manner there is attention given to processes of regularization that confirm and reproduce existing structures, as well as to processes of situational adjustment, in which events generate behavior that causes structural changes (Moore 1977; see also Ortner 1984; Sahlins 1985). In the course of time, people give meaning to what occurs to them, whether they reproduce or change structures. Research should have a historical dimension, and power processes must receive attention.

Pentecostalism in the Latin American context offers a striking example of this process. Conversion is viewed by believers as a radical change; social scientists would say a structural change. The convert adopts new social and symbolic structures. Certain events, often related to cognitive and material problem-solving, lead the potential convert in that direction. We have hardly begun to understand the complexity of these processes and personal strategies. Structural change not only occurs on the individual level, but also in society. Structural changes in society create problems for people and inspire and even oblige them to look for a solution to their problems. In any case, where individual and societal processes of regularization fail to combat indeterminacy, processes of situational adjustment occur (Moore 1977). What happens in the religious sector is a more specific illustration of this: if the joint familiar solutions of popular and official Catholicism do not solve the problems, alternatives like the Pentecostal become attractive. As a religious movement, Pentecostalism has its own social and symbolic structures that contain aspects that attract people. In other words, Pentecostalism should not only be explained by external factors, reducing it to a reflection of societal trends or of religious competition. The internal process should be studied in detail and in context. Power, within the groups under study, and in their societal context, is an important aspect of such studies.

Cognitive anthropology can be seen as a helpful tool for this type of study of Pentecostal praxis. The central question is how people organize their knowledge—understood in a wide sense, including emotion—within a cultural context. This again includes the relationship between actor and structure, because it is through cognitive processes that people internalize structures and reinterpret them. Cognitive processes are rooted in experience, including physical experience. People use schemes that consist of cognitive elements in their bare, simplified form, sufficiently summarized to be remembered. These schemes are completed in daily praxis. People think not only in a syntagmatic manner putting cognitive elements in a discursive order, but they also have a paradigmatic capacity, through which they can consult and manipulate several schemes simultaneously.

In the study of Pentecostalism, attention should be given to the schemes that are current and also to the way in which they are used. Conversion is, of course, a prime schema completed in each particular case. But there are other cognitive schemes and processes that are learned, reproduced, and reinterpreted in the Pentecostal's life including emotional dimensions. They often have to do with problem-solving and with physical experiences. Dualism is an example of a way to organize knowledge about society. The way healing occurs provides another example of a set of schemes. The Charismatic gifts of glossolalia and prophecy also represent schemes. In general, schemes in Pentecostalism have a dramatic character. These schemes should be compared to those that are characteristic of popular religion, especially popular Catholicism. A cognitive approach to Pentecostalism will show aspects of its dynamism despite the religion's reputation of rigidity and inflexibility.

With regard to globalization, the central question is which tendencies occur worldwide. Globality is consciousness of the world as a whole, as a single place (Robertson 1992, 6). This perspective looks beyond modernization as a process of westernization. It gives special attention to processes that influence all societies including western societies. Globalization works at the supranational level cutting across state lines. Culture is becoming deterritorialized, as is visible already in mass media and in communication technology. Though globalization theories are focused on the global level, the parallel question is how these worldwide influences are translated to the local level. Some speak of globalization (Robertson 1992, 173). It is also clear that at the local level fragmentation occurs simultaneously, often motivated by ethnic and religious motives, as when former states collapse and fall apart. As far as religion is concerned, globalization does not only mean privatization and secularization, but also new chances for religionization most evident in the spread of fundamentalism (Beyer 1994).

For the study of Pentecostalism in the Latin American context, the globalization perspective suggests that the movement not only grows because of North Atlantic influence, a thesis studied critically by Stoll (1990), but that it is very much part of a global movement. Martin (1990; 1994), comparing it to Methodist growth, presents Pentecostal expansion in Latin America as a—partly endogenous—expression of liberal pluralism that puts an end to Catholic monopoly and creates a free social space. His approach resembles Willems' anomie interpretation of Latin American Pentecostal expansion linking it to global processes. The globalization perspective points out another aspect: Pentecostals feel part of a worldwide movement, a true transnational enterprise. They will couch this in religious terms as the coming of the Kingdom. The already mentioned Brazilian Universal Church of the Kingdom (!) of God makes a case in point, being a "southern" initiative that now has branches in dozens of other countries, including "northern" nations. It is also known for its ability in using mass media and electronic devices. Globalization theory offers a framework that cannot be neglected in the study of Pentecostal expansion in Latin America.

Gender approaches represent a turning of feminist and women's studies to the study of the cultural definition of the relation between men and women, men and men, and women and women. Gay studies form a special branch of gender studies. The focus is no longer on what characterizes women as a category, but on difference between women. Gender is viewed as continuously constructed and reconstructed, as subjected to a process of symbolism and meaning-making.

Since Latin American Pentecostalism attracts many more women than men and paradoxically has an almost exclusive male leadership, gender approaches must be included in the set of tools to be used in studying Pentecostal expansion. Pentecostals generally condemn gay behavior, so a gay studies perspective must be added to this set of tools. A gender approach must include critical reference to the stereotype of religion in Latin America as a female affair. The approaches discussed in this article can be rethought with regard to the gender dimension. A situation of anomie will demand a renewed definition of gender roles and the corresponding values and norms. Pentecostal churches may offer stability by maintaining tradition and may also offer new chances of leadership to women. Similarly modernization can be studied from a gender perspective especially with regard to the changed position of women in the economic process and its consequences for the Pentecostal women.

Finally, postmodernism must be mentioned. In certain respects, it is similar to the eclectic approach proposed here. It deeply distrusts any exclusive and ultimate framework of orientation and explanation, most of all modernity. It presents reality as fragmented and knowledge of that reality as even more fragmented. Consensus is difficult to reach since knowledge is always under construction and deconstruction. Representation of reality is, therefore, problematic and always incomplete. In a more constructive way this has expanded the range of literary forms available to authors of research reports. Text has become a major metaphor in postmodernism.

To the study of Pentecostal expansion, a postmodernist approach can contribute first of all by relativizing unilateral approaches. If anything at all can be said, the student's discourse must be plural. This is a plea for an eclectic approach and for freedom in the literary expression of research results (for an example see Guerrero 1995). Furthermore, postmodernism's bitter criticism of the modernization project may oblige to a rethinking of explanations of Pentecostal expansion that refer to modernization theories. Finally, postmodernism, through its criticism of positivist conceptions of science, indirectly rehabilitates world views that do not obey the criteria of such conceptions. Though critical of all-embracing views, including religious ones, postmodernism relativizes the opposition between science and religion and shows the general incompleteness of knowledge in both. This may lead to a radical change in the attitude of those students of Pentecostalism who are interested in its attractive irrationality, to see it no longer as a strange and exceptional phenomenon, but as something normal and common, and, therefore, appealing to many people.

Acknowledgments

I am grateful to the members of the Pentecostalism Study Group at the Vrije Universiteit for their comments on an earlier draft of this chapter.

References

Alexander, Jeffrey C., "Analytic Debates: Understanding the Relative Culture." In *Culture and Society: Contemporary Debates*, ed. Jeffrey C. Alexander, and Steven Seidman, Cambridge: Cambridge University Press, 1990.

Baal, J. van, *Symbols for Communication: An Introduction to the Anthropological Study of Religion*. Assen: Van Gorcum, 1971.

Beyer, Peter, *Religion and Globalization*. London: Sage, 1994.

Bonilla, Plutarco, ed. "Pentecostalismo y Teología de la Liberación," *Pastoralia* 7, no. 15 (1985), 7-111.

Boudewijnse, Barbara, André Droogers, and Frans Kamsteeg, ed. *Algo más que opio. Una lectura antropológica del Pentecostalismo latinoamericano y caribeño*. San José, Costa Rica: DEI, 1991.

Bourdieu, Pierre, *A Economia das Trocas Simbólicas*. São Paulo: Perspectiva, 1974.

Brown, Diana DeGroat, *Umbanda: Politics of an Urban Religious Movement*. Ann Arbor, Mich.: Xerox University Microfilms, 1974.

———, *Umbanda: Religion and Politics in Urban Brazil*. New York: Columbia University Press, 1994.

Burdick, John, *Looking for God in Brazil: The Progressive Catholic Church in Urban Brazil's Religious Arena*. Berkeley, Calif.: University of California Press, 1993.

Camargo, Cândido Procópio Ferreira de, ed. *Católicos, Protestantes, Espíritas*. Petrópolis: Vozes, 1973.

DaMatta, Roberto, *Ensaios de Antropologia Estrutural*. Petrópolis: Vozes, 1973.

———, *Carnavais, Malandros e Heróis: Para uma sociologia do dilema brasileiro*. Rio de Janeiro: Zahar, 1979.

———, *A casa & a rua: Espaço, cidadania, mulher e morte no Brasil*. São Paulo: Brasiliense, 1985.

———, *Explorações, Ensaios de Sociologia Interpretativa*. Rio de Janeiro: Rocco, 1986a.

———, *O que faz o brasil, Brasil?* Rio de Janeiro: Rocco, 1986b.

———, *Carnivals, Rogues, and Heroes: An Interpretation of the Brazilian Dilemma*. Notre Dame and London: University of Notre Dame Press, 1991.

Dominguez, Enrique, and Deborah Huntington, "The Salvation Brokers: Conservative Evangelicals in Central America," *Nacla Report on the Americas* 17, no. 1 (1984), 2-36.

Droogers, André, "From Waste-Making to Recycling: A Plea for an Eclectic Use of Models in the Study of Religious Change." In: Wim van Binsbergen, and Matthew Schoffeleers, eds. *Theoretical Explorations in African Religion*. London: KPI, 1985.

Fernandes, Rubem C., "O Debate entre Sociólogos a Propósito dos Pentecostais," *Cadernos do ISER* 6, (1977), 49-60.

Fernandez, James W., *Persuasions and Performances: The Play of Tropes in Culture*. Bloomington: Indiana University Press, 1986.

Fry, Peter H., and Gary N. Howe, "Duas Respostas à Aflição: Umbanda e Pentecostalismo," *Debate e Crítica* 6, (1975), 75-94.

Guerrero J., Bernardo, *A Dios rogando...: Los pentecostales en la sociedad aymara del norte grande de Chile*. Amsterdam: VU University Press, 1995.

Hoffnagel, Judith Chambliss, *The Believers: Pentecostalism in a Brazilian City*. Ann Arbor, Mich.: Xerox University Microfilms, 1978.

Howe, Gary N., "Representações Religiosas e Capitalismo: Uma "Leitura" Estruturalista do Pentecostalismo no Brasil," *Cadernos do ISER* 6, (1977), 39-48.

———, "Capitalism and Religion at the Periphery: Pentecostalism and Umbanda in Brazil." In *Perspectives on Pentecostalism: Case Studies from the Caribbean and Latin America*, Stephen D. Glazier, ed. Washington, D.C.: University Press of America, 1980.

Ireland, Rowan, *Kingdoms Come: Religion and Politics in Brazil*. Pittsburgh, Pa.: University of Pittsburgh Press, 1991.

Kamsteeg, Frans, *Prophetic Pentecostalism in Chile: A Case Study on Religion and Development Policy*. Amsterdam: Vrije Universiteit, 1995.

Lalive d'Epinay, Christian, *O Refúgio das Massas, Estudo Sociológico do Protestantismo Chileno*. Rio de Janeiro: Paz e Terra, 1970.

———, "Religião, Espiritualidade e Sociedade, Estudo Sociológico do Pentecostalismo Latinoamericano," *Cadernos do ISER* 6, (1977), 5-10.

Marcus, George E., and Michael M.J. Fischer, *Anthropology as Cultural Critique: An Experimental Moment in the Human Sciences*. Chicago and London: Chicago University Press, 1986.

Mariz, Cecilia Loreto, *Coping with Poverty: Pentecostals and Christian Base Communities in Brazil*. Philadelphia: Temple University Press, 1994.

Martin, David, *Tongues of Fire: The Explosion of Protestantism in Latin America*. Oxford: Blackwell, 1990.

———, "Evangelical and Charismatic Christianity in Latin America." In *Charismatic Christianity as a Global Culture*, ed. Karla Poewe. Columbia, S.C.: University of South Carolina Press, 1994.

Moore, Sally Falk, "Epilogue: Uncertainties in Situations, Indeterminacies in Culture." In *Symbol and Politics in Communal Ideology: Cases and Questions*, eds. Sally Falk Moore, and Barbara G. Myerhoff. Ithaca, N.Y. and London: Cornell University Press, 1977.

Novaes, Regina, *Os Escolhidos de Deus: Pentecostais, trabalhadores e cidadania*. São Paulo: Marco Zero (Cadernos do ISER 19), 1985.

O'Dea, Thomas F., and Renato Poblete, "Anomie and the 'Quest for Community': The Formation of Sects among the Puerto Ricans of New York." In *Sociology and the Study of Religion; Theory, Research, Interpretation*, ed. Thomas F. O'Dea. New York and London: Basic Books, 1970.

Ortner, Sherry B., "Theory in Anthropology Since the Sixties," *Comparative Studies in Society and History* 26, no. 1 (1984), 126-166.

Poewe, Karla, ed. *Charismatic Christianity as a Global Culture*. Columbia, S.C.: University of South Carolina Press, 1994.

Poblete, Renato, *Sectarismo Portorriqueño*. Cuernavaca: CIDOC, Sondeos no. 55, 1969.

Robertson, Roland, *Globalization: Social Theory and Global Culture*. London: Sage, 1992.

Rolim, Francisco Cartaxo, "Expansão protestante em Nova Iguaçu, " *Revista Eclesiástica Brasileira* 33, no. 131 (1973a), 660-675.

———, "Pentecostalismo," *Revista Eclesiástica Brasileira* 33, no. 132 (1973b), 950-964.

———, "A propósito do pentecostalismo de forma protestante," *Cadernos do ISER* 6, (1977), 11-20.

———, "Pentecôtisme et Société au Brésil," *Social Compass* 26, no. 2-3 (1979), 345-372.

———, *Religião e Classes Populares*. Petrópolis: Vozes, 1980.

———, "Gênese do Pentecostalismo no Brasil. In: *Revista Eclesiástica Brasileira* 41, fasc. 161, 119-140.

———, "Igrejas Pentecostais,"*Revista Eclesiástica Brasileira* 42, no. 165 (1982), 29-60.

———, *Pentecostais no Brasil, Uma Interpretação Sócio-religiosa*. Petrópolis: Vozes, 1985.

———, *O que é pentecostalismo*. São Paulo: Brasiliense (Primeiros Passos 188), 1987.

———, "Popular Religion and Pentecostalism." In *Popular Religion, Liberation and Contextual Theology*, ed. Jacques van Nieuwenhove, and Berma Klein Goldewijk. Kampen: Kok, 1991.

———, *Pentecostalismo: Brasil e América Latina*. Petrópolis: Vozes, 1995.

Sahlins, Marshall, *Islands of History*. London: Tavistock, 1985.

Souza, Beatriz Muniz de, *A experiência da salvação, Pentecostais em São Paulo*. São Paulo: Duas Cidades, 1969.

Stoll, David, *Is Latin America Turning Protestant? The Politics of Evangelical Growth*. Berkeley, Calif.: University of California Press, 1990.

Tennekes, Johannes, "De Pinksterbeweging in Chili: een uitdaging," *Wereld en Zending* 1, no. 2 (1972), 148-163.

———, *El movimento pentecostal en la sociedad chilena*. Iquique: CIREN, 1985.

Valderrey, José, "De sekten in Centraal-Amerika: Een pastoraal probleem," *Pro Mundi Vita Bulletin* 100, (1985), 1-43.

Willemier Westra, Allard D., *Axe, kracht om te leven, Het gebruik van symbolen bij de hulpverlening in de candomblé-religie in Alagoinhas (Bahia, Brazilië)*. Amsterdam: CEDLA, 1987.

Willems, Emilio, "Protestantism and Culture Change in Brazil and Chile." In *Religion, Revolution and Reform*, eds. W. d'Antonio, and F.B. Pike. New York: Praeger, 1964.

———, "Religious Mass Movements and Social Change in Brazil." In *New Perspectives of Brasil*, ed. E.N. Baklanoff. Nashville, Tenn.: Vanderbilt University Press, 1966.

———, *Followers of the New Faith*. Nashville, Tenn.: Vanderbilt University Press, 1967.

Yinger, J. Milton, *The Scientific Study of Religion*. New York and London: Macmillan and Collier, 1970.

2

The Modern, the Magic, and the Ludic

The Pentecostal View Toward an Insecure Life, an Argentinean Case

Daniel Míguez

The question of whether Latin American Pentecostalism favors or opposes modernization is already a classic one in Pentecostal studies. It is interesting to note that, in general, authors choose to make "strong" claims in relation to this issue. There are those who conclude that Pentecostalism is a conservative force and others that assert that Pentecostalism, on the contrary, is a progressive force on the traditional-modern axis. A few authors have observed the possible ambiguities that, in these terms, Pentecostalism may present. In the following text I will attempt to show that the concept of *ludism* allows us to provide new answers to the old question. This perspective is not meant to definitively answer "yes or no" the question of whether

Pentecostalism favors or opposes modern life. On a different vein, my intention is to demonstrate how, for certain social sectors, the Pentecostal worldview allows people to, as it were, live at the margins of modernity, sustaining an ambiguous relation with it.

This paper will be presented in the following order: First, I will briefly summarize some of the analyses that have been offered on the subject. Second, I will describe the social situation of some of the members of the congregation in which I did fieldwork and from whom the evidence I will use in this article will be extracted. Third, through the use of a few examples I will demonstrate how Pentecostalism allows a sort of back and forth movement between modern and magical views of the world. Then I will try to explain how this is possible, using the concept of Ludism (Droogers, forthcoming). Finally, I will establish certain possible parallels between the ambiguities of the Pentecostal worldview and people's positions in the social structure.

Brief Bibliographical Review

The debate on the character of the relationship between Pentecostalism and modernization is already present in the classic studies of Emilio Willems (1967) and Christian Lalive d'Epinay (1968), who focus mainly on Brazil and Chile. These studies identify and place the emergence and growth of Pentecostalism between the 1930s and 1950s. Both authors propose some sort of association between Pentecostal expansion and the processes of industrialization and urbanization that Brazil and Chile underwent during this period. Willems asserts that the ascetic values of Protestantism present in Pentecostalism induces a type of conduct which contributes to the structural transformation of Brazilian and Chilean societies. For Willems this transformation proceeds from micro on to macro contexts. First, Pentecostal values of hard work, thriftiness, and the importance of family life promotes the upward social mobility of converts, making this behavior particularly meaningful to them. Because these transformations of behavior occur in sectors such as family, work, state relations, etc., it is possible to assume that these values will expand across society favoring modernity (1967, 164-179). Willems also argues that Pentecostal's traditional abstention in political activities is actually another form of protest against society. This is due to the fact that political corruption was so rampant in the traditional order that any form of participation implied support for the status quo.

As I said, Lalive d'Epinay strongly disagrees with Willems. On the one hand, he argues that the authoritarian relationships between Pastor and parish "reproduce ... the paternalist model of the expanded families which are based as the Hacienda in the antithetic concepts of oppression and protection, grace and arbitrariness in sum, tyranny and paternalism" (1968, 167). On the other hand, Lalive d'Epinay does not agree with the idea that Pentecostalism brings the "spirit of capitalism" to Latin America. For him, in Pentecostalism "neither progress nor hard work are essential values, the last one is seen as related to sin, since to go to work it is necessary to abandon the protective shell of the religious community" (1968, 188). Finally, Lalive also disagrees with the idea that refraining from political and social involvement is another form of social protest. To Lalive this implies the abandonment of the role as citizens required by modern state (1968, 165).

This debate, which one could assume is the product of a certain time period and a particular theoretical approach, has pervaded studies on Latin American Pentecostalism for almost two decades without coming to a conclusion. In 1980, for example, Judith Hoffnagel entered into the Willems-Lalive d'Epinay debate, with a position more aligned to Lalive d'Epinay than to Willems (Hoffnagel, 1980, 121). In 1986 and 1992 the question was addressed by Jean Pierre Bastian, who again sees a conservative force in Pentecostalism (1968, 168). However, in 1990 the well-known sociologist of religion David Martin argues through several examples for a positive relationship between Pentecostalism and modernization. In general terms all of these texts do not present great novelties in relation to the original terms in which the debate was established. Gary Howe developed a more original approach to the subject. Howe (1980) presents a critical perspective on the way many of the previous authors thought of Latin American modernization. To him, Latin American modernization does not represent a clear passage from a traditional social order to a modern one. Modern institutions in Latin America grew during the 1930s to 1960s, but they incorporated an ambiguous function. Therefore, the prevailing order is one in which the modern and the traditional are mingled: State institutions do not follow strict rational bureaucratic principles or the idea of citizens with rights and duties. Instead, they are pervaded by clientelistic ties which undermine their rational functioning. The market does not operate as a space for open competition, but as space in which the corporate behavior of industries struggling for state-guaranteed privileges is rampant. Furthermore, the job market does not provide rural migrants with jobs in the industrial sector, but they are instead incorporated in to the informal market pursuing "ill defined" economic activities. Therefore, some of the institutions of modernity—the state, the market, and the cities—were consolidated as a result of the Latin American structural transformations between 1930 and 1960. However, this "consolidation" of modern institutions did not mean the substitution of the traditional for a modern social order. Instead it meant the incorporation of both kinds of orders into a new type of institution.

Howe then compares Umbanda religion with Pentecostalism for the Brazilian case. He concludes that while the symbolic structure of Umbanda reflects what Brazilian society has of clientelistic and traditional, Pentecostal structure reflects what it has of rational and bureaucratic. The majority of the population integrated into some of these clientelistic ties would be reflected in Umbanda. Those excluded from clientelistic networks must establish "modern" relationships with the state, and they are reflected in the Pentecostal value system (Howe, 1980, 135-136). Hence, even though Howe considers some of the complexities of Latin American modernization, he concludes that there is a positive association between modernity and Pentecostalism.

As I claimed at the beginning, even if there are elements which allow one to argue on one side or the other of the Pentecostalism-modernization equation, authors normally gave rather one-sided answers. Looking at this issue André Droogers (1991) suggested that it is possible to think of a paradoxical relationship between modernization and Pentecostalism. I hope to advance in this line of reasoning through the use of the concept of Ludism. I also hope to explore another element that has not been thoroughly examined by authors when defining and analyzing modernization processes. Normally, modernization has been defined by looking at urbanization, state transformation, market development, and job relationships. Less attention has been paid to the diffusion of scientific rationality that accompanies modernization. Only Johannes Tennekes (1985, 68) makes a brief remark on the subject, arguing about the difficulties that popular sectors might have in incorporating scientific symbolism.

Insecure Life

As Howe has demonstrated in his comments on Latin America, many social sectors, because of their particular situation in the job market and in their relationships with the state, are left in an ambiguous situation in relation to the institutions of modernity. Due to certain recent transformations in its social structure some authors (Alberto Minujin, 1993; Alberto Barbeito and Rubén Lo Vuolo, 1992) assert that more people have fallen into these ambiguous positions in Argentina since 1976. There were basically two processes that have provoked this fall: a) a reduction in social policies and programs, meaning a reduction of the Argentinean welfare state; and b) a reduction in the formal job market. People therefore "backslide" into the more informal economy. This produced certain transformations in the Argentinean social structure. On the one hand, those individuals who previously lived below the poverty line become even more socially vulnerable due to the reduction of favorable social policies and programs—for example, their access to health care and education diminishes. On the other hand, social sectors that traditionally stood above the poverty line and within the formal job market start to fall below it and develop survival strategies within the informal economy. It is notable that the greatest expansion of Pentecostalism occurred in Argentina during the eighties when this process was at its peak.

The Pentecostal church where I did fieldwork is located in a neighborhood in which this economic and social transformation has had certain impact, and is also a social sector that lives in the ambiguous zone in relation to modern institutions. To illustrate this I will briefly describe the position in the job market, the access to education and health care, and the relationship with state offices that people of the neighborhood have.

Position in the Job Market

In order to assess the neighborhood population's position in the job market, I referred to school registration records which indicate the

professions of the student's parents. The records illustrated that most
of the women were homemakers. However in the majority of cases
working women were employed as housemaids (21.1 percent). Men
were mainly construction workers (27.7 percent). It is interesting to
note that 19.12 percent of all those working independently, and 12.18
percent of those working with no fixed income pertain to the construction industry. Only 9 percent of those working under official
contracts belong to this branch of the industry (Barbeito y Lo Vuolo,
1992, 174). Besides construction workers, people in other professions
in the informal economy included almost 50 percent of the total regis-
trations. In many other cases it was hard to tell if the registered profession implied involvement in the formal job market or in the informal
economy. However, it is possible to infer from these numbers that a
significant percentage of the neighborhood's population works in the
informal economy.

Education and Health Care

The *Mapa de la Pobreza en La Argentina* (Poverty Map of Argentina)
declares that only 3.2 percent of the children between six and seven
years in the neighborhood in which I did fieldwork is located do not
attend school. Therefore, we may infer that most of the children of
the neighborhood do in fact start primary school. However, according to the neighborhood school data it is notable that many of the
students have difficult schooling careers. During 1985 repeaters oscil-
late between 15 percent and 29 percent depending on grade. In that
same year there were 44.33 percent over-age students in the seventh
grade—the last grade in primary school. With passage into secondary
school, difficulties in continuing in the educational system become
aggravated. There is a massive exodus from the schooling system in
the fourteen to nineteen age group. Data from the *Censo Nacional de
Población y Vivienda 1991* (1991 National Census) exemplifies the
point. In the neighborhood 3104 children between ten and fourteen
years old were attending school while only 890 in the fifteen to nineteen age group attend. There are also clear restrictions in access to the
health care system for people belonging to this social sector. Given
their insertion into the informal job market many of them do not
have access to health insurance or other forms of health coverage. The

document *La Pobreza en el Conourbano Bonaerense* (Poverty in the Suburbs of Buenos Aires, 1989) indicates that between 42.6 and 54.5 percent of the poor have no health care coverage (1989, 42). Medical services to these sectors is provided by public hospitals, which are overwhelmed by an increasing demand and see their resources diminished by cuts in social policies (Alicia Gershanik, 1993, 158-160).

Relationship with the State

To illustrate how relationships between the neighborhood population and the state occur, I will use an interview which I did during my fieldwork. I have used this interview in previous work but I will use it again due to its eloquence. The interview allows one to clearly perceive the way that the state is pervaded by clientelistic relationships associated to the way political parties function in Argentina. The interviewee was Elvira, a young woman about twenty-six or twenty-seven years old. She had recently had a baby and urgently needed milk for him and also some clothing for her other children. She turned to the Consejera Vecinal (Neighborhood Councillor) to get them through a social plan that the municipality implemented to assist families in need. The Consejera Vecinal is also, and not coincidentally, a local leader of the political party in power at the municipality at that time. As Elvira asks for the milk and clothing she needs, the Consejera Vecinal asks her to affiliate to her party. Elvira tells the story in the following way:

> [Elvira]—Chichi? I don't like her at all.
> [Researcher]—You don't like Chichi?
> [Elvira]—No, she's a bitch, she's a self-interested bitch.
> [Researcher]—And she's a Peronist Councillor?
> [Elvira]—I think she's a Neighborhood Councillor, I don't know what that means.
> [Researcher]—Ah, a Neighborhood Councillor.
> [Elvira]—Well that's what she is. She's one of those.
> [Researcher]—And she is a Peronist?
> [Elvira]—Well of course. The other day they signed me up to be a Peronist.
> [Researcher]—And you don't like Peronists?
> [Elvira]—No. Because they call you compañera [partner, companion], but they say it in a way ... you can see that they are being false from a

mile away. And the other day I signed up to be a compañera as well, at least in that way, I said, they'll give me something.

[Researcher]—You signed up to get what, the food that Chichi distributes?

[Elvira]—I signed up because she asked me if I wanted to affiliate to some party, and if I wanted to affiliate to hers. So I said sure, why not? Like as I said it's the same for me.

[Researcher]—And then what happened?

[Elvira]—Well, one day I went, I don't know if she was giving out milk, I don't remember what she was giving—oh yes—she was distributing some school clothes for the kids, so I signed up to get some clothing for Adrian [one of Elvira's sons] and that same day they asked me if I wanted to join to the Peronist party. So I say—okay—since I am here; if we are dancing let's dance.

To conclude this section we can say that neighbors do not fully participate in modern institutions. Their position within the job market are not typical of modern life, their relationships with the state are also not clearly mediated by the institution of citizenship, their access to modern medicine is limited, as well as their access to the schooling system. In relation to this last point it may be important to stress that the limits that these social sectors experience in their access to the educational system implies a restricted socialization in scientific rationality. This hinders their ability to understand many of the issues and processes that affects their daily life, such as the functioning of the economic system or medical language.

The Modern and the Magic

In this section I will try to show how certain doctrinal elements of Pentecostalism have an ambiguous character; they promote both modern and magical perspectives on life. I will try to show this by examining how Pentecostal doctrine addresses two issues. First, I will examine the doctrine on economic issues, what is known (at least in Argentina) as the "doctrine of prosperity." Then I will look at how Pentecostal doctrine addresses the issue of divine healing. It is important to point out that conflicts on these topics exists among Pentecostals themselves, therefore different churches within the Pentecostal field construct different doctrines pertaining to these issues. In this study I will refer only to the way doctrine was expressed in the specific church where I did fieldwork.

Prosperity

During my stay in the Pentecostal congregation, references to the job market and household economy were frequent. These subjects were repeatedly referred to at Sunday services, some doctrinal courses which I attended, and were also present in some of the interviews which I conducted with members. What was said about these issues I think is well summarized by presenting three different occasions in which the subject is referred to in one of the doctrinal courses I attended. These three references were made by the same person, the course instructor, on three different occasions, each during one of three different classes. During one of the classes the instructor read a section of the Bible: "You will earn your bread with the sweat of your forehead." After reading it, he looked at the audience and made the following remark:

> Man must work, God says that he has to do so ... if not he'll be misera-
> ble. He must be responsible in his work, he's responsible for sustaining
> his wife and children, he's the head of the family and the wife must
> submit to him. It's not like the man has to be a machista that when he
> enters the house everybody starts to shiver because they say "iuuuhaa,"
> here comes the monster, no, no, no. The men sometimes may help the
> women in the kitchen with the dishes just to help his mate ... and the
> women must be at home and also be careful of the household economy
> ... not just buy anything or be careless about prices and everything ...

These assertions seem to sustain Willems claim that Pentecostalism promotes rational economic behavior and an emphasis on family life. However, during another class in the same course, one of the instructor's comments favors the sort of claim which Lalive d'Epinay makes. Reproducing the instructor's discourse:

> It is important that you save Sundays for God and the family—if you
> can't, you can't. I know there are professions like nurses, or policemen,
> or even bakers that sometimes have to work on Sundays and it is very
> hard for them, but a real believer will seek to change his profession.
> God will provide him with an even better position. You must know

that sometimes it's the devil who provides jobs ... jobs in which you
may earn a high salary of 2000 pesos [US$2000] and get a car and every-
thing, but many times in order to comply with that job you must leave
the church.

Having said this, a man attending the course commented: "Yes, that's
true, once I got a job in a factory with a good salary and everything
and we started to stay away from church. Before I realized it five years
had gone by in which we didn't come to church."

The third reference to family economy is also the most frequently
preached in services and presented in the numerous testimonies that
members of the congregation deliver. This is how the instructor presented it:

We must give God what belongs to Him. He asks only for us to tithe, he
gives us 100 and from those 100 he asks only for 10, and if we give those
10, he will bless us greatly. If you give with a shovel, God in return will
give you a truck full of blessings. I want to tell you the story of when I
converted. To tell you the truth, my wife and I were very bad economically. I had only enough money with me for our trip back home ... well,
we entered this church when it was only a small tent. In that moment
the Pastor was preaching exactly about this subject and I felt moved, I
was touched by the Holy Spirit and I gave the last coins I had in the
offerings. We had to walk 20 blocks back home ... the next day I had to
look for a job and ... well I don't remember if I borrowed money from
my mother-in-law or ... how it was that I ... the thing is that the next day
I went to apply for that job. I got there and there was already a pretty
long line, I took my place at the back of the line. On top of that all the
guys in the line were handsome so I said: no, I already lost this job, they
won't hire me. However, of all those that were in that line the only one
hired was me. I had no words to thank the Lord, I didn't know how to
... [thank him].

Before going on to the next example I will briefly analyze the three
references the instructor gave to show why I say that the Pentecostal
worldview allows an ambiguous relation with modern institutions. In
the first case, as I have already mentioned, it is easy to see the relationship between certain values of modern life and Pentecostalism. An
emphasis on rational economic conduct and ordered family life would
comply with the kind of rationality that—supposedly—a modern job
market demands. However, in the second case we find a double depar-

ture from this view, which is deepened more still in the third example.
On the one hand, we find the elements mentioned by Lalive d'Epinay,
with the job market being depicted as an area in which satanic forces
intervene. The Devil may "provide" jobs, especially those "good" jobs
that set people apart from the church. The idea that family economy
and the job market is intervened by transcendental forces is expanded
in the third example. In this case, it is God who opens the doors of a
job to a faithful follower. In these last two cases, components of the
economic sphere are explained as being the result of the intervention
of transcendental forces. Here we have a jump from a modern and let's
say "rational" explanation of how the world of economy functions, to
a sort of magical explanation in which transcendental forces act. I
think this is where we may perceive why I said that the Pentecostal
worldview allows this coming and going, accepting and denying, the
values of modernity. The view allows one to follow the values of
modernity—hard work, ordered family life, and saving as channels for
economic progress—and at the same time accepts a departure from
them—the intervention of transcendental forces as causes for economic progress.

Divine Healing

The doctrine of divine healing assumes that there is a satanic origin to
every disease: The Devil or one of his demons convinces the patient by
"whispering in his ear" or "talking to his mind" that he is really ill.
This being the origin of sickness, a cure is achieved by asking the Holy
Spirit, or Jesus himself, to set the ill person free from the bad spirit's
influence. Normally, church leaders pray to God for Him to do this
job and set members of the congregation free. Given that God,
through His power, is able to free people from illness, the antidote
against any possible physical injury rests in a solid faith in God. As the
Pastor preaches: "Since I got hold of the benefits of the Cross I have
never been ill, in 28 years I have never been sick." Even though this is
the official doctrine of the congregation, in practice the majority of
the church members consult a physician or take medicines even for
the slightest cold. Pastors then face a conflict. On the one hand, it is
risky to tell people not to go to the doctor—which is illegal—and also
because there is always the risk that people may become more ill or

even die. On the other hand, it is possible that even if the Pastor does instruct people not to go to the doctor they will probably still continue to do so. The Pastor resolves the conflict in the following way: "I have nothing against medical doctors: they are brought to earth by God, in his immense mercy, to alleviate the suffering of those that don't have enough faith." We can see here again how the Pentecostal worldview presents this ambiguous character towards modern world institutions. At the same time there is a magical view in which the causes of illness are transcendental forces, but still the practice is clearly entrenched in modern life. People go to the physician even if the sort of scientific-rational explanations offered for disease clearly contradict possible magical explanations.

The Ludic

The dualistic character of the Pentecostal worldview and practices has caused many researchers to ask whether or not Pentecostals truly believe in the direct intervention of transcendental forces in everyday life. Many times during my observations I have perceived simulation and forced "sacred interpretations" of daily events. However, my observations also allow me to say that many times a great part of my informants really accept the alternative of transcendental forces acting in their daily lives. In spite of this, as I have tried to show, these same people often behave following a modern paradigm that leaves very little space for magical life perspectives. The obvious question then, is: how is this possible? Although it is difficult to give a definitive answer to such a question, I think the concept of Ludism (Droogers, forthcoming) may allow a certain explanation. In the rest of this article I will try to develop the sort of explanations that this concept enhances. I must admit that this concept is new to me and that I am far from being able to fully grasp its pros and cons; however, I still think it is worth the exercise.

Johan Huizinga sees an element in play that pervades the whole of human activity. His definition of play—"specific and temporary worlds within the habitual world, that allow to carry an activity that is fulfilled in itself" (1957, 23)—highlights some of the central elements I want to point to when I speak of ludism. The possibility of play implies an alternative to momentarily interrupt one set of rules in order to adopt others which in turn may also be suspended in order to reestablish the former ones. It is important to mention that Huizinga, like other authors, asserts that there is seriousness in play. What I mean is that the concept of play does not imply that the activity developed as play is not taken seriously. For this reason, as Droogers does, I will use the term *ludic* instead of play since the term play is more associated to nonserious activities. Droogers' concept of Ludism basically has two differences with that of Huizinga. It does not imply that adopting one set of rules necessarily means abandoning the other. For this reason, and here is the second difference, man's ludic capacity is his ability to sustain, at the same time, two or more paradigms of reality, managing the contradictions, paradoxes and dichotomies that this provokes. In this view, life and culture are not a coherent whole, but instead are the sum of imperfectly articulated fragments. Man uses a series of rhetoric elements and ambiguities present in the different paradigms to create an illusion of totality, and of unity, where in fact there is conflict and diversity (Ewing 1990, 262). This concept of Ludism, I think, will provide us a certain vantage point in order to understand some of the Pentecostal views and practices. My hope is that in this way we may discover other things in Pentecostal views and practice than what questions on simulation and manipulation have allowed us. If we admit as part of human nature this ability to, as it were, maintain a multiple view of reality, the ambiguities we have been pointing to in Pentecostal views and practices may appear to be ludic exercises. From this perspective, for example, the ambivalence present in the doctrine of divine healing could be viewed as a ludic exercise in which a modern practice—going to the doctor—and a magical understanding of disease are combined. Illness is explained as the result of a spiritual war between the forces of good and evil, but at the same time is treated as a biochemical process. As we said, life appears as the sum of fragments which many times enter in conflict. In this case a rhetorical element—the idea that doctors are created by God for those lacking faith—is used to create the illusion of coherence, where in fact there is contradiction.

In the case of the doctrine of prosperity, ambivalence may also be understood as a case of ludism. Economic progress is first presented as a result of personal effort and rational behavior. Then we discover that it may also be the result of the way transcendental forces—God or

Satan—act. As in the case of divine healing there are multiple and contradictory views of things in Pentecostalism. In one human forces
dominate, in the other transcendental forces reign. Issues in the job
market or in the family economy may be explained by referring to
either of these two paradigms. In this case contradiction between both
kinds of explanation are not so obvious as in the case of divine healing
doctrine. Although, from our external perspective, there is tension
between these "magical" and "rational" interpretation of issues, in
emic terms this is not so apparent. There is not such a clear contradiction between the idea that one who works hard will make progress in
life and the assertion that God may economically help the faithful.
Pentecostals seem to rely on this ambiguity of doctrine to maintain a
sense of unity and totality.

Pentecostal Views and Social Structure:
A Meaningful Parallelism

There is an element in what has been said up to here that surely has
not escaped the reader's attention: both Pentecostalism and the positions of people in the social structure imply an ambiguous relation
towards modern institutions. I think this general parallelism may be
pursued a bit further. I will venture then to explore more precise
forms of it in order to show why the Pentecostal worldview may
make sense for people of this social strata.

Given people's insertion into the informal economy, the possibilities of finding jobs and making a living does not only depend on the
accumulation of a good working reputation, in terms of talent and
dedication. These values may help them, but they are not enough by
themselves to guarantee a successful career. Fortune and uncontrollable situations are very important in one's capacity to make a living.
I will give an example using some of my fieldwork observations.
Those who work as informal construction workers doing small re-
pairs in peoples homes, will find a job partly in relation to their reputation as good, honest, and skillful workers. However, their possibility of getting a job depends as much on the fact that someone within
their network of relatives and friends will require their services in a
particular moment. Job demand does not flow in an orderly manner.
At times there may be a peak of demand in which the worker may

even have to reject some offers. Two weeks later he may suddenly be out of work and remain unemployed for two or three months. Hence, family economy and economic progress depends in part on the modern values of hard and dedicated work, but it also depends on uncontrollable forces. The doctrine of prosperity presented earlier reflects this ambiguous situation of people in the informal economy. It provides an alternative that combines rational and magical elements in explaining why and how personal economic progress is achieved. This reflects the kind of forces that guide the destiny of people who search for jobs in the informal market.

As I indicated earlier, access to scientific medicine by the congregation's social sectors is limited. Basically, the limitations are expressed in two ways. First, there is an "objective" way: they are offered scant opportunities to be effectively assisted by medical services. Their access is materially limited. On the other hand, they also have a limited subjective access to medicine, since—due to scarce socialization in the scientific paradigm—they are hardly in a position to understand medical procedures and speech. This allows magical explanations of health problems—that in many cases are part of people's cultural traditions–to be more satisfactory than medical ones. On the other hand, people perceive that scientific medicine is generally more effective in dealing with illness than the traditional one. Therefore, people of this social sector find that the kind of medicine to which they have a more fluid—material and subjective—access is less effective, and that the more effective kind of medicine is less materially and subjectively available. The kind of perspective that Pentecostalism provides again reflects the ambiguous status that these individuals have towards a modern institution such as scientific medicine: it allows the use of scientific medicine while at the same time it provides alternative explanations and forms of cure.

The concept of ludism has allowed me to develop this sort of parallelism, but it has not been my intention to present them in a conclusive manner. However, I think that this ambiguity towards modern institutions that both specific forms of Pentecostal doctrine and certain social sectors sustain—coincidentally the sectors more responsible for the recent expansion of Pentecostalism in Latin America—is at least suggestive and worth exploring. At the same time I must confess that I still have certain doubts towards this concept. These doubts originate above all in that the concept implies an ontological claim: either man is in itself ludic thus creating this multiple views of things, or man lives a ludic life, and therefore multiplicity is an undeniable part of life itself. Whatever the case, I tend to be suspicious of ontological claims, in part—I must admit—out of my own prejudice, but also because ontological claims are always hard to prove. Even so, if the concept of ludism serves at least the purpose of introducing new questions and framing new perspectives it will fulfill part of its mission.

References

Barbeito, Alberto, and Rubén Lo Vuolo, *La Modernización Excluyente.* Buenos Aires: UNICEF/CIEPP/LOSADA, 1992.

Bastian, Jean P., *Breve Historia del Protestantismo en América Latina.* México D.F.: CUPSA, 1986.

——, "Les Protestantisms Latino-américains: un Object á Interroger et a Construire," *Social Compass* 39, no. 3 (1992).

Droogers, André F., *Methodological Ludism: Beyond Religionism and Reductionism.* Amsterdam, Forthcoming.

——,"Visiones Paradójicas de una Religión Paradójica. Modelos Explicativos del Crecimiento del Pentecostalismo en Brasil y Chile." In *Algo Más que Opio. Una Lectura Antropológica del Pentecostalismo Latinoamericano y Caribeño*, eds. Barbara Boudewijnse, André Droogers, and Frans Kamsteeg, San José, Costa Rica: DEI, 1991.

Ewing, Katherine, "The Illusion of Wholeness: Culture, Self and the Experience of Inconsistency," *Ethos* 18, no. 3 (1990), 251-278.

Gershanik, Alicia, "Salud de los Niños y Empobrecimiento: Su Atención." In *Cuesta Abajo*, Alberto Minujin. Buenos Aires: UNICEF/Losada, 1992.

Hoffnagel, Judith Chambliss, "Pentecostalism: A Revolutionary or a Conservative Movement." In *Perspectives on Pentecostalism: Case Studies from the Caribbean and Latin America*, ed. Stephen Glazier. New York: University Press of America, 1980.

Howe, Gary, "Capitalism and Religion at the Periphery: Pentecostalism and Umbanda in Brazil." In *Perspectives on Pentecostalism: Case Studies from the Caribbean and Latin America.*, ed. Stephen Glazier. New York: University Press of America, 1980.

Huizinga, Johan, *Homo Ludens.* Buenos Aires: Emecé Editores, 1957.

INDEC, *La Pobreza en el Conurbano Bonaerense.* Buenos Aires, 1989.

——, *Censo Nacional de Población y Vivienda 1991.* Buenos Aires, 1991.

Lalive d'Epinay, Christian, *El Refugio de las Masas*. Santiago de Chile: Editorial del Pacífico, 1968.

Martin, David, *Tongues of Fire. The Explosion of Protestantism in Latin America*. Oxford: Blackwell Publishers, 1993.

Minujin, Alberto, *Cuesta Abajo*. Buenos Aires: UNICEF/Losada, 1992.

Tennekes, Hans, *El Movimiento Pentecostal en la Sociedad Chilena*. Iquique/Amsterdam: Ciren/VU, 1985.

Willems, Emilio, *Followers of the New Faith. Culture Change and the Rise of Protestantism in Brazil and Chile*. Nashville, Tenn.: Vanderbilt University, 1967.

3

Pentecostal Women in Chile

A Case Study in Iquique

Hanneke Slootweg

This contribution is based on research carried out between March and September 1986, in the city of Iquique in northern Chile. The purpose of the study was to inquire into the appeal which Pentecostalism offers women from the most underprivileged social groups, who were previously involved in activities related to popular religiosity or considered themselves to be Catholic.[1] The majority of Pentecostal faithful are women.

Pentecostal conversion was analyzed in respect to the gains and losses involved in being a member of the Pentecostal Congregation, in order to find out whether it is possible to view women's conversion as a personal strategy in response to a specific social situation. It was also important to inquire about the relevance of Pentecostal symbols in this situation. The question was operationalized by focusing on the changes that conversion brought to women's lives. The study considered and analyzed changes regarding women's religious experience, male-female interactions, health, and material conditions.[2]

This contribution is structured in the following manner: first, there is a brief historical introduction of the Chilean Pentecostal Movement. This is followed by a characterization of the group of interviewed women. Next, women's own testimonies are presented in order to show the range of changes produced on their lives by conversion into the Pentecostal faith.

Origins of the Pentecostal Movement in Chile

The Pentecostal church in Chile was born in the year 1909 from a rift within the Methodist church. This rift was preceded by highly emotional events which occurred in the Methodist Church of Valparaíso and were perceived by the exalted faithful as "possessions" or "baptism by the Holy Spirit." These events were characterized by extended periods of fasting, atonement, and prayer. The American missionary Hoover, who testified regarding these phenomena, believed that these experiences were produced by an authentic Christian inspiration. Missionaries leading the Chilean Methodist Church, however, condemned these events. To the officialdom, the events in Valparaíso were "hallucinations or craziness (madness)" (Willems 1967, 10).

This intolerant attitude on the part of the ecclesiastical authorities resulted in the banning from the church of the group involved. In 1910, three organizations led by Hoover were established. This common front, known as the Methodist National Church, developed from a local movement into a national organization with affiliations throughout the country. In 1932, the movement split further into two separate churches: the Methodist Pentecostal Church and the Evangelical Pentecostal Church.

The great expansion of the Pentecostal movement occurred during the 1930s. Each of the above churches produced a number of autonomous Pentecostal congregations which varied in size and geographical distribution. Aside from these national movements, other North American groups were also established in Chile (Willems 1967, 11).

While these events were occurring, there were other social processes taking place in Chile. The end of the nineteenth century in Chile was marked by a transition from a *latifundista* society into an industrial society. This period was marked by a high degree of confusion and insecurity. In the twentieth century, the Chilean economy appeared to function fairly well. In the North, the mining of copper and nitrate flourished. In the South, the mining of coal was started in Concepción and an increase in migrations sparked agricultural development. These changes in turn resulted in increasing exports.

Nevertheless, this economic boom was not only of brief duration, it was also associated with unequal distribution of wealth. At the beginning of the 1930s economic development was waning. High inflation coupled with an agricultural crisis caused an increase in rural-urban migration which was not met by working opportunities. Thus, urban stratification processes began, with the rise of a middle class employed in the public sector and a growing mass of urban proletariat searching for means of survival which gave birth to the informal sector. In the political sphere, there was a tendency towards alternative forms of democratic governments of short duration and dictatorships of longer term (Lalive d'Epinay 1969, 30-32).

From the thirties until the present, the general structural picture has not changed much. The external debt increased until recently, there were economic recessions, almost continuous political repression (particularly in the period 1973-1989) and the proletarianization of the working classes.

The Catholic church became politically active in reaction to the Pinochet regime, which in turn restricted the church's privileges, while the Pentecostal church continued to grow steadily (Slootweg 1987, 19).

A Characterization of the Women Interviewed

The twelve women interviewed[3] are members of the Iglesia Evangélica Pentecostal (Evangelical Pentecostal Church) in Iquique. This church consists of 900 members and two-thirds of the congregation are women. The congregation was founded in the 1940s and has members from birth as well as members by conversion. It is a fast-growing congregation through conversions. The converted membership is primarily lower class while the birth membership is largely middle class.

All of the interviewed women are converted members, raised in a strong popular Catholic faith and/or participants in popular religious festivities.[4] The age range of the women is between thirty and sixty years of age, with an average of fifty. The level of schooling is also generally low. Approximately half of the women had not finished primary school, although some did have technical training. Half of the women were housewives and the other half held jobs in the informal sector, for example, domestic work, ironing clothes, sewing, etc. Two-thirds were married and one-third were "single" in varying forms. The spouses of those married worked in the service sector or as skilled workers.

The Conversion Experience

Some women were experiencing difficulties prior to their conversion. There were marital problems, financial problems, illnesses, and loneliness, which motivated them to search for assistance in the Pentecostal church. They were acquainted with the practices of the church through converted friends, relatives, or through public activities such as street preaching. Others experienced revelations from the Holy Spirit in spontaneous ways, without any previous contact with the Pentecostal church.

The first manifestation of the Holy Spirit was a realization by the women that they were sinners. They felt resentment and cried uncontrollably, sometimes for hours. After, the Holy Spirit would provoke extraordinary sensations and the forgiveness of their sins, revealed to them in symbolic ways. All of this fostered a state of great happiness. Sister Eduina testifies to this as follows:

> One day I was in a congregation with six brethren and I felt the presence of the Lord. I felt raised and there was a light illuminating my heart. At that moment, I felt happy and I was able to speak about the wonderful things of the Lord. I started preaching that the Lord can heal and in the hospital we formed a group of twenty-five people who called for the Lord ... I saw a tree in the water. At the beginning the tree was turning green and I knew that the Lord had forgiven me. And I was healthy again (Slootweg 1987, 21).

And Sister Silvia comments on her conversion:

When I was at a mission, the Lord arrived in my soul (heart). I felt as if two bags of potatoes were falling from my shoulders. The Lord raised me and I saw how he took my heart from my body, charged it, and put it into my body again (Slootweg 1987a, 33).

The testimony of Sister Alvina is also fairly typical:

When I left the church, I went home and I went to bed. In my dream I saw an animal, a big snake crawling along a large avenue with many trees. The snake looked at these tress, creeping from one to another. There was a vessel. The snake looked at the vessel from top to bottom (I was this vessel) and started to cry. I was very afraid and I ran away. Then I woke up and felt sad, for I thought the snake had baptized me. But one day, I told this dream to the minister of the church and he told me that it wasn't a baptism of the devil, but it meant that the snake could not find a place in my heart and he fled crying (Slootweg 1987a, 33).

The cause of grief is thus eliminated immediately (this is often an illness) or else it disappears after a short period of continued prayer. Some of the women were converted recently or a few years ago. Others converted ten or twenty years ago. But all of them declared that conversion had changed them. They were no longer suffering from depression or fears because their soul had found comfort. Many of them lost their interest in worldly matters and concentrated completely on the salvation of their souls. This change was frequently expressed by the women in religious symbolic language, such as "after baptism of the Holy Spirit the Lord changed me. Instead of being a daughter of darkness I am now a daughter of Light" (Slootweg 1987a, 41).

These words mean that this woman knows the will of the Lord and tries to practice it. The assurance that their sins have been forgiven is one of the most important elements of the women's faith. Further, the possibility of a personal communication with the Lord, which did not exist before, is a fundamental part of their religious experience (Slootweg 1987a, 34, 41).

Changes in Male-Female Interactions

The life of married women changed in a radical manner after their conversion to the Pentecostal church. If the husband also converted, marital interactions improved greatly. The opposite occurred if the husband did not convert. Sister Silvia describes this as follows:

> Formerly, my husband was an alcoholic, a fighter, and when he came home drunk he wanted to start a row and I insulted him. He insulted me, he struck me, and I took revenge by beating him when he slept. It was a marriage ruled by "an eye for an eye and a tooth for a tooth." Now everything has changed. We sometimes become angry with each other, but we no longer fight, we don't insult each other any more. When my husband goes out, I am sure he isn't going to drink, but he is visiting his relatives (Slootweg 1987a, 35).

The testimony of Sister Elvira is also a good example:

> My marriage wasn't very happy. My husband drank and he was like a child, not taking any responsibility. He hit me and spent all the money drinking and on other women. There were many fights. I had a child every year. I wanted to kill my husband, my children, and myself. My boss, who knew me, saw my bitter face and told me that I needed faith in my life. She advised me to speak with a priest. The priest advised me to speak with my husband and told me how to prevent fights, but it didn't work out and the feeling of bitterness persisted. A friend in the neighborhood was a member of the Pentecostal Church and I wanted to go to the religious services with her. Once, after having been to a service, I had a dream. The Lord had opened my heart and he entered and forgave me. That night my husband came home drunk. He was mad but I didn't answer him when he wanted to start a fight. My husband noticed that I had changed very much and he allowed me to go to services. I asked the Lord to change my husband too. Now he is responsible for the children and he doesn't squander his money, he is more concerned about what is lacking at home. He doesn't fight any more and he drinks less. In the past I was filled with hatred, I couldn't see a happy couple, I was very jealous because I wasn't happy and I wanted to destroy that marriage. Now there is more love in our home (Slootweg 1987a, 35).

These examples show that the women had problems prior to their conversion. They complained about their husbands spending their earnings on drinking and on other women, that they behaved like children showing no responsibility towards their families and thinking only of their own needs. This mode of conduct and the resulting problems to the women involved are phenomena commonly found in the lower classes of Chilean society, which is the status of the majority of the Pentecostal faithful.

The ideal type of woman and man which guides female and male behavior can be summed up in the concepts of the "machismo-marianismo complex." This complex presents both contradictory and complementary elements. In machismo, for example, women are considered both inferior and passive beings. It suits them to follow their man in everything, to obey, and respect him. As a women, she deserves no respect and her natural disposition towards evil cannot be averted. Hence her need for tutorship from her male relatives. She is only honored and respected in her role of virgin (purity) and mother (self-denial). Men are thought to be active beings, authoritarian, aggressive, and virile, who can allow themselves more sexual freedom because their honor is related to their virility. In marianismo, this positive-negative value is reversed. Woman is perceived as superior in comparison to man, spiritually and morally. Women are considered self-disciplined and wise while men are seen as irresponsible children (Steenbeek 1985, 37, 40-43).[5]

The ideology of Pentecostalism offers a solution to these problems because its norms and ideals concerning marriage and male-female interactions are somewhat different to those of the socio-cultural context. The directives of the church guide recently converted women towards a strategy of changing the existing situation by adopting reconciliatory conduct towards their husbands. Additionally, women testified that conversion caused a great change in their personalities and this provoked them to modify their conduct. In the Pentecostal church, members are educated in "correct marital behavior patterns" in separate sessions for men and women. The text of Ephesians 5, 21-24[6] is discussed in the congregation and used to illustrate the position a woman has to occupy in relationship to a man.

Some sisters expressed their opinion regarding the ideal behavior of a Pentecostal woman. Sister Veralda states: "a woman must always submit to the authority of a man because the Evangelist commands that man orders woman just as woman orders children." And Sister Ana says: "when a Christian woman marries she has to please her husband in everything, she has to follow him in everything" (Slootweg 1987a, 42-43).

The sessions offered by the church focus not only on the appropriate rules of conduct for women, but also on the fact that Pentecostal males also have to change their attitudes towards their wives. Most important is the fidelity of the Christian man towards his wife. They ought not to be jealous, but loving. Some men also gave their testimony during the church services regarding the changes they had experienced in their marriages. The following text is symbolic of this improvement in marital interactions:

> Before my conversion, I was very poor and I spent all my money on drinking. I had only one suit but that did not matter. I treated my wife badly (abused her physically) many times. I treated her so badly that she had to stay in bed for a long time. One day, when I went home and was so drunk that I could hardly stand on my feet, my wife wanted to kill me, but the Lord stopped her hand with the knife and changed her heart. At the beginning I resisted change, I did not want to be converted, I did not want to listen to the voice of the Lord because I thought I already had my religion. But I was converted anyway. The Lord changed my heart. One day he showed me that I shouldn't continue cohabiting with my partner, but I told the Lord that I couldn't marry because I did not love her. So, I asked the Lord to put love for her in my heart. One night I had a dream in which the Lord showed me a beautiful lady, elegantly dressed, and I fell in love with her, although I only saw her from the back. I called out to her and when she turned around I saw that she was my partner. From that moment on, the Lord put the fire of love in my heart and I never stopped loving her (Slootweg 1987a, 36).

The Pentecostal male has to be more responsible as a father, to participate in the education of their children, and seriously assume his role as supporter of the household. While the woman has the major responsibility for domestic tasks, men have to contribute in this domain as well, in order to run the home when the wife goes away on a mission in fulfillment of her religious duties. Women can appeal to the ecclesiastical authorities when men fail and revert to their old ways. The directives of the church have a sanctioning power in these cases. When the new faith is important to both husband and wife and they are both full members of the church, the feeling of sharing the faith and sharing the same hopes leads the couple into a better integrated pattern of interaction (Slootweg 1987a, 35).

When we compare the norms for male and female behavior within the Pentecostal church with those of the broader socio-cultural context we can observe a paradox of break and continuity. For example, male authority and female subordination are not being challenged within the church. Rather, they are legitimated on the basis of the teachings. There is also an appeal to an assumed sense of tolerance on the part of women. In a meeting of Dorcas, the Pentecostal women's organization, the minister advised women to "be wise" and search for the flaws in their husbands' character so that they could be reconciled when he became angry with them. In this situation, a wife has to show all of her love and tenderness to prevent an argument. If the husband has not converted to the faith, the wife has to act with wisdom in choosing the right moments for fulfilling her religious duties, which is to say that she must first fulfil her domestic obligations. According to the ministers, women who are "inefficient" and "awkward" destroy their homes (Slootweg 1987a, 43-44).

For the interviewed women, the conversion of their husbands meant a significant improvement of their position within the marital situation, due to a lessening of the macho attitude. The responsibility for the home (including the economic aspects) becomes shared, there is a certain protection against infidelity, and the physical abuse caused by drunkenness is eliminated altogether. On the other hand, if the husband does not convert, the marital situation progressively deteriorates. The family is conflict-ridden from the fact that the wife wishes to impose her new way of life on all of its members while the husband wishes to maintain his own habits. This causes an increasing alienation of the couple. There is no understanding between them and their struggle continues, often vehemently, sometimes subtly. At first, these women have difficulty obtaining permission to participate in religious services. The husbands are jealous and resent their wives' independence. The women have to hide on the way to church and rely on lies to explain their absence. Sister Sofia tells the following story:

> My husband did not want me to leave the house. He didn't want me to be independent. Previously, I had been submissive and shy. I would go to church, but I had to hide it from my husband. However, the Evangelist changed all of this. Since we lived in Pozo Almonte, I would say that I was visiting my children who were studying in Iquique. And then my husband became ill. I asked him for permission to go to church to pray

for his health, but he retorted that I might get used to going to church.
It was one year before my husband would allow me to attend services.
Then I was very happy and I wanted to give my name to the Book of
Life.

In most cases, the husbands gave in, but those women had to be watch-
ful of the time they returned home to avoid conflicts, and they could
not participate as intensely as their sisters.[7] These women have to
learn to avoid problems with their husbands in order not to endanger
their attendance to services.

The church's instructions on spirituality to those women whose
husbands have not converted indicate that they are allowed to act
independently. But this does not mean that they are not to obey their
husbands in all other matters, since, according to the Evangelist they
must always submit to him, even if he is not a Pentecostal. Women do
not always adhere to these instructions of the church, however, as we
may conclude from the following testimony:

> I begged the Lord continually to set me free in whatever way. It didn't
> matter whether the Lord used the death of my husband as a means to set
> me free, because serving the Lord was most important to me (Slootweg
> 1987a, 37).

Additionally, women are not allowed to separate. According to the
Evangelist "it is forbidden for men to separate what the Lord has united." It is only in cases of cohabitation without marriage that women
are allowed to separate, since this kind of relationship is not sanctioned by the Evangelist. For women in this situation, the church's
teachings might be used to legitimate the woman's wish for a separation in a troubled relationship. Women whose husbands are not converted may discuss their problems in the Dorcas meetings and thus
relieve themselves of their pressures. They can invoke the help of their
sisters by means of community prayer. Prayer is these women's only
instrument, given their belief that only the Lord has the power to
change human beings. Neither the wife, nor the minister nor other
members of the church have any power over the husband's soul
(Slootweg 1987a, 36-37).[8]

The Evangelical Pentecostal Church of Iquique has many single
women as members. Some are widowed, others are separated or aban-

doned. This group was also included in my research as a matter of comparison and contrast. The most important feature in these women's conversion experiences is the sense of protection they feel after joining the church. The knowledge of the Lord prevents them ever feeling lonely again. They now have a spiritual "heavenly husband" who is always concerned about them, even in material aspects. The heavenly husband takes more from them than their earthly partners. Sister Ana states this as follows:

> Before, the earnings from the altiplano did not arrive, or they had been spent or something like that, I didn't know where. Now, neither I nor my daughters are working, but clothing and food are never lacking (Slootweg 1987a, 38).

None of these women work, but, as they say, "the Lord has blessed them." He chose to reveal their poverty-stricken condition to the members of the congregation who could help them. The Lord can also provide an earthly husband in place of the heavenly husband for these women, as the following examples show:

> When my previous husband left me, I was very depressed. I felt lonely and was hoping that he would return. I waited every night for him. I wanted to take my life. I tried four times. But the Lord always protected me because I always told people of my intentions. For this reason, every time they took me to hospital and I survived. Once, I was very afraid that I might survive with mental damage and attempted another suicide. I asked the Lord to take my life because until that moment all I had known was foolishness. The Lord spoke through a Pentecostal brother. I like the Evangelist very much, although I also like the man through whom I had come to know the Evangelist. We fell in love and lived together. I didn't know of the things of the Lord as yet and I didn't know if this was good. I asked my husband to take me to church. I liked the church very much and asked the Lord to illuminate my heart. I thanked the Lord because he had given me a Christian husband so as to make up for all the misery I had suffered with my other husbands. Nevertheless, one day I read in the Bible (Galatians), chapter 5 and understood that I had lived in adultery because I was not married and I could not therefore enter the Kingdom of Heaven. We separated. Now I don't need a husband in the flesh because I am happy with my heavenly husband in my heart.

One of the women married at a very early age and was abandoned after a few years of marriage. She was left alone with two small children. She felt humiliated and despised by her husband. After she knew the Lord, she felt rehabilitated by her "heavenly husband." Her comfort is grounded on a biblical passage in Isaiah 54, 4-6:

> Fear not, for you will not be ashamed; be not confounded, for you will not be put to shame; for you will forget the shame of your youth, and the reproach of your widowhood you will remember no more. For your Maker is your husband, the Lord of hosts is his name; and the Holy One is Israel is your Redeemer, the God of the whole earth he is called. For the Lord has called you like a wife forsaken and grieved in spirit, like a wife of youth when she is cast off, says your God.

In Chilean culture, marriage is the normative ideal for women and the Pentecostal faith can offer legitimation as well as compensation (in the economic and emotional spheres) for separated, abandoned, and widowed women (Slootweg 1987a, 38-39).

The Improvement of Material Circumstances

The women interviewed told me that before their conversion they were very poor and afterwards the Lord had blessed them in the sense that although they were not richer than before, they lacked nothing essential. According to the teachings, this is consistent with the promise made by the Lord that neither bread nor water would ever be lacking. This is not to say that after their conversion there were no difficulties. Sometimes the women had to wait a while before receiving the Lord's blessings. In the majority of cases, this blessing arrived in the form of a revelation of these needs to other sisters or brothers of the church. Sister Ana recalls:

> There were a lot of years when we were very poor and I did not complain. I prayed to the Lord. One day, one of my sons brought home a basket full of food which had been given by a sister of the church.

And Sister Maria states:

> When I did not work I went through poor times. Sometimes I had no shoe polish and I cleaned them with water. Once I went to church and

my shoes needed mending and I complained to the Lord in my prayer. I
fell to the ground. The Lord made me fall to the ground in order to
show me that his will be done. I said to him: Lord, it is not my will that
counts, but yours. I rose to my feet and felt very happy. The next day, a
young boy came and gave me a new pair of shoes. He was not a member
of the church, but the Lord had revealed to him my need (Slootweg
1987b, 20).

The material situation improved for the majority of women who had
a converted husband because he would stop spending all his money on
his own needs. Although some women have to work since their husband's salary is insufficient to cover their needs, often this work conflicts with their religious duties. It is quite possible that women's faith
diminishes when their participation is curtailed. It is unclear why
some members of the congregation are more blessed than others.
According to the minister's wife and some of the brethren, there are
hardly any unemployed members in the congregation, thanks to the
church and the blessings of the Lord. One brother told me that within
his church people inform each other about the possibilities of having
better jobs and in this way they support each other.

As members of the church, women have access to friendships that
provide them with the help they need. They persist in praying, waiting for divine solution to their problems. This solution normally
comes through other people, but is always interpreted as a blessing by
the Lord.

Droogers (in this volume) states in his introduction that it is not
simply a network of mutual help which characterizes a religious organization and this network alone does not explain the extra-religious
needs of people. In my opinion, the reciprocity which governs the
Pentecostal church's network organization is of a different kind from
a secular organization. In the view of the Pentecostal faithful, it is not
that people can be dependent on the goodwill of their fellow members. Rather, the brethren feel motivated by the providence of the
Lord to provide their assistance, and do not expect direct reciprocity.

The Evangelical Pentecostal Church of Iquique is characterized by
values such as solidarity and love among fellow members. There is an
obligation on those who are economically better off to contribute in a
higher degree towards ecclesiastical funding. With these funds, the less
fortunate can be supported in emergencies (Slootweg 1987b, 25).

Sister Juana testifies to this by stating that "the sisters practice Christian love very well. They worry about what I am lacking both in material and in spiritual ways" (Slootweg 1987b, 24).

Membership in the Pentecostal church, while it requires a regular contribution from each member, also helps them economically in case of need. In a country such as Chile, where unemployment rates can at times be high and the salaries of the working classes are always rather low, membership can provide a sense of security to satisfy basic necessities (Slootweg 1987a, 70).

Healing

After their conversion, the women received the blessing of the Lord in healing from their ailments. They do not only receive these blessings for themselves, but their husbands and children were also healed when the women asked for the Lord's help. In the majority of cases, the illnesses cured were of a serious nature or it was a case of a crisis, such as cancer, rheumatic fever, tuberculosis, appendicitis, typhus, a hernia. Sister Juana tells the story of her own healing, thus:

> I was acquainted with the Pentecostal church because I had a neighbor who was a member of this church. At that time, I was quite ill and for ten years I had two tumors in my breast. At the time when the neighbor spoke to me of his faith, I felt like something was falling down from my head, as if I had been blind, and I believed that the Lord could heal. I asked my neighbor to heal me. Sisters and brothers from Arica arrived at the house of my neighbor and promised to heal me, but on condition that after I was healed I would preach in the street, because at that time there were only a few preachers. The brethren danced and danced and after a certain moment I was cured. I felt something like a fire burning in my breast.

It is well known that the Pentecostal faithful who are ill before and after their conversion address themselves to the Lord and do not acknowledge the usefulness of the health care system. The testimony of Sister Sofia is typical of this fact:

> At the moment of my conversion I was more seriously ill than ever and all I wanted was to go to church. I didn't know that the Lord healed and I had had an ulcer for six years. My husband told me to go to the doctor,

even though the Lord spoke to me and told me that there was no need
to go, that he would heal me in the church (Slootweg 1987a, 39-40).

One of the possible explanations for these women's reliance on divine
powers rather than the health care system might be attributed to the
fact that the national health care system is rather poor and does not
function very efficiently.

Additionally, people of low income have little access to health care,
hence the search for alternative forms of healing, particularly in situations of crisis. In a study by Maria de Bruyn conducted in Iquique, and
published under the title *They say that some people have good hands*
(1987) she looked at how people select treatment options and she revealed some of the disadvantages perceived within the national health
care system.[9]

With the exception of social and economic factors which play an
important role in choosing a form of religious healing, the practices of
the Pentecostal churches of northern Chile have some shared elements
with the Aymara worldview and also with some features of popular
Catholicism. Indeed, the Aymara find solace in their religious specialist while the Catholic faithful ask the Lord for help when they suffer
health problems. The healing is not solely physical in all of these cases.
Rather, physical illness is a manifestation of an impure and sinful state
of the human spirit.

In this respect, Sister Alvina's interpretation of illness is a clear
example:

> One day when I wanted to go to church I vomited blood many times.
> My brothers were very worried. Nevertheless, I felt healthy enough and
> mocked my brothers, because I knew this was God's work. He wanted
> to change me completely. My body threw out the bad that was in me. I
> fainted when they took me to hospital, but I wanted to leave the hospi-
> tal. The doctors told me that I only had two days to live because I had a
> tumor in my lung. I didn't believe them, though. Then the vomiting
> stopped. It has been two years since and I am still very healthy.

In this way, the healing event symbolizes a complete change within
the person after the forgiveness of her/his sins. This event is known in
Pentecostalism as the "baptism of the Holy Spirit" and leads to the
acknowledgment of good and evil. The mental changes produced sig-

nify a complete break with a former way of life (sin) and makes possible a new way of life (Pentecostalism).

Conclusion

In summary, we can state that the new model of life as a member of the Pentecostal church offers a solution to some fundamental problems to women of the lower classes in Iquique. The religious ideology of the church provides answers to marital problems by partially differing from the broader social context and reduces the weight of machismo on the husbands. Thus a relative improvement of women's position is effected.

For many women, marital life improves after conversion of the husband. Male abuse of alcohol and its consequent misery disappears completely. The husband no longer stays out as often and is more involved with his family. Women gain much more confidence in the fidelity of their husbands and in some cases the husband's role in the domestic domain is also enhanced, together with a greater involvement with the education of their young.

All of these changes occur in response to the teachings of the church. The Pentecostal church supports the women's position, so if the husbands transgress the rules, women can appeal to the church's authorities. This institution educates the women as well as the men in matters of the Christian marriage, according to which the woman has to submit to the man, but he also has obligations towards her.

For women whose husbands are not converted, membership in the church offers a legitimation for their independent attitude in regard to their husbands, in certain matters. Additionally, they are supported by the congregation in difficult situations.

For single women, who are in an exceptional situation within Chilean culture where marriage is an important and normative ideal for women, the teachings legitimize their status. While for married women, both the economic and emotional status of the family unit is greatly improved by conversion, which imposes a different pattern on spending. Also, the incorporation of the family in a network of interactions within the church provides greater security for their basic needs. The latter also applies to the single women.

The Evangelical Pentecostal   practices Christian neighborly love, as well as the conviction that the Lord is rewarding their religious zeal in the material sphere. These are convincing arguments for the potential faithful.

The objective situation of the health system which results in poor attention to women of the lower classes, forces this group to search for alternative healing practices. The Pentecostal church offers one alternative, while also offering more than the healing itself. Healing and membership are related to a new way of life which provides structural solutions to diverse, concrete needs.

Does this mean that women's conversions can be considered as strategies for changing their social position? When we compare the needs of the potential faithful with what the Pentecostal faith offers them, it becomes clear that women of the lower classes would find these solutions appealing. Women in the lower strata struggle through marital difficulties and find themselves in poor economic conditions, having to raise a family in poverty. If these women do not have a partner, their economic and social position is extremely vulnerable. Their duty in taking care of the family includes the responsibility for their complete well-being.

It shouldn't surprise us then, that all the women interviewed had taken the initiative to contact the Pentecostal church and later on intended to convert their husbands to accompany them. In many cases, the process of conversion of the husband was initiated when he became ill and the wife obtained the church's support in healing him. As a result of these actions, the men gave up and converted.

Although we have seen a correlation between people's needs and the church's offer of support, it is more difficult to identify the specific features of the women's social and personal strategies. Did the women convert to Pentecostalism in order to improve their situation and did they know in advance the possible consequences of their conversion? The women's persistent efforts to convert their husbands would indicate that this is so. One of the problems associated with this question is that the women never talk about the conversion as a consciously selected course of action to improve their situation.

At any rate, this contribution clearly shows that the Pentecostal churches are capable of resolving people's dilemmas and in respect to the other questions, we will let the women's testimony speak for itself.

Notes

1. Popular Catholicism in Iquique is expressed most clearly in the organization of religious dancers who perform yearly in honor of the *Virgen del Carmen* during the festivities in her honor.

2. A comparative investigation on this topic by Cornelia Butler Flora was very valuable in planning for the present study.

3. Twelve women were interviewed and through participant observation other information was obtained. In a six-month period, I attended church services five times per week and the meeting of women organized by Dorcas, once a week.

4. This research compared the advantages offered to these lower-class women by popular Catholicism and those offered by the Pentecostal church. The inquiry sought to find out if the women had sought assistance in problem-solving from the Catholic church or from popular Catholic organizations. There was also comparison with a control group of Catholic women.

5. Both women and men appeal to machismo and marianismo ideal types, depending on circumstances.

6. "Be subject to one another out of reverence for Christ. Wives, be subject to your husbands, as to the Lord. For the husband is the head of the wife as Christ is the head of the church, his body, and is himself its Savior. As the church is subject to Christ, so let wives also be subject in everything to their husbands."

7. The Pentecostal church services have no pre-established length, since the arrival of the Holy Spirit cannot be forced.

8. In my opinion, wives are forced into a passive position by awaiting Divine aid. A more active stance would induce them to change their own attitudes. There is an underside, however. By forgiving their husbands and maintaining a submissive attitude, they deal in very subtle ways with inequity. This may arouse a feeling of guilt on the part of the husband who would then change his conduct.

9. The national (public) health care system in Chile (SNS) operates with a 7% contribution from monthly earnings of those working in the public sector. To a certain limit, all benefits are free. This service provides for a basic social security, but there are many problems, such as bureaucratic inefficiencies and a lower quality of care. Also the waiting period for consultation is rather long and even though patients are seen for free, medication is not covered by the system.

References

Bruyn, Maria de, *They Say Some People Have Good Hands: How Patients Choose Treatments for Illnesses in Iquique*. Amsterdam: Vrije Universiteit, 1987.

Butler Flora, Cornelia, "Pentecostal Women in Colombia: Religious Change and the Status of Working Class Women," *Journal of Interamerican Studies and World-Affairs* 17, no. 4 (November 1975): 411-425.

Hoogen, Lisette van den, "Gezegend onder de vrouwen: rituele genezeressen in katholiek Minas Gerais," *Sociologische Gids* 4, (1987): 248-270.

Lalive d'Epinay, Christian, *Haven of the Masses: A Study of the Pentecostal Movement in Chile*. London: Lutterworth Press, 1969.

Slootweg, Hanneke, *Religie en haar gevolgen voor het leven van vrouwen in volkswijken te Iquique*. Utrecht: RUU, 1987a.

———, *Religieuze bewegingen en sociaal protest: een empirische toepassing van Laeyendecker op de Chileense Pinsterbeweging en de Noord-Chileense bedevaartverenigingen*. Utrecht: RUU, 1987b.

Steenbeek, Gerdien, "Wie niet sterk is moet slim zijn: vrouwen en het machismo-marianismo complex in Latijns Amerika," *LOVA-Nieuwsbrief* (1985): 36-58.

Willems, Emilio, *Followers of the New Faith: Culture Change and the Rise of Protestantism in Brazil and Chile*. Nashville, Tenn.: Vanderbilt University Press, 1967.

4

Pastors, Lay People, and the Growth of Pentecostalism

A Case Study from Arequipa, Peru

Frans H. Kamsteeg[1]

> And then the pastor showed me God's leaders. He said, "even the pastors always depend on God. But they have the example of Moses and Joshua. Neither of the two was able to become a leader by himself, but with the help of God they could. And God in his great love has not only helped them, but others as well." That is what my pastor told me and it encouraged me a lot. From that moment I knew that I could do it (that is, become a pastor, FK) with Gods help, and I soon took charge of the La Blanca annex. We just started right away, but God has been blessing us ever since; the church is growing now.

This quotation is from a Pentecostal pastor running a church in a popular neighborhood of the South Peruvian city of Arequipa. He is one of many church leaders responsible for the continuous expansion of Protestantism in Latin America.[2] This expansion has increasingly

worried the Catholic church in many countries to such a degree that
the formulation of an adequate response to the Protestant challenge
has become a basic concern of many Catholic bishops.[3] Protestant
growth is strongest in Chile, Brazil, and some of the Central American countries, though the figures in use often show considerable variation.[4]

Most studies on the Protestant issue in Latin America have a broad
scope; whether they deal with the continent as a whole or with a particular country, they always pay much attention to growth figures
(Martin 1990 and Stoll 1990 are the clearest examples), not infrequently combined with a clearly pastoral (Catholic) perspective. Very
seldom do we see these Protestant believers at work, or hear their
opinion. This article focuses, from an anthropological perspective, on
Pentecostal meaning-making and the consequences for Pentecostal
growth. The central question is what aspects of Pentecostal discourse
are used to legitimate lay leadership, and how does the expansion
process stemming from that discourse work in practice? I will argue
that power and (symbolic) meaning are the main constituents for any
explication of the steady growth of these Protestant communities.

The analysis rests upon data which I gathered during my fieldwork
in one particular Pentecostal congregation of the neighborhood of
Cerro Negro in Arequipa.[5] This means that I only sporadically refer
to macro-sociological models explaining Pentecostal growth. These
models often use concepts like anomie, modernization, and others,
which do clarify the complicated process of growth, but only to a
limited extent (see Droogers' article in this volume). In my opinion,
however, to deepen our understanding of the phenomenon we need
more in-depth studies of local situations, and particularly those studies
which include internal religious and symbolical aspects.[6]

To start with, I give a general impression of Pentecostal churches in
Peru and a brief sketch of the economic and religious situation of the
city of Arequipa. Subsequently, I present some sermons, prophesies,
and interview pronouncements by pastors and other leaders of the
Pentecostal community in Cerro Negro, in order to demonstrate how
(symbolical) power is divided between leaders and lay people. The
position of the pastor is particularly highlighted. The concrete examples taken from field experience allow me to answer the question of
the impact of Pentecostal discourse on the practice of church growth.

Pentecostal Churches in Peru

The number of studies on the Pentecostal movement in Peru is limited if compared to other Latin American countries, such as Chile, Brazil, or Central America. The other Andean countries—Colombia, Ecuador, and Bolivia—have also attracted more attention (Bamat 1986; Butler Flora 1980; Muratorio 1980; Gill 1990). For Peru, there are hardly any scientific works; the articles and papers available often have clearly evangelistic purposes.[7] The absence of data is not so surprising, given the fact that the start of Pentecostal growth in Peru only dates from the late seventies. Of course there are Pentecostal churches whose history is much longer—the Assemblies of God were founded in 1939—but the first to obtain a foothold in Peru were the traditional (historical) Protestant churches: Lutherans, Anglicans, Presbyterians, Methodists, and later also the Baptists. Alongside these churches, Peru has had the national *Iglesia Evangélica Peruana* since 1922. The latter is the third biggest church in Peru, after the Catholic church and the Seventh Day Adventists. The Adventists have been a fairly stable denomination since the late nineteenth century, whose members are predominantly found in Lima and among the Aymara Indians in the highlands around Lake Titicaca (Kessler 1967; Barrett 1982, 559-661; Lewellen 1978).[8]

By way of introduction, I will dedicate a few words to the development of the Pentecostal movement in Peru so far. It is characterized by what Tennekes has compared to the cell partition process (1985, 21). The Assemblies of God, for example, have experienced so many schisms in their history of more than fifty years that it can only surprise that it is still the largest Pentecostal church. Another characteristic of Peruvian Pentecostalism is that most churches have been founded by foreign, mostly North American, missionaries. Some managed to broaden their scope to the whole country, yet the majority never gained significance beyond the local level.

Given the scarce historical sources, it is not easy to give a clear picture of the growth process. Apart from the book by Kessler, we only have at our disposal the *History of the Pentecostal Movement in Peru* by Huamán and some preliminary studies by the Evangelical Seminary (see note 8; Escobar 1981; Kessler 1981). Huamán is an enthusiastic defender of the Pentecostal cause. His book well illustrates the way

Pentecostalism has spread through Peru. He gives a central role to the individual missionary, who initially is often a foreigner, but in most places is soon replaced by a Peruvian. Personal initiative and the so-called "calling" decide where evangelistic work is started and churches are established. If results are considered promising and church growth permits it, local church members leave their congregation to "push the gospel forward" by founding new churches. These may continue to belong to the original denomination, but often they constitute the start of a new independent church. Separation and schism are of almost daily occurrence. Generally, local pastors take their followers with them in a separation from the mother church; the reasons given for such behavior often indicate organizational problems, though occasionally doctrinal motives are advanced, too. The following quotation from Huamán is illuminating:

> For many years, this was a flourishing congregation of the Assemblies of God. But there have always been frictions, too. Criticism was often expressed as to the forms and customs of the services and the way the church was run. Then, on 23 May 1979, [the congregation], including its 43 annexes, decided to separate itself from the Assemblies of God, to avoid further problems between the brothers and sisters (n.d., 108).

Within Pentecostal churches, this is the normal course of events, but this "growth through division" provokes contradictory feelings. It is in part considered inevitable and even salutary—in cases when separations do not result in a split off from the original denomination—but the negative result is a vast fragmentation resulting from eternal mutual quarreling. The same type of conflict also occurs within Peru's only interecclesiastical organization, CONEP, as a result of which this organization has a rather poor reputation. Moreover, Pentecostals are badly represented in it, despite constituting the vast majority of Protestants in the country.

Arequipa

Economy

Arequipa, situated at 2,300 meters above sea level, is the second largest city of Peru and had about 700,000 inhabitants during my last visit in

1989. It is surrounded by three impressive volcanoes, at the edge of an extensive plateau which occupies a large part of Southern Peru. In fact, the city lies at the fringe between the desert and the mountainous highlands. Its climate corresponds to this position: it is a dry place, with abundant sunshine and moderate temperatures.

Its favorable geographical situation makes Arequipa a center of commerce and services: it is the economic nucleus of Southern Peru, relatively close to both Bolivia and Chile, the commercial bonds with both countries being of major importance (by train, car, and airplane). Additionally, it serves as the nucleus of transit trade between the capital Lima, both adjacent countries and Arequipa's own hinterland, South Peru. Arequipa is also the principal industrial center in the South; it has breweries, a substantial mining industry, milk plants, and an important leather industry. Irrigated agriculture and wool processing (*llama* and *alpaca*) are other economic activities of considerable importance (for an overview see Flores-Galindo 1977; Zarauz 1984).

All these economic sectors together, however, are insufficient to give work to the rapidly growing population. Many people have to seek "employment" in the informal sector. Moreover, the city constantly faces a huge flow of immigration from the highlands, as a result of general underdevelopment and regular economic crises. These migrants, mainly from the Cuzco and Puno areas, seek to survive in street commerce. Many of them are highland Indians, who abandon their natural habitat, as a result of population pressure and prolonged periods of drought alternated by floods, in the hope of better chances in the city. Thus Arequipa becomes the destination of many highlanders, and often serves as an intermediate station on the road to Lima.[9] Given the magnitude of the problem, migration is also a major issue for local politicians. For the Pentecostal churches, the stream of migrants is the main source from which they try to gain followers.

Religion

Catholicism is strong in Arequipa. According to 1981 census figures, around 95 percent of its inhabitants declare they belong to the Catholic church (INE 1984, 196). The remaining 5 percent are Protestants —mainly Pentecostals, Adventists, Jehovah Witnesses, and Mormons. Catholicism is not only dominant numerically, the Arequipan clergy is also very influential at the level of the national church hierarchy. To give an example, most archbishops from Lima have had their roots in Arequipa; the city is therefore named "the Rome of Peru." The present archbishop carefully nurtures this reputation, for example by mentioning this at the occasion of the visit of Pope John Paul II to the city in 1985.

However, various threats affect the dominant position of official Catholicism. There is a constant shortage of priestly callings, while church revenues are seriously decreasing. Church services are, therefore, increasingly performed without the presence of official church representatives—that is, without priests. This problem is acute in the provinces, but also in the rapidly expanding number of the city's *pueblos jóvenes* ("young villages", a euphemism for slums), where a proper Catholic church building and a priest are becoming a rarity.[10] Not only is the church practically absent in most neighborhoods, official Catholicism with its Mass, sacraments, and other rituals also has an increasingly limited appeal to people. Instead, "popular Catholicism" enjoys broad support. The Virgin of Chapi occupies a central place in the worship of ordinary Arequipans. The sanctuary is situated in a remote desert place, some fifty kilometers outside the city. In May, especially May 1, the place is visited by large numbers of people, but veneration is not limited to this period. Moreover, Chapi's Virgin is the Patron Saint of Arequipa and her image is inseparably connected to people's daily religious practice, although there are several additional saint cults playing a pivotal role in Southern Peruvian popular Catholicism. These saints are supposed to give their attention and help people cope with their daily problems. Problem-solving is also the main characteristic of another form or popular religion, which has its roots in a mix of indigenous Indian religion and Catholicism: the Cross feasts. These are particularly popular among slum migrants from the highlands. Marking holy places is an old Indian tradition, which under the influence of Catholicism was often done by placing wooden crosses, sometimes wrapped in a cloth or with an image of Christ hung on them. In the city, crosses have become like saints, and are believed to be easily accessible and open to communication in the same way as "personal" saints (Irrarázaval 1980). The variety of Catholic practices, both official and popular, together constitute the principal bone of contention for Pentecostal preachers. They fiercely fight against what they consider "a world of superstition." Catholicism happens to be a tough enemy, though, since in Peru's "Rome" Pentecostal growth is relatively slow.

Growth of a Pentecostal Church in the Neighborhood of Cerro Negro

In the 1981 census, 16,614 people were registered as *evangélico* in Arequipa, which was about 3.5 percent of the city's total population. Protestants as well as their Catholic opponents agree that this figure is most probably too low, given the recent increase of the number of churches in the city. Exact figures are lacking, but there are certainly more than eighty Pentecostal congregations, varying in size between 25 and 500 members. The *Iglesia Evangélica Peruana*, the biggest non-Pentecostal church in Arequipa has more than twenty congregations of its own. Taken together the total number of Protestants must now be around 6 percent. The biggest individual church is the Pentecostal Assemblies of God, whose central congregation now has more than 500 members. This principal congregation has many "daughters" in the city's neighborhoods and in the provinces, and is constantly promoting the formation of new ones. Most of the time these newly established congregations have their own pastor, who is firmly dedicated to the growth of his church. Yet growth is more often accomplished by multiplication of churches than by the expansion of single churches. Some pastors manage to keep their members within the church boundaries and finally reach their dream of a mature and big church; most of them, however, have to face constant division and the foundation of new, competing groups.

Such groups often function in private rooms, for newly started groups lack the means to buy a piece of land to build a church on. The modest housing of the groups does not prevent them from growing. Their modest appearance may even encourage people to enter more easily, as they hardly notice the threshold. In any case, meetings are generally not attended by people who live at a distance of more than two blocks, which is a constant source of complaint by the respective pastors. This type of practical reasoning is also responsible for the fact that people prefer to attend or even start a new congregation instead of continuing to belong to their original church.

The fact that Pentecostal growth goes by multiplication instead of expansion of single congregations brings us to the question of what exactly the mechanism responsible for it is and how is it rooted in the Pentecostal belief system. In short, what is the religious basis of all this "mushrooming" and how does it affect power relations in the Pente- costal churches? To answer these questions I present a few testimonies from the Cerro Negro congregation.

> There were three of us at that time. Together we built this temple here and all three of us have a ministry now: Alberto went to La Joya, Alfre- do to the Maranatha Church—his father is still a musician at our church—and I conduct the congregation in which the three of us started and which belongs to the *Centro Evangelístico Pentecostal* (CEP). It is going well now, the church is growing. (pastor Francisco)

> Well, all of us have our different plans for the church. In the musical group, for example, we think that some day I will set out to some place to take an active part in God's work, to preach the gospel, and establish a church. I mean, me alone, but it is still too early. (lay brother Juan)

> I have always been very anxious to really learn about God's word. I have never been a back-seat person; my place was in front, preaching, but I still had to learn so much. My pastor told me to pray and fast abun- dantly in order to know how to serve the Lord. Every instruction by the pastors, I obeyed. So, once I went to a distant mountain to pray and fast. I asked, "Lord, I want to serve you, could you allow me this gift?" Actually, I never thought of myself as a leader. The Lord summoned me to be one. (Valentín)

These three testimonies from the CEP congregation in Arequipa's biggest slum, Cerro Negro, are fairly revealing as to the way Pentecos- tal communities manage to widen their range. The congregation these Pentecostals come from was only fourteen years old at the time the interviews were held. Pastor Francisco was one of its founders, who decided to start working in a church after a miraculous cure of his friend and co-founder of the congregation. Brother Juan also joined the church after being cured of a gastric ulcer through the prayer of a friend. Brother Valentín converted when "God brought him to his senses" at a time when he was on his way to commit another robbery somewhere in the neighborhood. This, he reported, was such a tre- mendous experience that his whole life was turned upside down. In his "new life" (see also Tennekes 1985) he had only one goal, and that was "to serve the Lord by being a worthy disciple."

The church building itself is a typical Pentecostal chapel; it is a small building, almost an annex of the pastoral home. In fact, the pastor originally handed over the plot for this purpose. It is quite a busy place; people very often come to play, sing, or pray, and frequently use the opportunity to consult the pastor if they have a problem. The approximately eighty church members all live within a stone's throw of the church building. In the neighborhood there are dozens of other Pentecostal communities, which are organized in the same territorial way. Most of the believers are Indians who migrated from the Cuzco and Puno region. The majority of them cannot read nor write and speak Spanish only with great difficulty. Consequently reading the Bible is far from simple for them, which gives the few members who do read without problems a pivotal position within the community. Let us now have a closer look at how this church community in the Cerro Negro neighborhood is actually run.

Church Services

Apart from the main Sunday afternoon service (*culto*), there are four nightly meetings during the week. The Sunday service is attended by almost the complete membership. It lasts for about three hours, and starts with extensive individual prayer during which people freely express their emotions and "present their daily tribulations to the Lord." Pastor Francisco has his own prayer seat, at the platform near the pulpit. As time goes by, the room slowly gets crowded and the prayers gradually fade away. Then the service really starts with the reading of a Biblical psalm, followed by a new prayer. The pastor then steps back and one of the brothers steps forward to lead the worship. This part, the singing, again carries on for quite some time; it ends with intensive praying during which several people get very excited and go into ecstasies. They may start "speaking in tongues" or "dancing in the Spirit." People really look as if they are in a trance, and this is also the moment when some use the opportunity to utter "prophecies." These public manifestations are often made by a select group of congregation members, among whom the members of the music band and the annex leaders are especially prominent. The "prophecies" generally have a strong defensive theme: the church congregation must be defended against the hostile outside world. An example:

> Thus says the Lord, that we be vigilant in the present bad times. There is so much that endangers our spiritual life. The enemy is strong! Trust the Lord and obey him, says the Lord. Put your trust in the church leaders and pray for them, pray for the church, that light will shine from it. Thus says the Lord: I see rivers of living water starting from this church. Leaders will stand up and preach God's word in the world. Pray for them, because the world is a dangerous place. May they bear fruit, says the Lord ...

While this prophecy is spoken, the faithful remain silent, but when it finishes thanksgiving abounds in loud prayer. After this prayer, it is time for special requests (*súplicas*). Anybody may come forward to sing a hymn, give his or her testimony, tell of a miraculous event from the past week, relate "God's compassionate intervention" in their life, or simply request other congregation members' "intercession before the Lord" to remove "temptations." If it is felt necessary another song is sung and the usual collection of money is made. This is also when people say pay tithes for the maintenance of the pastor.[11] The latter reads the weekly announcements and then turns to his principal contribution to the service, the sermon. After this normally quite lengthy episode, the meeting is quickly drawn to a close and people return to their homes, spiritually prepared to face the trials of the coming week.

Sermons: On Discipleship

Most Pentecostal churches only have a loosely constituted (and equally loosely observed) set of church rules. The pastoral task is usually one of the best-described functions. The pastor's[12] rights and privileges include the reading of the Sunday sermon, though preaching is not usually the exclusive pastoral monopoly. Every convert may be "used by God's Spirit for the preaching of His Word."[13] In fact lay leaders often sermonize, though the Sunday sermon is usually the privilege of the pastor.

The sermon is used to "awaken the community." People are urged to deepen their spiritual life through abundant praying and Bible reading. Public testifying is another task people are incited to. The latter usually takes place during open-air evangelization raids in one of the city's squares, parks, or markets. But the personal network of friends and relatives—within and outside the neighborhood—is also regularly exposed to conversion efforts. This "recruitment" theme returns in practically all the sermons. The way this is done is crucial to the understanding of Pentecostal church growth.

In his sermons, the pastor frequently relates his dreams or visions concerning the congregation. What I present below as a single sermon is basically a synthesis of a series of different sermons given by pastor Francisco and some visiting preachers in his church community of Cerro Negro. The biblical image of "rivers of living water" (referred to in several psalms) frequently returns in these sermons (as in the prophecy I mentioned above). This "water" is said to flow out of the church into the world. The message of the sermon goes as follows:

> The canals these living-water-streams flow in have to be dug by Christ's followers, by you believers. Only then can the Gospel (=the water) reach the unbelievers who are aching for it. How do you believers acquire the necessary knowledge to build these canals correctly and make the water really flow? To do so you have to "build your house on the rocks of the Bible, God's Word." These foundations, the "solid rocks," enable us to cope with the severe trials of this world; they make us sufficiently strong to lift our heads and face this miserable world in order to convert it. Are we prepared to put our trust on him and change the world? Is this church really such a source of living water? Are you really disciples of the Lord?

This type of question really awakens the congregation. Almost in trance, the pastor describes what he sees when he closes his eyes. He see "the workers leaving the vineyard into the empty field, the hostile areas of the countries which are desperately longing to be conquered." Francisco relates how he once experienced this divine command to "go out and preach the gospel." He especially addresses himself to the youth, urging them to obey the apostle Matthew's commandment to "go ... and make disciples of all nations" (28:19). He tries to give his message extra impact by citing examples of disobedience he personally knows of. He tells of a woman "who at the moment she entered heaven could not answer the question of how many people she had managed to convert, and therefore had to go back on earth." Or tells the moving story of a dying pastor who "had to continue evangelizing because the youth of this congregation failed to assume their responsibility." This example is applied to the Cerro Negro congregation: "I know I have a group of successors, but do they really want to take up their discipleship?" This rhetorical question is emphasized by adding threatening prospects: "You must obey, as time is running out and the apocalypse is imminent." Francisco does not fail to impress his congregation by stating that through him "God is speaking directly to them, for a pastor is only the vessel of God's Word, the messenger of his commandment to evangelize."

Religious Specialists versus the Laity: Pastors and Disciples

The preaching examples I gave above constitute the core of Pentecostal discourse. The pastor, pretending to possess direct access to God, feels he has a mandate to mobilize his flock and make them assume their responsibility as disciples of the Lord. Of this chain of relations between God, pastor, and congregation members, only relations between the last two are open to scientific research. The first, though for the believers probably the most important, should be respected but consigned to the realm of actors' categories. The relationship between pastor and lay believers is without question a power relation, though as we shall see a rather ambiguous, or paradoxical, one. It is, however, the most fruitful relation in terms of Pentecostal church growth. It works at the lowest church level, the congregation, and is the building-stone out of which the movements' success is made. A neutral definition of power, "the capacity to achieve outcomes," may well serve if we are to explain the very effective mechanism of Pentecostal discipleship, because it leaves open the possibility of ambiguity and paradox. What concerns us in this paper—something that in my opinion is often lacking in analyses of power relations in religious context—is the question of the sources of power and their use in particular situations.

I am looking for religious sources of power which are expressed in religious leadership positions, or in other words, for the way religious capital is acquired and invested in power positions. This capital consists of the access to and degree of appropriation of symbols, dogmas, and ritual performances by people. Usually, there is a special group of religious specialists controlling most of the capital flow (Bourdieu

1971, 303). In Catholicism, these are the priests and monks; in Protestantism, they are the theologians and pastors, while in Pentecostalism we only find pastors without much schooling, but with a considerable amount part of religious/symbolic capital at their disposal (see also Rolim 1985, 129ff). The simple fact that these religious specialists possess special—and sometimes secret—knowledge is responsible for the widely accepted view that religion, particularly in societies with strong social differentiation, constitutes a (semi-)autonomous field, separate from the economy and other fields.[14] However, it should be stressed that this autonomy is limited to the "erudite domination" (Bourdieu) of a relatively limited number of specialists manipulating—or even monopolizing—the religious capital. Lay people, the common believers, have far less grip on the flow of symbolical capital.

There are, however, religions in which domination by specialists is less noticeable. Bourdieu characterizes them by the label "religious self-service." In such situations of "practical domination" (Bourdieu 1971, 305), the religious apparatus is almost undifferentiated, and the very believers themselves administer, reproduce, and spread the religious goods. In the case of erudite domination, specialists produce religious goods for consumption by their customers, in the other case the consumers are themselves producers of these goods. This could also be described in terms of a range of religious power (Bourdieu 1979, 82-85). Is the religious—often symbolic—power exerted by a limited number of specialists, or do ordinary believers manage the flow of symbolic capital, thereby dominating the power balance? In this particular case study, the question related to this issue is what positions Pentecostal pastors and lay people occupy in the range of power. To answer this question we turn again to the Cerro Negro neighborhood and the congregation of pastor Francisco. Using the terminology introduced in the foregoing paragraph, we may consider Francisco as the religious specialist within the church community. At first sight he pulls all the strings of religious power: the church is built on his site, he has spent most on its decoration and on the educational material; he decides the main content of the services and last but not least he has a big say in all other congregational matters, and even in the private lives of the members.[15]

Maybe the pastor's symbolic power is even greater, since he is also the chief interpreter and guardian of church discipline. That allows him to control the moral conduct of his congregation: he is the only person who can punish someone who has offended church rules or who has otherwise gone astray.[16] A more subtle way of wielding power is by organizing the content of the religious teaching, principally through Sunday School. Since the pastor is also the first person to be consulted in case of illness, faith healing is another major source of power for him.[17] At his visits to sick people's houses, the pastor has ample opportunity to spread his views and control the observance of his, usually biblically founded, advice. A considerable number of people from outside the church community also consult the pastor for healing purposes.

Yet, pastor Francisco is far from almighty. His CEP church operates the rule that all congregations are responsible for the maintenance of their pastor. Francisco therefore depends for his living on the tithes (*diezmos*) of his followers, though in this case the danger of becoming vulnerable to economic pressure is not great, because Francisco runs a small weaving trade alongside his pastoral duties. Other pastors sometimes have a really hard time when their people "punish" them economically, for, as a common saying among Pentecostals goes, they want to get their money's worth. Apart from reducing tithes, believers may threaten to transfer to a rival Pentecostal church, which in fact happens quite often. Not feeling at ease with the pastor is the reason most often given by those who desert a church; they apparently feel they can no longer realize their own ideas and objectives.

Here we come to a crucial point in our argument, which is the paradoxical situation with respect to Pentecostal leadership. It is true that, according to biblical principles, the pastor wields absolute authority within his congregation, but at the same time every church member who tries to become a good disciple has all (s)he needs at his/her disposal to defy him. Let me explain this a little further. A crucial point concerning Pentecostal leadership is the position of the pastor as Christ's "deputy" on earth. Francisco, for example, believes he has received his mandate directly from God. His pastoral office is not the result of prolonged theological studies, but indeed the result of what he considers a heavenly calling. As he maintains, even the exact location for assuming his pastorship, Cerro Negro, was revealed to him by God in a dream. Only several years after running his congregation successfully did he obtain the authorization of his pastorship from the headquarters of his denomination in the capital Lima. Until then, he had defended his leadership position with reference to his divine calling and a number of supporting Bible texts. Now that he possesses the formal position of power, Francisco continues to emphasize obedience to God, as well as to himself as the pastor who has been singled out by God for this job. For this purpose he also teaches well-known examples from the Old Testament, referring, among other significant passages, to the sacred office of priesthood and to the great leaders of Israel such as Abraham and Moses.

On one occasion I witnessed a sermon by Francisco on the theme of discipleship. For Biblical support he first read Exodus 18: 1-27, the story of Moses and Jethro. The latter told Moses, who was having a difficult time with his people on his way to Israel, that he should appoint a series of leaders to govern his people, and no longer do it all by himself. Subsequently, Francisco explained in great detail and with little room for objection that the situation in Peru was remarkably analogous to the biblical story. In his community, there was a strong need for leaders who could assist him in governing and lifting the church spiritually. These very leaders could even play a decisive role in the church's expansion by winning new converts and establishing new annexes, he asserted. Francisco supported this vision by referring to the type of prophecies I related earlier, and he was sure his appeal was going to be effective. When Francisco consequently started a long and intense prayer for the rise of new leaders, the obstacles to announcing oneself were minimal. It appeared to me that for several church members this special session served to confirm their calling and to persuade them to discuss it with the pastor, who, as they apparently thought, had to give his consent.

Since this was not the only occasion when summons like these were made, there is no reason to be surprised that the greater part of the lay members are anxious to hold some sort of church office. There are elders and deacons; there is a youth group, a musical band, an evangelization group, and even a special prayer group. The majority of the people are committed to the church through one office or another. Though in this article I only base myself on observations in one particular church community, what I describe fits the general pattern in Pentecostal churches all over Peru and most of the rest of Latin America.

Women are emphatically not excluded from church office (except in most cases from pastorship). Women's opportunities to take public offices are more restricted than those of men, at least according to Pentecostal discourse. Dressing prescriptions and the general code of conduct are rather strict as a result of a literal reading of the Bible, particularly the letters of the Apostle Paul. The subordination of women to men is also a recurrent topic during teaching sessions. However, women are ordinary church members; they have the right to vote and are bound to propagate their faith as much as men. Discipleship is open to both sexes. For women, this discipleship even has special consequences. Faithfulness to a calling is a serious and legitimate affair which may undermine the traditional male dominance (by their husbands) which is in force inside as well as outside church boundaries. Women in Pentecostal churches are, therefore, constantly maneuvering between the poles of obedience to and dependence on the pastor and men in general on the one side, and personal initiative and resistance on the other. This constitutes a delicate affair for women, for they have to apply their strategies in two different, though related, domains: the church and their family. Yet for women this double promise of liberation is one of the most appealing aspects of Pentecostalism; it is probably the principal reason why Pentecostal churches are overcrowded with women (see also the contributions of Boudewijnse, Slootweg, and de Theije in this volume).

Religious specialism is one of Pentecostalism's main paradoxes. The office of pastor, the specialist par excellence, is open to all (male) church members. This is in itself nothing much, but what makes the Pentecostal case special is that this theoretical possibility is practiced on a broad scale. Within these churches, all are religious specialists, or "intellectual agents," as Rolim (following Gramsci) ascertains (1985, 140-141). All believers may—and indeed do—actively play their part in the prevailing (symbolical) power game, thus considerably altering them at times. Of course not all make use of this possibility, but it is emphatically not reserved to a specific intelligentsia. Within churches this often means that the official ideology—all believers are equal to God—is in reality at odds with a very clearly observable, though very changeable, hierarchy (see for a similar observation Lalive d'Epinay 1969, 48).

Religious specialism in Pentecostalism is not in the first place based on theological knowledge; the first step for a career as a specialist is taken when a person accepts the biblical commandment to become a disciple, which is often followed by the experience of divine intervention, for example, by means of a message received in a dream. The next step may in some cases consist of intensive Bible study in one of the various Pentecostal institutes in the country. The CEP has such a school in Lima, which is open to all church members who express their wish (and calling) to become a pastor. In most cases, however, it does not come to this. People stay in their neighborhoods, pass through a number of offices within their churches and eventually come to lead a church annex or a congregation of their own, without ever finishing any type of religious training. Pastor Francisco is a self-made man like this and the two young men in his congregation who aspire to become pastor will most probably never receive professional training either. Let us hear what two of them have to say about this matter:

> Maybe the Lord will call me to go to that place. We, the youth of Cerro Negro, want to go and find a congregation straight from where we are now. In the Lima Seminary they study a lot, but I think pastor Francisco has not been there either. He went to work for the Lord right away. I believe the most important thing is having faith. By praying and reading the Bible, we can receive everything that others acquire by studying in Lima. (Juan)

> Well, I do not know how the pastor did it exactly, but what I do know is that his faith is firm as a rock. I myself never went to any seminary, but thanks to the Lord I believe I have learned even more in daily practice, through all the experiences I went through. Maybe it is even better so. When one is serving with all one's heart, nothing is impossible, the Lord does it all. (Valentín)

Both Juan and Valentín want to follow pastor Francisco's route. Others within the Cerro Negro community are also infected by the idea of becoming a pastor at some time. Both young men have a long-lasting relationship with this congregation and they have held most religious offices at least once. Valentín is now the music group's leader and deputy pastor in the annex La Blanca, where eventually he plans to become pastor himself. He is consulted by the pastor and the church board about all major decisions. Juan leads the evangelization group and is the second man in the musical group. Together with four other young people he is responsible for the recently founded annex of San Bartolomé. This is a desolated irrigation village, far away from the city, where a small church has been founded after an intensive evangelistic open-air campaign. It is in this nascent Pentecostal community that Juan hopes to settle as pastor in the future. In fact, to aim for the pastorship appears to both men a logical "last step" in their religious career.

Yet both incipient congregations are supervised by pastor Francisco and the youngsters have respected that so far, since they share the conviction that any local authority comes "from the Lord" and it was Francisco who founded both annexes. Nevertheless both Valentín and Juan do their utmost for these two annexes, hoping to enlarge them to such an extent that they become acceptable as independent congregations, in which case they can logically succeed pastor Francisco. So far, the latter has never raised the subject of succession. He enjoys serving the three communities, and for the time being keeps the aspiring youngsters at bay by emphasizing the heavy responsibility of pastorship and the inadequacy of the two men's experience and knowledge. However, he does not rule out their chances in the future. He even encourages them to dedicate and prepare themselves for such a future task, for, as we have seen above, Francisco actively preaches discipleship on biblical grounds. Valentín and Juan, however, have the feeling they are being kept on a string, though both do their best to avoid expressing this too openly.

The hidden tension between pastor Francisco and two of his congregation members is not just an example of the typically ambiguous relations between religious specialists and the lay believers. What makes this case special is that Francisco has himself trained them to become his rivals. The young men's ambition to become good disciples is constantly fed by Francisco's encouragement to open themselves to the inspiration of the Holy Spirit. This situation may be described in Bourdieu's words as one between dominating and dominated specialists (1971, 324). The dominant Pentecostal pastor fosters a group of well-equipped lay leaders, who in the future are very likely to become dominating pastors themselves.

What we witness in the CEP congregation can easily be character-ized as a power struggle, a conflict between rival men, however much similar terms are avoided in daily Pentecostal practice. The source of the conflict lies in the broad accessibility of leadership positions in Pentecostal churches. The extensive possibilities for gathering sym-bolic capital, the basis for successful power exertion, make this reli-gion very attractive to people, but it is at the same time potentially highly disruptive. In this sense Pentecostal leadership does not differ essentially from other types of leadership in Peru, and, more generally in Latin America. Extreme personalism is traditionally very strong in Latin America; it is therefore not without significance that Lalive d'Epinay (1969) sees great similarity between the traditional large estate holder and the Pentecostal priest.

The kind of conflict described above clearly cannot be kept nor resolved within church boundaries. It is obvious that the protagonists see the solution to the problem only in terms of expanding their scope of action. Though I have lost touch with the people I describe in this article, the case is very likely to have ended in the following way. Valentín is most probably administering his own Pentecostal commu-nity in La Blanca. This congregation might even have left its CEP mother church altogether, and if not, will sooner or later be fully recognized by the Lima church board as an independent congregation. Juan may very well have followed Valentín's track in San Bartolomé. If neither man has succeeded in establishing himself as an independent pastor, this is most probably because others have come to the fore even more successfully. Whatever the outcome it is a perfect demon-stration of the mushroom-like character of Pentecostal growth, in which conflict proves to be highly fruitful. Particularly since this is a process which tends to repeat itself under many, often very different, circumstances, Pentecostal growth seems to be guaranteed for quite some time.

Conclusion

By applying Bourdieu's ideas on the role of the laity and religious specialists, I have built an argument around the question of whether in Pentecostal churches ordinary believers play the dominant role or their pastors. The Arequipa data from the Cerro Negro neighborhood brought me to the somewhat paradoxical conclusion that both sides do. Thus I reach the same conclusion as does Willemier Westra elsewhere in this volume, who sees paradox as the driving force behind the Afro-Brazilian Candomblé religion. In his introductory contribution Droogers put a strong emphasis on Pentecostalism's paradoxical character as well, though to him the usual explanations for its success are equally paradoxical.

What I have attempted here is to show how the Pentecostal pastor manages to get his authority recognized by imposing a sophisticated discourse, which allows him a strong power position. However, this success is balanced and to a large extent neutralized by the same pastor's own teachings on the accessibility of leadership positions for all. By emphasizing the divine calling he easily awakens slumbering desires and feeds ambition among his congregation members. "Discipleship" is the clue to understanding this process, as I hope to have demonstrated. A congregation full of disciples can in the long run never remain homogenous; it blows apart into new cells for Pentecostal growth. As long as the pastor manages to control the pressure caused by ambition, his church is bubbling over with (spiritual) life. If the situation runs out of (pastoral) control, schism is often unavoidable. Thus, the tragedy—or better the paradox—of the pastoral figure is that he is constantly digging his own grave by preaching this message of discipleship, which once aroused his own pastoral ambitions.

The key to the explanation of Pentecostal success has to be sought in its paradoxical nature and the ensuing practice. In Pentecostalism believers are always close to the pulpit, both literally and figuratively. Inspired by biblical texts, they are given the floor so often that aspiring to leadership positions becomes the most natural thing for them to do. The spectacular growth of Pentecostalism worldwide proves that this process resembles a snowball. Using Droogers' words from the introduction, in Pentecostalism the tension between hierarchical tendencies and the more egalitarian or democratic ones is highly fruitful. The movement's rapid expansion is the best proof of this. This case study also shows that in order to reach such broadly valid conclusions, they have to be supported by detailed studies of daily Pentecostal life in local church communities like the one we visited in the Arequipa's Cerro Negro neighborhood.

Notes

1. I did fieldwork among poor Pentecostals in Peru (mainly in Arequipa) during 1987 and part of 1989 as part of a research project at the *Vrije Universiteit* Amsterdam, The Netherlands. This fieldwork was made possible by a grant from WOTRO (Netherlands Foundation for the Advancement of Tropical Research). Recently, I finished a Ph.D. on the vicissitudes of "progressive" Pentecostalism under the Pinochet regime in Chile (Kamsteeg 1998).

2. The majority of these Protestants are in fact Pentecostals. I use the term Protestant as a sort of "umbrella" word, despite the fact that it means little to most Latin Americans. They prefer the term *evangélico* (evangelical), which has, however, different connotations in the Anglo-Saxon world. I also make a distinction between church and congregation. By church I mean a denomination with its proper rules and articles of faith. The local church community I prefer to call congregation; the latter may in their turn have (a series of) dependent annexes.

3. The vast number of publications on the theme of "sects," as Protestants are often pejoratively called, confirms this ecclesiastical concern. Typical examples are *50 respuestas a los protestantes*, published by the joint Colombian bishops, in which strong warnings are made against Pentecostal sects and their proselytist practices (more than a million copies were sold), and *Look Out! The Pentecostals Are Coming*, written by Peter Wagner, a North American Protestant (the book has been translated into Spanish).

4. For Peru, I base myself on figures by Barrett (1982), two national sources (INE 1984; Concilio 1986), as well as personal estimations.

5. I did fieldwork in three different neighborhoods during my fieldwork in Arequipa–Cerro Negro, Miraflores, and Paucarpata. For this article I have only used material from the first one. On the request of the people whom it concerns, I changed the names of the neighborhood, church, and persons.

6. Most of the works alluded to are dealt with in Droogers' introduction. Willems (1967), Lalive d'Epinay (1969), Rolim (1985), and Howe (1980) are among the most important. I comply with the plea made by Droogers (1985) for an eclectic use of theories.

7. In 1988, Manuel Marzal published a study on the religious tendencies among working-class people in Lima, in which he also paid attention to Pentecostals. The single really comprehensive work on Peruvian Protestantism by Kessler (1967) only indirectly deals with Pentecostal churches.

8. Despite its somewhat unreliable character, I give some statistical material based on the limited sources available. Barrett estimates that the number of Protestants was 400,000 by 1975, that is 2.5% of the total population. His prediction for the year 2000 is a growth to only 3.5% (1982, 559). A diagnosis by Lima's Evangelical Seminary, which is supervised by the CONEP (*Concilio Nacional Evangélico del Perú*), maintains that only 2% of Lima's population

was Protestant in 1986, excluding the Adventists. Of the 610 churches counted, 128 had been founded between 1980 and 1985 (Concilio 1986, 10), which
clearly indicates accelerating growth during the last decade. Additional research concerning the rest of the country is underway. Yet given the size of
the project and the character of its methodology, any new figures should be
taken with a broad margin of reliability.

9. Migration is a complicated process, only superficially studied in Peru so far.
A first synthesis is *Problemas poblacionales peruanos II*, edited by Róger Guerra
García (1986). Migration is often given explanatory value in relation to the
growth of Pentecostalism (Willems 1967; Lalive d'Epinay 1969). A state of
anomie resulting from migration is considered to be responsible for the attraction and subsequent conversion of people to Pentecostalism. Its stable and
unambiguous worldview are supposed to be attractive to people in a situation
of transition.

10. All emerging neighborhoods plan to have a Catholic church building, but
its construction is seldom realized for lack of financial means. The idea that
almost certainly no priest will come to the place can hardly make people
enthusiastic about contributing to the church building. Pentecostals take
notice of this weakness of the Catholic church. Once they succeed in obtaining a plot for themselves, they rapidly build a small chapel on it with the help
of the church community.

11. Tithes normally supply the pastor with an income, but, depending on
church rules, they may also be used for church maintenance. However, Pentecostals do not observe the rule of tithing as closely as the pastors would like
them to do, but it is still the main cork that keeps the Pentecostal ship (pastor)
floating.

12. I never came across a Pentecostal church which allowed women to become
pastors.

13. Curiously, at this particular moment of writing my article I was visited by
two Jehovah's Witnesses.

14. Therefore it is no wonder that anthropological monographs generally deal
with religion in a separate chapter.

15. He does so in total agreement with the *Centro Evangelístico Pentecostal*'s
own church regulations, which assign maximum authority to the pastor.
Consequently, every initiative needs his prior consent. He also presides over
the church board and is chairman of every commission established.

16. The castigation (*disciplina*) most often consists of a prohibition on taking
part in the main church activities and the prescription to pray intensively.

17. Elsewhere I have given a more elaborate description of how pastors (and
lay people) take advantage of their gift of faith healing (Kamsteeg 1991).

References

Bamat, Tomás, ¿Salvación o dominación? Las sectas religiosas en el Ecuador. Quito: Ed. El Conejo, 1986.

Barrett, David B., ed. World Christian Encyclopedia. Nairobi: Oxford University Press, 1982.

Bourdieu, Pierre, "Genèse et structure du champ religieux," Revue française de sociologie XII, (1971), 295-334.

———, Outline of a Theory of Practice. Londen: Cambridge University Press, 1977.

———, "Symbolic Power," Critique of Anthropology 4, no. 13/14 (1979), 77-85.

Butler Flora, Cornelia, "Pentecostalism and Development: the Colombian Case." In Perspectives on Pentecostalism. Case Studies from the Caribbean and Latin America, ed. Stephen D. Glazier. Washington, D.C.: University Press of America, 1980.

Concilio Nacional Evangélico del Perú, Directorio Evangélico 1986, Lima, Callao y Balnearios. Lima: PROMIES, 1986.

Droogers, André F., "From Waste-Making to Recycling: a Plea for an Eclectic Use of Models in the Study of Religious Change." In Theoretical Explorations in African Religion, eds. Wim van Binsbergen and Matthew Schoffeleers. London: KPI, 1985.

Eliécer Sálesman, P., 50 Respuestas a los Protestantes y Comunistas, Supersticiones, Masones y Espiritistas. Bogotá, no date.

Escobar, Samuel, Las etapas del avance evangélico en el Perú. Lima: Seminario Evangélico, 1981.

Flores-Galindo, Alberto, Arequipa y el Sur Andino, siglos XVIII-XX. Lima: Editorial Horizonte, 1977.

Gill, Lesley, "Like a Veil to Cover Them: Women and the Pentecostal Movement in La Paz." American Ethnologist 17, no. 4 (1990), 708-721.

Guerra García, Roger, ed. Problemas Poblacionales Peruanos II. Lima: AMIDEP, 1986.

Howe, Gary N., "Capitalism and Religion at the Periphery: Pentecostalism and Umbanda in Brazil." In Perspectives on Pentecostalism. Case Studies from the Caribbean and Latin America, ed. Stephen D. Glazier. Washington, D.C.: University Press of America, 1980.

Huamán, Santiago A., La primera historia del Movimiento Pentecostal en el Perú. Lima, no date.

Instituto Nacional de Estadística, Censos Nacionales VIII de Población II de Vivienda, 12 de julio de 1981, Departamento de Arequipa A (tomo I). Lima: INE, 1984.

Irrarázaval, Diego, "Fiesta de la Cruz - del campesino o del misti," Pastoral Andina 32, (1980), 5-16.

Kamsteeg, Frans H., "Pentecostal Healing and Power, a Peruvian Case." In *Popular Power in Latin American Religions*, eds. André Droogers, Gerrit Huizer and Hans Siebers. Saarbrücken/Fort Lauderdale: Verlag Breitenbach Publishers, 1981.

———, *Prophetic Pentecostalism in Chile. A Case Study on Religion and Development Policy*. Lanham, Md.: Scarecrow Press, 1998.

Kessler, J.B.A., *A Study of the Older Protestant Missions and Churches in Peru and Chile*. Goes: Oosterbaan & Le Cointre, 1967.

———, *La historia de la Iglesia en América Latina*. Lima: Seminario Evangélico, 1981.

Lewellen, Ted, "The Adventist Elite." In *Peasants in Transition. The Changing Economy of the Peruvian Aymara*. Bolder, Colo.: Westview Press, 1978.

Martin, David, *Tongues of Fire. The Explosion of Protestantism in Latin America*. Oxford: Basil Blackwell, 1990.

Marzal, Manuel M., *Los caminos religiosos de los migrantes en la Gran Lima*. Lima: Fondo Editorial de la Pontificia Universidad Católica del Perú, 1988.

Muratorio, Blanca, "Protestantism and Capitalism Revisited, in the Rural Highlands of Ecuador," *The Journal of Peasant Studies* 8, no. 1 (1980), 37-61.

Rolim, Francisco C., *Pentecostais no Brasil, uma interpretação sócio-religiosa*. Petrópolis: Vozes, 1985.

Stoll, David, *Is Latin America Turning Protestant? The Politics of Evangelical Growth*. Berkeley: University of California Press, 1990.

Tennekes, Hans, *El movimiento pentecostal en la sociedad chilena*. Amsterdam: Vrije Universiteit/Iquique: CIREN, 1985.

Wagner, C.P., *Look Out! The Pentecostals Are Coming*. Carol Stream, Ill.: Creation House, 1973.

Willems, Emilio, *Followers of the New Faith. Culture Change and the Rise of Protestantism in Brazil and Chile*. Nashville, Tenn.: Vanderbilt University Press, 1967.

Zarauz, Luis, *Parque industrial de Arequipa y crisis del sector empresarial*. Lima: CIED, 1984.

5

A Farewell to Mary?

Women, Pentecostal Faith, and the Roman Catholic Church on Curaçao, N.A.

H. Barbara Boudewijnse

The events presented in this contribution took place in the early 1980s on Curaçao (Netherlands Antilles), a Caribbean island approximately 70 miles to the north of Venezuela.[1] Traditionally, more than 80 percent of its population is Roman Catholic. As elsewhere, the Curaçaoan Catholic Church has been challenged by the Pentecostal movement, which has grown continuously throughout the last four decades.

In 1975, partly in response to this challenge of Pentecostal growth, Catholic priests launched the Catholic Charismatic movement on Curaçao. Since that time, the Charismatic and non-Charismatic clergy alike have had to face the problem of keeping those *guias* (leaders of prayer meetings), who monopolize leadership in their prayer groups, under control. The danger that a guia might leave the Charismatic movement, taking part of the prayer group with her or him, is not unrealistic. When I was doing fieldwork on Curaçao among Charismatic groups, I was confronted with the aftermath of this kind of schism.

What had happened? The female guia of one of the three prayer groups in the parish of a Charismatic priest refused to recite the rosary prior to the Charismatic prayer meeting. The other two groups did not refuse to do so. The guia, informed that it was wrong to dispense with the rosary as a fixed devotion prior to Charismatic prayer, denounced the veneration of the Virgin Mary as practised on Curaçao, and eventually refused to say the Hail Mary at all. Finally, the priest saw no other way to make her change her mind than to deny her the right to lead the group. The guia left the Catholic church and joined "Bida Nobo," one of the Pentecostal churches on the island. She was followed by some hundred members of the group. Shortly thereafter, she founded her own independent Pentecostal church.

How are we to interpret this conflict? What did the rosary and Hail Mary mean to the contending parties? What was at stake here? In this contribution, I would like to clarify the circumstances generating this particular conflict. Basically the dispute can be seen as a power struggle between the established church (represented by the priest) and a number of laymen (represented by the guia and her Charismatic prayer group). This, however, only partly explains the events. It is crucial to note that the laymen were all women. The important question is what Pentecostalism had to offer these women. It can be said that by refusing to say the prayer to Mary, the women were protesting against a church they experienced as patriarchal. But does this imply that Pentecostalism does more justice to women than the traditional Curaçaoan Catholic church? As we shall see, this question cannot be easily answered. In order to fully grasp the issue, it is necessary to first present a general overview of the Charismatic Renewal movement and its relationship to the Catholic church.

The Catholic Charismatic Renewal Movement

What is the Charismatic movement? In general, the term is used to denote the Pentecostal movement within the established churches, a movement which has developed since the 1950s. The Catholic "branch" originated in 1967 in the United States and has since spread all over the world.

The Charismatic movement differs from classical Pentecostalism in various ways. Classical Pentecostalism, which originated at the beginning of this century, comprises diverse autonomous, often locally organized groups. In general, fundamentalism and a rigid moralism are considered typical, as are the exclusive character of the groups and the emphasis they put on "withdrawal from 'the world'" (society and its institutions, norms and values).[2] Classical Pentecostalism has often been seen as a movement of the poor and deprived (e.g. Lalive d'Epinay 1969; see also Droogers, in this volume). After the Second World War, Pentecostalism experienced a widespread revival. Sometimes this revival itself is called neo-Pentecostalism. More often the term neo-Pentecostalism is used to specify a qualitative dissimilarity from classical Pentecostalism. Whereas classical Pentecostals unfailingly used to leave the established churches, neo-Pentecostals hold their ground within their churches of origin. They do not wish to found new churches, but to renew the church in which they were born and raised. To make it clear that they want "renewal" and not "secession," the adherents of the Pentecostal movement within the established churches call it the Charismatic movement or Charismatic Renewal, the term Charismatic pointing to the *charismata*, the gifts of the Holy Spirit.[3] Neo-Pentecostalism is usually typified as a middle-class movement and is described as ecumenical. Charismatics reject excessively stringent moralism and feel no need to withdraw from "the world." As such, they clearly differ from classical Pentecostals.

The Charismatic Renewal movement first originated within established Protestant churches. In 1967 the movement also reached the Catholic church. In that year, a few Catholic staff members and students at Duquesne University (Pittsburgh, Pennsylvania) joined to pray for and eventually experienced the Baptism in the Holy Spirit. They were assisted by Pentecostal believers whom they had asked for advice. These meetings initiated the development of the Catholic variant of the Pentecostal movement.

The attraction of Pentecostalism to Catholics was not new, but until the birth of the Catholic Charismatic movement, the transition to Pentecostal practices usually meant a breach with the Catholic church, which from an early stage had strongly condemned Pentecostal ideas and practices. The fact that the Catholic church has accepted the Charismatic Renewal movement within its ranks has been interpreted as a consequence of its general loss of authority in society. Nowadays, in our pluralist society, the Catholic church offers just one among many worldviews. In these circumstances, church authorities must of necessity be more tolerant towards renewal movements and have to find more subtle ways to control them. In this respect, the history of the Catholic Charismatic movement demonstrates a policy of cooptation and routinization.[4]

The Catholic Charismatic Renewal movement was initiated by a group of laymen. Through the personal networks of relatives and friends, it quickly spread all over the United States and from there all across the globe. Although at first the movement mainly attracted students, by 1970 according to McGuire (1982, 5) most of its membership could be characterized as middle aged. McGuire further estimates that by 1978 the movement had approximately 600,000 members. Since then, she observes, the movement fell somewhat into decline (1982, 6). According to Bord and Faulkner, the stagnation had set in by 1974 (1983, 9).[5] Moreover, they observe a growing clericalization of the movement (1983, 39-40).[6] This pattern of stagnating growth and an ageing membership also characterizes the Catholic Charismatic movement in the Netherlands and on the Netherlands Antilles.[7]

How to interpret these developments? What has been noted above seems to imply that, as far as the Catholic church is concerned, the Pentecostal renewal has been rendered harmless. Catholics who are attracted to Pentecostal spirituality, may set up and visit prayer groups. They do not have to leave the Catholic church. Moreover, church authorities seem to have a firm hold on the Catholic variant of the Pentecostal revival. However, the aforementioned processes of stagnation and ageing membership set one thinking, as does the schism on Curaçao: considering the fact that worldwide Pentecostalism is a rapidly expanding movement, the lack of growth of the Catholic

Charismatic movement is remarkable.[8] To suppose that there is a connection between the stagnation of Catholic Charismatic growth and the explosive expansion of Pentecostalism, does not seem too far-fetched. As will be demonstrated, Pentecostal faith holds the seeds of rebellion against established church structures.

Life in the Spirit

Catholic Charismatics themselves refer to the movement as one of *renewal*: they speak of the Charismatic Renewal. They thus express their view that the church (and Christianity in general) needs to be spiritually renewed. This religious renewal should, and according to them can only take place through the spiritual renewal of the individual. In turn, individual spiritual renewal can only be achieved by means of the manifestation of the Holy Spirit. The Charismatic movement goes back to those parts of the New Testament in which the Pentecost and the gifts and workings of the Holy Spirit are described. People believe that every worshipper can receive Baptism of the Holy Spirit, including laymen. According to Steve Clark, one of the originators of the Catholic Charismatic movement in the United States, one has to aim at a "life in the Spirit," the life in which a person experiences the presence of the Spirit and his working. The Life in the Spirit is the norm for the Christian life. The individual has to experience "baptism in the Holy Spirit" (Clark 1976, 15-6).

While personal religious experience is central to the Charismatic belief system, prayer groups constitute the basis of Catholic Charismatic activity.[9] The prayer meetings are of central importance to the creation of "religious power." In order for the individual to experience the presence and power of the Holy Spirit, he or she has to take part in a Charismatic prayer group. In this respect we can speak of a paradox: attention is focused on the spiritual experience of the individual, but the group is central in bringing about that experience.

One can be baptized in the Spirit without the help of any other Christian. Only God (the baptizer) and the Holy Spirit are essential. All one has to do is ask for the Holy Spirit (Clark 1976, 52, 55). Baptism in the Spirit changes one's relationship with God. When a person is living the life of the Spirit, he or she knows by experience that the Holy Spirit is inside. One begins to experience the Holy Spirit making

it possible for one to praise God and worship God with a new freedom. One experiences the Holy Spirit making the Scriptures come to
life and giving Christian doctrines new meaning (id., 10-11). Baptism
in the Spirit also means that one can receive the fruits of the Spirit
(love, joy, peace, patience, etc.) or some of the charismatic *gifts* (the
charismata: tongues, prophecy, healing, etc.) (id., 64-5). People believe
that when the Holy Spirit comes to them, they know it; that people
can experience the Holy Spirit coming to them in a way that they can
recognize. What happens at the moment that people are baptized in
the Spirit varies a great deal. Sometimes it feels as if an electric current
is running through one, or people experience "a strange warmth"
filling them. Many simply feel a deep peace, or a joy (id., 19-20).

The Catholic Charismatic movement aims at renewal of the Catholic church through the spiritual renewal of the individual. From
early on, its leaders have emphasized that Pentecostal practices and
Catholic doctrines, such as those concerning the authority of the clergy, the liturgy, and the sacraments, are not contradictory. This point
of view is not shared by everyone.[10] McSweeney, for instance, characterizes Pentecostalism as an antisacramental movement (McSweeney
1980, 210). He observes that, since Charismatic Catholicism makes
experience the crucial test of the relationship with God, this means
that there is no objective test of moral, doctrinal, or sacramental validity. Since experience is incommunicable, each individual is his own
judge of his relationship with God. The traditional structure of the
Roman Church, McSweeney continues, is built upon a contrary principle: it is not experience which matters but the content of belief
which can be expressed verbally, communicated, and tested for validity against the measure of the church (McSweeney 1980, 215-16).

On the whole, the Catholic Charismatic movement can be characterized as a lay-movement. Not only its adherents, but most of its
leaders are laymen. On Curaçao most of the members and guias were
women: more than 85 percent (Boudewijnse 1991, 182). The prominent role of the laity in the movement was legitimized by the belief
that the Holy Spirit can work through *any* person and not just
through members of the clergy. Anyone having the true faith can
receive baptism in the Holy Spirit as well as the *gifts of the Spirit*, such
as the gift of prophecy, the gift of speaking in tongues, or the gift of
healing. This doctrine, and the ensuing prominence of the laity, con-

fronted Curaçaoan church authorities with the problem of how to control the movement. In practice, this problem was very real, since many of the prayer groups functioned autonomously and eluded the grip of the church. So while Charismatics explicitly avow to be part of the Catholic church, Charismatic ideology and practice may in fact pose a threat to traditional Catholic authority structures.[11]

The general statement that people, as always, strive for power and esteem, explains nothing. The question is why particular people in a particular context choose the means they choose. In this instance, Charismatic ideology presented the guia with a symbolic instrument to handle the confrontation with clerical authorities. To the guia and her following, the Holy Spirit was the symbol of their being in the right. The Holy Spirit provided them with religious power: the power to speak up to the religious authority of the priest, the power to legitimately decide on religious truth themselves. The resulting schism was justified, as they saw it, on the grounds of the "unchristian" and "diabolical" veneration of Mary as practised by the Catholic church.

This brings us to the main issue of this contribution, which is the question of why the symbol of *Mary* proved to be the focal point of battle. Why refuse to recite the rosary and why is this of such importance to the priest?

Charismatic Attitudes to Mary

All over the world, Catholic Charismatics have demonstrated an ambivalent attitude towards Mary. This ambivalence clearly comes to the fore in a leaflet tellingly entitled *Mary is Pentecostal* (Pfaller and Alberts 1973), where the authors write:

> ... many Christians today do not see eye to eye on the place which Mary and the Holy Spirit have in our lives today. They suppose that there is a dichotomy. I have friends who are dedicated to the blessed Mother who look with fear and apprehension on those who are in the Charismatic Movement and pray for the conversion of those straying brethren. And there are sincere people in the Charismatic Movement who think that devotion to Mary detracts from the true worship of God and has no place in the life of the Spirit. With a foot in both camps, I have been pained to witness this needless antagonism. Though it is not true that all Charismatics are opposed to Mary, and all Marian

devotees against the Charismatic Movement, there has been much
opposition due to mutual misunderstandings (1973, 5).

As will be clear, the authors want to make it clear that Mary was "the
first and greatest Pentecostal." Thus, the leaflet illustrates the ongoing
debate on the position of Mary. Leaders of the movement continually
emphasize that Pentecostal spirituality is *not* incompatible with Catholic devotion to Mary and will even foster it. In practice, however,
Catholic Charismatics are often little inclined to give attention to
Marian devotions. In fact, Catholic Charismatic devotion tends to
shift from Mary to the Holy Spirit. In the United States, where the
movement originated, studies of Catholic Charismatic prayer groups
have demonstrated the existence of unorthodox beliefs, such as the
idea that devotion to Mary or the Saints is equivalent to idolatry
(Fichter 1975, 42). Bord and Faulkner indicate that Mary is seldom
mentioned during prayer meetings. Only 18 percent of their respondents agreed that Mary ought to receive more attention at prayer
sessions (1983, 114).

The Curaçaoan case, it will be clear, is not unique. Still, in order to
understand this particular event, the Curaçaoan context has to be
taken into account.

The Catholic Charismatic movement was introduced on Curaçao
to defy Pentecostal competition.[12] Although the movement developed
into a movement of laymen, with only a small number of nuns and
priests involved, participants and outsiders both identified the movement with the Catholic church. While the participants saw the movement as one of renewal, Pentecostals saw it as an extension of the *traditional* Catholic church. The ongoing strife between Pentecostals and
the Catholic church invariably manifested itself in conflicts about the
significance of Mary and the saints.[13]

The leaders of the Catholic Charismatic movement on Curaçao
emphasized that Mary is the perfect intermediary. Anyone offering
prayer to Mary can be certain that she will personally plead his case to
her Son. But although Mary generally occupied a prominent position
in the Curaçaoan movement, it was nevertheless striking that some
prayer groups gave her much more attention than others.[14] Not every
Charismatic priest or nun put Mary in a central role. One of them told
me:

The prayer meeting always starts at 6:30 p.m. with prayer of the rosary. At 7:00 p.m. the rest of the people arrive. The rosary is really a legacy of the former pastor. He wanted a Catholic make-up. But it doesn't fit in.

And another priest said:

In the United States one didn't recite the rosary either. The problem is that people think they *have* to recite the rosary. But it is a special prayer, a mystical prayer. The rosary and Charismatic prayer are two different kinds of prayer.

It is no coincidence that the strife between the Pentecostal movement and the Catholic church on Curaçao continually focused on the Holy Virgin. On Curaçao, Marian devotion has traditionally been widely and strongly practised. To Pentecostals, Mary was therefore a symbol of traditional Catholicism. They labelled Marian devotion "stupid" and "diabolical." They emphasized that a Christian should turn directly to Jesus. When I asked Pentecostals why the veneration of Mary was "stupid," they would tell me that "the church" had always kept the people ignorant. "We were not allowed to read the bible," they would say. "But now," they emphasized, "we have learned to think for ourselves," "now, we know that we ourselves can talk directly to God. We don't need the priest to mediate, nor do we need Mary as an intermediary."

These statements show how in their experience Marian devotion is closely linked to being kept ignorant, being made subordinate. As a Charismatic priest explains:

There are seven churches of Mary here [on Curaçao] ... The position of Mary has been heatedly debated, especially in groups with members from the Legion of Mary. In one prayer group there was a married couple from the Legion. They were pro-Mary, but [somebody else] was against the Virgin. They did not formally split up, but the couple left for a new group that had recently been established. The new group was pro-Mary. Considering the context of the experience of many people here, that is, first, a deeply rooted devotion to Mary which is, generally speaking, old and conservative, problems were bound to arise. What are the ideas of the group against Mary? ... Jesus Christ is the *only* Salbador [Saviour] and people oppose any trace that sees Mary as a kind of intermediary. Maybe you could say that this is an anti-clerical tendency. Within the Charismatic movement people experience their religiosity in their own way. People want to feel knowledgeable by contrast with the past and the priests: the people themselves became expert on religious matters. They no longer let themselves be told everything by the priests. Normally, one says "pater" [father], but in the Charismatic movement one says "ruman" [brother or sister]. This is also an aspect of liberation.

Here, a few aspects are mentioned that are important for our discussion. First of all, the fact of the wide-spread devotion to Mary. Next, the fact that this devotion is generally associated with a conservative church. One of the new aspects of the Charismatic movement is that people can experience "their own religiosity." An illustration of this is the breach with "pater," the traditional form of address. Thus, the priest is not only differently perceived, but also one's self-perception has changed: the lay person has come on equal footing with his or her "brother," the priest. The faithful get a different view of themselves and their relationship to God. In the words of another Charismatic priest:

> Especially the sectarian aspects of sects flowered in the Charismatic movement in the United States, such as the abandonment of the Eucharist, the criticism of Mary, the opposition to the authority of the church, the refusal to be guided. This is not nice. The bible becomes a new idol: "God will tell me what to do."

The authority of the priest, traditionally the link between the faithful and God, comes under pressure.

But the newly acquired confidence in religious matters did not necessarily lead to conflicts. In a conversation with a priest who was not involved in the movement, he said in this respect:

> In the Catholic church the high point is the Mass, the Eucharist. Around this, the church is built. When I came to this parish, there was a prayer group from 6:00 to 9:00 p.m. At 7:00 p.m. Mass was said, so I thought "that is perfect. I can attune my sermon to it and so enrich them." But at 7:00 p.m. most of them left. It means nothing to them. In their eyes liturgical prayer is no prayer. Some of them stay on. But when I speak of the charisms, it goes in at one ear and out at the other. Once, I left for a vacation. When I came back, I did not see the prayer

group. They had shifted the meeting to another day of the week, because in that way they would no longer be "disturbed" by the Mass. I ask you! I gave up hope, then, that anything can be done with it [the Charismatic movement].

In this particular case the prayer group had achieved a great deal of autonomy. The group had succeeded in effectively avoiding traditional Catholic habits, devotions, and celebrations. Its activities took mostly place outside of the pastor's view. But connections were not everywhere that loose. In the parish in which the schism occurred, the parish priest himself was Charismatic and deeply involved in the movement. He had even been officially proclaimed "director of the Charismatic movement on the Netherlands Antilles" by the bishop of Willemstad. In this particular parish traditional devotion to Mary was deeply rooted.

A Closer Look at the Conflict

The laymen in the Curaçaoan case were *women*. These women had joined a movement combining Catholic and Pentecostal elements. It paved the way, as it were, towards a more radical breach with traditional Catholic practices. It offered them a new way to express their religiosity. One significant aspect was the new form of addressing fellow Christians as "brothers" and "sisters." They had come to be, so to speak, on equal footing with the priest, who had become their "brother." In this respect it is relevant to wonder what it is that Pentecostal faith had to offer these women. Are we to conclude that Pentecostal faith does more justice to women than the traditional Catholic church? This question cannot be answered unambiguously. Before any answer can be given, it is necessary to know more about Rosa, the guia with whom all this began.

One of the persons involved in the conflict gives the following account:

[Rosa][15] was one of the leaders. She had experienced a dramatic conversion. Although she had little education, only a few years of primary school, she had many talents. But she was very stubborn. There were always problems with the other leaders. Because of that I sometimes did not feel like going to the core group meeting. It got worse after Jamaica.[16] There she came in touch with the Pentecostal movement. After that a non-Catholic element encroached. But there has to be unity. The core group meetings became awful. Then she left the core group. After a while she asked if she could have her own prayer group. [The pastor] agreed, although he had some doubts. She started her own group, then, on Friday, [in a building] behind the church. Increasingly, it became evident that unknown people who did not belong to the parish visited the group. Testimonies! ... There was clearly something wrong. The drop that made the bucket ran over was that they decided that they would no longer pray the Hail Mary. There was to be a talk between her and the pastor, but it never took place. Later we heard that they said "we have been kicked out of the church." This is nonsense. They were free to leave. It was a matter of authority, a matter of control ...

Also, at that time, one of the important Jamaican leaders visited Curaçao. We thought it was ecumenical, but it wasn't. He was like a Trojan horse. He had been in Rome; in Jamaica, he had afterwards been put on the sidelines. [Rosa's] son-in-law also comes from Jamaica. I think he was a Baptist preacher who left the Baptists.

One of the women belonging to the group that left describes her first meeting with Rosa in her later experiences:

I met [Rosa] in the church. She was in the Charismatic movement. She lead the Friday prayer group. Here they just preached the gospel, it was a great blessing. There was laying on of hands, many miracles happened there. They had a simple faith. They just did what it says in the Bible. There were about 300 people. But then jealousy came up in the church. The other groups were not as big and they became jealous. Then we had a conference. Its theme was "Jesus: Way, Truth, and Life." Afterwards problems developed because they did no longer prayed the Hail Mary. But the Catholic church worships Mary and the saints. In Timothy it is written: only Jesus is the link between God and man. The *only* link. The pastor said that if they would not pray the Hail Mary anymore, she would no longer be allowed to lead the Friday prayer group. That was in May.[17] They had to choose. The pastor had preached that one had to pray to the saints. But in Jeremiah 7 it is written that he who bows to the queen of heaven, to Mary that is, is evil. Together with a friend I went to the pastor. He was so angry, he turned us out of the house. He said he had studied for ten years and that we could teach him nothing. But those saints, like Miguel and San Antonio, they are also used in witchcraft, in brua. Therefore, it can't be good, can it? If it were good, the Lord would not allow that. After-wards we all went to Bida Nobo. But the Lord told us that we had to come together. Elder sisters in particular came to tell us time and again that we had to come together. On Tuesday we had a meeting; we much prayed for our needs. On Playa Kaliki they prayed for three weeks. In November, they first came here [at her place, HBB], with about twen-ty-five people. Afterwards we were with approximately 200 people. Since that time, we also have a pastor from Jamaica ...

They say we wanted control. That we were disobedient to authority. But in the Catholic church they are not open to the Holy Spirit. By raising Mary they try, because of the criticism, to push the saints into the background. I love Mary as mother of the man Jesus. But Mary also lies in her grave waiting for the resurrection. However, her submission to the Lord I want to follow ...

Only in Jesus I find peace. In nothing else. In him I have found respite. I don't have to search anymore. I have given my life to Jesus. And he has kept his promises. Jesus is the husband of my soul. Now, I'm happy even when I'm sad. In the past, it was like dying ...

When karismátika [the Charismatic movement] came here, it came by way of Trinidad. It started there ... When karismátika began, it was focused on the Holy Spirit. The emphasis on Mary has increased since the group left. The pastor has even visited the pope; he and the bishop were reprimanded by the pope because of the group's refusal to pray the Hail Mary ...

Nobody has manipulated us, the Word has awakened us. For that reason in the Catholic church they have kept the Bible closed to the people. And the pope is not the only ambassador of Jesus, we all are. The Holy Spirit leads our services.

Next to the tension between the parish priest and the guia and her fol-lowers, another element comes to the fore in these personal reports. It is said that Rosa had great capacities, although she had had no formal education. And also that she had experienced a "dramatic conversion." In the second story the pastor's education ("ten years of study") are contrasted with the woman's own reading of the Bible. As a result of this reading devotion to Mary is condemned, as is the veneration of the saints. On top of that, the saints are linked to witchcraft. As such, two aspects are indirectly touched upon that need closer inspection: the position of Curaçaoan women and "brua."[18]

Regarding brua, a guia from a different parish says:

Brua and religiosity are tied together. Brua comes from African rites that survived Christianization. Brua people are religious, they are not looking for material benefits. When the Charismatic movement came [to Curaçao], they were happy: they were finally able to express themselves. The Dutch and the Spaniards were of the opinion: in church one has to be serene. But one wants to sing with one's entire body. That is why the Charismatic movement caught on. They could do their own thing. It meant liberation. Especially those people from brua: they could not switch to "silent night," but they could to karismátika. But it's quite a job to channel it. At the time, the pastor called together a group of people to assist [him]. Among them there was a woman from [Rosa]. She was really deeply affected! She was heavily in brua and then, all at once, she wanted to completely renounce it. The pastor needed leaders and he chose her too. For her, this wasn't good at all. Suddenly, she wanted to convert the whole world. But she had come to the fore prematurely, she wasn't ready for it. On Monday morning[19] there were about 500 people. She is so nice. She is a maternal woman. I can imagine getting completely in her sway.

And a Charismatic priest says:

In the Charismatic movement, the danger of brua is fairly great, for many brua people come to the Charismatic movement. But from the depths of their being things come to the surface that tell me they have not really been liberated. Take for instance [Rosa]: the absolute refusal to accept, to be humble, the lack of will to reconcile herself to the view of others, this points to diabolical influences ...
They also talked with Tardif.[20] Tardif tried to persuade them to humility. But they didn't even want to bow to the monstrance. How deeply rooted these evil practices are in their attitude! The inhuman pride! They have a magic persuasion.

Before her conversion to Charismatic faith, Rosa had been a well-known *hasidó di brua* (literally: a "brua-maker") with many clients.[21] As such, she had been used to running her own "business." A significant part of her activities in that respect concentrated on illness and healing.

The fact that most brua-makers are women has to do with this practice of healing. As is generally the case in Latin America and in Afro-American households, women are confined to the domestic domain. A woman's place is at home, she runs the household and is often the head of it. Socially speaking her position is subordinate. She often has a hard time making ends meet and providing for her children. Usually the only field where she can assert herself is the religious sphere.

Rosa also found herself in that position. Of humble birth and without schooling, she was forced to provide for herself and her large family. However, she was talented and gifted with a natural authority. As a brua-maker she had been very successful. Brua, however, has a low status, even though it is widely practised. This is why brua is practised secretly, hidden from view. Conversion to the Charismatic movement enabled Rosa to come out into the open. She had nothing to hide anymore. Her brua activities were translated, as it were, into the "gift of healing": in the prayer group guided by Rosa, faith healing occupied a central place. This was not normally the case in other groups, which partly explains the enormous popularity of Rosa's prayer group.

The Denouncement of Mary and the Emancipation of Women

It can be said that there is a great deal of continuity between the household tasks of Curaçaoan women and their religious activities. Conway, writing of Haiti, states:

> Most of the converts to Pentecostalism in Haiti are women. The principal reason for this is that it is women who are primarily responsible for the health of their families. If a child becomes ill, its mother may convert on account of it. The father may encourage the conversion, but will not often convert himself ... But it is significant that in the Vodoun system as well women seek treatment through initiation more often than men. Women are active not only as recipients, but also as performers of Pentecostal health practice (Conway 1980, 21).

A Dutch author (Ter Steeg 1980), writing of Mary and the emancipation of women, acknowledges that the veneration of Mary may theoretically raise the status of women and has undoubtedly provided a haven of refuge for many women. In actuality, she argues, women have venerated in Mary a symbol that contributed to their own lack of freedom. Marian devotion raised the esteem of women but ultimately taught them the virtue of submission. She finds that Mary has mostly been venerated in countries where women hardly participate in public life, are confined to the home, and are victims of double sexual standards.[22]

In this light, the rebellion of Rosa and her sisters comes into perspective. In their refusal to say the Hail Mary, they revolted against an ideology that kept them subordinate; an ideology that told them to be humble, docile, and mute. The symbol of the Holy Spirit, on the other hand, enabled them to speak up, to assert themselves. Rosa and her following, in their outright refusal to say the prayer devoted to Mary (as the ideal woman), expressed their protest against a church experienced by them as patriarchal in nature.

Does the refusal to pray the Hail Mary mean a definite farewell to all that this prayer has traditionally implied? Has Pentecostal faith inaugurated the liberation of these women? The answer is both yes and no. In a social respect, nothing has changed. Whether a woman practices brua, attends the Catholic church, or adheres to Pentecostal faith, her life unfolds within the confines of family life and religion. However, as far as religious power and status are concerned, it seems that the Pentecostal movement has more to offer to women than the traditional Catholic church. The Holy Spirit manifests itself through all the faithful. Women can receive the gift of prophecy, explain the bible, speak in tongues, or guide a prayer meeting.

There is, nevertheless, as is noted by Kamsteeg in his contribution to this volume, a certain ambivalence in Pentecostal faith concerning the position of women. Everyone is considered equal in God's eye, but, in reference to the letters of Paul, the distinctive role and position of women is preached, a role considered to be subordinate to that of men. Therefore, in many Pentecostal churches again the men predominate.

Although the switch to Pentecostalism has not been reflected in a better social position for the converts, it nevertheless means a breach with the past. The symbol of the Holy Spirit implies that women are no longer principally addressed as "women," but as "individuals." If "Mary" emphasizes their "womanhood," the ideology of the Holy Spirit emphasizes their "personhood." Pentecostal ideology offers a handle to reformulate their personal histories. It enables them, as Lawless (1991) has termed it, to "rescript" their lives. The past and the future are viewed from a new perspective. If Pentecostal practice can be seen as an extension of their former religious life, in other ways it embodies their protest against the establishment.[23]

Notes

1. An earlier version of this article (Boudewijnse 1993) was published in *Op zoek naar vrouwen in ketterij en sekte*, eds. D. van Paassen & A. Passenier. Kampen: Kok, 1993.
2. See for instance Quebedeaux 1976, 25-51. For a critical evaluation of fundamentalism as a characteristic of Pentecostalism see Spittler 1994.
3. For a general treatment of the Charismatic Renewal Movement see McDonnell 1976; Quebedeaux 1976; Poewe 1994. For a general analysis of the Catholic Charismatic movement see O'Connor 1971; Fichter 1975; McGuire 1982; Bord and Faulkner 1983; Csordas 1994.
4. *Cooptation*: the process through which members of the clergy increasingly take part in a new movement, thereby enabling the church to get a hold on the movement. According to McGuire (1982, 218), cooptation "implies the opposite of renewal. Instead of the new movement gaining control over the old institution and changing it from within, the old institution gains control over the new movement." *Routinization*: in this context the process whereby Charismatic spirituality becomes routinized into a form of devotionalism comparable to pre-Vatican II devotionalism (McGuire 1982, 218).
5. For the second half of the 1980s I have no reliable figures from an independent source. There is no reason to assume that this period has seen a renewed, significant growth.
6. Clericalization means that members of the clergy increasingly participate in the prayer groups and gradually determine the movement's character, which means a general fading of its lay character and origin.
7. See Boudewijnse 1991. My conclusions regarding the Catholic Charismatic movement in the Netherlands are mostly based on anthropological fieldwork (1991-1993) and interviews.
8. See Martin 1990; Stoll 1990.
9. McGuire (1982, p. 12) emphasizes in this respect that people join the local prayer group, not the general movement.
10. For a analysis of the (in)compatibility of traditional Catholic theology and Pentecostal doctrines, see Breckenridge 1980.
11. The organizational pattern of Pentecostalism as a religious movement is characterized by Gerlach (1974, p. 680-681) as *segmentary, decentralized, polycephalous* or "many-headed", and *reticulate*. That is, the movement is composed of semiautonomous cells or segments (the local prayer groups), each having its own temporary head, who can retain leadership only by proving his or her worth. The individual cells are tied into a loose and informal network of

reticulate structure by the personal interaction of cell leaders, overlapping membership, the sharing of a common ideology, common cause, and common opposition. In her study *Pentecostal Catholics* (1982) McGuire discerned "open" and "closed" prayer groups. The terms "open" and "closed" refer to the degree in which ordinary members are allowed to influence the meetings or to do the talking. Closed groups are characterized by a more hierarchical organization. The meetings are highly structured. Procedures are less definite with open groups. The more "open" the group, the more likely it is that all the gifts of the Holy Spirit will manifest themselves in the group. My own findings are that closed groups are more often lead by members of the clergy than open groups, which are mostly lead by laymen. In practice, these lay groups function almost autonomously and elude the grip of the church.

12. For the history of the Catholic Charimatic movement on Curaçao, see Boudewijnse 1991.

13. Other regular conflicts concerned baptism by immersion as practised by Pentecostals, and the rules propagated by Pentecostal churches, forbidding alcohol consumption, the wearing of jewels or make-up, and forbidding participation in carnival (which is characterized as a "diabolical event"). The conflicts concerning Mary, however, are the most prominent.

14. Generally speaking, there was less attention given to Mary in "open" prayer groups than in closed groups. See also note 9.

15. For reasons of privacy I have given the guia concerned a fictitious name.

16. There had been a Charismatic conference at Jamaica that had been visited by members of the Curaçaoan movement.

17. In the Roman Catholic church the month of May is dedicated to Mary!

18. *Brua* (from the Spanish word *brujería*, "witchcraft") is the umbrella term for a complex of magico-religious beliefs and practices. On Curaçao a distinction is made between "white" and "black" brua, comparable to white and black magic. Many Antilleans, when confronted with misfortune—or in order to prevent this—turn to brua to propitiate fate.

19. Before the Friday group was started, Rosa was part of the core group of the Monday prayer group. Conflicts between the guia's resulted in her leaving the Monday group and starting her own group on Friday.

20. Emiliano Tardif MSC, a Canadian priest from the Catholic Mission in the Dominican Republic, is an important figure in the Catholic Charismatic Renewal movement. Since the seventies, he has travelled all over the world to give testimony of a personal healing experience that heralded his faith healing activities. He has visited The Netherlands as well as Curaçao more than once.

21. Elsewhere I have explained how the switch from brua to the Charismatic movement or Pentecostalism is linked to the association of brua with the lower classes. By renouncing brua, one distances oneself from the common people. At the same time, Pentecostal faith enables the converts to personally acquire supernatural power—as does brua—but this time in a socially legitimate way.

See Boudewijnse 1991; Ackermann 1981.

22. On "double sexual standards" see also Stevens 1973. For more specific analyses of Marian devotion and the symbol of Mary, see Warner 1976; Johnson 1985; Carroll 1986; Zimdars-Swartz 1991.

23. Alexander (1991) has argued that Pentecostal rituals are not just a passive expression of rebellion against society, but also further social change because they actively contribute to consciousness-raising. Cucchiari (1988-1990) has pointed at the link between the spread of Pentecostalism and the transformation of patriarchal societal structures. According to him, this becomes evident in a more feminine interpretation of God. In patriarchal religion the Holy Family forms the core image (with a stern Father God, a loving Mother Mary, and the Son Jesus); in Pentecostalism the central focus is on the Holy Trinity. All the feminine values and attitudes that used to be condensed in the symbol of Mary are now absorbed in the images of God the Father and his Son Jesus.

References

Ackermann, S.E., "The Language of Religious Innovation: Spirit Possession and Exorcism in a Malaysian Catholic Pentecostal Movement," *Journal of Anthropological Research* 37, no. 1 (1981):90-100.

Alexander, Bobby C., "Correcting Misinterpretations of Turner's Theory: An African Pentecostal Illustration," *Journal for the Scientific Study of Religion* 30, no.1 (1991):26-44.

Boudewijnse, H. Barbara, "The Development of the Charismatic Movement within the Catholic Church of Curaçao." In *Popular Power in Latin American Religions*, eds. André F. Droogers, Gerrit Huizer, and Hans Siebers, Saarbrücken: Breitenbach Publishers, 1991.

Boudewijnse, H. Barbara, "Een vaarwel aan het weesgegroet? Over vrouwen, het pinkstergeloof en de katholieke kerk." In *Op zoek naar vrouwen in ketterij en sekte*, eds. Dorothée van Paassen and Anke Passenier, Kampen: Kok, 1993.

Bord, Richard J., and Joseph E. Faulkner, *The Catholic Charismatics: The Anatomy of a Modern Religious Movement*. University Park, Pa.: Pennsylvania State University Press, 1983.

Breckenridge, James F., *The Theological Self-Understanding of the Catholic Charismatic Movement*. Washington, D.C.: University Press of America, 1980.

Carroll, Michael P., *The Cult of the Virgin Mary*. Princeton, N.J.: Princeton University Press, 1986.

Clark, Steve, *Baptized in the Spirit and Spiritual Gifts*. Pecos, N.M.: Dove Publications, 1976.

Conway, Frederick J., "Pentecostalism in Haïti: Healing and Hierarchy." In *Perspectives on Pentecostalism. Case Studies from the Caribbean and Latin*

America, ed. Stephen D. Glazier, Washington D.C.: University Press of America, 1980.

Csordas, Thomas J., *The Sacred Self. A Cultural Phenomenology of Charismatic Healing*. Berkeley: University of California Press, 1994.

Cucchiari, S., ""Adapted for Heaven"; Conversion and Culture in Western Sicily," *American Ethnologist* 15 (1988):417-441.

———, "Between Shame and Sanctification: Patriarchy and its Transformation in Sicilian Pentecostalism," *American Ethnologist* 17, no. 4 (1990):687-707.

Fichter, Joseph H., *The Catholic Cult of the Paraclete*. New York: Sheed and Ward, 1975.

Gerlach, Luther P., "Pentecostalism: Revolution or Counter-Revolution?." In *Religious Movements in Contemporary America*, ed. Irving I. Zaretsky and Mark P. Leone, Princeton, N.J.: Princeton University Press, 1974.

Johnson CSJ, Elizabeth A., "The Marian Tradition and the Reality of Women," *Horizons* 12, no.1 (1985):116-135.

Lalive d'Epinay, Christian, *Haven of the Masses. A Study of the Pentecostal Movement in Chile*. London: Lutterworth Press, 1969.

Lawless, Elaine J., "Rescripting their Lives and Narratives: Spiritual Life Stories of Pentecostal Women Preachers," *Journal of Feminist Studies in Religion* 7, no. 1 (1991):53-71.

Martin, David, *Tongues of Fire. The Explosion of Protestantism in Latin America*. Oxford: Blackwell, 1990.

McDonnell, Kilian, *Charismatic Renewal and the Churches*. New York: The Seabury Press, 1976.

McGuire, Meredith B., *Pentecostal Catholics: Power, Charisma and Order in a Religious Movement*. Philadelphia, Pa.: Temple University Press, 1982.

McSweeney, Bill, *Roman Catholicism: The Search for Relevance*. Oxford: Basil Blackwell Publisher, 1980.

Pfaller OSB, Louis and Larry J. Alberts BOC, *Mary is Pentecostal*. Pecos, N.M.: Dove Publications, 1973.

O'Connor CSC, Edward D., *The Pentecostal Movement in the Catholic Church*. Notre Dame, Ind.: Ave Maria Press.

Poewe, Karla, ed. *Charismatic Christianity as a Global Culture*. Columbia, S.C.: University of South Carolina Press, 1994.

Quebedeaux, Richard, *The New Charismatics: The Origins, Development and Significance of Neo-Pentecostalism*. New York: Doubleday, 1976.

Spittler, Russell P., "Are Pentecostals and Charismatics Fundamentalists? A Review of American Uses of these Categories." In *Charismatic Christianity as a Global Culture*, ed. Karla Poewe, Columbia, S.C.: University of South Carolina Press, 1994.

Steeg, Maria ter, "Maria en de emancipatie van de vrouw," *Tenminste* 1 (1980): 59-65.

Stevens, Evelyn P., "Marianismo: The Other Face of Machismo in Latin-America." In *Female and Male in Latin America*, ed. A. Pescatello. Pittsburgh, Pa. : University of Pittsburgh Press, 1973.

Stoll, David, *Is Latin America Turning Protestant? The Politics of Evangelical Growth*. Berkeley: University of California Press.

Warner, Marina, *Alone of All her Sex. The Myth and the Cult of the Virgin Mary*. London: Weidenfeld and Nicolson, 1976.

Zimdars-Swartz, Sandra L., *Encountering Mary. From La Salette to Medugorje*. Princeton, N.J.: Princeton University Press, 1991.

6

Market Behavior among Brazilian Consumers of the Divine

Public Opinion Regarding Pentecostalism and Afro-American Religiosity in the Provincial Town of Alagoinhas (Bahia)

Allard Willemier Westra

Religion as a Marketplace

We walk the unpaved streets of Alagoinhas, a provincial town in Bahia. The place is virtually deserted. No wonder—the heat is oppressive. The unrelenting wind gives no solace. Instead, it shrouds the brightly colored dwellings in a grim gray blanket of dust. On the shaded pavement in front of one of the houses sit two black women. We overhear them talking about people in the neighborhood. In great detail, they discuss what has been going on, rehashing the local gossip. The news must be engrossing; they don't seem to notice the clouds of dust that the wind keeps stirring up.

The exchange is more than an assessment of human fallibility and virtues. The women dwell on the worrisome life of every day. The conversation reveals their view of religion: an important means to lighten one's burden. One of the women says:

> Oh, you know what a strong believer I am, but I just don't know which way to turn. Every day I light a candle for Cosmo and Damian [two saints whose images grace the home altar] but it doesn't help. I have already been to see dona Matamba [a priestess of Candomblé, an African cult of possession]. I made an oath in the [Catholic] church of Nosso Senhor do Bonfim [in Salvador, the capital of the province, about 110 km from Alagoinhas]. Now I just don't know any more. Chico [her son] is just not getting better. Those temper tantrums he gets [that are sometimes followed by an epileptic fit] are terrible. Her friend is silent for a long time and then sighs. Finally, she suggests: "Why don't you just see what the *crentes* [Pentecostals] can do for you? People say they have the gift of healing [*dons*]. My neighbor had a difficult child too. Everybody thought it was possessed by an evil spirit [*exu*]. Now, she goes to the Assembléia de Deus [a Pentecostal church] a couple of times a week and he is doing a lot better now."

In Brazil, this kind of conversation is by no means unusual. Particularly the disadvantaged do not to tie themselves to one single religion. People tend to take an easy-going attitude toward worship in order to increase their chances of survival. The question people ask themselves is: "which religion, or more precisely, which religious authority is most helpful to me in dealing with a given material or spiritual problem?" We should point out that sources of aid other than religious ones are extremely scarce. The ease with which people move from one belief to another is thus not mere opportunism; their fickle devotion is born of necessity.

Furthermore, Brazil has a long history of blending of beliefs (Warren 1970). The population has become accustomed to vague boundary markers between the diverse religious tendencies. This open attitude is greatly reinforced by the precarious living conditions under which a large share of the populace has to live. Overall, about two-thirds of the Brazilian population do not even earn minimum wage (which is much too low anyway). And the situation in Alagoinhas is certainly no better. It is estimated that only 15 to 25 percent of the population have adequate food, clothing, housing, and health care (Willemier Westra 1987, 29). This means that an extremely high proportion of the population is preoccupied with the struggle for a bare existence.

The example cited above—the conversation between the two women—highlights a fundamental characteristic of this struggle for survival. Above all, people perceive their travail as a spiritual problem. This is not surprising. We should realize that almost the entire population is painfully aware that life on earth rests on a religious foundation.

That religious basis is articulated differently in the diverse beliefs. In Candomblé, for instance, people believe that the foundation consists of (magical) "power." Ultimately, that power may be traced through numerous hierarchically ordered spiritual beings back to God. (People hold the same view in the Umbanda religion, which is related to Candomblé.) Most Catholics believe that the saints exert a great influence on their lives. Likewise, those saints derive their "power" from God. The followers of Pentecostalism distinguish themselves by their much more straightforward version of the foundation of their earthly existence. From their point of view, that basis is none other than the Holy Ghost—God.

For various reasons, the above differentiation in three currents of belief is too simplistic. First of all, Alagoinhas has more religious denominations, such as the Seventh Day Adventists and the Baptists. Together, these comprise a few percent of the population. Secondly, most of those who call themselves Catholic are seldom if ever seen in church. On the other hand, those same individuals participate in the ubiquitous cult of Candomblé. We suspect that three-fourths of the population take part in Candomblé rituals, some sporadically and others on a regular basis. Yet even more important is the observation made above about the prevailing attitude toward worship. People here are not very principled—at least from a European perspective—in their religious thought and action. They simply try to buttress the spiritual foundation of existence wherever feasible. They seek spiritual redemption where they can, in the hope of raising their chances of survival.

Pentecostal believers (who comprise roughly 5 to 10 percent of the population) are formally known as being dogmatic in religious affairs. Nonetheless, several of these Evangelicals are definitely exceptions to this general rule. I myself have heard many stories—at least in Alagoinhas—demonstrating that people do not hesitate to seek deliverance in Candomblé, even though that cult is vilified in Pentecostal circles as devil worship. Actually, these are mainly cases of emergency, where people seek help in life or death situations. As an experienced Candomblé medium explains:

> Those people from the Pentecostal church always come after dark. Then they come "round back," so nobody sees them. They feel guilty about coming here. So I say: "Listen, we work with God, just like you do. All *orixás* [powerful African deities] have to obey God too. Without God they can't do anything for you." But I don't think they believe that. Even so, if they are desperate enough, they come anyway.

As an effect of this religious latitude, a large share of the population respond to the offer of assistance (both spiritual and material) that is made by the diverse religions in the town. As we have seen, this commodity, which people themselves define as religious, is not the exclusive product of just one religion. One could say that people are consumers of problem-solving redemption, actors in a religious market that is served by various religious agencies.

In this article, I attempt to chart this market. In doing so, I elaborate upon a few notions that play a role in this consumer behavior. My focus is on the two main competitors that operate in this market: Candomblé, an established cult of possession; and Pentecostalism, a religion that is on the rise in Alagoinhas. But first, I very briefly describe the local Catholic church, as it operates in the same religious market. That discussion reflects my point of departure for this article: that consumers are not the only actors in this market; we should also give due attention to the supply side.

This approach may be somewhat unusual. Yet I feel it sheds light on a particular characteristic of the Brazilian religious experience. Of course, along with clarification, this perspective gives some distortion as well. Shopping for a chicken to make soup is undeniably different from making overtures to join a church or temple. People do not generally determine their religious affiliations by weighing the costs and benefits; and they do not do so in Alagoinhas.·

Spiritual events of all kinds are part of everyday life for a most inhabitants of the city. They perceive their religious experience as the main criterion in evaluating a religious agency. Yet even this basic fact is subject to the market mechanism. The religion wherein people undergo the deepest spiritual experience—or suppose they can do so —is where they expect to find problem-solving redemption. Many people in Alagoinhas feel that their living conditions are so precarious that they have no choice but to actively seek deliverance.

This consumer behavior is influenced by a large number of considerations, some of which are touched upon in this article. These factors are summarized schematically as an appendix. By putting these notions into a matrix, I hope to help the reader relate the cases discussed here, along with the market considerations pertaining to them, to the entire religious market.

General Overview of the Catholic Market

Official Catholicism, with its churches and chapels, is predominant in Alagoinhas in more than one respect. Besides its physical presence on the streets, it is perceived as a powerful opponent by the leaders of the Pentecostal churches and the Candomblé. With the exception of the Pentecostals and other Protestants, everyone in the city claims to be Roman Catholic, including the numerous followers of Candomblé. In this article, I concentrate on those who believe in both Candomblé and Pentecostalism. Therefore, with respect to the Roman Catholic church, I restrict my comments to a few characteristics that are relevant to the competitive position of the church.

As we shall see below, both Candomblé and Pentecostalism are characterized by a high emotional content in the services. It is no exaggeration whatsoever to speak of religious ecstasy in both cases. It is striking how little scope there is for religious experience of this type within the official Roman Catholic church, or in the basis communities attached to it. With few exceptions, these institutions appeal more to common sense and public decency than to the need for release of religious emotion. This is one reason why the believers from the poorer segments of the population feel a wide gap between themselves and the Catholic church. Among this population, religious rapture and spirituality have not been differentiated since time immemorial.

This need for a special type of religious inspiration, which is difficult to measure, is just one factor at play. In Alagoinhas, other factors—more down-to-earth ones—also influence the attitude of (potential) believers. First of all, we notice that people ascribe little practical utility to the official Roman Catholic church. It is generally seen as a rich man's church. In other words, it is not firmly embedded in popular culture. Thus, the church does not know how to strike a chord with the public at large. People do not feel especially comfortable in the dignified ambience of the church. There, everything seems to be very distant from everyday life.

For instance, people regret that the Catholic church is the only one to ignore the existence of black magic (or sorcery). Of course, the church will therefore not defend the interests of its members who feel threatened by such forces. That negligence is felt to be all the more galling because the entire city is in the clutches of paranoia induced by this antisocial magic (compare Fry 1976). A young woman, disappointed in the contacts that she maintained with the church through a basis group, says: "Once, when I asked something about black magic, I didn't even get an answer. And you should realize that my aunt was very gravely ill at that time. That was because somebody had cast a spell on her. I really felt abandoned then. I have never been back; not in the church either."

Both Candomblé and the Pentecostal churches take the belief in sorcery serious, each in its own way. In comparison, the Catholic church is at a great disadvantage in this sense. This is somewhat compensated by a number of attractive characteristics that people ascribe to the official church, unbeknownst to most of the clergy. Priests, for instance, are said to be the most powerful sorcerers that exist. A Communion wafer that has been consecrated by a priest can be put to very good service by someone practicing white (i.e., healing) magic. Unfortunately, it can also be used to perform black magic. Furthermore, Roman Catholic priests are considered able to make holy water "powerful." Then it can be used to "charge up" the images that stand on the home alter or the Candomblé altar. Moreover, attendance at Holy Communion is also seen as a good occasion to absorb protective and healing "power" for the struggle for survival. There is no need to understand anything about the Mass, or even to be physically present in the church building. Just hanging around near the entrance is seen to be more than sufficient. One of the main ways in which the Catholic church touches everyday life is through baptism. With the exception of second-generation Pentecostal believers and other Protestants, virtually everyone has been baptized as Roman Catholic (including followers of Candomblé). However, people link baptism to attracting salvation and warding off disaster. As a priest recounts:

> I was called out of bed at eleven-thirty at night. Before me stood a big black man about twenty-five years old. He needed to be baptized, he said, because he had found work far away in the interior and had to leave town. His parents were no longer alive, and he couldn't remember having been baptized before. His friends and traveling companions insisted that he had to get himself baptized. Otherwise they would not take him along the next morning out of fear for an accident with the [indeed, very old] automobile.

The activities of the Roman Catholic church are certainly not limited to inadvertent aiding and abetting of magical mischief. In Alagoinhas and elsewhere in the country, this is evident in the social significance of the religious basis communities (*comunidades eclesiais de base*). These communities are an outgrowth of the solidarity that the church endeavors to display toward the disadvantaged. This policy is not restricted to setting up new structures at the basis. It includes efforts to give the believers a voice in social issues (see Krischke 1986, 188 ff.).

In Alagoinhas, this was translated (in 1979 and a few subsequent years) into a large-scale program (*promocão humana*). That program encompassed a number of highly divergent activities, such as literacy campaigns, potable water security, women's clubs, and legal counsel. Opinions differed, even among the clergy, about what basis communities actually were. In the widest sense of the word, the concept even covered thirty-five neighborhood catechism groups (Brasilien Team 1976). In a narrower sense, people referred to an entity as a basis community only if it were explicitly engaged in social or political activities. Examples of such engagement include a house-building cooperative, an agricultural co-operation, a group resisting land dispossession by the local elite, and a group fighting the oil company that had contaminated their water source. Using this narrower definition, Bishop dom José Cornelis identified a mere seven basis communities. Only a few hundred persons (out of a population of slightly over 100,000) were involved in the activities of those seven.

In Alagoinhas, basis communities in both the narrower and the wider sense share an attitude of opposition to folk religion. They attack not only the ubiquitous cult of Candomblé but also the guidelines of the Catholic church. Of course, this offensive stance towards the church may have changed somewhat over the past few years. If so, the gap will undoubtedly have been narrowed between the everyday experience of the believers and the activities that take place in the basis communities (see Azevedo 1986, 135, 144 ff.). Nonetheless, the appendix to this article reflects the situation as I found it at the end of the seventies.

I will not dwell on the topic of folk Catholicism here. Once a major religious movement, it has been severely undermined by the negative attitude of the official church. Already under pressure, the cult of Candomblé aggravated the situation by co-opting a major share of the devotion to the saints. As a priest of the cult says: "The Catholic church, that is us! If you don't believe me, you should just take a look in my altar room. That is where the images are standing that they threw out of the [Roman Catholic] church down the road. Shame on them!" Be that as it may, the cult of Candomblé has been able to benefit from the antipopulist attitudes held by many Roman Catholic clergymen. Folk Catholicism is only thriving in the sphere of private devotion. For example, rarely do people doubt the special powers of the prayer specialists (*rezadoras* or *rezadores*), who are called to the home for special occasions. Moreover, in some cases, people consider pilgrimages to be just as useful as ever to resolve personal problems.

Pentecostalism

Many people in Alagoinhas view followers of Pentecostalism with mixed feelings. On the one hand, people respect them; on the other hand, people think they are very strange. A woman who calls herself Catholic, even though she has never set a foot in the church, made the following comment:

Pentecostal people drink no alcohol, not even the men. I can't understand that, although I do admire them for it. It even saves money. I wish my husband would give a little thought to money once in a while too. Sometimes he drinks up all his earnings and then my children and I have nothing to eat. Oh well, men have to keep themselves going somehow. Girlfriends or prostitutes, they are out of the picture if you are a Pentecostal believer. So they say, but I know a prostitute who still gets regular visits from men of that church. I don't really trust them. What they say is too good to be true.

In a rural town like Alagoinhas, gossip serves just about the same purpose as a tabloid does for us. Many stories circulate about the Pentecostals (*crentes*). They seem to have a skeptical undertone. Apparently, people do not believe that the beast in the man can ever be tamed. A key element of this attitude is the concept of machismo. That is an ideal type of the man as a male animal, emphasizing the display of brute force and unbridled virility. For this reason, people have more difficulty with the phenomenon of pastors than of male *crentes*, the latter are also nearly superhuman creatures in the eyes of many. As one middle-aged man said:

> Aw, you're a man yourself, sir. You know how we are. You just make a fool of yourself if you don't go along with your friends. Now take Alfonso, down the street. You used to be able to have a good laugh with him, but now he just stays home with his wife and the kids. I ask you, is that a life for a man? He has no more friends, only that church of his. That's not for me.

People have less trouble with the idea of women becoming Evangelicals. Men generally assume that women are by nature domesticated creatures; conversion only confirms that opinion. This stereotype generally includes the idea of sexual modesty (the *marianismo* complex). But women see another side to Evangelicals. They often point out that marriage among Pentecostal believers is markedly stable. Furthermore, women usually draw the connection with a regular family income and better educational opportunities for the children. A young woman who knows several Pentecostal believers who live in her own street recounts:

Crentes are thrifty. The men bring their money home. Their religion tells them to. Yes, they do give a lot away to the church. I think that's a shame, but oh well, that's up to them. They have to work hard and study too. They learn to read and understand the Holy Bible. Everybody knows that *crentes* work hard. Their church says they have to. Any boss would love to hire them. As for me, I think they're crazy to work hard for a boss, but if you're the wife of a Pentecostal believer, that is real nice, of course.

Favorable opinions such as this, albeit with a trace of envy, are fairly common. On one side of the balance, people express both amazement and admiration. On the other side, they usually heap real or supposed disadvantages of the Evangelical faith. To my mind, this ambivalence is not only connected to the conversion and the abrupt change in behavior that this entails. Indeed, I think it reflects the Pentecostal ideal of setting an example for every nonbeliever by living according to the Gospel. My view is shared by Michel Bergmann, a sociologist (and Taizé brother) who lives in Alagoinhas. This is what he had to say on the topic in a taped interview:

For the Pentecostal believer, one of the most appealing points is deliverance from fear. If this liberation is to be truly successful, the Pentecostal church has to have credibility. That can be demonstrated in visible signals, such as when someone quits drinking alcohol, when someone leads a monogamous life, and so forth. Only then is it convincing. This conviction is necessary to be freed from fear [of black magic]. The new life must be visible, manifest in daily life.

In this passage, Bergmann says that in order to be liberated from fear, the follower of the Pentecostal faith must convince him/herself as well as others that the conversion is real. By convincing the others, it becomes more real to oneself (and vice versa). By employing internal and external means, an indisputable conviction is put into practice, even when the individual is not yet entirely convinced of the conversion. One could say that the desire to be free of fear begets the actual liberation.

This release is not merely psychological, however important this aspect may be. To be liberated also means that people no longer need to spend great sums of money on healing and protective rituals that may be purchased from one of the numerous traditional healers representing the diverse strains of folk medicine that abound in Alagoinhas. Many of those who do not follow Pentecostalism actually feel precisely the opposite about such rituals. Indeed, they consider folk medicine to be a more rewarding investment than outlays for better schooling, for instance.

Besides offering a way to prevent the continual financial blood-letting for "healing," the Pentecostal belief offers another advantage. It offers people the chance to extricate themselves from their social network. Obviously, this is not particularly attractive to those who feel a need for familial support. On the other hand, if one is going to belong to the social climbers—which is a distinct possibility for Evangelical followers in Alagoinhas—then the situation is quite different. Thrift and investment in a better financial future are just not compatible with a continual onslaught on the extremely limited monetary resources for the sake of helping out relatives, friends, and neighbors. There are indications that aid to family members declines sharply after one converts to the Pentecostal belief. This is induced by the high pledge required by the church (amounting in some cases to 10 percent of the household's income). After making this contribution, not much is left for outsiders. Moreover, the Pentecostal belief demands such a high degree of participation that little time remains for relations outside the church. In this way too, the obligatory social network is thinned out.

In sum, people in various echelons of society realize that a Pentecostal believer has better job opportunities and thus better chances of upward social mobility. In addition, people are aware that the believers can look forward to a life without fear of magically induced violence (sorcery). Strangely enough, this image is affirmed by one of the most renowned priests of Candomblé in the area. As he puts it:

> Many people who used to give their money to the cult of Candomblé have now switched to the *crentes*. It is much cheaper. There, a healing ritual is free, and for a lot of people the expense is important, like it or not. In Candomblé, the rituals are expensive, while over there everything is much more simple. But even more important is that Candomblé doesn't save anybody. Candomblé is no more than a duty, an obligation to the spirits, but the safest road is of course the path to God. He is the only one who is able to oppose the many evil things that we do. God sets us free, Candomblé does not. In my religion, you are always busy

making offerings and serving the [lesser] spirits. In the Pentecostal church, they do that better.

Candomblé

In Alagoinhas, people have mixed feelings about Pentecostalism. But feelings are also mixed about followers of Candomblé. The latter are seen as individuals who help the poor and needy, but also as individuals who can cause incalculable suffering if they so desire. The attitude of outsiders is thus a blend of appreciation and admiration, on the one hand, and suspicion and fear on the other. From an anthropological point of view, the cult of Candomblé is an amoral religion. In other words, this religion refrains from passing judgement on social issues. Someone who joins the cult generally does not have to change his or her habits, good or bad, to any great extent. Members are mostly interested in finding practical solutions to problems they are wrestling with in their daily lives. These practice-oriented actions are called "healing" (cura). Clearly, this term has a wider application than in Europe and the United States.

An aspiring member of the Candomblé cult simply expands upon the array of characteristics he or she was raised with by adding a number of magical skills. The adept does not usually undergo a clear transformation in thought and behavior. Therefore, no clearly defined breach will occur in someone's social relations. Everything continues as usual. The difference is that people believe that there is now a link between the adept and the spiritual beings. Because of that tie, the new believer is considered to have a firmer grasp on life—his or her own, and that of other people.

In some cases, this intimate contact with spiritual beings implies that preexisting aspects of one's character can be legitimated. A young woman tells about her promiscuous companion, who is a medium in the cult of Candomblé: "It is his spiritual being [orixá]. His Candomblé priestess said it herself. Men who are dedicated to Ogun [a very masculine spiritual being] need more than one woman. And men who belong to Oxóssi are hunters. He [her companion] has both. There is nothing to do about it."

Pentecostal converts display remarkable changes. We saw a notable difference in their sexual and drinking behavior, for instance, after conversion. But this is hardly or not at all the case when people join the cult of Candomblé. The Pentecostals' change in behavior improves their chances of upward social mobility. But outside their own circles, such changes have little appeal. In general, the fact that Candomblé is so easy-going is considered a great advantage of this religion.

Still, membership in the cult does entail some restrictions. These pertain to sexual behavior and alcohol consumption. However, the applicability of the rules is limited. For instance, people are aware of the likelihood of contracting an evil spirit (*exu*) from a prostitute. Indeed, this can happen in other "impure" places as well. Then too, people are wary of bringing discredit upon one's own priest(ess). To avoid that, they only need to live more carefully in general. Moreover, the *orixás* prescribe sexual abstinence for a few days prior to participation in rituals. At the same time, the participants are subject to restrictions on alcoholic beverages. An optimal contact with spiritual beings is clearly incompatible with living it up. Thus, this contact offers a moral incentive that is implicit yet clear. In general, however, this does not lead to behavior that conflicts with what people consider appropriate in the local context.

An exception to this rule is found in the reversal or the breakthrough in attitudes toward gender roles. Men who start to exhibit behavior that is designated as typically feminine make themselves ridiculous in the eyes of their fellow men unless their deviant behavior develops under the influence of an *orixá*. It is not only homosexuals who legitimate their behavior in this manner; heterosexual men who like to keep house do likewise. Also the behavior of women that is considered masculine, such as actively seeking different sexual partners, can be legitimated with the aid of the *orixás*. Orixá Iansã, a female *orixá* known to be extremely voluptuous, is often mentioned in this connection. In other words, in the area of sexual morality, Candomblé offers just about as much new leeway as it imposes new restrictions.

With regard to the (highly prevalent) abuse of alcohol, the cards are stacked differently. Alcoholism, which gives rise to a great deal of grief, is not legitimated by those *orixás* that are known to be beneficial. On the contrary, it is disqualified by bringing it into connection with evil spirits (*exus*). People believe that these demons have an exceptionally destructive influence on human beings. Thus, alcoholism is condemned, in a symbolic sense. Yet this does mean that the alcoholic is exempt from blame. He or she is merely an unwitting victim of the manipulations of malevolent forces. In this case, one could say that morality is depersonified. The notion that a personal sin may have been committed—for which penance would have to be done or for which forgiveness would have to be asked (as in the Pentecostal belief)—is unknown in this religion. It gives people reprieve from their personal sense of guilt, regardless of how terribly they have treated others. People can start anew with a clean slate, even from the point of view of those who have suffered from their actions.

In the long term, this relative amorality means that initiates to the cult do not feel any need to make a drastic change in their life style. For instance, they would not suddenly become frugal and then invest in a serious educational program. In contrast, such change does occur frequently among Evangelical converts. In Candomblé, people do not invest in things that could eventually improve their well-being. Instead, followers of the cult tend to invest in rituals that safeguard one's relation to the *orixás* and other spiritual beings. This relation is seen as the only firm foundation for attaining well-being and affluence. In many cases, membership in the cult does provide people with a degree of economic security. They help each other in emergencies. And through the priest(ess), people have a better chance of getting jobs passed their way. If one succeeds in building up a career as a medium, the path to an independent future is clear.

Summarizing, it may be said that Candomblé is usually concerned with offering relatively easy solutions to the problems confronting people. Moreover, these are generally short-term solutions, unless one is lucky enough to be a medium gifted with long-term visions.

An important point is the way in which Candomblé deals with fear. Indeed, fear can be dealt with for a fee. But that is done by counteracting its magical sources. Meanwhile, the social antecedents of fear remain unaddressed. Thus, problems related to that fear can recur at any time. In this respect, participation in Candomblé is something like mopping up with the faucet open (as we just saw, even in the eyes of some fervent believers).

Strangely enough, this perpetually maintained atmosphere of terror actually enhances the effect of rituals that are performed to assuage one's fears. People know how much terror Candomblé can inspire, and they do not hesitate to put this potential to work. It serves as a means to exert pressure upon members of the local economic and political elite, inducing them to grant favors of all kinds. Those favors are subsequently redistributed among one's own constituency in the form of miracles. Obviously, this kind of help does a lot of good for the reputation of Candomblé, at least among the poor. In the same vein, people can use this potential to exert political pressure if they so desire, and they often do (Willemier Westra 1982; 1987, Ch. 7).

This intimates that priests of the Candomblé cult have a great deal of external power, albeit largely informal. Of course, like other religions, the leaders of this cult are able to influence their own constituency. They are even known to be extremely authoritarian and to demand absolute obedience (Lima 1977, 56 ff.). When necessary, compliance is enforced by terribly frightening magical means. As a result, membership in the cult is experienced by many as a burden, despite the advantages it offers. Indeed, only rarely do people describe their own belief as a joyful experience. On the contrary, they generally call it an obligation (obrigação).

Pentecostal Churches and Candomblé Compared

At first glance, Candomblé appears to offer its constituency a great many advantages that Pentecostalism does not have. One of the main attractions of this cult of possession is that the gap between religion and everyday reality is narrow. It is true that Candomblé imposes a number of restrictions on alcohol use and sexuality. Yet these guidelines do not cause people to place themselves outside the generally accepted moral frameworks.

In contrast, this does happen to those who subscribe to the Pentecostal belief. In fact, converts intentionally seek to create a breach with the established norms and values. As we have seen, people take a strictly monogamous approach to marriage and consider alcohol consumption to be fundamentally wrong. On the basis of these attitudes alone, the Evangelicals set themselves apart from mainstream society; but there is more. As a result of joining the Pentecostal church, one's social relations with friends and neighbors are diminished. The same applies to contacts with relatives, although familial ties are affected somewhat less. At times, the limitations on social interaction outside one's own group creates major psychological tensions among the believers. People have been known to switch to Candomblé as a result, since this cult does not impose such far-reaching social restrictions.

There are several other criteria on which an Evangelical church is considered less appropriate than a cult of possession. Candomblé (and to a lesser degree Umbanda) offers an appealing sensory experience. There is always something of interest going on to keep people talking for days. The songs, the dancing, the costumes, and especially the capricious deeds of the spirits that make an appearance add up to free entertainment. As far as the people in attendance (who are not necessarily regular members) are concerned, a Candomblé ritual is a wonderful performance of popular theater. Moreover, people attending can enjoy a delicious (offering) meal for free. In no way are people coerced into joining the group. The recruitment tactics of Candomblé are geared to giving everyone the feeling they can come and go as they please. The followers seem to be convinced—and not without reason—that everything that goes on in the temple is so fascinating that most visitors will come back again on their own accord. From an outsider's point of view, Pentecostal groups offer a less attractive show. Their tactic is to give people the feeling that they are taken up into the circle of brothers and sisters from the outset. Some people like that feeling, while it prevents others from setting a foot inside the door of a Pentecostal church.

The population of the city is poor, for the most part. Thus, the costs and benefits of the various religions are crucial to one's decision whether or not to join. It is known that the Pentecostal churches claim a considerable percentage of the household income, be it high or low. It is hard to make an exact comparison of the costs of the two religions. But people generally feel that Candomblé is cheaper, at least after the expensive initiation period. In addition, the latter religion has the reputation of being able to deliver more benefits in the short term. These take the form of favors, which the Candomblé leaders pass on to the regular members. In fact, the cult leaders might even exert pressure or use blackmail in order to deliver those favors (Willemier Westra 1982).

The increase in prestige among people who join the cult of Candomblé or the Pentecostal church is not too great at first, in most cases. In the longer term, however, joining may definitely lead to a significantly higher social status. It is interesting that the increased respect for Candomblé in popular opinion is the result of its divergent qualities. People feel a mixture of admiration for someone's healing and problem-solving gifts, on the one hand, and fear of that same person's potential to work black magic, on the other. The threat of terrifying acts is ever present. With regard to the Pentecostal believers, in contrast, notions that lead to more prestige are much less ambivalent. Indeed, people see these believers as rather self-righteous do-gooders. But this does not diminish the admiration people feel for the Evangelicals' way of living, which seems superhuman. Nor does it reduce the appreciation of the way the members of the Pentecostal church have raised their social position, which not seldom goes hand in hand with that life style. Moreover, this approval is not mixed with fear.

Over the past years, the Pentecostal churches seem to have won some ground from the cult of Candomblé in Alagoinhas. The relative unambiguity of Pentecostal theology has been a key element in this process. The life of the underprivileged population is already insecure, without adding fear of magic to their worries. Pentecostalism is a religion that presents its message with conviction: that the Holy Ghost is able to repulse any and all threats of black magic. For that reason alone, this Evangelical church appeals to many people. Pentecostal churches fervently expound their stance against black magic. While assailing black magic with fire and sword, they condemn Candomblé just as vehemently. In fact, they refer blatantly to that cult as the work of the Devil. In contrast, Candomblé does not cast aspersions on Pentecostalism, nor upon the Roman Catholic Church, for that matter. The members of the cult are content to take in those who defect from the Pentecostal belief. For the rest, they just ignore the negative publicity. Actually, this attitude reinforces the image of Candomblé as a source of extraordinary "power." The fact that this image is partly based on fear does not detract from its force.

The ambivalence of the public opinion with regard to Candomblé is also found in the stories that circulate about the internal discipline in this religion. Most of the priests and priestesses of this cult are all too eager to present themselves as devoted father and mother figures, who would spare no effort to please their followers. Nonetheless, stories regularly emerge in the local gossip circuit and even in the press that conflict with this idyllic picture. One notorious affair is a method used to punish recalcitrant members, by which the chastisement is left to a spiritual being that is sent by the priest(ess). People say that those punished in this manner can incur very serious injuries. Reports like this clearly indicate that the power structure within Candomblé is extremely authoritarian. Moreover, it is highly charged with fear. In that way, joining becomes an act whereby the believer gives up an inordinate degree of control over decision-making regarding his or her own life.

Pentecostalism, in contrast, offers a greater degree of personal freedom. As in Candomblé, an effort is made to keep people in the faith when they want to leave. It is true that this is done by exerting psychological pressure. At any rate, apostates are not kept in the fold by magical methods, as they would be in Candomblé. In the Pentecostal church, moreover, the gift (*dom*) of grace of the believer prevails over the official relations of authority—at least in the churches of Alagoinhas. Anyone who is touched by the Holy Ghost has a recognized position in their religious circle, a position that cannot be retracted by higher authorities. With regard to the relations of authority, the local variant of Pentecostalism is thus considerably more horizontal than the cult of Candomblé, and burdened with less fear.

This is perhaps most clearly manifest in the "healing" (*cura*, which in its wider sense includes solving problems) that has a central place in both religions. In the Pentecostal belief, *cura* is seen as the result of the benevolent influence of the Holy Ghost. In practice, this comes down to the celebration of the goodness of God.

In the cult of Candomblé, however, "healing" is a highly paradoxical procedure. Its essence is use evil to drive out evil, to dispel calamity with calamity, and to get rid of trouble with trouble. People believe that it is precisely acts that inspire fear, cause illness, and make trouble that provide the best chances of "healing." In this vein, *cura* has some elements of a "celebration" of fear. Nevertheless, even in these exceptional cases, the fear is ultimately reduced, if not entirely dispelled. The *cura* usually leaves the "patient" with the feeling that the problem at hand has been brought closer to a solution and that he or she can once again deal with life.

Final Remarks

The religious market of Alagoinhas is fairly hard for outsiders to fathom. For instance, the architectural design of the city is dominated by buildings of the Roman Catholic Church. In contrast, the Candomblé temples and the Pentecostal churches, though numerous, go virtually unnoticed. Moreover, Candomblé is not even included in the statistics. The reason is that the followers of this cult of possession call themselves Catholic (as do followers of the cult of Umbanda elsewhere in the country).

Furthermore, it is a tactic of Candomblé to keep this market from becoming transparent. The members feel no need to profile themselves as competitors of any religion whatsoever. As far as the leaders of the cult are concerned, the believers do not have to make an exclusive commitment to their own religion. In part, that explains why this religion contains conflicting elements of belief. We have just seen this same paradoxical tendency in the discussion of the essence of Candomblé, that is, the *cura*. This paradox also pervades public opinion about this religion in general.

The image of Pentecostal churches in Alagoinhas is considerably less contradictory. Although people sometimes think the believers are naive, they still warrant respect. The choice to follow this religion is exclusive, in principle. This in itself lends some clarity of direction to everyday action. Likewise, the theological core of this religion is ambiguous. It is absolutely clear to the believers what is good and what is not. Paradoxality is nowhere to be found.

Nevertheless, I can endorse the conclusion that Droogers makes in his introductory article of this volume. From the standpoint of the scientist (etic), Pentecostalism does indeed contain a number of fundamental contradictions. The ones to which the believers do not subscribe I will call etic paradoxes. In my view, Droogers rightly observes that a number of paradoxes may be traced back to contradictory theoretical models applied by various scholars. This means that the theory itself is the source of the paradox in those cases. This special kind of paradox—one caused by model-building—I would like to call a modeling paradox. In such cases, opposing models evoke a contradictory image of a religion. On the other hand, I would refer to a paradox that emerges within one single theoretical framework by the general term of etic paradox. It is valuable that Droogers points out this distinction in regard to Pentecostalism (with regard to Candomblé, see Willemier Westra 1987, 221 ff.).

Still, it would be unfortunate to identify the lack of consensus among model-builders as the exclusive source of Pentecostal paradoxalities. (And indeed, Droogers does not do so.) For instance, in another contribution to this book, Kamsteeg points out that hierarchical and egalitarian tendencies go hand in hand in the Pentecostal churches. He even suggests that the structural tension that this engenders actually promotes the expansion of this church (by fostering internal conflict and fractionalization).

Similarly, in another article in this book, Hoekstra sheds light on one more paradoxical tendency in Pentecostalism. She lends credence to the idea that both conservative and progressive orientations may coincide in the same group or church. According to Hoekstra, the aspect that will predominate is determined by what is considered to be beneficial to the church or group in question. Hoekstra seems to refer to etic paradoxes, whereas the article by Kamsteeg is unclear in this respect. This brings me to a brief discussion of another type of paradoxes.

Besides etic paradoxes, there are also paradoxes that are recognized by the believers themselves. I refer to these as emic paradoxes. Following Van Baal (1971), Droogers sees paradoxes as the foundation of every religion. Despite being ubiquitous, paradoxes are given more emphasis in some religions than in others. My first proposition is that emic paradoxes are prominent in Candomblé. I even think that they are intentionally heightened. In contrast, they are minimized in the Pentecostal churches, as they are in scientific pursuits (see Horton 1973). Indeed, Pentecostalism is closer to Western rational thought than Candomblé is. Interestingly, Droogers hardly mentions emic paradoxes in his discussion of the Pentecostal churches, whereas such paradoxes are actually prominent in the cult of Candomblé.

My second proposition is related to the first. At least in the long run, the lower degree of paradoxality in the Pentecostal belief leads to an advantage over paradoxical religions such as Candomblé and Umbanda. The latter offer more solutions on the short term. Pentecostal groups primarily provide clarity and support with regard to the exigencies of daily life. That support does not have to be continually wrested from God by performing private rituals, as in Candomblé. The support that is given in the Pentecostal religion is thus not only less ambiguous but more permanent than in Candomblé. This enhances the clarity with which the members of the Evangelical church present themselves to outsiders.

The second proposition leads me to make another theoretical distinction that is important when comparing Pentecostal churches with the cult of Candomblé. Emic paradoxes may be divided into two types: those related to the structure of the group and those embedded in the system of belief. I call the first type structural and the second theological paradoxes. A comparison of the structural paradoxes of both religions would certainly bring some interesting differences to light. Nevertheless, I will restrict my discussion to theological paradoxes. Like the other guidelines for daily living, the structural aspects of a religion are also derived from theology. This also applies to the way in which people resolve daily problems and treat illness (*cura*). The Pentecostal churches contend that *cura* is identical to the exclusive orientation toward God. Thus, the behavioral model they promulgate is both simple and consistent. In contrast, in the realm of *cura*, Candomblé applies a paradoxical method. Problem-causing forces and powers are summoned forth with the intent of exorcizing them.

Fry and Howe (1975, 89), mentioned in Droogers' introduction, are correct, however, in referring to the "dramatic cogency" of the Umbanda ritual (and, by implication, that of Candomblé). Indeed, the cult of Candomblé has an impressive arsenal of ritual elements, like rousing music and dance, which have a wide appeal. These instruments also serve to create a sense of solidarity with respect to outsiders (*communitas*), an awareness that transcends everyday experience. Where this consciousness prevails, all sense of social differentiation subsides, but that not alone. Most notably, the paradoxality inherent to this religion then dissipates. Its disappearance is particularly striking with regard to methods of providing assistance to people in need, whether in the public or private sphere.

The public rituals of the Pentecostal churches are considered to be much less attractive by people who are not members. But the rituals are not intended to have a wide appeal. These churches do not face the same problems as the Candomblé temples. Indeed, the churches do not have to publicly reconcile a paradoxical system of aid with a paradoxical theology. Furthermore, they employ a different method of recruitment. This entails a demonstration of righteous living. The change in behavior that occurs in a new believer must be apparent to everyone. The recruitment methods also involve some advantages that only become manifest over time. These are the long-term social and economic advantages of commitment to the faith. In this respect, the solutions that Pentecostalism offers are more appropriate to the needs of a modernizing country like Brazil. Thus, though taking a different perspective, I can also endorse the findings reported by Howe (1981; discussed by Droogers in his introduction to this book). And at the same time, this convergence provides me with a hypothesis to explain the relative gains made by the Pentecostal churches in Alagoinhas over the past several years.

References

Azevedo, Marcello, *Comunidades eclesiais de base e inculturaçao*. Sao Paulo: Ediçoes Loyola, 1986.

Baal, Jan van, *Symbols for Communication: An Introduction to the Anthropological Study of Religion*. Assen: Van Gorcum, 1971.

Brasilien Team, *Bilanz nach 8 Jahren*. Passau: Diözese Passau, 1977.

Fry, Peter, *Regional Cult or National Religion: The Predatory Expansion of Umbanda in Urban Brazil*, 1976. Unpublished paper.

Fry, Peter, and Gary N. Howe, "Duas respostas a afliçao: Umbanda e pentecostalismo," *Debate e Crítica* 9 (1975): 75-94.

Horton, Robin, "Paradox and Explanation: A Reply to Mr. Skorupski," *Philosophy of Social Sciences* 3: 231-256, 289-312.

Howe, Gary N., "Capitalism and Religion at the Periphery: Pentecostalism and Umbanda in Brazil." In *Perspectives on Pentecostalism: Case Studies from the Caribbean and Latin America*, ed. Stephen D. Glazier. Washington, D.C.: University Press of America, 1980.

Krischke, Paulo, *A Igreja nas bases em tempo de transiçao*. Porto Alegre: CEDEC, 1986.

Lima, Vivaldo Costa da, *A familie-de-santo nos candomblés Jeje-Nagôs da Bahia - um estudo de relações intra-grupais*. Salvador: Universidade Federal da Bahia, dissertaçao de mestrado, 1977.

Warren, David, "Notes on the Historical Origins of Umbanda," *Universitas* 6/7 (Salvador), 1970.

Willemier Westra, Allard, "Religie en dagelijks overleven: hulpverlening in de candomblé-religie van Brazilië," *Internationale Spectator* 17, no. 1 (1982): 151-153.

———, *Axê, kracht om te leven: het gebruik van symbolen bij de hulpverlening in de candomblé-religie in Alagoinhas (Bahia, Brazilië)*. Amsterdam: Cedla, 1987.

Table 1 Overview of a segment of the religious market of Alagoinhas

	Catholic			Noncatholic	
	Official R.C. Church	Base Communities	Folk Catholicism	Candomblé/Umbanda	Pentecostal Churches
Cultural gap religions vs daily life (sex, morality, alcohol, abuse, etc.)	Elite: small, lower class: large	Large (rational approach)	Very small	Very small	Very large
Psychological Factors — Fear of black magic	Ignored	Ignored	Not ignored, not attacked	Individually removed, socially exacerbated	Liberation from fear of black magic
Celebrations etc.; "theatre" and entertainment	Practically inaccessible to the poor population	Absent	Sharply declining demand	Very important	Less important, religious ecstasy
Social Relations — Social contact with relatives	Not affected	Not affected	Fostered in some case	Not affected	Usually less
Social contact with friends and neighbors	Not affected	Not affected	Godparents, thus fostered	Not affected	Very sharply diminished
Take on new social obligations; obedience	Not applicable	On voluntary basis	In some specific cases	Sacrifice some personal freedom (initially)	On voluntary basis but large
Expansion of social network	Via ritual kinship	Legal, educational, and other support (expertise)	Via ritual kinship	Very large, internal and external	Especially internal relations

Table 1 Overview of a segment of the religious market of Alagoinhas (*continued*)

Chances of Survival	Take on financial burden	Church obligations for ordinary believer are expensive	Sometimes but usually with help	In personal cases but then sometimes expensive	Ritual burden very large in the beginning	Permanently very large
	Financial benefits	None	Depending on the project, sometimes large	None	Only large for experienced mediums	Substantial in the long run
	Chances of income form work	Chance no greater	Depending on the project, sometimes better in the long run	No greater (according to believers, via miracle)	Greater for the faithful, sometimes greater for "patients"	Greater, reliable, schooling
	Solutions to concrete problems of everyday life	Chance no greater	Depending on project, usually greater	Same as above	Definitely possible, certainly in material sense	Especially effective in the long run
Social Status and Power	Increase in personal prestige	Great in personal prestige	Probably negligible	Only in specific cases	Major increase for experienced medium	Considerable
	Chance of exerting political pressure	High for the elite, not for the poor	Via official church organ when needed	None	Definitely for well-known mediums	Not sought after

7

Rural Pentecostalism in Pernambuco (Brazil)

More than a Symbolic Protest

Angela Hoekstra

In 1918 two Swedish priests began to preach the Pentecostal belief in Pernambuco, a federal state in the northeastern part of Brazil. Counting only a few hundred members in 1920, the movement in that area grew to 56,000 members in 1974. This fast growth of Pentecostalism is a phenomenon that can be observed in the whole of Latin America. The period from the beginning of this century until now is characterized by fast, radical changes in society. Processes occurring are rapid urbanization, industrialization, and rationalization of the predominantly export-oriented agriculture. The application of modern technology in the plantation economy of Pernambuco at the beginning of this century is a typical example of a development which caused many farmers to be expelled from their land. A worsening situation, especially in the countryside—certainly for the smaller farmers—caused an enormous migration-flow to the cities. So the rise of Protestantism in the nineteenth century was correlated to changes in societal structure as well (Willems 1967).

The enormous growth of Pentecostalism has led some authors to search for an explanation of this phenomenon. Explanations tend to center on the urban situation, where lots of migrants coming from the countryside were converted. However, in the countryside changes also occurred, and Pentecostal movements sprang up. The question arises how these are to be explained. In search of an explanation I want to make a comparison between rural and urban Pentecostalism. I will therefore discuss both phenomena, based on general literature on the subject and specific literature on Pernambuco. In this chapter I intend to make clear how in both forms of Pentecostalism response is made to different kinds of problems happening to people who find themselves in a situation of rapid social development.

For the purpose of describing urban Pentecostalism I will use Willems (1967) and Hoffnagel (1978). This last author completed research in Recife, the capital of Pernambuco. Pentecostalism in rural areas, I will illuminate by studies by Novães (1985) and myself (Hoekstra 1991), both of which were conducted in rural towns in Pernambuco, in northeast Brazil.

Before making comparisons, I will describe traditional society, which was totally centered around the *fazenda* (large-scale land-ownership), to enable an understanding of which elements of traditional structure are continued in Pentecostalism. This continuity in structure is an important factor in explaining the success of the Pentecostal movement, both in rural and in urban areas. However, elements of a break with tradition have to be taken into consideration as well, and therefore will also be discussed.

As Droogers has already commented in the introduction, some authors emphasize continuity with the past, others tend to focus on aspects involving rupture. In this chapter we will see that exclusivity is not appropriate, but that different points of view are of complementary value in explaining the attraction of Pentecostalism. For Hoffnagel (1978) continuity with traditional social structure leads her to believe that Pentecostalism is a conservative movement. Willems (1967), on the other hand, views Pentecostalism as a (symbolic) protest movement, paying attention to elements of break with the status quo and especially to the egalitarian ideology. The rural example given by Novães will clarify the view that Pentecostalism can in fact mean more than a symbolical protest, and even in a concrete socio-economic sense can mean rupture with traditional society. The tendency in these explanations of the growth of Pentecostalism is to view the phenomena as a solution to problems resulting from the crisis that people are facing. A problem that arises is that these explanations often lack specification, and can be applied to other religions as well. In my research I choose to look beyond these functionalist models of explanation, and take the content of the Pentecostal ideas into consideration.

Traditional Social Structure

When the Portuguese first arrived in Brazil, they did not find as the Spanish did, enormous treasures and established realms, but tribes of hunters and gatherers. Because the exploitation of Brazilian wood did not turn out to be lucrative enough, and precious metals were only discovered in the eighteenth century, the colonists started to lay out numerous coffee and sugar plantations. Commercial agriculture, aimed at European and African markets, dominated the economic development of Brazil. The colony was officially ruled from Bahia, Salvador being the capital. But in reality guidance and control by the state were very weak. Aristocratic families dominated colonial society (Lang 1979, 35-73). An important element in the socio-economic system was the *fazenda*, a large-scale plantation or estate in private hands, that still today represents the dominant form of landownership. Production is aimed at external markets. In addition, the laborers, subject to the *fazendeiro* (landlord), produce for their own consumption. Freyre (in Kliewer 1975, 36-45) emphasizes the autonomic functioning of the *fazenda*, forming a more or less closed system for the tenants, not only with regard to production, but also in the aspects of religion, family-planning, and politics. The relationship between the *patrão* (landlord) and the tenant farmers is one based on vertical power. The system has developed its own special social ethics, defining the economic as well as the moral and psychological involvement with the *patrão*. Both suppression and affection are part of the relationship with the landlord. The latter factor prevents outbreaks of antagonism between the owner of the property and his subordinates. Kliewer (1975) in this connection mentions an appearance of caring and humanity, institutionalized to restrain the laborer from protesting. The very existence of the vertical social structure happens at the cost of horizontal solidarity.

The fact that the agrarian laborer is willing to submit himself to an unequal relationship with the landowner is out of pure necessity because of an existing lack of ground for cultivation. This inequality is also being fed by a series of general predispositions towards submission to authority. There is socio-cultural agreement with dependency on the *patrão*, which forms the ideological base of class structure in the countryside (Forman 1975, 76).

Traditionally, the task of the Catholic church was to provide the symbolic meaning that would integrate different parts of society. Religion obviously had a normative function, propagating values of an authoritarian society such as obedience and submission. Colonial society in this respect can be called a *sacral* society, in which hierarchical norms were given by divine power and were looked upon as sacred and unchangeable. The religious practices of the lower strata were determined by popular Catholicism, in which the notion of a natural presence of the supernatural in this world, especially in the form of saints, formed the central element. Submission was the only religiously legitimate attitude people could assume towards the saints. This is not to state that by definition a believer was apathetic, because there was always the possibility of reducing the pain by prayer. The supernatural was hierarchically organized, with God at the top, not available for direct contact. Below that were Maria, Christ, and numerous saints. These saints were specialized, meaning they were connected to a certain person, place, or situation. The religious hierarchy was a mirror image of social structure, in which the power of God and the king were parallel, and the *patrão* as well as the personal saint had to be put in the right mood to obtain a certain favor. The supernatural world and its attendant meanings had a tremendous impact on people's attitude to life, and led to almost universal submission to higher powers and acceptance of the "earthly" faith (Kliewer 1975, 45-51).

Continuity of Pentecostalism with Traditional Elements

Willems states that the success or failure of an attempt to introduce new elements into a society depends on the extent to which these are matchable with existing values and attitudes (1967, 15). In other words, there has to be a certain continuity with the traditional. Evidence of this continuity would be a factor explaining the successful rise of the Pentecostal movement both in cities and in the countryside. Distinguished in this theory may be historical, symbolic, and social continuity. Let us see the extent to which these can be applied to the Brazilian situation.

With regard to historical continuity, the northeast of Brazil has a longstanding tradition of messianism (belief in the second coming of Christ), that can be traced back to the sixteenth century Sebastianism (ibid., 134). Particularly during the nineteenth and twentieth centuries, messianistic and millenistic (belief in the coming of a Thousand Year Reign of Peace) protest movements emerged in the Brazilian back lands. These were mainly an expression of economic dissension, in which conflicts about ownership of land were the central issue. In this context, messianistic religion served as a means of social mobilization, in which leadership in addition found a religious legitimation (Forman 1975, 221-237). For these messianistic movements, with the message of a religious leader being relevant to a large group of underprivileged people, the following of an ascetic way of life can be seen as a necessary sacrifice in order to find a solution to their problems. So the acceptance of an ascetic way of life is not unique to Protestantism and Pentecostalism in Brazil, but finds historical precedents in messianism. Both these movements and Pentecostalism can be looked upon as answers of traditional society to the problems that occur in times of fundamental socio-cultural change (Willems 1967, 51-53).

In the second place, there is a demonstrable symbolic continuity with elements from popular Catholicism. A central issue in popular Catholicism is the expectation of direct and relieving intervention by the supernatural in daily life (ibid., 36). The belief in the performance of miracles and the healing of sickness by saints is continued in the Pentecostal beliefs, where the Holy Ghost takes over these tasks (Kliewer 1975, 97). Even the *pagar votos*, the carrying out of vows to saints in trade for a favor, is being continued in a certain manner in the Pentecostal movement, although believers make their vows to God (Hoffnagel 1978, 152-153). Furthermore people could establish an emotional bond with the supernatural by getting into a state of ecstasy. True, Pentecostalism distances itself firmly from the phenomena of ecstasy and trance, which are branded as the work of the devil, but emotional contact is possible through the workings and appearance of the Holy Ghost. Inspirations, revelations, and prophecies, formerly attributed to various powers, for Pentecostals are the working of the Holy Spirit. Like popular Catholicism, Pentecostalism can be called a faith of providence, in which people are absolutely dependent on the will of God (Kliewer 1975, 97-99).

Finally, there may be considered to be social continuity with elements of the traditional *fazenda* system. On the *fazenda* numerous and extensive family relationships form the key to social organization. Within the Pentecostal movement, these are being replaced by a family-like network of brothers and sisters in the faith (Lalive d'Epinay 1969, 129-131).

Both the *fazenda* and the Pentecostal group are exclusive systems, making a total appeal to their members and secluding them from the outside world. On the *fazenda* the owner willingly tries to keep his tenants politically unemancipated. In the Pentecostal movement political emancipation can be prevented by consciously avoiding "worldly" affairs (Kliewer 1975, 144ff). Lalive d'Epinay describes the Pentecostal movement as a reincarnation of the traditional system, on one side characterized by narrow personal bonds, on the other by a concentration of power in the hands of the landlord. In the traditional system, the individual only had indirect connection to the outside world. In the Pentecostal movement, the pastor (minister) takes over the role of intermediary from the *patrão*. Both the leaders of the *fazenda* and the Pentecostal movement not only play a protecting role, but are authoritarian as well. They expect their members to be obedient. In conclusion, the paternalistic and authoritarian structure of the traditional *fazenda* system is maintained in Pentecostalism (Lalive d'Epinay 1969, 129-131).

Break with Tradition

Although, as illustrated above, Pentecostalism shows many signs of continuity with traditional elements of society, aspects of break with that tradition can be traced as well. I described both the *fazenda* and Pentecostalism as exclusive, closed systems. However, it also has to be taken into consideration that this exclusivity in the case of the *fazenda* is based on economic exploitation by the landowner. He is maintaining his position of power for the sake of controlling labor. In contrast, in the Pentecostal movement this exclusivity is rejected precisely at the economic level, because labor relationships for the believers form the most important contact with the outside world. In the same way, the protective function of the *fazenda* is based on economic power of the patrão and serves his interests. In Pentecostalism, protection is the result of a well-integrated group.

Another important difference is that most of the time people are born on the *fazenda*, while joining the Pentecostal church is by individual choice. This also implies that followers are able to leave the group. It is therefore necessary for the pastor to stimulate mutual bonds. In contrast, the *patrão* will try to discourage horizontal solidarity. Leadership of the *fazendeiro* is connected to possessions, that of the *pastor* to charismatic qualities. The laborers at a *fazenda* are dependent on their leader in an economical way, Pentecostal believers are dependent in an ideological manner. In addition, the pastor also depends on the church members, sometimes for financial support, but definitely for the maintenance of his leadership (Kliewer 1975, 144-147).

In contrast to the Catholic church, where the clergy stands above the people, the Pentecostal movement has an egalitarian form of organization. Every member is a potential leader and has direct access to the supernatural world. Kamsteeg, in this book, points out that there is a certain tension between the fact that the minister is a recognized authority with a lot of power, but at the same time this powerful position is open to any ordinary member. Ideally, Pentecostal society forms a classless society, in which status does not depend on possessions, profession, class, or personal relationships (Lalive d'Epinay 1969, 130-131). The receiving of the Holy Spirit is the only recognized way to legitimate power. Social egalitarianism is a dogma, and aspirations for leadership must be ratified by divine power (Willems 1967, 137ff).

Pentecostal ideology sets strong bounds to personal behavior, in the sense that it forbids "worldly" pleasures and hedonistic conduct. Gambling, dancing, drinking, and smoking are forbidden. This is also a break with traditional society, where someone could be both a hard worker and participate regularly in the lottery. For Pentecostalism such things are irreconcilable. For respectable women drinking, gambling, and extramarital sex were already not respectable things to do. Because women had already internalized rules of correct female behavior, strongly determined by an androcentric society, their traditional lifestyle seems to be very compatible with Protestant ethics. This may explain why women seem to be more attracted to Pentecostalism. In Pernambuco, for example, the percentage of Pentecostal women is 13.9 percent higher than the figure for men (Mariz 1989, 72-73).

Willems points out the existence of a double standard with regard to sexuality. The male role is centered around a set of values that can be called the virility complex, in which frequent sexual intercourse, drinking, and expressions of aggression are essential to prove masculinity. The female role, enhanced in the virginity complex, stresses an early separation of the sexes, virginity, and therewith, the saving of the family honor. The goal of the Protestant ethic is to eliminate this double standard (Willems 1967, 45-50). Hoffnagel states that female Pentecostal believers are indeed more able to control their husbands than nonbelievers, and that there is more moral equality between the sexes. However, it cannot be forgotten that the Pentecostal movement, as does traditional society, still strongly values women as mothers and wives. Bringing up children is still predominantly seen as a task for women, which in addition enables them to gain a certain status within the group (Hoffnagel 1978, 185-189).

Urban Pentecostalism

The growth of urban Pentecostalism has been explained by the movement's function as a mechanism of reorganization for migrants who came in large numbers to the cities due to the worsening situation in the countryside. For them, Pentecostalism has an adaptive function in

a society facing fast socio-economic change. The lower strata especially have been radically affected by migration, urbanization, and
industrialization (Willems 1967, 247-267). In their new urban environment, the migrants fell into a state of anomie, in which they lost the
sense of security provided by the traditional social structure and the
customary way in which status was defined (Kliewer 1975, 82). For the
migrant to refind his lost identity, these changes called for a reconstruction of primary group relations in the city. In this respect, the
Pentecostal movement, strongly emphasizing cooperation, personal
responsibility, and mutual aid, provided an adequate answer to the
need to create a new "personal community." This group provided
both a new social identity and a feeling of security (Willems 1967, 83,
123).

For the lower strata, Pentecostalism offers a way of compensating
for the power, prestige, and status that are denied to them in society as
a whole (Hoffnagel 1978, 1-4). Willems states that in a society with
strong class consciousness, the migrants have to overcome feelings of
inferiority, for which the supernatural power of the Holy Spirit can
compensate. The attraction of the emotional Pentecostal beliefs and
the asceticism going with it, lies in the fact that it denies the very existence of this world, in which the believers are underprivileged. Instead, it creates an alternative society, the kingdom of God, in which
they themselves form the elite. Before conversion a believer was just a
nobody, but now he or she is a person receiving supernatural powers
and belonging to the chosen few (Willems 1967, 139-144).

In the chapter by Droogers in this volume we have already seen
that models of anomie have a number of shortcomings. First, they
lack specificity for Pentecostalism. Also, according to Fernandes (in
Droogers), the anomie and social vacuum experienced are not as great
as suggested. However, Droogers concludes that the simple fact that
people find a so-called "personal community" and experience some
social progress, have been demonstrated at least for some churches.

The question arises of why popular Catholicism no longer meets
the needs of migrants. Popular Catholicism in the first place is a rural
religion, adapted to problems happening to peasants. The religion is
strongly associated with crops and cattle, with droughts and floods.
Moreover, the pantheon of saints has a local connection, so that migration not only alienates people from their relatives and friends, but

from their saintly protectors as well (Willems 1967, 131-134). In this paper we have seen that Pentecostalism shows so much symbolical continuity with popular Catholicism that we can state that the Pentecostal belief offers lost elements of the traditional religious way in a new form.

According to Willems (1967) Pentecostalism not only functions as an adaptation mechanism, but also contains elements of protest. He suggests that at first sight the Pentecostal movement may seem totally irreconcilable with the traditional social structure of Brazil. The frequent flourishing of messianistic protest movements however suggests that at least part of the population at times is capable of rebelling–be it secretly or openly—against the established order. Even Protestant ethics, stressing diligence, thrift and chastity, are not essentially different from elements present in this historical precedent. Certain parts of the population, by which Willems means the underprivileged strata, were and still are capable of expressing their feelings of hostility by both spontaneous organization and deviant religious interpretations.

The egalitarian form of organization of the Pentecostal church leads Willems to label Pentecostalism as a protest movement. The absence of the ecclesiastical hierarchy so important in the Catholic church, the priesthood now being open to ordinary members, a charismatic form of leadership enforced by the Holy Ghost, and local autonomy, all imply a symbolic inversion of traditional social order. As a result, Pentecostal beliefs form a symbolic protest against the religious monopoly of the Catholic church and her traditional ally, the elite. It is to be expected that the further the ideology and structure of a certain Protestant denomination is removed from the established social order, the more appealing it will be to lower, hostile segments of the population. In this regard, the organizational structure of the Pentecostal church offers an especially useful option. For the lower strata conversion to Pentecostalism is the most meaningful symbolic protest against traditional rulers. In fact besides regarding Pentecostalism as a mechanism of adaptation to an altering social situation, Willems views it as a motor behind further change.

Taking quite a different view, Hoffnagel (1978), having done research on the *Assembléia de Deus* in Recife, pictures Pentecostalism as a conservative movement, retaining many elements of traditional social structure, supporting the status quo, and therewith delaying

social change. According to Hoffnagel, the differences in the organization of the Pentecostal church compared to the traditional organization stressed by Willems, are only an unrealized ideal. The majority of
the members have but a small say in the selection of new leaders, or
none at all. They tend to view their leader as superior, and he in an
authoritarian way exerts an influence on their lives. There is a clear
relationship between the way power is exercised within the Pentecostal movement and the way it is in broader Brazilian society.

Hoffnagel states that the church integrates its members in the status
quo. Politically speaking, urban Pentecostalism supports dominant
power structures. The believers are very aware of the fact that maintaining connections with local political elites can be very useful. An
example of this is the fact that members of the movement belong to in
the city council of Recife. Moreover, the Pentecostal followers are
expected to vote, as good citizens are supposed to do. On the other
hand, Pentecostal ideology discourages any political involvement. The
solution to this contradiction lies in defining politics as action with the
goal of altering the status quo. According to this interpretation, by
voting for governing parties and not for the opposition (branded as
communistic by Pentecostal believers), people are not engaged in
politics.

Moreover, Pentecostalism is not contributing in any way to societal change. Membership of the Pentecostal church for the individual may lead to a small improvement of socio-economic position,
because the money formerly spent on "worldly pleasures" now serves
to provide more useful things such as better housing and education.
Therefore membership has to be viewed as a successful strategy to
maximize limited economic resources. This can result in a certain
amount of social mobility, especially over several generations. However, the fact that the Pentecostal ideology in general produces disci-
plined, honest, and obedient workers, benefits the finances of the rich
more than the economic situation of the laborers themselves. Economic improvement is not social, but limited to an individual level,
and only in a moderate way. The Pentecostal ideology does not foster
class consciousness at all. Separation from the world and the notion of
the temporary character of this world do not encourage the search for
a social solution to problems. The believers live in a religious world, in
which pain and suffering are explained, and in which their problems

find solutions, either now on earth or, if not, certainly later in the
Kingdom of God. In conclusion, Hoffnagel states that Pentecostalism
has a clear tendency towards supporting the status quo, and that potential changes at best take place at an individual level. In her view, the
religion does not contribute to social change.

Rural Pentecostalism

In the mid-sixties the *Assembléia de Deus* settled in a rural village in
Pernambuco, fictionally named Santa Maria. Novães (1985) researched the meaning and consequences that joining the Pentecostal church
would have with regard to the social behavior of the believers. The
members of the *Assembléia de Deus*, all farmers in a subsistence economy, do not have a collective form of organization. They are spread
all over the region, where they cultivate their plots. Characteristic of
all farmers, including those who are not Pentecostal believers, is that
production is based on family labor, and that they struggle with scarcity of land. Within the household, the physical, social, and most of
the economic production are realized. In this the farmers distinguish
themselves from wage-earners and tenants, who predominantly have
to look outside the group for economic survival. The produce of the
small farmer, with the number of acres varying from a half to fifteen,
is meant for his own consumption. The main crops planted are maize,
manioc, and beans. They also keep poultry and other small animals,
and perhaps some cattle. In addition they produce a small amount of
crops meant for selling on the market, such as sugar, coffee, and fruits.
    Both quantitative and qualitative scarcity of land presses these
farmers during the low season to look out for additional jobs in the
capital of the state, Recife, or to go further southward to engage in
seasonal labor on the sugar plantations. Another possible "survival
strategy" is to look for uncultivated areas in the vicinity, which can be
found at *fazendas*, but also at the properties of smaller landowners.
This may seem paradoxical, but some farmers at times have to face a
shortage of family labor due to the life cycle of the family, the children
being too small or having married and left the house. In addition,
some farmers may lack the necessary financial reserves at the beginning of the season, for example because of high expense incurred by
the illness of a family member. Another possibility, from which Pen-

tecostal members are of course excluded, is the renting of *Terra do Santo*, land owned by the Catholic church. In the last decades major changes have occurred in the model of land use at the *fazendas*. In the mid-fifties patterns of urban consumption changed. New urban demand caused a growing request for the production of meat and dairy produce, which stimulated cattle-raising. In the sixties especially there was an enormous rise in the amount of farmland allocated to stock-breeding. This happened at the expense of the production of other traditional commercial crops like coffee and cotton (Clay 1989).

Before this change farmers were enabled to use a plot at the *fazenda*, in the form of *arrendameto*, which was leased at a previously agreed price. However, when cattle-breeding turned out to be so lucrative, *fazendeiros* were less interested in *arrendameto* contracts with small farmers. They were only interested if the agreement would lead to an expansion of the amount of pasture. For this purpose, a new sort of agreement was invented, called *foro pelo pasto* (pasture lease). *Fazendeiros* who still used part of their property for the production of cotton, but wanted to switch to stock-breeding, allowed farmers to grow maize and beans among the cotton plants, which they had to take care of as well. After harvest the farmers could keep all the products in exchange for planting the plot with *palma* (a cactus species), pangola, or elephant-grass, which could serve as forage. In this way the *fazendeiros* were enabled to make the transition from cotton to cattle-breeding without high costs. The choice of using *fazenda* land as a survival strategy was only made in the case of extreme necessity, for the farmers were well aware of the subordinate position they found themselves in. But when more and more land became occupied by *palma*, pangola, and pasture, the importance of having access to the landlord's property became clear, because the problem of scarcity of land became ever more serious.

In this agrarian context the Pentecostal members do not distinguish themselves from the nonbelievers in Santa Maria. Existing social relationships within the domestic group are maintained (and some family members may even follow another religion), because a good *crente* (Pentecostal believer) lives up to his obligations. So conversion does not mean the breaking of existing social networks. There is a religious dimension to it; a fanatical believer will try to convert the rest of his family. But there is a materialistic benefit as well in maintaining bonds with kin: the religious community does provide a new network of people which can be relied on for help, but it cannot replace the old one, because economically speaking it is not self-supporting.

But conversion in Santa Maria has far-reaching consequences in terms of political participation. The *crentes* of the *Assembléia de Deus* pursue an effective strategy of cooperation with the only body representing the rural laborers: the *Syndicato dos Trabalhadores Rurais*. This organization offers the farmers legal assistance for example. Politically speaking, the Pentecostal members fight for land rights. According to Novães, the so-called corporate character of Pentecostalism, lying in the local autonomy and in the fact that both material and intellectual sources are of local origin, means that the acknowledgment of the farmer's problems and the solutions are in the hands of the religious organization.

Gramsci (in Novães 1985) states that where the national political system restrains the opportunities to express protest and get organized, the religious apparatus represents the essential way in which the lowest social strata can express themselves. Indeed the *Assembléia de Deus* shows the farmers a way to make their wishes recognizable.

In the opinion of Novães (1985, 131) the experience of conversion and the intensity of religious life for the Pentecostal believers creates a common feeling, a strong sense of "belonging together." The *crentes* legitimate their struggle for land rights on the basis of the contents of psalms and the Bible. In this way, there is a strong connection between religious and social aspects. For the Catholics in Santa Maria this is less true, and their feelings of togetherness are weaker.

Due to the fact that the *fazendeiros* do not want to make any more land available for *arrendamento*, but through the system of *foro pelo pasto* allocate more land for cattle-breeding, and moreover buy small plots from the farmers, differences between the classes are being accentuated. The Pentecostal movement in Santa Maria cannot be called a defender of the status quo. Its members assume an antagonistic attitude against the dominant class (the *fazendeiros*) and against the Catholic church, the traditional representative of this class. The chance to join the Pentecostal movement for small farmers means a opportunity to be able to live amongst equals. In other terms, Pentecostalism organizes the poor and stimulates them in the struggle for land rights. The traditional domination of the *fazendeiros* is seriously questioned. Now that the landlords are refusing to rent plots to the farmers, the farmers are striving to break down traditional clientelistic relationships with this group.

Novães (1985, 153) suggests that the weakening of social bonds with the *fazendeiros* in a way creates the necessary space for the existence of the Pentecostal church in Santa Maria. For the possibility the *Assembléia de Deus* offers small farmers to loosen the ties of dependency with the landlords can be a significant factor in motivating them to join the Pentecostal movement. The rupture with traditional social structure that Pentecostalism implies is, therefore, an important part of the explanation of the growth of Pentecostalism in Santa Maria.

Pentecostalism in a Larger Rural Town

My research (Hoekstra 1991) was conducted in Pernambuco as well, but unlike that of Novães, in a town of about 35,000 inhabitants. The economy in the town is largely dominated by agro-industrial processing of tomatoes and fruits. There are also some smaller industries, like the production of lace. Eighty percent of agricultural land is used for cattle-raising, the other 20 percent for agro-industrial products and subsistence.

A small majority of the regular members of the Pentecostal church *Deus é Amor*, where the research was done, lives in the town itself, the others are small farmers or tenants in the region. In addition there is a group of members who visit the church only once a week on market day and miss the other services because they have to travel a long way.

Members inhabiting the town have histories and present situations similar to those of migrants in large cities as described by Hoffnagel and Willems. But because others live fairly traditional farmers' lives in the countryside, the anomie model developed for migration situations does not explain the growth of this Pentecostal church sufficiently. Nor can the attractiveness for the farmers be explained by stating that the Pentecostal church supports politically and economically advantageous behavior, as Novães described. The church does not engage in any action of this kind.

As I stated at the beginning of this chapter, the explanations discussed so far have one thing in common: they all perceive crisis to be the most important factor of explanation of the Pentecostal phenomena. In other words, authors tend to focus on the function of the Pentecostal religion, on the role it plays in society. However, these functional explanations lack specification, and can also be applied to other religions. According to Droogers (1990), this is due to the fact that the emphasis in research has been on the relationship between Pentecostal members and society. The relationship believers have with the supernatural world should be taken into consideration as well. In this way, more justice will be done to the specific character of the Pentecostal religion itself.

Sepúlveda (1989) notes that until now religion has been looked upon in social sciences as opium for the people, as a means of dominance and social conformism or as a heaven for the masses. He pleads for religion to be viewed from a more inclusive perspective, emphasizing the meaning religion has to its believers.

Cavalcanti (1985) notes that among people in a socially deprived situation feelings of combativeness exist, in which people find themselves frustrated, because living conditions exclude actual opportunities to fight. They do not have access to means of power to influence their situation. However, the psycho-social means people have at their disposal to express the struggle for survival cannot be disregarded. People attempt to create a new consciousness that better fits reality. Supported by a new set of ideas, which can be a religion, solutions are invented both on an individual and on a community level.

According to Cucchiari (1988), religion is not purely to be seen as a survival strategy, but also as an expression of religious needs. He stresses that conversion is not primarily related to a psychology of deprivation, but to a psychology of creativity. Agreeing that conversion is impossible without crisis before, Cucchiari states that instead of emphasizing the causes of the crisis, we should look more at the "creative potential" of the crisis. In doing so, justice is done to the existence of two relatively autonomous worlds, one being that of the external conditions, the other being that of the subjective interpretation of those conditions. He calls conversion a psychological-moral process of self-transformation, which has to be accomplished within the existing religious tradition.

In my study (Hoekstra 1991) I have stated that the notion of crisis is predominantly connected to the relationship between believers and society, because changes occurring in society marginalized the believer. On the other hand, the notion of creativity is primarily linked to the relationship the believer has with the supernatural world, where he can expect divine powers to support him. It is in this realm that Pentecostals look for creative solutions to make daily life bearable. Both domains are closely interconnected. The position a believer has in society influences the way he organizes his religious worldview. But the opposite is true as well. The way he pictures the world of gods and spirits determines his attitude towards society. I want to clarify this interconnection of the realms by describing the millenistic beliefs, divine healing, and the exorcism of demons in the church of *Deus é Amor*.

Talmon defines millenistic movements as religious movements which expect a near, total, irreversible, and collective salvation (1966, 156-169). All these criteria can be applied to *Deus é Amor*. Although the Pentecostal church *Deus é Amor* is not primarily a millenistic movement, as are for example the cargo-cults described by Worsley (1970), in which all religious and social-economic behavior was aimed at bringing in the cargo, millenistic, and messianistic conceptions constitute an important part of the religious discourse. For the members of *Deus é Amor*, the coming of Christ is in the very near future. To prepare for his coming, people pray a lot because, as they put it, "praying is the key that opens the windows to Heaven." On the other hand, in a practical, economical sense they do not change their lives at all. This in contrast to the Milne Bay movement in New Guinea, for example, whose followers ate the whole harvest and slaughtered all their pigs because the cargo would arrive any moment (ibid.).

Characteristic of millenistic movements is a collective orientation. Salvation is for all believers as a group, who will be allowed to live in the divine city on earth, and then will have eternal life in heaven. This goes beyond the salvation of individual souls. At the same time, it implies that the millenistic worldview is strongly dualistic: the world is divided into believers and nonbelievers. The importance these millenistic themes have for *Deus é Amor* is illustrated by the fact that one of its most popular songs, sung at practically every service, is about the future salvation, and contains the words "these are the people who are going to live in heaven; they left the world with all its vanity behind them." Although members of other churches also know that the coming of the Millennium is predicted in the Bible, in the religious discourse of *Deus é Amor* this element is especially strongly present.

These millenistic expectations express the hope that the group of believers will soon be saved from worldly suffering. The supernatural world will in the near future alter the relationship between believers and society, and will solve the crisis. But in their relationship to the supernatural world the believers also set in motion a creative process of transforming actual suffering caused by poverty into a proud pre-paredness for self-sacrifice, because, as was the case with Christ, it is perceived to be the only way to salvation. In this interpretation, depri-vation within society becomes functional in the relationship with the supernatural. Orsi states that religious sacrifice represents the human claim to self-respect in a context of suffering (1985, 223). The experi-ence of power and dignity is essential in counteracting feelings of ano-mie and in destroying other negative consequences of a situation of great deprivation. A change in self-perception is essential in any search for improvement in life (ibid., 82, 220-237). In other words, by enlarg-ing feelings of dignity, Pentecostalism motivates people to endure poverty and to avoid self-destructive behavior. People's attempts to differentiate themselves from "the world" seem to be a strategy for reinforcing self-esteem.

Both the dualistic worldview inherent in and the self-respect de-rived from millenistic beliefs, which are subjective interpretations of present conditions, are part of a creative process employing psycho-social means that will support the church members in their struggle to survive. This clarifies the interconnection between the supernatural world and the earthly world, the first influencing the realm of believer and society because the requirements for survival in everyday life are provided on a supernatural level.

Another feature of the belief system of *Deus é Amor* that clarifies the two-way relationship between the earthly world and the spiritual world, is the strong belief in divine healing. During my research I learned of numerous stories of diseases which were miraculously heal-ed by prayer; cases in which people were often helped by a minister of the church in person, or in one case, on the radio. Sometimes the mere fact of conversion is enough to be cured. But in most cases people try to accomplish the healing of a certain individual by collective prayer during church or street services, where all the believers as a group ask

God in loud voices for assistance. In this sense it differs from traditional Catholicism, where seeking a cure is an individual concern. Moreover, the members of *Deus é Amor* are convinced that their church is the only one that preaches divine healing. Although this is a participant view, it stresses the importance of this religious theme for the members, and is part of the attraction of this particular church. Although most of the divine healings are not necessarily spectacular, where there is no doctor around these healings can be an essential resource supporting the believer in his struggle to survive. We have to bear in mind that Pentecostals have a psychosomatic approach to health problems, meaning that in their opinion psychological stress, conflicts, and frustrations—caused by poverty—can affect one's health. In this context it is fundamental to the poor to have an efficient means of attaining health (Hoekstra 1989, 238). This is certainly true for the members of *Deus é Amor*, who although they have free access to medical assistance, cannot afford to buy the prescribed medicines. People living in the countryside face the extra problem of a long distance to the nearest doctor.

For the members of *Deus é Amor* the term divine healing means more than only the healing of illnesses and diseases. Some of these just happen to a person, but others are caused by demons. In that case, the successful exorcism of demons means healing at the same time. Among the members of the church, there is a constant threat of being "seized" by a demon. Most of them know only four demons by name and character, which are derived from Afro-Brazilian religions, and in addition a group of *viramundos*—those who turn the world upside down. Their leader is Satan, who is constantly trying to send his demons to intrigue in the church. Those whose faith is insufficiently firm can be victimized. The preoccupation with demons endangering church members is a frequently recurring theme during services.

Samandu (1989) notes a strong contrast between the scarcity and poverty of everyday life and the richness of the way in which people picture the supernatural world. An explanation is to be found in the dualism that is characteristic of the Pentecostal belief, which we have already found in the millenistic aspects of the religious discourse. The world is the realm of the evil forces, the supernatural realm that of the good ones. Looking at the vision the Pentecostals have of the supernatural world, the same dualism can be distinguished here, with Satan and his demons on one side, and God and his angels on the other. The way the supernatural world is organized symbolizes the way life on earth is arranged. The fact that the believers are able to conquer evil spirits by collective prayer, singing, and clapping of the hands can be projected onto the relationship between church members and society. In that context it means a symbolic victory of the group over the wickedness of the world.

Mariz states that for Pentecostals poverty is primarily understood to be an individual problem, part of God's plan for a certain person, and therefore economically speaking, improvement is sought on an individual level, mostly by being a good worker (1989, 222-246). This in contrast, for example, to members of CEBs[1], which see poverty not as an absolute but as a relative problem, as a consequence of class exploitation. The fact that conversion to Pentecostalism is a dramatic experience for the individual, which requires a conscious option, reveals that there has to be a belief in the ability of an individual to change his life. The attempt to unify faith with life by adopting a special lifestyle and morality, means that religion must change everyday life. Moreover, the fact that Pentecostal beliefs and lifestyle are not traditionally accepted, and therefore need a special justification, proves that Pentecostals assume that religious adhesion is a matter of reasoning. These elements, according to Mariz, are all part of a rationalization process in the Weberian sense, substituting myths and rituals for reason, and therefore may be carriers of modernization. However, the experience of dignity provided by Pentecostalism, the direct relationship to the supernatural which increases self-esteem and the destroying of the experience of powerlessness by the ability to perform miracles, by Mariz are merely seen as elements that counteract feelings of anomie. They are more useful as tools with which to endure poverty because it makes individuals better equipped and motivated to endure poverty and abstain from self-destructive behavior, like drinking, gambling, and weakening the family structure which is essential for economic stability, rather than being instrumental for collective upward mobility.

But this point of view only takes into consideration the realm of believer and society. When regarding the domain where the Pentecostal is guided by supernatural beliefs in the coming of the millennium, divine healing, and the overcoming of evil forces, the interesting fact emerges that on this level a community effort is made to find solutions. Unlike Afro-Brazilian religions and popular Catholicism, where supernatural favors are only granted by the intermediation of mediums, priests, or saints, Pentecostals have direct access to the highest power to find solutions to illness and to psychological problems caused by poverty. Therefore, on the level of subjective experience the Pentecostal church is the only one that offers the opportunity to participate actively and directly in combating evil forces, and in this way accomplish a symbolic victory over the world. In this psychological battle, its members are able to express collectively the feelings of combativeness Cavalcanti noted among the poor. Looked at from an inclusive perspective, it becomes clear that the crisis does indeed have a creative potential, in which subjective solutions are found, containing a whole new set of ideas to interpret reality and leading in their turn to a reorientation of poor people's position in society—victors instead of victims. The collective reaction to the problem of poverty leads me to believe that poverty for Pentecostals is perceived as not merely an individual problem, and that therefore the sense of being able to cope with problems as a group has the potential for concrete socio-economic action which can make a contribution to social improvement.

Conclusion

This chapter has made clear that Pentecostalism shows historical, symbolic, and social continuity with the traditional, *fazenda*-centered society. Elements of a break with tradition lead Willems (1967) to regard Pentecostalism as a symbolical protest movement against the established social order. Hoffnagel and Mariz on the other hand, based on research also done in an urban situation and looking especially into whether the movement supports economically or politically advantageous behavior, concluded that in a concrete sense the Pentecostal movement does not contribute to social change, and only contributes to minor individual economic improvement. However, Novães (1985) in her study showed that membership of the Pentecostal movement can certainly motivate active political participation, a process in which class conflict between small farmers and landlords is strongly emphasized.

Moreover, survival is not merely economic and physical. Since people are symbolical beings as well, survival also requires motivations and meanings on a subjective level. Analyzing the relationship between believers and the supernatural shows that there is more to be taken into consideration than only the concrete socio-economic consequences of conversion to Pentecostalism, and that the process of psychological self-transformation taking place is important in itself in resulting in a reorientation of the poor in society. In the realm of believer and the supernatural, Pentecostalism means a psychological battle that leads to victory.

In conclusion, Pentecostalism carries conservative as well as innovative elements. It is too much a prolongation of traditional social structure to be viewed it as a revolutionary movement without qualification. On the other hand, the political function of Pentecostalism in the situation described by Novães, and the potential for collective action inherent in the way the struggle for life is expressed in the believers' relationship to the supernatural, demonstrates that the movement cannot be described as purely conservative either.

The solution to this paradox lies in the acknowledgment that, given the fact that both kinds of elements are abundantly available, it would appear that the *crentes* have the option to apply Pentecostalism in the way which will be most beneficial in their specific situation. Depending on the social context, the Pentecostal religious view may generate different behaviors. In any case, Pentecostalism means more than only a symbolic protest against a fast-changing society.

Notes

1. *Comunidades Eclesiais de Base*, Catholic Base Communities strongly encouraging political participation.

References

Cavalcanti, Helenilda Wanderley de V., "Syndróme da Falta de Poder da Classe Pobre," *Cadernos de Estudos Sociais* 1, no. 2 (1985): 141-160.

Clay, Jason W., *The Articulation of Non-Capitalist Agricultural Production Systems with Capitalist Exchange Systems: The Case of Garanhuns, Brazil, 1845-1977.* Ithaca, N.Y.: Cornell University Press (dissertation), 1979.

Cucchiari, Salvatore, "Conversion and Culture in Western Sicily," *American Ethnologist* 15, no. 3 (1988): 417-441.

Droogers, André F., *Macht in zin: Een drieluik van Braziliaanse religieuze verbeelding.* Amsterdam: Vrije Universiteit, 1990.

Forman, Shephard, *The Brazilian Peasantry.* New York: Colombia University Press, 1975.

Hoekstra, Angela, *Deus é Amor; Crisis en Creativiteit in een Braziliaanse Pinksterkerk.* Utrecht (M.A. Thesis, University of Utrecht), 1991.

Hoffnagel, Judith C., *The Believers: Pentecostalism in a Brazilian City.* Ann Arbor, Mich.: University Microfilms International (Ph.D. Thesis, Indiana University), 1978.

Kliewer, Gerd U., *Das neue Volk der Pfinstler: Religion, Unterentwicklung und sozialer Wandel in Lateinamerika.* Frankfurt: Peter Lang GmbH, 1975.

Lalive d'Epinay, Christian, *Haven of the Masses; A Study of the Pentecostal Movement in Chile.* London: Lutterworth Press, 1969.

Lang, James, *Portuguese Brazil: The King's Plantation.* New York: Academic Press, 1979.

Mariz, Cecilia L., *Religion and Coping with Poverty in Brazil.* Boston (Ph.D. Thesis), 1989

Novães, Regina R., *Os Escolhidos de Deus; Pentecostais, Trabalhadores e Cidadánia.* Rio de Janeiro: ISER, 1985.

Orsi, Robert A., *The Madonna of 115th Street. Faith and Community in Italian Harlem, 1880-1950.* New Haven, Conn.: Yale University Press, 1985.

Samandú, Luis, "De andere kant van de medaille; het succes van de sekten in Midden-Amerika," *Alerta* 14, no. 149 (1989): 10-18.

Sepúlveda, Juan, "Pentecostalism as Popular Religiosity," *International Review of Mission* 78, no. 309 (1989): 80-88.

Talmon, Yonina, "Millenarian Movements," *Archives Européennes de Sociologie* 7, no. 1 (1966): 159-200.

Willems, Emilio, *Followers of the New Faith. Culture Change and the Rise of Protestantism in Brazil and Chile.* Nashville, Tenn.: Vanderbilt University Press, 1967.

Worsley, Peter, *The Trumpet Shall Sound; A Study of "Cargo" Cults in Melanesia.* Aylesbury: Hazell Watson and Viney, 1970.

8

Family, Sexuality, and Family Planning

A Comparative Study of Pentecostals and Charismatic Catholics in Rio de Janeiro[1]

Maria das Dores Campos Machado

One of the things that most impressed me on my first visit to a Charismatic community in Rio de Janeiro was the physical expression of the women, gaily swinging their hips to the rhythm of the hymns, who at a certain point began to develop a sort of choreography, sequentially marked by handclapping, crossing, genuflection, and finally, standing with their hands stretched toward heaven. Composed for the most part of middle-class women of over fifty years of age, this community had managed to bring together approximately 1800 people for a service at 2 P.M. on a Monday afternoon who, for two hours actively participated in the service. Their spontaneity, freedom of movement, and gestures were in total contrast to the cold ceremonies of more

conservative priests and the contrition and rigidity of the more fervent Catholic women, with their slow, lamenting pacing in traditional
processions.

Their emotional participation, spontaneous speeches, and testimo-
nials reminded me of scenes which I had witnessed at a revival meeting
put on by the Universal Church of the Kingdom of God[2] (UCKG) in
a football stadium where predominantly lower-income believers were
assembled. On that occasion, having read about the first Pentecostal
churches founded in Brazil[3]—which not only segregated men and
women, but also prescribed rules of behavior, emphasizing the use of
chaste clothing—I was surprised not only by the style of the pastors
and of the service itself, but also by the way women were dressed, and
the happy intermixing and freedom of movement among participants
during the mass meeting. Obviously change was under way that
touched not only the Catholic tradition, but the Protestants as well.[4]

Since the end of the 1980s, studies of the growing number of "emotional communities" in European societies have called attention to the
more corporal, rather than verbal, interaction they promote
(Hervieu-Léger 1993). In Brazilian studies (Velasques Filho 1990;
Bittencourt 1991), however, one of the most frequently used criteria
for differentiating Charismatics from Pentecostals has been the social
origin of the former, which is at the root of their more contained body
gestures. With that in mind, several questions arose: How were
women of this social strata and advanced age able to break their in-
grained restraints and appear so uninhibited and at ease with their
bodies? Was this gaiety a special quality of the movement in Rio de
Janeiro?

I had already been to Charismatic services in other states where the
women were certainly emotionally involved, but it was nothing like
what I saw in Copacabana.[5] Could this festiveness have something to
do with the carioca[6] culture where dancing and the body are so present
in the celebration of Carnival? How does secular culture affect religion? I later saw a carnival parade based on a samba praising Jesus,
organized by a Pentecostal denomination, the Evangelical Community, which would show me that my questions were indeed valid, and
that, even though they openly criticized the "festival of the flesh,"
Pentecostal believers had begun to incorporate the gaiety and some of

the corporal expression of Carnival into religious rites, giving it new meaning.

It is true that through the issues of death, sickness, procreation, and even sex, the corporal dimension has in some way always been present in religious ethics (Riis 1993). Nevertheless, there is a consensus among researchers that the theologies of salvation impose both a devaluation of the human body, as well as a regulation of believers' sensuality. We know that in the Christian universe, the duality established between the body and the soul in the early centuries of the church created a hierarchy of these dimensions, placing the first in an inferior position and in opposition to the spirit.[7] "The body is the world of instincts which must be controlled" and it is exactly this potential of control which differentiates men from animals. Thus, "rational objectives should orient and even repress the appetites of the body," including sexual desire and pleasure (Gudorf 1993, 4). The consequences of this policing of the body are not restricted to behavior in the religious sphere, but depending on the historical circumstances can be seen in the economic and even political spheres as well.

Weber, in his *The Protestant Ethic and the Spirit of Capitalism* showed us how, in the initial phases of capitalism, strong ethical precepts were employed to discipline the body through inner-worldly asceticism and channel human energies into labor.[8] Contemporary analyses (Simpson in Riis 1993, 379) however, affirm that the capitalist system itself would stimulate a redefinition of the use of the body as it became an object of consumerism. The growth of alternative therapies and ritualistic healing practices combining body and mind are, for some researchers (e.g. McGuire 1990), a reflection in the religious field of these changes in contemporary societies.

In comparing these experiences to our observations in the field, we are led to hypothesize whether these Brazilian neo-Pentecostal, Catholic, and Evangelical movements, which also stimulate corporal expression, are not following a similar tendency to rearticulate the body and the spirit, even though they may still emphasize the latter.[9] What are the limits to this new appreciation of the body for believers? Is it merely ritualistic? Do the changes we see in the use of the body in relation to Jesus, particularly in moments of praise, express changes in the exercise of female sexuality as well? How do Pentecostals and Charismatics deal with their own sensuality? These are some of the questions with which we will be occupied in this study, although we will concentrate on the examination of values relative to the sexuality and reproductive behavior of believers involved in the Movement of Charismatic Catholic Renewal (MCCR) and in Pentecostalism.

The Christian Sexual Tradition

If we go back in the history of Christianity we can see that from the second century until the middle of the 1900s, a negative perception of human sexuality predominated and was most radically expressed in the writings of Saint Augustin and Saint Jerome.[10] Based on the previously mentioned separation of the body and soul, this tradition may be summarized in three main points: 1) the condemnation of sexual desire and pleasure; 2) the linking of the sexual act with procreation; and finally 3) the imputation of an inferior status to women in relation to men, which is expressed through the emphasis on her reproductive role. For these religious thinkers, sexual intercourse was only justifiable for human reproduction, and its practice, even in marriage, could be considered sinful, given that carnal pleasure is so difficult to avoid. After Saint Thomas Aquinas, an instinctive and bestial characterization of sex would predominate over the sinful qualification, but sexuality would continue to need a justification beyond itself: that of procreation.

There is an unequal treatment of the sexual partners which underlies this entire tradition, awarding women an inferior status. It exalts the spiritual dimension of the masculine gender, presenting him as created in "the image and likeness of God," while it emphasizes the physiological dimension (carnal) of the feminine gender (thus the direct association between women and the idea of temptation), justifying her existence in terms of motherhood. In both Saint Augustin and Saint Thomas we see that it is the woman's place to assist man only in the task of reproduction, for in all other endeavors men are undoubtedly superior, and in no need of female aid (Gudorf 1993, 4).

According to specialized studies, the religious reform movement of the middle ages, which repudiated the devotion of the saints, particularly the female ones, went a long way in reinforcing the importance of the masculine gender in the Protestant world. After all, if Catholicism emphasized the masculine qualities of God, there was also "the feminine alternative of the Virgin, to whom women could turn in moments of need" (Davis in Tarducci 1990). This imbalance in the treatment of the sexes by Christian theologians would be reinforced through the rise of Pentecostalism at the onset of the twentieth century, which in opposition to the most liberal tendencies of the Protestants would restore the belief in the natural inferiority of women, placing women at the foot of a "divinely ordained hierarchy which awards power and authority to God and to men" (Gill 1990). Founded on the individualistic, but still patriarchal tradition of the nuclear bourgeois family in the United States in the early twentieth century, this ideology would run into ambivalent and paradoxical consequences (Droogers 1991; Burdick 1990). These would not be restricted merely to the internal structuring of religious organizations and the distribution of power between masculine and feminine members, but would also affect the private behavior of followers in these religious communities, as it reinforced masculine authority in the home.[11]

However, while one line of enquiry relating gender and religious conversion is being consolidated, contributing significantly to our understanding not only of the rapid growth of Pentecostalism in Latin America, but also of the changes in the model of the family for followers of this religious tradition, in terms of the first two pillars of the Christian sexual tradition there is still much to be investigated. On the doctrinal level, we know that both the devaluation of sex and the norm of "sex for procreation only" remained basically the same through the first few decades of this century, sexual abstinence being the only legitimate method available for birth control.

In 1930, Anglicans gathered at the Lambeth Conference defended the use of birth control methods in cases where there were "serious restrictions to procreation," thus paving the way for a rupture with the Christian insistence that reproduction be the ultimate end for conjugal sex, and for the first time showing that sexual activity within marriage could be justifiable in and for itself. The use of artificial means of birth control was no longer linked to the notions of illicit sex, adultery, and, above all, prostitution; but could be used by Christian couples, even if only for health reasons. Shortly thereafter, in 1931, the committee for marriage and the family of the Federal Council of Churches of the United States approved the use of contraceptives, transferring the decision-making responsibility to professionals in the medical area and to the believers themselves. The economic and social context, particularly the economic slump which followed on the heels of the second world war and the global urbanization which took place during the middle of the century, favored the spread of these liberal and secular positions, as other Protestant churches recognized that the responsibility and definition of contraception usage belonged morally to the individual, and technically to science.[12]

However, when we turn our attention to the Catholics, we see that the process of revising values has been much slower and more difficult. In 1930, in direct response to the birth control movement, but particularly to the liberal position assumed by the Protestants in Lambeth, Pope Pius XI published the Encyclical Casti Connubii, reaffirming the link between sexuality and reproduction and energetically condemning abortion and the limitation of births by artificial means. It was only in 1950, in his speech to the Catholic Society of Midwives, that the High Magistrate of the Church admitted the legitimacy of birth control for the first time. In this document, Pope Pius XII recognized the "rhythm method" as in keeping with God's laws, finally accepting the natural technique discovered in the 1920s by scientists Ogino and Knaus.

In the last thirty years, the behavioral revolution ushered in by the birth control pill, the rise of feminist movements bringing to the political arena their demands for sexual liberation, and the development of new technologies in the area of reproduction have incited new debates within the church hierarchy and among the more active lay workers, but have not been strong enough to force a revision of the ban on abortion nor of the traditional rejection of birth control methods.[13] Documents such as the Humanae Vitae (Pope Paul VI, 1968)[14] and Familiaris Consortium (Pope John Paul II, 1993) reinforce the condemnation of birth control methods, save natural ones, thus showing how difficult it is for the Papacy to accept the separation of sexuality and procreation, and to adapt to changes in reproductive behavior brought on by advances in science.[15]

In Brazil we find at least two different interpretations of the local reaction to Vatican directives. The first, frequently encountered in progressive Catholic spheres, points out the theological advances resulting from the doctrine of "responsible parenthood" (Gaudium et

Spes, Pope Paul VI, 1965). The very existence of distinct interpretations of this doctrine within the Brazilian clergy, however, underlines
a lack of consensus in terms of the absolute rejection of artificial means
of birth control.[16] The second, much emphasized by feminists, calls
attention to the role of the National Council of Brazilian Bishops
(NCBB) and other organizations in influencing public policy-making
and public opinion in general by both pointing out how the local
clergy furthers the Vatican line on procreation and showing the authoritarian nature of the Catholic interference in discussions on reproductive rights (Araujo 1993, 425; Ribeiro 1993, 403-4). Along these
lines, Avila (1993, 389) argues that the Catholic church

> holding to the principle of sex for procreation, ... does not allow for
> behavior deviant from its norm, even for those who are not in keeping
> with its doctrine and/or do not want to submit themselves to its law,
> this being the individual's prerogative, guaranteed constitutionally
> under the right to freedom of belief. Its action is not restricted to pasto-
> ral preaching to maintain its hegemony in the religious field, but also
> has as one of its goals to influence or even define social and legislative
> policy.

The Vatican's inflexibility has, in fact, not significantly influenced the
behavior of the majority of Catholics. A recent study commissioned
by the church itself (Jornal do Brasil 1994) reveals how disparate are
the clergy's norms from the sexual mores of young Catholics. According to the data from this study, 90 percent of the Catholics between
eighteen and thirty years of age approve the use of contraceptives, 70
percent consider masturbation normal, 65 percent accept sexual relations before marriage and 40 percent are in favor of abortion in special
circumstances.[17]

In the Evangelical world, studies (Pierucci 1989; Freston 1993) of
the participation of "believer" congressmen in the 1988 National Con-
stituent Assembly, point out their "moralistic political activism,"
demonstrated by the creation of a multiparty block of Protestants
who concentrated their efforts on committees dealing with the family,
and the sexual and reproductive behavior of Brazilian citizens. Since
the majority of representatives in this block were from neo-traditionalist denominations, their positions against homosexuality, abortion,

feminism, drugs, pornography, and even the dissolution of marriage predominated.

If, in the Catholic case, alliance to a confessional group may indicate different degrees of obedience to and assimilation of the values of church leaders, we should also confront the positions we have just pointed out with those of the leaders of other religious denominations and even with the conduct of members of these religious communities.[18]

The Neo-Pentecostal Movement in Brazilian Religious Sociology

In Brazil, where the rapid growth of neo-traditional groups of Protestant origin has begun to undermine Catholic hegemony and is beginning to constitute a true alternative to the more progressive tendencies of Liberation Theology, there is no tradition of quantitative research in the area of religion. Even qualitative studies on new affiliation to spiritual movements and family life are few, with the effects of religious conversion in domestic relations being secondary concern within the more extensive studies on the religious thematic. Further, there is a constant line drawn between Pentecostal groups, associated with the lower classes, and those called Charismatic, which researchers deem typical of the middle classes. Attention has been given mainly to the former; there are few studies on Catholic Charismatics, and none which specifically deal with the so-called Evangelical Charismatics.

Studies which deal with the Movement for Charismatic Catholic Renewal (Ribeiro de Oliveira 1978; Benedetti 1988) recognize the ecumenical origin of this movement and the Evangelical influences expressed in their renewed emphasis on the Bible, the belief in the power of the Holy Spirit, and the spontaneity and emotional involvement of believers during the services and celebrations. Nevertheless, they prefer to compare this to other movements within the Catholic church, particularly those of the middle sectors, and to analyze its relation to the institutional structure. Thus, they identify a certain continuity between traditional Christian Retreats and Meetings of Couples with Christ, and Charismatic Renewal, concluding that this adjusts itself to the church, and is not a movement in opposition to the Catholic hierarchy. Even those researchers who emphasize the

MCCR ideology which gives renewed importance to the family emphasize the function of the movement to preserve the religious institution, and fail to investigate the consequent changes in the attitudes and behavior of believers who adhere to such an ideology.

The results of a recent study on syncretism and religious transition (Mariz and Machado 1994) suggest, on the other hand, a great proximity between Charismatics and Pentecostals, with the first, without any class discrimination, considering the second to be the religious group they most admire and with whom they most identify. This study showed that Charismatics simultaneously attend Pentecostal services as well as talks by Evangelical pastors, and even frequent renewed Evangelical churches. As to parallel attendance, it was found that this occurred chiefly during the conversion phase, before the religious option had been completely made. As for visits to Pentecostal denominations, quite frequent among the lower-income population, albeit present in middle-classes groups as well, these seem to constitute a decisive moment for the quitting of syncretist practice, particularly those related to Afro-Brazilian religious groups.

The decision to include lower-income segments of the population in the study of Charismatics was important in order to verify the hypothesis of "adjustment" to the institutional structures of the Catholic church, for it was seen that there were many in this population who abandoned the church because of conflicts with its hierarchy, and thus turned to Evangelical groups.[19] Further, even temporary visits by Charismatics to Pentecostal communities shows that the line separating the two is neither as clear nor as strong as that which, until recently, divided the Protestant and Catholic universes, reinforcing the option of a comparison between them.

In the Pentecostal world, despite a vast bibliography on these religious communities and even on the public behavior of believers, there are few studies which include the influence of their beliefs and religious affiliation on the private sphere and, particularly on gender relations (Willems 1967; Page 1984; Novaes 1985; Mariz 1994; Burdick 1990). Further, the lack of a tradition of attitude studies in Brazilian sociology has resulted in a deliberate emphasis on the dimension of values, making the analysis of Pentecostal doctrine the central issue. Some case studies manage to confront these two dimensions, but suffer the inherent limitations of studies of this nature, which cannot generalize their results to the Pentecostal movement as a whole. Beyond this, the majority of studies call attention to the asceticism which follows conversion and restrict themselves to investigating the effects of the religious option on the alcohol consumption and sexual behavior of the husband, while failing to investigate what may be the consequences on the sexual orientation given to children, on the reproductive behavior of the couple, and even on female sexuality.

A Sample Study

We interviewed thirty-seven married women, three who were living with men, six who were single, two who were separated, and four who were widowed. Of these, twenty-six were of middle-class origin and twenty-six were from the lower-income sector, being divided equally between Charismatics and Pentecostals.[20] The Charismatics had an average age of forty-two and showed the highest educational level—five of those from the middle sectors were college graduates, while those from the second religious group[21] were slightly younger, having an average age of 39.6 years, but with fewer years of formal education—while only two from the middle sectors had completed their university studies. Among those from the popular sectors, the differences between the two religious universes are negligible, with half of those interviewed from each religion having completed grade school, two or three from each having finished high school, and the rest having had less than a first-grade education. There were three women who had had at least one previous union; one was a middle-class Charismatic, and two were Pentecostals—one from the middle and one from the popular class. After leaving their previous unions, the two Pentecostals were married in the church of which they are now members. The Charismatic, who was divorced from her first husband, has lived together with a divorced man for twenty years.

As for the men, we spoke with twenty who are currently married, ten from the middle classes and ten from the popular classes, equally distributed between the Charismatic and Pentecostal groups.[22] Their average ages were, respectively, forty-five and forty-one. The Charismatics showed the same tendencies found in the female sample, the male group having a greater level of formal education—four from the middle class held college diplomas—but here the difference in relation to the Pentecostals practically disappears, for three of this group had also finished their university studies. Within the lower-income Pentecostal and Charismatic segments we find a similar internal distribution where the vast majority of the men claimed to have finished only grade school, and the remaining two—one from each religious group—stated that they had dropped out before completing it.

Sexuality: From Learning to the Transmission of Values

Nearly all of those we interviewed from both communities revealed they had received no sexual education from their parents. Friends and schoolmates had been responsible for furnishing information, be it about menstruation and masturbation, be it about sexual intercourse and contraceptive methods. Besides feeling ill at ease with the subject, these parents, described by our informants as "traditional," seemed to hold a negative view of everything to do with sexuality. It is here that gender differences begin to show up. Whereas men, who had always had greater access to literature or to group conversations between adults where sexual questions raised saw no problem in this, the women regretted the lack of information, and the more educated among them were critical of this family attitude, some of them even relating this fact to difficulties they had with their own sexuality.

Considering that one of the things that most clearly distinguishes Catholics from Protestants in Brazil has been the moral rigidity of the latter, our examination of the sexual education received by our sample population took us back to their parents' religion, and for this reason we looked into their religious upbringing. The Charismatics unanimously declared their parents' religion to have been Catholic, and had long considered their membership in this church as inherited, but had not considered themselves to be practicing Catholics. It is interesting that in the popular classes we found a significant number of Charismatics who claimed to have begun their religious involvement in Pentecostal denominations. Of the ten married women from this social segment, for example, six had been members of Pentecostal churches before joining the MCCR. Two of the five married men had the same story to tell. All of them, men and women both, had come from nonpracticing Catholic homes when they began their religious search, initially in Evangelical churches, finding their way into the following denominations: three were "renewed" Baptists; three were from the UCKG; two were from the "God is Love" church; and two were members of the Assemblies of God.

Of the twenty-six female and thirteen male Pentecostals we interviewed, five and seven respectively had come from Evangelical backgrounds. The Assemblies of God came out as the denomination with the most staying power, the one most able to pass on its values from one generation to the next, being particularly true in the case of the males. Most of these men whose parents were Assemblies of God believers had either remained or had returned to the church after a period of absence, usually during their youth. As for the females, those young women who found the church's strict codes of dress and behavior to be unbearable had moved into other less strict denominations. A large number of Pentecostals, however, had come from Catholic homes and spoke both of their family's and their own syncretist religious practices before conversion to their present church. In these cases, the moral orientation they received differs little from societal norms and those of the hegemonic religious group, in other words, the encouragement or at least tolerance of the awakening and development of sexuality in the boys, and the severe control of sexuality in the girls, and the frequent passing-on of a negative perception of sexual contact. M.H.Q. (36 years old), daughter of middle-class Catholics, but a current member of Calvary Baptist Church, claimed that her mother taught her that "sex was disgusting, horrible, and rotten. When, as an adolescent, I found out that she did it too, I really thought her vulgar. After I tried it myself, I was angry at what she had done to me. I'm not doing the same thing to my daughters."

Here we must call attention to differences in male and female interviews. While many women were willing to talk of their sexual lives and even, spontaneously, of their discontentments in this area and of their early ignorance in relation to their sexuality, none of the men revealed any sexual dissatisfaction, even to the male assistant interviewer. Even those who admitted to extra-marital relations claimed no link between this and any sexual difficulty within the marriage. Their arguments fall into the usual line of moral deviance and the harmful influences of a secular and macho culture. It is also curious that most of the women who experienced difficulties with their sexuality did not relate these problems to the sexual performance of their partners. At this point social differences come into play; women from the lower educational strata blame themselves for their lack of sexual fulfillment and feel guilty for the excuses they give to their partners. Furthermore, when they shared with us the instruction they had received from church-sponsored classes, lectures, and sermons we saw that these seem to encourage their conformity to the sexual patterns established by their partners, and deal with sexuality as a matrimonial responsibility.

A positive attitude toward sex in marriage seems to be something shared both by Pentecostal, as well as Charismatic leaders, but the view they take does not always aid women in questioning the performance and responsibility of their partners in relation to their dissatisfaction. Charismatic leaders follow official church doctrine, which, though still lagging behind society as a whole, already in Gaudim et Spes (1965) viewed procreation not as an end in itself, but as the result of conjugal love. Certainly, though, their condemnation of non-natural methods of contraception shows the ambiguity of this position, and paves the way for very different attitudes towards and perceptions of sex. At retreats and encounters, as well as at the weekly Charismatic meetings which we attended during our two-year study, we saw that when the issue of sexuality appeared, it was accompanied more frequently by moralizations such as the denunciation and censorship of the "depraved behavior" of homosexuals, unfaithful spouses, and sexually active singles, than by discussions of the difficulties normally encountered by men and women in their intimate relationships. From interviews with members of this movement, we concluded that questions of this nature are dealt with either by seeking the counsel of elders, or by going outside the church to other sources or family-oriented movements parallel to MCCR such as the Couples' Meetings, the Group of Our Lady, the Encounter groups for Dialogue, etc.

In the Evangelical world, as Reverend Caio Fábio, president of the Brazilian Evangelical Association told us, "the great moment of change in the evaluation of sexuality came about nearly fifteen years ago, with the explosion of books on the market dealing with sex and pleasure" and the intense, subsequent discussion of the issue among religious leaders. Among the women we interviewed, those who were members of the UCKG were most able to share the guidance received through their religious community, pointing out the availability of assistance, either in the form of private counselling by the pastor or his wife, or in vigils and lectures on the importance of sexuality in the preservation of the family. This denomination holds emotional vigils and in its sermons, encourages believers to be more affectionate with their sexual partners in their daily lives. Other denominations deal with the issue in a more discreet fashion, promoting Couples' Meetings, Courses for Newlyweds, or, in the case of the smaller denominations, through informal talks with older women from the religious community. Within the middle classes we saw that the pastor's office was an important place for consultation, though most of the women sought the counsel of the pastor only in extreme circumstances. In the more popular groups, information was more frequently gleaned from the informal conversations occasioned in Women's Meetings.[23]

In the case of the Universal Church of the Kingdom of God, despite great creativity on the part of its leaders, who, in their all-day-Thursday family encounters offer a "chocolate kiss," a "rose of happiness," or some "holy oil" to be given to one's spouse as a token of affection, the lack of sexual preparedness and the low educational level of pastors and lay workers constitute a real limitation to any true aid the church might be able to offer to women with problems. By presenting sexual difficulties often as the frigidity of the wife or as a problem basically of the woman, religious guidance seems to run on the line of a greater understanding of men's sexual needs by women. N.M., a forty-three year-old housekeeper and UCKG member with a first-grade education told us:

> Before joining the church I didn't want to have sexual relations with my husband and I avoided him for a long time. But when I joined the UCKG and began to hear the pastor say that a woman shouldn't turn from her husband, I began to make an effort and I'm beginning to get better. Before, I felt no pleasure at all and tried to get away from it, but now I turn to God, really ask for his help to be willing; but to be honest, I don't really enjoy it when he comes to me.

For this woman the explanation for her sexual disinterest in her husband lay in her "defects, difficulties, and selfishness," which she was "trying to battle with and make better." But in middle-class sectors, among more highly-educated women from both the Pentecostal as well as Charismatic worlds, we found women who told us of sexual problems, but presented them not as difficulties in meeting their partners' desires, but as the inability to find satisfaction for themselves. M.M., forty-four, from the upper-middle class, a graduate of journalism and currently separated, told us she had had extra-marital relations before converting to Pentecostalism and becoming a member of the UCKG, because she "couldn't have an orgasm with her husband." She was the only one of all those we interviewed who used this expression, but despite her liberal behavior and language, she had been sexually inactive since her husband left her three years ago. S., a lovely woman of fifty who had also completed university studies, a member of the MCCR and a recent widow, also told us that her sex life had been rather frustrating and that she had never felt completely fulfilled. In her own words:

> I knew that F. loved me a lot and I never doubted that he was faithful. But I needed him more than he needed me. There were long periods [without sex] which he wasn't bothered by. It was very hard on me and I asked him if it was a problem with me, but he said no, it was his problem. But he never really faced it. I tried to talk about it several times, but he was never very open, he never liked to talk about these things.

Testimony such as this shows that more than religious affiliation, age, or educational level influence the way women feel about their sexual activity, though having once joined one of these Pentecostal movements, they have little choice but to deal with their sexual dissatisfaction by trying to make their partners more sensitive to their needs. The possibility for dialogue is greater when both partners share the same religious values. According to Gill (1990, 717) one of the consequences of male conversion to Pentecostalism is that men are encouraged to cultivate virtues traditionally allocated to women, such as humility, which to a certain extent facilitates understanding between partners and helps them to overcome some of the male chauvinist behavior so present in Latin American culture.

Another important point is how believers who had received no sexual education from their parents were dealing with the issue in their own families. In both Pentecostalism and the Charismatic movement, we saw that for both sexes, conversion leads to a greater preoccupation with the sexual education of the children. When we compared the testimony of women who had joined Pentecostal movements without their husbands (25) with that of women who had been successful in converting their spouses (16) we found that in the first case the women, more than the men, were concerned with preparing their children and with not repeating their own parents' pattern of neglect. In the case of couples who had both converted, this became a shared concern, showing that men had become more involved in the raising of the children.

On the whole, we found that parents end up guiding their offspring according to the questions the children themselves pose. In other words, education means establishing rules of behavior and answering questions asked by youngsters. If they neither contest nor question, the parents need not touch on the issues of sexuality. One woman of thirty justified her mother's never having spoken to her about sex by her own early pregnancy, leading her mother to assume that she already knew all there was to know, since she was already obviously sexually active with her boyfriend. As for the Charismatics, where a greater number of women join the movement on their own, we find the typical Brazilian double standard of control over female sexuality and tolerance of male incapacity to remain chaste. AIDS, though a strong motive for conversation between parents and children, served in this religious group to reinforce the double standard, strengthening the defense of virginity for girls, and guaranteeing the right to sexual activity for boys, as long as it is not promiscuous and includes the use of condoms. "After all, men can't get by without sex," one Charismatic woman of thirty-eight put it. Although she had herself been an "expecting bride," her advice to her daughter was "to save herself for marriage," while at the same time reminding her son not to forget to take condoms with him on a date, "just in case he and his girlfriend decided to stay out late."

Pentecostals, for the most part, follow traditional Protestant guidelines for sex, countering looser Catholic ideals; they encourage chastity before marriage for both males and females and extend the vow of fidelity to both spouses. Thus the more radical group becomes the more egalitarian in terms of gender as well, denying both partners any extra-marital dallying. Their advice runs from the warning to boys that they "do not even converse with certain girls, certain women of the streets" to the suggestion that they respect their girlfriends, treating them as they would a sister. G.A., a seventeen-year-old, middle-class student and member of the International Evangelical Center told us that "love between believers lasts because before calling a woman your wife, you call her your sister and before any carnal embrace, any carnal love, there is spiritual love."

It is interesting that among women who confessed to having got married after becoming pregnant—fourteen out of the forty who were married—ten currently belong to Pentecostal groups and three came from Evangelical homes, meaning that they had received the kind of orientation described above.[24] All these were daughters of Assemblies of God members, one of the most traditional Pentecostal denominations. S.N., thirty-four, had been baptized in the church at thirteen, but had shortly thereafter gone with her parents and siblings to a "renewed" Baptist church, where the younger members of the family felt more at ease. She is currently a member of the New Life Church. M.N., twenty-nine, attended Assemblies of God services and celebrations with her family until the age of fourteen when she abandoned the religious community, returning to religious life only after marriage, joining the Christ Lives Church. Finally, we have R.S., twenty-six, who, in conflict with the strict Assemblies of God rules of behavior, was baptized in the Congregational Church at fifteen and has been there ever since. On her pregnancy she was temporarily suspended from the church, but shortly thereafter found support and aid which eventually led her into a religious marriage. She, like the others who had married while pregnant, today preaches chastity for singles, and speaks of the guilt of having betrayed God as an obstacle to true happiness after marriage.

The fact that these young women went against their religious communities' rules of behavior demonstrates the difficulty many believers of both sexes have juggling conflicting norms "with the attitudes and behavior socially expected for this phase of life" (Novaes 1985, 76). Adolescence and the beginning of adult life are tense times. Restrictions on drinking, smoking, and dancing, the control of dating and strict dress codes put off a good number of those whose parents belong to more radical denominations, and even those who continue in the religious community show occasional dissatisfaction with the moral strictness of the group. We heard from the Coordinator of the Youth Group in one Charismatic church, that the majority of requests for counsel stem from young people's uncertainty as to how to deal with sexuality while dating and contemplating marriage, and that her advice to both boys and girls was to remain chaste until marriage. It is a position similar to that of the Pentecostals, but need not necessarily apply to one's own son or to non-Charismatic young people, as we saw a few pages back.

Infidelity: Moral Deviance Fought with Prayer and Sessions of Deliverance

Specialized literature on the subject has emphasized (Willems 1967; Page 1985; Brusco 1986; Burdick 1990; Mariz 1993, 1994) the emotional, and at times material, support that conversion to Pentecostalism offers women who face problems with their spouses, be they adultery or the consumption of alcohol. Within our sample study, drug use and particularly alcohol dependence, was mentioned by both male and female respondents more frequently than infidelity as a source of domestic conflict. Nevertheless, several of the women interviewed told us that their first visits to religious communities had been brought on by the extra-marital affairs of their husbands. Again, there were a greater number of Pentecostals who were able to speak of their husbands' deviant behavior. Of the seven women who claimed to have gone through, or were currently dealing with such a situation, five were Pentecostals and only two were Charismatics. Most of the first group were from lower-income backgrounds, while the Charismatics had middle-class origins.

Although the number of Charismatics who admitted having this kind of problem or having had premarital sex was smaller than that of the Pentecostals, this does not mean that their husbands were necessarily more faithful, or that they themselves had married as virgins. There were only two male interviewees who admitted having been unfaithful to their wives before converting to the MCCR, but in later interviews with their wives this fact was never mentioned as a motivating force leading to their joining the movement (one said she had been depressed for several years and the other said she could no longer get along with her husband). By the same token, during one interview, a woman was scolded by her husband because she admitted to having had sex before getting married. This is an indication that the Catholic tradition of censorship and condemnation of deviant moral behavior remains strong, even among followers of the MCCR, and that Pentecostals are more at ease talking about the problems, even very intimate ones, they had faced before conversion.

In Gill's view (1990), one of the advantages of Pentecostal beliefs is that is offers an alternative for women to interpret "their experiences in a new light of changed social identity." This perhaps explains the fact that in this group we found a greater number of women who spoke of having had abortions, as we will shortly see a highly condemned practice in the eyes of neo-traditionalist Christian groups. M.M., forty-four, a middle-class housewife and worker for the UCKG who attended services at least twice a day, spontaneously told us that she had begun her sex life at fourteen, had had three abortions before getting married and two more after, and had been involved in extra-marital affairs. Hers was the only admitted case of female infidelity within our sample study.

Through both the men who spoke of a polygamous past and the women whose husbands had behaved in such a manner, we came to realize that most men had only given up extra-marital relations at an already advanced age, in general after fifty, and only two had been motivated to do so by their own conversions. The more commonly cited reasons of the husband's inability to keep up two relationships, his abandonment by the female lover, and the financial difficulty of maintaining this type of situation were to reinforce the wives' efforts to reestablish the marriage.

We must here call attention to the distinct ways in which Charismatics and Pentecostals explain moral deviance. On the one hand, believers predominantly cite religious arguments to explain the probable reasons for infidelity, homosexuality, and deviant sexual behavior, while on the other hand revealing the influence of social origin and level of schooling. Arguments such as "absence of God, lack of prayer, and lack of religion" came up independent of gender, class, or educational level. However, answers such as "the influence of demonic forces, the Devil's work," etc. appear more frequently in the popular sector and were much more common among Pentecostals. Explanations based on antagonistic supernatural forces—God and the Devil—are not mutually exclusive. In the Pentecostal view, evil spirits interfere in conjugal life when there is a lack of prayer and dedication to

God. However, the lack of a Christian religious life does not necessarily imply that there is a belief in the existence of the Devil.

Pentecostals, despite differences in emphasis on one or another of the powers of the Holy Spirit—speaking in tongues, healing, and exorcism—consider deviant behavior, be it sexual or some other vice, as symptomatic of a spiritual crisis.[25] Evil spirits or demonic forces are thought to act on the individual, destroying the personality. Without being aware of what is happening, this individual begins to lose control, becomes involved in extra-marital relations, spends money and distances himself from his family; or he experiments with promiscuous and "depraved" relations which also place the institution of the family at risk. It was precisely among the more popular groups, where the level of schooling was lower for both sexes, that we found a greater tendency to blame the Devil for episodes such as extra-marital and homosexual sex. Some middle-class believers also link infidelity and homosexual practice to the Devil, but given their higher level of education, it is a less common explanation than for those from the lower-income group.

It is important to point out the consequences of blaming the Devil for these types of moral deviance for the believer and for the religious institution. On the one hand, the believer need not carry all the blame for his actions, allowing for greater understanding and tolerance on the part of family members and the religious community itself. On the other, it strengthens the institution even further, for if the problem is spiritual, only religion can help to solve it; moreover, it can only be a religion which guarantees deliverance—a religion which can exorcise occult forces. Currently, the denomination which gives most emphasis to the power of the Holy Spirit is, without a doubt, the UCKG. However, we should point out that in the competition for converts, other denominations are now adopting such rituals as the public exorcisms common to the UCKG. Among denominations which have appeared since the UCKG we also see the tendency to liberalize the rules of "classic" Pentecostalism dictating behavior, particularly concerning dress and hair, as well as an effort to institutionalize Charisma through the creation of preparatory courses for religious leaders. In other words, the competition between Pentecostal denominations has undermined the academic differentiation between "classic" and "autonomous" Pentecostalism.[26]

In the Charismatic world, where there is less influence from Afro-Brazilian religions, explanations of deviant behavior emphasize the absence of religious values or the submission of these values to those of the secular world. Many of those we interviewed added psychological and sociological arguments to their religious discourse, citing "the individualism of modern societies, Brazilian macho culture, and the lack of understanding of other family members." Of course, just because most of these participants did not explicitly mention evil influences does not mean that Charismatics deny the existence of the Devil.[27] Nevertheless, the mere mentioning of the Devil when referring to deviant behavior did not eliminate the individual's responsibility for his actions, and was always accompanied by a value judgement.

Means of Family Planning

The ways in which participants dealt with birth control is also an expression of how the questions of desire and sexual pleasure are addressed by believers in these religious movements. Among our Charismatics, the married women of fertile age and the men whose spouses were in this same phase were, respectively, fourteen and eight in number. Of this total, half claimed to use natural methods, according to Catholic doctrinal teaching and avoided the use of artificial contraceptives. This was the overwhelming preference for men from the popular classes, a fact which may be understood in part by the material difficulties they face which make the limiting of births a necessity; and, in part by the fact that these methods require a period of abstinence which is more easily tolerated by husbands who share the same religious values as their wives. S.V., a thirty-six-year-old systems analyst who used the Billings method justified this choice of birth control thus:

> The same problem you have with drinking you have with sex. It's who controls who. Either you are a puppet to your own needs, or you learn to control your own sexual functions. You can't just be controlled by your own sexual desire. When you control it, you can use the natural method. It's easy. You do it when you want to, how you want to, and don't become a slave to passion.

In general terms, participants who employed natural methods of family planning related their choice to the position of the church, making it clear that they were concerned with following the directives of religious leaders, in particular, of the Pope. The similarity between the period of time they had participated in the MCCR and the use of this method appears to confirm the relationship between belonging to a religious group which encourages sanctification—therefore requiring observance to established rules—and the choice of this birth control method.

However, while half of those interviewed who were in the fertile period of life demonstrated this type of concern, there were a significant number who opted for feminine sterilization; no fewer than ten had chosen to have their tubes tied.[28] These sterilized women were in the 33 to 46-year-old age group and the great majority claimed to have made the decision before joining the MCCR, and after the prolonged use of the birth control pill, this being the most common of the artificial methods, particularly among members of the middle class.[29] C.P.R., a thirty-eight-year-old housewife and mother of three, told us that since she had married, she had been aware of the teaching of the Catholic church as to the use of only natural methods of birth control, but her fear of having children while facing financial instability forced her to opt for the use of condoms; it was only when they decided to undergo sterilization that they felt guilty for disobeying the Pope.

> Before having my tubes tied I asked for advice from three priests who didn't know me. I really wanted to do it, but I was afraid of going against the church. They said I should be aware of how many children I wanted and could support. And that if I decided to do it they saw no problem, so I did it. That was before I joined the MCCR, but I still feel ok about it because I asked those priests beforehand.

Here we become aware of two levels of orientation within the Catholic church: official and pastoral discourse, which result, at times, in contradictory positions and concurrent clerical ideologies in relation to birth control practices. According to specialists (Pierucci 1978; Ribeiro 1989; Bingemer 1992) the "doctrine of responsible parenthood" affirmed in papal documents in the 1960s, particularly in the Humanae Vitae (1968) opened up the possibility for members of the church hierarchy, when counselling individuals, to approve the limitation of births, to a certain extent responding to pressures from believers. The ambivalence of a family theology which, on the one hand tells parents to have only the number of children they can adequately educate, feed, and raise with dignity, meaning, of course, to limit the number of births, while at the same time condemning the use of artificial contraceptive measures exhorts priests into greater understanding and mercy toward those who cannot follow these instructions. This, according to Pierucci (1978, 71), results in a casuistic application of the rules on the part of most of the lower clergy, who "assume a liberal and permissive posture in relation to birth control," principally in the case of the Brazilian poor.

To a certain extent, our research can confirm the pressures put on the clergy who minister to these segments of the population. Among those we interviewed, the only Charismatic women who seemed dissatisfied with the official position of the Catholic church were those of lower-income background, confirming the importance of the class variable. The other women who used artificial contraceptives were able to justify their choice either because they made it at a time when they were distanced from the Catholic community, or even before entering the MCCR. Exposure to poverty and violence, however, led participants from the popular groups toward opposition and even criticism of the church hierarchy. T.S., wife of an alcoholic, mother of a daughter and with three abortions behind her, told us: "the church condemns it, but that's just not the way things are nowadays. You just can't have a houseful of kids. Now that's sinful, filling a house with kids who end up starving to death. Even if I were fertile now, even after joining the MCCR, I'd take the pill, because life is just too hard."

One other woman besides this one, also from the popular sector, mentioned abortion as an option for avoiding having an unplanned child, and according to her testimony, it was just this guilt-laden experience which led her to have her tubes tied. Confession after the decision to use such methods and the search for forgiveness was common among women who were searching to alleviate their feelings of guilt; and, with the exception of abortion, priests proved understanding to the situation of women from this segment of society.

Nearly all the married Pentecostals in the fertile phase of life claimed to use birth control. Only one man, A.S., a forty-four-year-old driver and the second president of an Assemblies of God congregation took a stand against birth control, declaring that "we live according to the word of God, and any person who avoids having a child is disobeying God's laws. The word of God is to let children come unto me, so there is just no way to condone it." His position may have been the result of the fundamentalism of his denomination, or even of his position in the religious group. For this reason we sought to hear from members of his congregation, and out of the group of four married and fertile participants, two stated that female sterilization had been their preferred option. These were P.P., thirty-eight, a deacon in an Assemblies of God church, who told us that his wife had taken the pill until eventually deciding on sterilization, and R.D., daughter of Assemblies of God parents, and herself a practicing member for seven years. She was the youngest of the all women we interviewed who had opted for this type of surgery: twenty-two years of age. Such cases show that if until recently the Assemblies of God were against birth control, in particular by artificial means, there is currently no single orientation shared by pastors in Rio de Janeiro; and that the material difficulties faced by the poor are at times more important than the literal translation of the Bible. Other denominations adopt a more historical interpretation of the holy book, at least in respect to family planning. J.C., a doctor of forty-four and member of the UCKG told us:

> The pastors tell us, and even Bispo thinks that the best thing for a couple is to have two children ... First, because the world is over-populated, and secondly because the commandment to grow and multiply came at a time when there was nobody in the world—just Adam and Eve ... Our Bispo is totally in favor of the pill and of birth control as long as the couple already has as many children as they want.

This position, much closer to the values of modern society than to the Catholic church, explicitly defining the medical difference between abortion and the use of contraceptives which inhibit ovulation, was considered "progressive" by our participant. It was progressive because it both adopted scientific values and recognized the many difficulties believers would have in supporting large families. This position is not unique to the UCKG, the denomination of this particular respondent (Machado 1993). There were a significant number of participants from other Pentecostal churches who were willing to accept the use of artificial birth control methods, as we have already seen. We further saw signs of greater masculine participation in family planning, for on one hand we found two cases of male sterilization, both UCKG, and on the other, a greater number of references to the use of condoms. Whereas only one of the married Charismatic women cited the use of this method, among Pentecostals four women and one man affirmed having used them at some point, and in one case they were the only method ever employed.

Female sterilization surgery also seemed more common in this religious group when we looked at the middle-class segment. Six out of a total of ten women and two out of five men had opted for this method. Of this group only two were no longer fertile at the time of the interview and both had had the operation before their religious conversions. The remaining women were in the 34 to 46-year-old age group. M.H.Q., a thirty-six-year-old housewife who had been a member of the Calvary Baptist Church for seven years told us that, contrary to what most people who are not Evangelical think,

> we believers have very open minds about sex. I mean about all that stuff they told me when I was a child, about the hole in the sheet, just isn't true. Believers discover that sex is a gift from God. The only difference is that God allows it only in marriage, between a husband and wife. We take the pill, use condoms, and I have even had my tubes tied by a doctor from my church.

It is interesting that even when the decision to have children or not was made independent of religion, or was made prior to conversion, all of our participants justified their option by citing the attitude of the church.[30] In other words, we found here none of the tension between the concrete practice of these believers and the teaching of the religious institution that was so present in the case of the Charismatic Catholics who, though having used different forms of birth control, were nevertheless unable to shake off their feelings of unease at not being completely in line with church doctrine. In the lower-income group, the number of women with their tubes tied dropped to levels comparable to the Charismatics, though this was certainly due more to the cost of having the operation done than to any negative feeling about it. One of our participants, who was not sterilized, considered it "a blessing from God" that a doctor had tied her granddaughter's tubes

free of charge. In this group, the age of sterilized women fell to between twenty-two and thirty-six years of age, which calls our attention to the fact that some Pentecostal communities not only educate
believers as to family planning, but also, through the solidarity of the
brothers and sisters in faith, often help to raise the necessary funds for
the operation.

In the popular segments where average time since conversion was
the lowest among all the religions, we also found a greater number of
women who had had abortions. Half of the Pentecostals in this social
group admitted to having had at least one. They all claimed to have
had the abortions prior to their conversions and expressed regret at
having done so. Their motivation was always the financial situation
they faced, either the unemployment of the spouse or his inadequate
salary, and two claimed to have been forced into the decision by their
husbands and mothers-in-law, with whom they lived. No male interviewed admitted to his wife having had an abortion.

Conclusion

We began this chapter by recounting the feeling of surprise and wonder the researcher felt at the freedom and gaiety of Charismatic
women at a worship service in the southern zone of Rio de Janeiro. At
first sight they seemed out of sync with the traditional behavior of
middle-class believers and those who looked to the Bible for guidance
in their daily lives. They just did not fit into the Christian sexual tradition that for centuries had devalued the physical dimension of the
relation between man and the sacred. Our central question would be
to investigate the extent to which this appreciation of bodily expression in celebrations and religious services, evidenced in both Charismatic and Pentecostal circles, was evidence of a change in the evaluation of the physical dimension of believers and, consequently, in human sexuality itself.

A comparison of neo-Pentecostal movements within distinct religious traditions—the Charismatic within the Catholic world and the
Pentecostal in the Protestant tradition—has shown us that, in spite of
the historical hegemony of the Catholic church, there has been a
growing process of "Pentecostalization" in the Brazilian religious arena, where believers have been adopting the practices and forms of

religious celebration common to this group. Observations of denominations which are able to fill football stadiums and defunct movie theaters have turned up changes in the Evangelical universe itself, encouraging criticism from both progressive Protestant as well as "classic" Pentecostal leaders. The first tend to consider these denominations as agents of healing, while the second criticize the more liberal, and less restricted ethic they promote. In any case, changes as to dress—tolerance of commonplace clothing used by young people in general: exercise outfits, shorts, sleeveless shirts, etc.—or even a happier and more spontaneous climate in the services are obvious throughout the Pentecostal world.

Our observance of religious services and our interviews with believers made it clear to us that competition in the Brazilian religious field has closed the gap of differences between religious communities, who scramble to copy the elements which attract believers to their competitors, thus reinforcing the tendency toward a homogenization of Christian religious groups. Nevertheless, we also found that for Evangelicals, anybody who goes off the moral track must be suffering from some form of demonic influence over their personality, a view which serves both to promote a more tolerant attitude from the group and to lower the tension and suffering of the transgressors and their families alike. Here, the variables of class and educational level come into play, with among the more needy and less educated this ideology holding greater sway, causing this population to resort more frequently to the practice of exorcism. On the whole, we found that the women of all social spheres were more open and willing to speak of their sexual lives and reproductive behavior.

In the case of Charismatics, we found that the Catholic tradition is a weighty one, which forces followers of the movement to deal with the tension between Pentecostal beliefs, and the norms and doctrine of the Catholic church. In the middle strata, a greater degree of schooling goes hand-in-hand with a desire to preserve status and Catholic identity, making MCCR participants wary of questioning church hierarchy, and causing them to reject demonic influences and public exorcisms. Deviant behavior is strictly reprimanded, and in this sense, Charismatics differ greatly from Pentecostals, who tend to suspend moral judgement be it in relation to cases of unfaithfulness, single motherhood, or homosexuality.

The fact that the Catholic church still does not accept the use of contraceptives creates another type of tension for followers of the MCCR. Its rejection of birth control methods expresses the difficulty of the Catholic hierarchy in separating sexuality from procreation, and considering desire and sexual pleasure in a more favorable light, a position directly opposed to changes in secular culture and advances by minorities. Highly-educated, middle-class Charismatics, though concerned with obedience to the Pope, are torn between following institutional norms on the exclusive use of natural methods of birth control, or ignoring them, with this second option normally bringing on feelings of guilt. Here, the principle of authority seems to weigh more heavily than the educational level of the believer, who to a certain extent has access to information as to how contraceptives work. The variable of both spouses being active participants in the religious group is also important to this issue, with the exclusive use of natural methods being more frequent among believers who share religious values with their spouses. For their part, Charismatics from popular segments, though less exposed to information about contraceptives, not only use those that are available to them, but are more willing to criticize the doctrinal position of the Catholic hierarchy.

Finally, if we are truly witnessing changes in the rituals and celebrations of both Catholic and Evangelical neo-Pentecostal groups, reflecting a renewed appreciation of gestural and bodily expression, we do not yet believe we can extend these changes to the sexuality in general of these believers without further investigation. For the time being, we can only state that sexuality seems to have been stimulated in the second group, where a positive attitude toward sex within the marriage is more evident and less ambiguous than in the Catholic universe. We observe, however, that both groups hold to their condemnation of sexual activity for singles, widows, and unmarried persons in general.

Notes

1. This contribution was presented as a paper at the XVIII Annual ANPOCS, Caxambu, November 1994, and financed by the MacArthur Foundation, through an award for Research on Reproductive Rights (PRODIR II).

2. This church was founded in 1977 and quickly rose to the third-place position among Evangelicals in number of churches in the Rio de Janeiro metropolitan region (191) according to the Evangelical Census of the ISER Research Center (CIN 1992).

3. In particular on the Christian Congregation of Brazil and the Assemblies of God denominations founded in 1910 and 1911 through schisms in the Presbyterian and Baptist Churches, respectively (Rolim 1985, 1987).

4. A study by Datafolha in 1994 and based on a sample of 20,968 Brazilians showed that 74.9% and 13.3% respectively, of those interviewed claimed to be Catholic and Evangelical, and the rest were distributed as follows: followers of Kardec (3.5%), Afro-Brazilian (1.3%), other religions (2%) and no religion (4.9%). Focusing on the two traditions with which we are concerned, the Catholic and Protestant, we see that of the total number interviewed 61.4% claimed to be Catholic by birth, 3.8% were Charismatic Catholic, 1.8% belonged to CEBs and 7.9% participated in other movements; while 3.4% claimed to be Protestant and 9.9% Pentecostal. In Rio de Janeiro State, of a total of 2204 cases: 62.8% were Catholic and 16.1% were Evangelical, of which 54.9% had been raised Catholic, 1.6% Charismatic, 0.9% were members of CEBs and 5.5% were involved in other movements; while 5.5% claimed to be Protestant and 10.6% Pentecostal (Prandi and Pierucci 1994:22).

5. A middle-class region of the city of Rio de Janeiro.

6. Pertaining to the specific culture of Rio de Janeiro.

7. For Gebara (1989, 19) "this battle, in which the body was the loser, the greatest loser, "condemned to death," was the body of woman. Her body would carry the wounds of all bodies exiled from theology." The Brazilian Catholic theological position is revolutionary not only because it attempts to restore the importance of the body, desire, and pleasure for theology, but above all, because it attempts to grant women equal rights to men. After all, the Christian doctrines on the female body value it for its reproductive capacity and even in this, never fail to accentuate the suffering and pain of childbirth, rather than the pleasure.

8. A similar mechanism can be identified in progressive Brazilian Catholic groups. According to Botas (1981, 54) "it is not overdoing it to say that the emotional upbringing of most Catholic Action believers was based on the *channelling* of their life potential, in other words, the *erotic*, into the task of changing the world. This great discipline was composed of learning to suppress *sensuality, emotion, feeling,* and *pleasure*—and the aesthetic of the sexual—for the creation of VIRGIN and, in most cases, *heroic* workers."

9. In Latin America, progressive sectors of the traditional churches, women and a few male theologians linked to Liberation Theology, attempt to question the body-spirit relationship, based on a "unitary" anthropology and not the patriarchal and hierarchical one preferred by most Christian religions (Gebara 1988, 21). This is, however, a very recent discussion in the Brazilian religious sphere.

10. Through study on the renunciation of sex in primitive Christianity, Brown (1990) states that "up to the second century, the great emphasis on speculation as to "human frailty" was centred on the fact of death. During the second century a new way of thinking came about in Christian circles transferring emphasis to sexuality."

11. The author who most objectively profiled these paradoxical consequences for women converts to Pentecostalism was Brusco (1994) who, making use of Molineux's conceptual distinction between "strategic interests" and "practical interests," has repeatedly affirmed that one of the effects of conversion to Evangelism in Colombia is the redefinition of female and male roles in the domestic sphere and the creation of a new family ethos. For the Brazilian case see Machado (1994).

12. In the 1958 document *The Family Today*, the Anglican church held this position, leaving it to couples to choose the contraceptive methods they deemed most appropriate (Pierucci 1978, 40).

13. During the II Vatican Council, the Commission for the Study on Population, Family, and Births was formed. It concluded that "the church should only guide followers as to the meaning of true conjugal love, leaving a couple to choose, and to plan its family, using the techniques most accessible, adequate and less contradictory to their expression of love," but the Commission's draft was rejected by Pope Paul VI (Ribeiro 1989, 147-148).

14. According to Pierucci (1978, 38), Brazilian bishops, during the 1940s and 1950s avoided public debates on this question "so that it would not be the clergy itself that would spread knowledge about the various (condemned) means of birth control to believers who were not yet aware of them." In the late 1960s, however, when "the militancy of other institutions in favour of family planning ..., particularly the North-American Evangelical missionaries" became evident, the church hierarchy was forced to abandon their strategic silence, using their presses and documents of related organs to define their official positions. Nationalist and anti-imperialist arguments were intermixed with moral and religious justifications, showing that while the upper echelons of the Brazilian clergy held to papal doctrine, local bishops rejected such "neo-Malthusian" solutions to the problems of underdevelopment and poverty.

15. In the manual *How is your Family?*, brought out by Brazilian Bishops to orient discussions in the International Year of the Family this reaffirmation of the rejection of contraceptive methods is not discussed. Once again, the local clergy avoided confronting upper-level hierarchy by claiming that, if on the

one hand, the church was in favor of family planning (NCBB 1994, 85), on the other, they had no methods of family planning. Moreover, they condemn artificial means of birth control in official documents based on their insistence on natural methods, claiming that the institution holds a more global view of the human being which make "certain methods unacceptable."

16. The intense battle against campaigns for the prevention of AIDS, particularly those which encourage the use of condoms, leaves no doubt as to the convergent position of the hegemonic sector of the Brazilian hierarchy with the Pope in terms of the link between sexuality and reproduction.

17. Progressive Catholics, such as the theologian Bingemer (1992), have identified this disparity as the main reason for many believers' merely "festive and ritualistic" participation in the church, emphasizing that those born "under the star of sexual liberation" and of feminine emancipation frequently live outside the teaching of the ecclesiastic institution, having little Catholic influence in their family ethos. Their values and behavioral patterns are more strongly influenced by other means of communication as well as by mystical alternatives, be they religious or political.

18. Like the Catholics, Protestants have their own progressive group which attempts to discuss questions relating to sexuality and to abortion, defending its legalization. Within this group, we call attention to the theologians and pastors who try to show how the churches, focusing their discussion on abortion on the fetus rather than on the pregnant woman, deny the difficulties millions of women face, in particular those who live in conditions of poverty (see Jarschel 1988, 37-39).

19. The majority of cases were male believers who, on leaving the Catholic church, founded new Pentecostal churches or joined other growing movements.

20. These interviews were conducted as part of the data used in my doctoral dissertation entitled *Religious Choice and its Effect on the Private Sphere* (1994).

21. The Pentecostal women (26) belonged to the following denominations: UCKG (9), Assemblies of God (4), New Life (3), Calvary Baptist (2), Maranatha Evangelical Missionary Association (2), International Evangelical Center and Support Front (2), Evangelical Church of God in the Last Days (2), Church of Christ (1), Christ Renews (1).

22. The distribution of the men (14) in Pentecostal denominations was the following: Assemblies of God (4), UCKG (2), International Evangelical Center and Support Front (2), House of Prayer (2), Maranatha Christian Church (1), Christ Lives (1), Methodist Wesleyan (1), Christ Renews (1).

23. Authors such as Brusco (1994), Burdick (1990), and Gill (1990) have pointed out the importance of the public space opened for women by Pentecostal movements. In Gill's words, "the Pentecostal service offers women an institutional base in which to develop important and lasting relationships, and through its rituals to reinforce these emergent ties, thus aiding the creation of a

stronger feeling of community" (1990, 712). In other words, women are thus able to develop extra-domestic relationships where they can talk about their problems.

24. Here the age variable is very important. The majority of women who stated they were no longer virgins when they married were in the 23 to 36 year-old age group and were similarly distributed in both social segments. Thus we could not see an influence of schooling or social origin on this group. The greater number of Pentecostals than Charismatics can in part be understood by the fact of this group having a lower average age, and in part by the fact that in the Pentecostal world the responsibility for behavior prior to conversion is lightened, and individuals can feel better about previous deviant episodes.

25. Freston (1993), investigating three Pentecostal waves, found different emphasis on the powers of the Holy Spirit. According to this interpretation the first Pentecostal wave, marked by the founding of the Assemblies of God and the Christian Congregation, was characterized by speaking in tongues; the second, which occurred in the early 1950s, is marked by the power of healing; and the third, from the 1970s, by the power of liberation.

26. This differentiation was established by Bittencourt (1991) and is based on the fact that denominations such as UCKG arose from dissidents within classic Pentecostal churches and were structured around a few strong leaders. Based on the "triad of healing, exorcism and prosperity," this new type of Pentecostalism would draw its followers predominantly from the popular segments.

27. In an earlier paper (Mariz and Machado 1994), we analysed the unease of Charismatics with the so-called "manifestations of evil spirits."

28. According to data from the National Study on Maternal-Infant Health and Family Planning (BEMFAM) in 1986, 43.2% of the Brazilian women in the fertile age group had been sterilized. The index for women in Rio de Janeiro was also around 43% (Aguiar 1994, 111).

29. According to data from the *Jornal do Brasil* (3/31/94, 9) and based on a study by Susheela Sigh and Dierdre Wulf on Latin American countries, "the use of the pill is not popular among Brazilians, Colombians and Dominicans, due to their fear of negative side-effects; only 6% to 17% take them."

30. According to data from the *Jornal do Brasil* (3/31/94, 9), based on a study by the Alan Guttmacher Institute (New York) "around 53.8% of pregnancies in Brazil are unwanted, but 23.1% reach full term, with live births."

References

Araujo, M.J., "Aborto legal no Hospital de Jabaguara," *Revista Estudos Feministas* 1, no. 2 (1993).

Benedetti, L., *Templo, Praça, Coração - A Articulação do Campo Religioso Católico*. São Paulo (Ph.D. Thesis), 1988.

Bingemer, M.C., *Família e Instituição Religiosa: Tensões e Prospectivas.* Anpocs, Caxambu (Paper presented at the XIV Annual Meeting), 1992.

Bittencourt Filho, J. "Pentecostalismo Autônomo." In *Alternativas dos Desesperados: Como se pode ler o Pentecostalismo autônomo.* Rio de Janeiro: CEDI, 1991.

Botas, P.C., "Creio na Ressureição da Carne," in *Religião e Sociedade* 7 (1981).

Brown, P., *Corpo e Sociedade: O homem e a mulher e a renúncia sexual no início do cristianismo.* Rio de Janeiro: Jorge Zahar Editores, 1990.

Brusco, Elizabeth, "The Reformation of Machismo: Ascetism and Masculinity among Colombian Evangelicals." In eds. Garrard-Burnett, Virginia and David Stoll, *Rethingking Latin-American Protestantism.* Philadelphia, Pa.: Temple University Press, 1994.

Burdick, J., *Looking for God in Brazil.* City University of New York, 1990.

Droogers, André F., "Visões paradoxais de uma religião paradoxal: modelos explicativos do crescimento do Pentecostalismo no Brasil e no Chile," *Estudos de Religião* 8 (1992).

Freston, P., *Protestantes e Política no Brasil:da Constituinte ao Impeachment.* Campinas (Ph.D. Thesis), 1993.

Gebara, I., "Corpo; novo ponto de partida da teologia," *Tempo e Presença,* 1988.

Gill, Lesley, "Like a Veil to Cover Them: Women and the Pentecostal Movement in La Paz," *American Ethnologist* 17, no. 4 (1990).

Gudorf, C.E., *Redeeming Sexuality: Shifts in Christian Understanding of Moral Good.* Rio de Janeiro, (Paper presented at the Working Groups on Sexual Behavior Research, Conference on International Perspectives in Sex Research), 1993.

Hervieu-Léger, D. "Present-Day Emotional Renewals; The End of Secularization or the End of Religion?." In *A Future for Religion? New Paradigms for Social Analysis,* ed. W. Santos. London: Sage, 1993.

Jarschel, Haidi, "Aborto: Entre a fome e o desejo," *Tempo e Presença* 256 (1988).

Machado, Maria D.C., *Charismatics and Pentecostals: A Comparison of Religiousness and Intra-Family Relations within the Brazilian Middle Class.* (Budapest Conference of International Society for the Sociology of Religion), 1993.

———, *Adesão Religiosa e seus Efeitos na Esfera Privada - Um estudo comparativo dos Carismáticos católicos e Pentecostais do Rio de Janeiro, Religious Choice and its Effects on the Private Sphere.* Rio de Janeiro: IUPERJ (Ph.D. Thesis), 1994.

Mariz, Cecília, *Coping With Poverty.* Philadelphia, Pa.: Temple University Press, 1994.

————, "Pentecostalismo y alcoholismo entre los pobres del Brasil," *Cristianismo y Sociedad* 105 (1990).

Mariz, Cecília, and Maria D.C. Machado, "Sincretismo e Trânsito Religioso: comparando carismáticos e Pentecostais", *Comunicações do Iser* 45 (1994).

Novaes, Regina R., *Os Escolhidos de Deus: Pentecostais, trabalhadores e cidadania*. Rio de Janeiro: ISER. 1985.

Oliveira, Pedro Ribeiro de, and Leonardo Boff, J. Libânio, Estevão Bittencourt, *Renovação Carismàtica Católica*. Petrópolis: Vozes, 1978.

Page, John J., *Brasil Para Cristo: The Cultural Construction Of Pentecostal Networks in Brasil*. Ann Arbor, Mich.: University Microfilms International (Ph.D. Thesis, New York University), 1984.

Pierucci, A.F., "Igreja: contradições e acomodações. Ideologia do clero católico sobre reproduçào humana no Brasil," *Cadernos CEBRAP* 21, (1975).

————, "Representantes de Deus em Brasília: A Bancada Evangélica na Constituinte," *Ciências Sociais Hoje* (1989).

Prandi, José R., "Catolicismo e Família: Transformação de uma ideologia," *Cadernos CEBRAP* 21 (1975).

Prandi, José R., and A.F. Pierucci, *Religiões e Voto no Brasil*. Caxambu, MG, (Paper presented at the XVIII Meeting of the Anual da ANPOCS), 1994.

Ribeiro, I., "O Amor dos Cônjuges." In *Amor e Família no Brasil*, ed. M.A. D'Incao, São Paulo: Editora Contexto, 1989.

Ribeiro, Lúcia, "Ética e Reprodução: A vivência das Comunidades Eclesiais de Base da Igreja Católica." In *Meio Ambiente, Desenvolvimento e Reprodução: Visões da Eco 92*, Núcleo de Pesquisa do ISERRJ, Rio de Janeiro, 1992.

Riis, Ole, "The Study of Religion in Modern Society," *Acta Sociologica* 36 (1993).

Rolim, Francisco C., *Pentecostais no Brasil*. Petrópolis: Vozes, 1985.

————, *O que é Pentecostalismo*. São Paulo: Editora Brasiliense, 1987.

Tarducci, M., "Pentecostalismo y Relaciones de Gênero: Una Revision." In *Nuevos Movimentos Religiosos* 1, ed. Alejandro Frigério. Buenos Aíres: Centro Editora De America Latina, 1993.

Velasques Filho, P., "Sim a Deus e Não à Vida." In *Introdução Ao Protestantismo No Brasil*, ed. P. Velasques Filho and A.G. Mendonça. São Paulo: Edições Loyola, 1990.

Weber, M., *A Ética Protestante e o Espirito do Capitalismo*. São Paulo: Livraria Pioneira Editora, 1987.

Willems, Emilio, *Followers of the New Faith. Cultural Change and The Rise of Protestantism in Brazil and Chile*. Nashville, Tenn.: Vanderbilt University Press, 1967.

9

Deliverance and Ethics

An Analysis of the Discourse of Pentecostals Who Have Recovered from Alcoholism

Cecília Loreto Mariz

The high proportion of Pentecostal men that report having overcome drinking problems has attracted my attention ever since I started research on Pentecostal churches in Brazil. When Pentecostals, especially men, talk about their conversion experience, it is very common to hear them report past problems with alcoholism. There are various possible explanations for this. Alcoholism is indeed a serious problem in Brazil, especially among the poorer classes (Soares 1992) and hardly any efficacious therapies are available for treating alcohol dependence. The many problems this dependence creates for the individual and his family may urge him into changing his life and adhering to the anti-alcohol discourse that comes with adoption of Pentecostalism.

I recognize that alcoholism is an objective evil, whatever discourse is built around it, and like other of life's daily hardships may help explain the drawing power of these churches. In this article, however, my concern is not alcoholism in and of itself but the role it plays in the Pentecostal discourse and worldview. I will not be examining the objective reality of reported alcoholism, nor, consequently, will I address the concept of alcoholism—in other words, the issue is not whether those interviewed were ever really dependent or whether they truly recovered. Likewise, I will not detain myself on the anthropological literature on alcoholism.[1] Following Beckford's suggestions (1978), I am looking for meaningful connections between recovery from alcoholism and the Pentecostal worldview.

In order to understand this connection I have analyzed interviews with Pentecostals who claimed to have been addicted to alcohol and to have then managed to conquer the habit thanks to their conversion. Part of these interviews were collected during my research on Pentecostalism and coping with poverty in Brazil (Mariz, 1994). Another twelve interviews were conducted to supplement the earlier data.[2] In these lengthy, open-ended interviews, alleged ex-alcoholics who had converted to Pentecostalism were asked what they believed was the likely cause of their alcoholism, why they had resorted to drink, how they had become dependent, how they became aware of their dependence, why they gave up drinking, how they came to seek help from the Pentecostal churches, and what their recovery process and experiences with the church had been like. Most of the material reported was collected in Pernambuco and in Rio de Janeiro states. The Pentecostals interviewed belonged not only to traditional denominations, such as the Assembly of God, but also to more recent churches named by some social scientists *Movimento de Cura Divina* and by others autonomous Pentecostalism or neo-Pentecostal churches.[3] The majority of interviews were from the working classes but as a control group middle-class Pentecostals were also interviewed. An analysis of these interviews can help us understand the logic and suppositions behind Pentecostal reasoning and suggest some hypotheses that may account for these churches' appeal, especially to needy populations. The main hypothesis analyzed in these pages is that it is not an enchanted universe which is the mainstay of the Pentecostal church's success story among Brazilian lower classes, but rather *how* this religion conjoins enchanted or magical elements with ethical ones.

Above all, it is the Pentecostal concept of *deliverance* that makes this conjoining possible. In these pages, I hope to demonstrate that by offering "deliverance from evil" Pentecostalism enables the believer to perceive him or herself as an individual, with a certain degree of autonomy and freedom of choice, and to reject any self-conception that restricts individuals to traditionally prescribed roles and denies them the capacity to choose their own destiny. Despite the limits of the Pentecostal concept of individual freedom—being free means being able to reject evil—Pentecostalism does hold to a concept wherein the individual possesses a certain degree of autonomy, and this permits an ethical religiousness to develop.

The idea of deliverance presupposes that individuals do not deliberately choose evil but are dominated by it, and consequently are not responsible for their bad deeds but are, rather, mere victims of evil.[4] By thus denying that individuals are free to choose evil, Pentecostalism rejects the presuppositions of an ethical, rational worldview. Instead, it sees an identification between sin and sickness, between "values" and "facts"; indeed, in the cases analyzed in these pages, converts placed no emphasis on the notions of guilt or repentance. On the other hand, when Pentecostalism affirms that acceptance of Jesus is a choice that brings deliverance from evil and allows the individual to make a clean break with his or her past and former fate, it introduces elements of an individualist view. After being "delivered from evil spirits," the alcoholic individual is capable of being ethical because he is "free" to act in accordance with the chosen law and no longer has to let himself be ruled by unchosen and unexplained impulses. Therefore, although the idea of deliverance itself denies the rational assumption that individuals are able to choose good or evil, and despite the fact that the deliverance services look more like the practice of a magician than of a priest,[5] paradoxically, deliverance seems to be an important step in a process of religious rationalization in the Weberian sense, that is, the process through which religions emphasize a universal ethic while limiting enchanted elements and magical and sacramental procedures and experiences.

The analysis of this process of conquering alcoholism exemplifies the Pentecostal concept of deliverance/cure well, because alcoholism lies in the gray area between sickness and sin. On the one hand, alcoholism does not seem to be an illness, because being cured of it demands a moral concern for others and a decision to lead an ascetic lifestyle. On the other, it does seem like a sickness in that mere repentance and the individual's desire to regenerate himself do not suffice to overcome it. Like a disease, the desire to drink seems stronger than individual will; like sin, being cured does not depend on remedies or medicines but on one's own choices and, at times, on receiving assistance from a *force majeure*. The Pentecostal discourse on alcoholism and on recuperation and deliverance can thus help us understand this religious group's conception of the individual and of freedom.

The Pentecostal Concept of Individual Freedom

Ex-alcoholics tell us how they used to feel weak and at the same time guilty about their weakness. The experience of alcohol dependence erodes the individual's self-esteem and reinforces guilt feelings (Potter-Efrom 1987). Alcoholics begin to berate themselves not only because, as some interviewees stated, others see them staggering about and falling down, physically they become unattractive, and they behave in ways that leave them embarrassed afterwards, but also because they feel incapable of licking their habit. When they try to and fail, they realize they are dependent. Confronted by their impotence, they feel weak and enslaved. Understandably then, the promise of deliverance offered by Pentecostalism looks very attractive.

When they actually stop drinking, these alcoholics feel they have received a strength and power beyond their own. The freedom they talk about is that of acting according to rules they consider genuine and of no longer being slaves to irrational habits. They develop an ascetic concept of freedom and deliverance, achieved at the price of submission to moral laws. Their success constitutes a victory of the will over the body and of reason and rational choice over irrational drives. An example of how the definition of freedom is transformed appears in the statements of ED: "I resisted the church at first because I felt [it was] just like a prison; it would keep me from enjoying myself." But he concludes by saying he discovered that in the past he had been a prisoner of alcohol.

Nevertheless, the Pentecostals—and especially former alcoholics who have tested the limits of their will—do not see the individual as an autonomous being. They feel that even though they had many reasons to give up drinking, they were unable to follow their own reasoning or make their own choices. Alcoholism is perceived as a prison and an evil. They believe the deliverance offered by the church enables them to act in consonance with their own reasoning and will.

Pentecostalism assumes that all people depend on God, without whom individuals become the easy prey of malignant forces. The Pentecostal conception of individual freedom is, therefore, quite distinct from that generally found in modern psychology. It contrasts especially with the concept of freedom defended by authors like Richard Bucher and Priscila Costa (1985:77), who assume individuals are capable of absolute autonomy and who criticize recovery from alcoholism through reliance on support groups, viewed as merely trading one type of dependence for another and as a form of "ideological reintoxication." The Pentecostal conception of liberation is also opposed to that adopted by Reginaldo Prandi (1994) when he affirms that Afro-Brazilian religions (*Candomblé* and *Umbanda*) liberate individuals because they do not annihilate human passions. For Pentecostals, human passions are a threat to the individual's freedom, because they are a hindrance to ethical choice-making. It is thus clear that although Pentecostalism contends that "spiritual deliverance" (*libertação espiritual*) endows the individual with autonomy, it *does not* embrace a contemporary individualist view because it does not define the individual as wholly autonomous and self-determining. The concept of Pentecostal freedom entails submission to God, that is, to his dominion and his plan (Providence). Being free does not mean following individual desires but, rather, following the ethics and Word of God. Pentecostalism is, however, individualist in the sense that it assumes any transformation of society will depend on delivering individuals from evil.

Although the habit of smoking does not provoke as many personal and social problems as drinking, not being able to give it up may prompt an oppressive feeling of dependence, much as alcohol dependence does. It is perhaps for this reason that the interviewees spontaneously told of how they gave up smoking and commemorated the event as another deliverance. They talked about their "victory over the cigarette" and "over the bottle," speaking of these achievements with great pride and often using the word "deliverance." Achieving deliverance from drink through the church is not merely a means of leaving dependence behind but requires adoption of a new lifestyle, a new conception of the world, of "I," of liberty, in short, of a new *episteme*—which is the same experience as those who join *Alcoholics Anonymous* or AA (Fonseca 1989). Giving up drinking comes as a consequence of all these other changes.

The Role of the Group in Deliverance

When he reaches a certain level of dependency, almost every alcoholic recognizes the need to give up drinking and longs to do so. Repeated negative experiences, the awareness that they are destroying their own lives, and feelings of isolation and loneliness are identified by the interviewees as motives for giving up their habit. They recalled that they wanted to attain a balanced life and no longer bring trouble or suffering to their families (wives, children, and parents). Almost all mentioned a desire to improve their familial and emotional lives, but few showed equal concern for their occupational lives.[6] However, the motivation they felt did not seem to be enough in itself, since their desire to give up drinking apparently waned when they were faced by the difficult task of confronting their dependence alone.[7] As the psychological literature on alcoholism makes clear, frustration with oneself and the feeling of failure prompted by the individual's inability to quit the bottle substantially increases his need to drink. This helps explain why alcoholics need outside help to recover (Roazzi 1987).

The literature also mentions cases of alcoholics who recovered by themselves after having gone through an experience that caused them deep pain, referred to in the literature on alcoholism as a "limit experience" (Oliveira 1991), something that provides a very strong motivation for quitting. Various interviewees mentioned experiences of this nature. ED was involved in a car accident, and GI once tried to kill his wife when he was drunk. AD said he lost his family because of his habit. There was also one case of an interviewee who was abandoned by his partner, and another who had to be hospitalized. However, not everyone mentions going through something like this.

It can be seen that when an individual seeks help from a religious body, when he attends a "deliverance service" (*culto de libertação*), in all likelihood he has already decided to give up drinking and ardently desired to do so, but has been unable to. The Pentecostal church does not create the desire to leave drinking behind; it merely reinforces it and provides strong support for the individual's daily motivation to stay sober. The desire to give up drink is reinforced when alcoholism is defined as the devil's work; the individual perceives alcohol not merely as a threat to his physical survival but also to the survival of his soul. In addition, the church also reinforces this motivation insofar as the institution advocates total abstinence from drink. Coherent with its asceticism, any consumption of alcohol, and not just dependence, is condemned.

The interviewees cited their first visit to church as the fruit of a personal call from God. They generally commented that they had tried other things, but without success. Before seeking help from the church, two had tried to give up drinking through AA.[8] One interviewee had turned to Afro-Brazilian spiritism in his efforts to overcome his habit but now blames the failure of this attempt on the "evilness" of that religion. Another reported having taken medicine, but no one had sought out medical services, psychiatrists, or psychologists, not even the middle-class believers, who tended to use terms from psychological jargon in accounting for their alcoholism.

Although they emphasized that they had turned to their church after hearing the call of God deep inside themselves—that is, through their own choice—before the conversion of nearly all these former alcoholic *crentes*, family members already belonged to a Pentecostal church. They invariably remarked that their wife, mother, father, brother, or sister, or even an ex-alcoholic friend, had prayed for them before they were converted. As the alcoholic inevitably causes his whole family trouble, Pentecostalism appears as an instrument that the dependent's family can use to combat the situation. Furthermore, Pentecostals see themselves as responsible for the salvation of other family members, in other words, for the salvation of their souls and health. In these interviews, they often brought up the biblical promise that he who believes in God will reach salvation along with his whole household. These converts thus hope the conversion of their entire family will assure fulfillment of this promise. The fact that most members of the families of former alcoholics stated they were not originally either Protestants or Pentecostals seems to suggest they may have converted mainly because of this alcoholic family member.[9] The data also indicate that choosing to join the Pentecostal church as a means of recovering from alcoholism is above all a familial rather than an individual option. In the first place, Pentecostalism offers a new lifestyle not only for the alcoholics but likewise for those closest to them. The dependent's struggle with alcohol is not just the individual's psychological and internal fight against dependence but is also the whole congregation's fight and, in most cases, the alcoholic family's as well. In this way Pentecostalism offers the alcoholic's family support, particularly his wife, by helping her both cope with her troubled spouse and encourage his efforts to overcome his alcoholism.

The individual's deliverance thus occurs via the congregation and the family, especially through church and family prayers. Prayer is considered even more powerful if one or several church leaders lay their hands on an afflicted individual who wants, and needs, to be delivered. In this way, the alcoholic achieves deliverance through the group. At the discursive level, however, the group's, and even the family's, role in this process is lessened. These accounts of deliverance emphasize instead the intervention of the Holy Spirit, God's call to the individual, and the individual's decision to choose Jesus. In these accounts, the mystical experience is individualized and individualizing. This may have to do with the idea of individual responsibility that the deliverance experience seeks to create.

Furthermore, the fact that these Pentecostals emphasized their "individual experience with God" more than the particular religious denomination where their deliverance took place may reflect the individualist tendency of their new worldview. There is clearly only a weak link between deliverance and a given denomination, mattering little to interviewees whether their experience had occurred in a neo-Pentecostal church or a traditional one. Calling themselves Evangelicals (*evangélicos*), Brazilian Pentecostals adopt a broad Evangelical identity that is independent of any specific denomination. This generic identity becomes evident in accounts of migration from one denomination to another. ED's conversion, for example, took place in the Church of New Life but he later became a member of the Assembly of God. AL, who belonged to the Baptist Church Renewed in the Holy Spirit at the time of these interviews, underwent his conversion within the Wesleyan Methodist Church. JL, a Wesleyan Methodist, was converted at the House of Blessing and later joined the New Life.

This type of nondenominational Evangelical identity can also be found in the accounts of former alcoholics raised in Protestant families. Although these men were not brought up in the same church they later joined, and some had not been raised in any Pentecostal denomination, they felt that by accepting Jesus once again, this time as Pentecostals, they were going back to their origins.

On the other hand, once an individual has been delivered, he has an obligation to try to deliver others, and thus he feels somewhat responsible for transforming others and, to a certain extent, for transforming society. As an individual with autonomy in relation to society and to others, the Evangelical becomes responsible for them too, albeit this responsibility is restricted to individuals' private life.

Deliverance as an Individual Choice

Although the data suggest it is the family that dictates the decision to seek help from the church, almost all interviewees emphasized that they decided on their own initiative to attend a church or religious service. Although many had on various occasions been invited to church by family members, most state their decision was made independent of any family invitation. One interviewee, for example, said that he decided to actually go only after being handed a leaflet on the street, while another recalled that his decision came in response to an invitation made by a "strange woman who seemed to know [his] whole life." Even those who admitted to having gone at the direct invitation of family members or friends said their decision to accept the invitation was *their* response to some special circumstance, which they regarded as a supernatural "sign." They spoke of their decision to go to church as a profoundly individual experience.

For some, the decision to attend church came after or during participation in alcoholic support groups (for example, the *Esquadrão da Vida* or Life Squad). For most, however, their first contact with the church came at a regular service or as part of missionary work.

As I mentioned earlier, the Evangelicals' accounts of their first attendance of a church service are always filled with a sense of wonder and marked by mysterious circumstances, interpreted as part of God's personal call. RI, for example, said he first attended church after hearing a voice in a bar. In the case of AD, mentioned earlier, a woman who was a complete stranger told him he should go to church right away. ED had been feeling severe pain in his head when he decided to go for the first time: "My mother said it was the devil's work, and by the time I had gone half the distance between my house and the church, I didn't feel any pain any more."

It is not just the decision to go but also the very experience of attending the first service or missionary event that was generally described as a motive for strong emotion and a sense of wonder. The music and hymns profoundly touched most interviewees. SI recalled:

> My first visit to church was very nice because I had always liked music and the first thing that caught my attention was the hymns ... I particularly noticed one "sister": when she sang his praises, they came from her heart. I felt shivers down my spine when I saw that sister praising the Lord ... All the music and the sermon really held my attention.

The emotions described by SI are a constant. Many of the Evangelicals said they cried when they heard the hymns or preaching and commented that the sermons seemed to be for their ears alone. They felt that God was calling to them personally, like PB: "It was my life they were speaking about. In a few hours I heard the story of my whole life in the hymns of praise that were sung ... It was directed right at me, all that I needed to hear." He went on to say that: "I realized I was doing something which was causing problems to my body and to all humanity." By creating a new experience specific to that one person, the magic and emotions contribute to the development a new worldview and concept of the individual.

Various of those interviewed recalled that just as soon as they entered the church they felt "something different in the air" or were "overwhelmed by the presence of God." Almost all believe that the "experience of God" was a decisive factor in their decision to give up drinking. But since the interviewees did not delve very deeply into this question, it is not clear whether they were referring to trance-like experiences involving the gifts of the Holy Spirit. Although such experiences may be of fundamental importance in these denominations, Pentecostals do not readily bring up the topic. They are for the most part reserved and do not address the subject spontaneously or openly when talking to outsiders. But we may nevertheless suppose that what they call an "experience with God," often reported to have been of fundamental importance in changing their relation to alcohol, involved receiving the gifts of the Holy Spirit.

Society as a Source of Oppression

If we analyze Pentecostal discourse regarding the root causes of alcoholism, we perceive an indictment of society, which is accused of oppressing the individual and working against his autonomy. The Pentecostals are critical of contemporary social standards, with which they refuse to comply. As far as the Pentecostals are concerned, society fosters alcoholism. Most interviewees did not point to any particular event or catastrophe in their personal lives that induced them to drink. On the contrary, they stated that they had begun to drink because they were influenced by their friends and because they wanted to enjoy themselves, get more pleasure from life, and feel freer. ED, a ceramicist with only a primary school education, member of the Assembly of God, recalled: "I drank to relax. I thought I was making the most of life." Another member of the Assembly, BE, seventy-five years old and retired, said he took to drink because "it felt good and raised [his] spirits." The pursuit of pleasure was mentioned often. Only two people brought up negative experiences in their lives that allegedly drove them to alcohol dependence.

The influence of colleagues from work was singled out by several interviewees as the factor responsible for their initiation in drinking and their taking to "the vice." For example, SI mentioned that where he worked, 90 percent of the staff drank; drinking was their main form of relaxation. He recalled: "I wanted to hold my own and be able to say I could drink heavily." And so he became dependent. PA had a similar story to tell. Between the ages of sixteen and seventeen, he worked in a boarding house that was frequented by "the worst kind of people." Everything was a reason for partying, and commemorating meant drinking, buying rounds, and holding drinking contests. The interviewees thus recognized that drink plays a role in social integration. Many of them affirmed that they drank to gain social acceptance and be part of the group. Indeed, drinking and "knowing how to drink"—that is, being able to "hold your liquor"—are highly valued characteristics in the male world and important definers of the male identity (Jardim 1992).

In nearly all the interviews with Pentecostals from the lower classes, we can observe that the workplace is identified as the environment where dependence began, whereas it is within family life that the alcoholic will find the motivation and support needed for him to give up drinking. Their private world, in this case their families, offers them support and a reason to change their lives and "seek deliverance."[10] In contrast, in the public arena—their workplace—they are exploited and feel threatened. Testimonies like these help us understand the emphasis that the Pentecostal discourse places on the family and individual morality as well as its relative disregard for the public sector. This emphasis has attracted sharp criticism from many authors who see it as indicative of the political alienation and conservatism of Pentecostals.

The middle-class interviewees differed from their working class counterparts in that they did not mention the workplace as the environment where they first took up drinking. However, they also pointed to social factors in explaining their dependence. They stated that in addition to social influences, they also faced personal problems and conflicts. Among these personal conflicts, they nonetheless underscored the need for social acceptance and integration. WA claims his alcoholism was encouraged by his family environment, since his family drank heavily. RO mentioned that he began to drink when he started attending night school: "It was 'in' to drink, because the ones who drank were 'the best,' and they became my role models." The fact that they start working earlier and tend to be exploited more perhaps explains why ex-alcoholic Pentecostals from the lower social classes blame the work environment for their alcoholism more than middle-class converts do.

According to the Pentecostal worldview, the society outside the church—in other words, non-believers who "do not accept Jesus"—breeds alcoholism because it sees drinking as a way of relaxing and bonding with work colleagues or friends and as one of this world's instruments, perhaps the only one, for coping with life's conflicts, frustrations, and hardships. These ex-alcoholic Pentecostals were advancing a social critique when they did not deem alcoholism the outcome of any specific defect in an alcoholic's personality or physical constitution but rather the expression of a broader evil that impinges on a Godless society or on all those who lack faith in Jesus Christ.

From this point of view, the faithless despair when confronted by the normal problems of life, and even when not faced by any grave problem the humdrum of their lives leaves them feeling empty. This broader criticism was made by RI, a middle-class Pentecostal: "There are alcoholics who admit they are hooked and those who don't admit it. I think the social factor plays a big part. You begin to drink socially, like me, and eventually become alcoholic." Pentecostals thus reject not only dependence but the consumption of alcohol in any form, criticizing those that RI would call "closet alcoholics" (alcoólatras não assumidos) as well as society as a whole, which assigns so many social and existential functions to this habit. In the life of the Pentecostal, the church takes over such functions (Mariz 1990).

Pentecostalism thus clashes with psychiatrists and psychologists who, along with support groups like Alcoholics Anonymous, categorize alcoholism as a sickness and identify the causes of dependence in the mind or body of the individual. The definition of alcoholism as simply a sickness was not heard in any of these interviews, not even in the case of Pentecostals from the middle classes.[11]

Within both social classes, the discourse of these Pentecostals contained a social critique that has been underestimated by the literature, which defines Pentecostals as conservative and opposed to change. This literature has slighted the critical and transformational potential of Pentecostalism, probably because these criticisms do not address the economic or political system but morality and/or cultural life instead and, further, because Pentecostalism is primarily concerned with changing the individual and the private world. There has been a general tendency on the part of the social sciences to disregard the potential of proposals for cultural changes and to perceive culture as an epiphenomenon of the economic and political realms. The transformational potential of individual change has also been underestimated. In both the positivist line inspired by Durkheim as well as in the historical materialist approach, sociology has emphasized the power of society over the individual, thereby neglecting the power of individuals as social agents. For sociologists such as these, the public sector occupies all of history's stage while its actors are so powerless that any attempt to transform them is useless. To believe it may be possible to transform society through individuals or to propose to change private lives is criticized as a conservative and alienated position. Sociology has only very recently begun taking a close look at the lives of individuals and the private world.

For Pentecostals, however, society is not the sole nor even the main cause behind alcoholism or man's imprisonment to evil. Behind society there lies the "hidden enemy," a supernatural force that is the origin of all evil. To overcome this supernatural, unethical (unjust) force, man requires the power of an absolute, ethical (just) God.

The Supernatural as a Source of Oppression

Besides mentioning the social causes associated with alcoholism, these Pentecostals from the poorer social classes also pointed to the importance of the supernatural. "Malignant spirit," "evil spirit," "hidden enemy," "adversary," and "work of the devil" were some of the expressions used by interviewees to identify the culprit behind alcoholic dependency. So it is the devil who is really the instigator of this apparent need for relaxation and pleasure. It is likewise the devil who inspires those "friends" who push others onto the wrong path and who is responsible for this faithless society.

The devil is not only responsible for alcoholism but for all that is wrong with the world. The ceramicist ED put it this way: "When you're drinking, you're not thinking about anything; you drink surrounded by friends who are being guided by the devil." The security guard GI recounted: "In the beginning, I drank to relax, but then I began drinking to destroy myself, and drink was really a manifestation of the Evil Spirit ... He starts by letting you enjoy yourself, but then you begin to destroy yourself little by little." The search for pleasure in drink is consequently a subterfuge of the devil. Another ceramicist, AL, agrees with GI when he says that "people who don't have Jesus in their lives think that drinking is fun."

He also pointed out that the friends who induced him to drink were "false friends" doing the bidding of the "malignant enemy." Another interviewee, PB, recalled: "When I left the [Assembly of God], I looked for refuge in drink and tried to do what the Enemy invited me to do—the habit. So I took to the bottle ... What happens is that the devil himself puts these desires into your head."

Although they also acknowledge that supernatural causes lie behind alcoholism, the interviewees from the middle classes talked less about the devil. This may perhaps be due to their more secular vision of the world and their higher level of instruction, but it may also reflect their fear that by confessing such beliefs they leave themselves open to ridicule. Middle-class interviewees spoke in terms of psychological problems. They too mentioned the quest for pleasure, but less often, emphasizing instead "psychological reasons" and using expressions such as "frustration," "internal conflicts," "depression," "inferiority complexes," "despair," "emotional weakness," "loss of personal values," "loneliness," and "emptiness" in accounting for their alcohol dependence. In these interviews, terms borrowed from psychological jargon intermingle with terms bearing moral connotations.

Nevertheless, both the working-class and middle-class Pentecostals' accounts of conversion do not in any way emphasize a discovery of the supernatural or spiritual world. Conversion does not bring any re-enchantment of their worldview. Before adhering to Pentecostalism, most interviewees already believed in God and in a supernatural world, although most practiced no religion at all. Two had practiced spiritism (in the broad sense of the term, that is, including Kardecist Spiritism and Afro-Brazilian religions); one of them had, in his own words, attempted to defeat his alcoholism "through Macumba." The middle-class student VA had followed an Oriental religious path for some time. While he was still drinking, GI, the security guard mentioned earlier, says that he had participated in a prayer circle (*corrente de oração*) at a Pentecostal church because he wanted to see his brother get out of jail. What the analyzed reports seem to suggest, then, is that when people convert they do not acquire faith in the supernatural world or power—something they already have—but, rather, they discover or, better put, redefine the devil. Before conversion, in the words of ED, "you know the devil exists, but you're not aware of his plans." In their reports on conversion, interviewees emphasized that the discovery of the actual presence of the devil helped them make sense of their lives and sufferings.

These interviews suggest that the conversion to Pentecostalism does not reflect the discovery of a magical or enchanted world. What happened to these people that converted was not a return to a religious world or the rediscovery of a supernatural or enchanted universe. Their emphasis on the power of the Holy Spirit, who delivers them from evil, seems to reflect the discovery of a unique God committed to ethical values and able to destroy various other spirits that are not necessarily committed to any ethics or values and that are perceived as demons. The appeal of Pentecostalism therefore seems to have more to do with a search for ethics, order, and morality, as well as for supernatural support for these. Although magical, enchanted, and emotional experiences may be fundamental to Pentecostalism, what it offers that is novel, what makes it attractive for the people interviewed, lies more in the normative order and control it proposes.

When Pentecostalism assumes a clearly defined, rigid morality governed by strict universal laws, it breaks with the previous religious views of the new converts because it adopts a more rational, in the Weberian sense, conception of nature and cosmic order. Rejecting the Catholic tolerance to deviants and the flexibility and multiplicity, almost case-by-case, Afro-Brazilian moral rules, Pentecostalism advances an ethical order and a logic that is missing in the Brazilian society as a whole, afflicted by economic crises, inflation, and rampant crime and characterized by weak laws and widespread impunity (Fernandes, 1991). Individual disorders, expressed in alcoholism, in sickness, and in deviations similarly understood to be spiritual in nature, are seen as a reflection of this supernatural disorder caused by the absence of God and manifesting the presence of the devil. The Pentecostal approach seeks the order offered by a moral God. By defending an absolute God with a divine set of values and deeming demoniacal and evil anything else supernatural, Pentecostalism theologically proposes a program for people's lives that breaks with the broad society patterns.

The debility of Brazilian public institutions and law has been amply denounced and debated. The ethical crisis burdening our society affects minority groups most heavily. When there is no moral support underpinning laws, disadvantaged groups are the ones that suffer most, because minority groups are least protected by the law and the most likely to end up breaking it. Lower-income groups are eager to see strong laws and harsh punishment applied to wrongdoers, since their own physical and moral survival depends more on the rule of law than does the survival of members of the higher classes. Ever experiencing the affects of lawlessness in their daily lives, Pentecostals find no viable support for any system of ethics within the social sphere, and so look for it in the supernatural realm.

Despite the Pentecostal emphasis on miracles, cures, and deliverance or exorcism, the multiplication of such churches across Brazil does not negate the Weberian thesis that a greater rationalization of religion accompanies the development of modern society, nor do these churches symbolize the irrational or "primitive Brazil." On the contrary, they seem to represent a step towards the rationalization and individualization of mentalities. Pentecostalism offers charismatic and "enchanted" or magical support for an ethical rationalizing proposal. The magical elements of Pentecostalism do not stand in opposition to its ethical rules; instead, both elements reinforce each other.

Conclusion

The interviews with former alcoholics help us understand the importance that deliverance from alcohol or other vices or habits has in the Pentecostal church. Alcoholism, like any other type of dependence, be it smoking or drug-addiction, follows the model by which the Pentecostal worldview defines the relation between the individual and evil. According to this model, the individual is fragile and the force of his own will is not strong enough to escape evil. Even when he has done wrong, the individual is regarded as a victim of a malignant force. Sin is not viewed as originating from individual choice. For this reason, accounts of conversion do not stress repentance of sins but deliverance from evil, and evil can be an illness as much as a wrong or a vice.

If we analyze the reasons given to explain alcoholism, we see that Pentecostals are highly critical of the society in which they live, identifying within this society the root of all their suffering. It is not just the individual who drinks excessively and is dependent on alcohol who sins but society as a whole, which accepts and permits drinking. The struggle of an individual against his alcoholism is not only a subjective struggle with himself, but the struggle of the church against society. This criticism of society is present in the interviews with Pentecostals from both the lower social strata and the middle classes. However, the former tend to blame the workplace more, commonly regarded as the location where their drinking began.

While the working-class interviewees spoke explicitly of the power of the devil or hidden enemy, those from the middle classes adopted psychological terminology to explain their problems. However, no one deemed alcoholism merely a sickness, and no one had sought out a doctor or psychologist to help cope with the problem.

The decision to look to the Pentecostal church for a solution to these men's drinking problem seems to have been made by their family. Almost all interviewees mentioned family members who belonged to the church before they were converted and who prayed for them. The interviewees nevertheless underscored that the option itself was their own.

In order to deliver, or free, the individual from the oppression he suffers from society at large and from the devil, Pentecostalism creates a small society of "the delivered"—the church and the family—and appeals to a supernatural power stronger than the devil, to wit, the Holy Ghost. The small, cohesive community of "brothers" will help deliver the alcoholic from the world, while God's absolute, moral power will provide deliverance from the multiple powers bereft of morals. Pentecostalism thus helps the individual discover his autonomy by combating the oppression of society with another social model and by combating spiritual oppression with a stronger and ethical supernatural power.

My analysis of these interviews with ex-alcoholic Pentecostals suggests that the Pentecostal worldview lies midway between a traditional fatalist worldview, where the individual is borne along by destiny, and a contemporary worldview, which argues for a wholly autonomous individual. Pentecostalism likewise offers a middle road between a religiousness that seeks practical, magical solutions applicable to daily life and a religiousness that offers an ethical proposal of transformation. The seeming contradiction within this religion, underscored by Droogers (1991), derives from its straddling the border between the traditional and modern worlds. This "borderline" position makes Pentecostalism quite attractive insofar as it enables the group to: (1) blend individual and social issues; (2) attribute autonomy to individuals and assign them a role as transformational agents of other individuals, without blaming them for their failures, as a purely individualist worldview would do; (3) bring the mystical/magical poles of religion together with ascetic/ethical ones; and (4) support and reinforce individual efforts to achieve self-transformation and change reality.

Notes

1. In an earlier study (Mariz, 1991), I take a closer look at the anthropological literature on alcoholism. A detailed review of a bibliography about social aspects of alcoholism can be found in Heath (1975, 1986, 1987) and Barrows & Room (1991).

2. This research is part of a broader two-year research project (Mariz 1993) supported by the Brazilian Research Council (Conselho Nacional de Pesquisa - CNP) and by the Fundação de Amparo à Ciência do Estado de Pernambuco (FACEPE).

3. For a characterization of Brazil's so-called neo-Pentecostal churches see Ari Pedro Oro (1991).

4. This Pentecostal conception of man as a weak being easily dominated by evil and by the world has been observed by other authors, including Ireland (1992).

5. See Weber's (1972) distinction between magicians and priests.

6. Only one interviewee (who was from the middle class) mentioned work when explaining why he needed to stop drinking.

7. A previous study of a low-income community suggests that more than 60% of alcoholics do not succeed in efforts to give up their habit (Mariz 1993).

8. Although these interviewees reported they knew many alcoholics who had cured themselves with the help of AA, they did not explain just why this group could not work in *their* case and why they had turned to the church instead. One commented vaguely that he preferred the atmosphere of the church.

9. This would explain the relatively greater percentage of alcoholics in families of Pentecostals, as found in a previous study in a low-income area of Recife (Mariz 1993).

10. The exception to this line of argument among interviewees from the working classes was the night watchman, GI, who claimed to have started drinking under the influence of his own brothers, who encouraged him to take up the habit when he was still a child.

11. Only one interviewee, the one who had participated in AA before conversion, used the word "sickness" (doença) among those he employed in defining alcoholism. He explained that the cause of alcoholism "may be financial, familial, or caused by loneliness; it's a vice, a habit, a sickness." It is worth observing that in this broad, eclectic reply where distinct definitions overlap, the term "sickness" is not at odds with the idea of a vice, but rather the two terms complement one another.

References

Barrows, S., and R. Room, ed. *Drinking Behavior and Belief in Modern History*. Berkeley: University of California Press, 1991.

Beckford, James A., "Accounting for Conversion," *British Journal of Sociology* 29, no. 2 (June 1978): 249-262.

Bucher, Richard and Priscila F. Costa, "Modelos de Atendimento a Toxicômanos," *Arquivo Brasileiro de Psicologia* 37, no. 3 (July/September 1985): 70-83.

Fernandes, Rubem C., *Inflação e Desconfiança*. (Paper presented at the seminar "Inflação Ética e Felicidade" (Ethical inflation and happiness), Economics Department of the Universidade Federal Fluminense), 1991.

Fonseca, Márcia M., *A Experiência da Mudança; de Gregory Bateson aos Alcóolicos Anônimos*. (M.A. Thesis, Getúlio Vargas Foundation), Rio de Janeiro, 1989.

Da Matta, Roberto, *Carnaval Malandros e Heróis*. Rio de Janeiro: Zahar, 1980.

Droogers, André F., "Visiones paradójicas sobre una religión paradójica." In *Algo más que opio; una lectura antropológica del pentecostalismo latinoamericano y caribeño*, eds. Barbara Boudewijnse, Frans Kamsteeg, and André Droogers. San José: DEI, 1991.

Heath, Dwight B., "A Critical Review of Ethnographic Studies of Alcohol Use." In *Research Advances in Alcohol and Drug Problems* (2), ed. R. Gibbins, et al.. New York: John Wiley and Sons, 1975.

———, "Drinking and Drunkenness in Transcultural Perspective" (1), *Transcultural Psychiatric Research Review* 23 (1986): 7-42.

———, "Anthropology and Alcohol Studies: Current Issues," *Annual Review of Anthropology* 16, (1987): 99-120.

Ireland, Rowan, *The Kingdoms Come: Religion and Politics in Brazil*. Pittsburgh, Pa.: University of Pittsburgh Press, 1991.

Jardim, Denise F., *Tornar-se Homem; o Uso das Bebidas e Masculinidade*. (Paper presented at the 18th meeting of the Brazilian Anthropological Association (ABA)), Belo Horizonte, 1992.

Mariz, Cecília L., "Pentecostalismo y Alcoholismo entre los Pobres del Brasil," *Cristianismo y Sociedad* 105 (1990): (39-44).

———, *As Igrejas Pentecostais e a Recuperação do Alcoolismo*. (Unpublished Research Report CNPQ and FACEPE), 1993.

Oliveira, Vera L. de, *Alcoolismo: Fenômeno do Corpo, da Alma e da Cultura*. (M.A. Thesis, UFPE), Recife, 1990.

Oro, Ari P., "'Podem passar a sacolinha': Um estudo sobre as representações do dinheiro no néo-pentecostalismo brasileiro," *Cadernos de Antropologia* 9 (1992): 7-44.

Potter-Efrom, R., "Shame and Guilt: Definitions, Process and Treatment of ADDA Clients," *Alcoholism Treatment Quarterly* 4, no. 2 (1987): 7-24.

Prandi, Reginaldo, "Pombagira dos Candomblés e Umbandas e as Faces Inconfessas do Brasil," *Revista Brasileira de Ciências Sociais 26*, no. 9 (October 1994): 91-102.

Roazzi, Antônio, "Considerações sobre o Significado Ideológico das Toxicomanias," *Arquivo Brasileiro de Psicologia* 39, no. 4 (October/ December, 1987): 48-6.

Soares, Bárbara M., "Alcoolismo no Brasil," *Folha de Dados*. Rio de Janeiro: Núcleo de Pesquisa do ISER, 1992.

Thomas, Keith, *Religião e o Declínio da Magia*. São Paulo: Companhia das Letras, 1991.

Weber, Max, *Sociology of Religion*. Boston: Beacon Press, 1972.

10

Charismatic Renewal and Base Communities

The Religious Participation of Women in a Brazilian Parish

Marjo de Theije

Brazilian Catholicism recently gained a new manifestation with the emergence of the Catholic Charismatic Renewal Movement (*Renovação Carismática Católica*, henceforth RCC). According to the national media the RCC is the fastest growing religious movement in Brazil (Istoé 1991, 28). The RCC is a Pentecostal movement and shares many characteristics with the broader Pentecostal movement sweeping through Latin America. The most prominent likeness is its focus on the so-called gifts of the Spirit.[1] A significant difference from the Pentecostal churches is that the RCC is part of the established Catholic church. Therefore the religious doctrines and practices of Catholicism are also important for the movement. In this respect the veneration of Mary has a prominent place (see Boudewijnse 1991 and in this volume).

The growing popularity of the RCC in Brazil is often explained as a reaction to the progressive,[2] liberation theology Catholicism of the Catholic Base Communities (*Comunidades Eclesiais de Base*, henceforth CEBs) that have dominated the Catholic scene for so many years. At the institutional level conservative sections gave support to the RCC because of its focus on spirituality instead of political consciousness-raising. Under Pope John Paul II this faction gained influence and was backed by Rome (Della Cava 1990; 1992; Lernoux 1989; Lesbaupin 1990; Libânio 1990).

The declining influence of the progressive church at the level of ordinary believers is attributed to its neglect of the mystical part of religion (Veja 1991). Mariz (1993) pointed to the disenchantment of the world as a consequence of the rationalization of religion in a progressive discourse that does not fit in with the religious world view of most Catholics. The alternative offered by the RCC, with its emphasis on singing, praying, and the experience of the sacred, including healing, presents a re-enchantment of the world (Csordas 1995). The healing practices of the movement, in particular, receive much attention from the media. This is a "Catholicism of results" as Istoé put it (1991, 28) to emphasize the short-term perspective as opposed to the project of the construction of a just society aimed at by the progressive church.

This explanation implies that for the ordinary believer the differences between the various versions of Catholicism are clear and of importance. But is this so? How do these divergences look at the local level? And do they really matter? My research indicates that from the viewpoint of the ordinary believer the RCC and the CEBs have a lot in common. After all "we" are Catholics in the presence of "them" Protestants and (Afro-Brazilian) Spiritists. This suggests it may be worthwhile to pay more attention to similarities and harmony instead of confining our view to ideological differences and political strife in the religious realm. Both the CEBs and the RCC are often represented as being more ideological than they are in everyday practice. Instead of restricting our view to institutional, national, or global features of the RCC we need to include in our studies the reception and reproduction of the discourse and symbolism in the Catholic parishes.

A case study of local groups offers an opportunity to understand the processes of selection, reinterpretation, and adaptation bound up with the process of religious meaning-making. Most members of both lay associations were Catholics before they started to participate, and the new discourses, symbols, and religious practices were assimilated into the existing beliefs (cf. Drogus 1990, 63). The peculiarities of this process might help an understanding of the success of the RCC in the land of progressive Catholicism. In the next section I will start my analysis with a description of both groups and their place in the parish. But first I must introduce the main key to the argument of this article.

It is not only from the point of view of the people involved that the CEBs and the RCC share many characteristics. An anthropologist researching lay activities in the parish finds various similarities too. The most important commonality between both groups is that the majority of the participants are women. Traditionally women's involvement with institutional Catholicism is greater than men's (Bruneau 1982, 33; Van den Hoogen 1990, 172). It is no surprise then that the commitment of women to the CEBs and the RCC, is higher too. Researchers indicating the proportional participation of women report that the majority of CEB members are women, as high as 80 percent (Alvarez 1990, 381; Castro 1987, 140; Drogus 1990, 64; Hewitt 1991, 64; Mariz 1994, 44, 117). For the RCC fewer figures are available, but my observations give no reason to suggest a different sex ratio. Including gender in the analysis, then, may illuminate the practice and ideological significance of the Catholic lay movements under study. In section three of this article I will explore the general features of the participation of women in the groups and lay the foundation for a better understanding of the shape and significance of the lay groups in the following sections. This will be linked to an explanation of the fact that in practice the CEBs and the RCC are not as different as they are often said to be.

Anything Religious Is Good!

The parish of Saint Vincent is situated in the seat of the bishopric of Garanhuns (PE). The parish covers some of the poorer neighborhoods of this town, the so-called periphery, and an extensive rural zone with scattered towns and villages. The total extent of the area is 860 km².

According to estimates by the vicar 55,000 people live in the parish. The area is situated in the dry zone (*agreste meridional*) of Pernambuco State and most of the inhabitants live in poor conditions. The neighborhood of Colina to which I will restrict myself in this article, is the urban part of the parish. Here the main church is located and the priest lives. It is also the most populated part of the parish, including the thousands of people living in the *favela*, a squatter-area up on the hill.

Since the end of the 1960s, and especially after 1974 when a new bishop was appointed, the diocese of Garanhuns developed a pastoral practice of evangelization in which lay persons were stimulated to participate. This was done through a democratization of pastoral work. These changes were linked to the changes set out in the Second Vatican Council and the heyday of Liberation Theology. Garanhuns chose the "option for the poor" and in the region the diocese became known as progressive. Most pastoral activity concentrated on the (formation of) evangelization groups or CEBs.[3] It is hard to formulate a clear definition of the phenomenon of *Comunidade Eclesial de Base*, not only because theologians and priests give different meanings to the concept, but most of all because the members of these groups and other Catholic believers do too. In Garanhuns the groups are directed by one or two lay persons who organize meetings at their house or the house of another participant every week. At these meetings they read biblical texts and try to provoke discussion and reflection (*conscientization*). The lay leaders receive a guide (*roteiro*) every month, a booklet prepared by a pastoral coordinating group in their area (in the case of Colina four urban parishes) where texts from the Bible are selected together with examples from real life to stimulate reflection. The priest of Saint Vincent, Father Milton, agrees with the policy of the "preferential option for the poor" of the diocese and tries to put into practice the guidelines set out by the diocesan assembly.[4] During mass he calls on people to participate in the groups and he organizes Bible courses for their leaders. Beyond that the groups function without supervision and the priest seldom visits the CEBs in Colina.

Since the CEBs form the main aim of diocesan policy and the work of Father Milton in the parish, it sometimes looks as if they *are* the parish.[5] In many instances of Catholic celebrations the priest relies on the CEBs to organize church life in the parish. Some of the most active

CEB leaders are also members of the parish council, participants in various ministries, and act as readers during mass. This all adds to the impression that CEBs (or at least the members) are the backbone of the parish.

In this respect the situation of the RCC is quite different. It is organized independently of the parishes, which is not to say that it has no contacts with the priest. Father Milton was even invited to become their "spiritual leader." The priest did not accept this invitation, but once in a while he attends the prayer meeting and even visits meetings of the charismatic groups outside his parish, for example the *retiro* they organize every year at Carnival. He may be motivated by pragmatic reasons[6] but his behavior certainly helps to legitimate the RCC. The fact that the prayer group meets in the principal church of the parish adds to the image of close ties with the parish.

In Garanhuns the RCC was introduced in 1979, by a layman who had become familiar with it when hospitalized in the State capital of Recife. Today there are nine prayer groups in Garanhuns and the movement is expanding to neighboring parishes and towns. In the parish of Saint Vincent there is one group, which organizes a prayer meeting every Monday evening in the parish church. Every year there is a seminar for new members, where the basic doctrines of the Charismatic Renewal are taught. For people already involved there is a seminar going more deeply into the "gifts of the Spirit."

As already mentioned, the RCC is organized independently of the parishes. At the level of the diocese there is a coordinating committee which organizes the more important meetings, for example at Pentecost, and maintains contact with the prayer groups. Individual members may perform other tasks in the parishes, such as the catechism or evangelization, but they do not do so as representatives of the RCC. Until recently the Charismatics in Garanhuns did not have a priest as spiritual leader. Every time they needed a priest to say mass, they had to see if one was available. Nowadays there is a Dominican friar taking part in the coordinating group.

Both the RCC and the CEBs are clearly present within the neighborhood of Colina and are open to everyone interested. However, most Catholics do not participate in lay groups. Here it is important to remember that lay groups diverge from ordinary Catholicism because they invite Catholics to participate more actively in the church.

Within the current trend (since Vatican II) of emphasis on lay participation stimulated by the institution, the CEBs and the RCC can be
seen as an expression of what Benedetti (1988, 319) called a new "division of labor" or a rearrangement of the Catholic universe. In this
Catholicism the movements of the laity have a certain autonomy,
since neither priests nor any other "official" pastoral agent exert control over their meetings. At the same time they continue depending on
the hierarchy if only for the administration of the sacraments or the
use of the church building. In Colina leaders and members of both
groups also showed a need for the approval of the priest for their activities. They often feel insecure and only want to carry out their plans
after the priest has sanctioned them.[7] Many explanations can be given
for this attitude. For this article the most important is the value the
members of the lay groups attach to their membership of the Catholic
community—the unity of Catholics. The priest is an indispensable
part of this. It also is demonstrated in the nonproblematic coexistence
of the various groups in the parish.

Although the CEBs are part of the policy of the diocese and the
RCC is not, the Charismatics do not encounter strong opposition. All
priests agree that it is better to have a Charismatic Renewal within the
church than to lose the faithful to the Pentecostal churches in town.[8]
At the level of the parishes and neighborhoods I did not see any hostility between the two types of groups either. Participation in one of the
groups is considered to be more a question of personal preference than
of fundamental difference in belief. Only a few members and leaders
of the lay groups are conscious of the pronounced opposition depicted
in the national media. Some CEB members repeated to me the contrast between alienation and social activism as it is sketched in the
newspapers: "They only pray." Others, however, are impressed by the
appeal and fervor of the RCC. As one leader of a CEB expressed her
admiration while describing a man of the movement: "He is so Catholic!"

It is important to recall that participating in the groups is an easy
step to take, because it is not a change of church. People are Catholics
and continue to be so. It comes as no surprise then, that quite a number of women from Colina participate in both groups. Dona Joanina
for example never misses the prayer meetings of the RCC but also
loves the CEB meetings in her street. She was not the only one to

assure me that "anything religious is good." The experience of the unity of Catholicism, with its sacraments, Eucharist, and priests proves to be more important in everyday practice than ideological disputes between the different lay groups.

Groups for the Laity

In the Colina neighborhood about ten evangelization groups, or CEBs, function, and one RCC prayer group. This prayer group has thirty to forty regular participants and usually there is an average of fifty persons present at the weekly gathering. The typical CEB is much smaller with only about ten persons participating in the weekly meeting, so in Colina roughly a hundred Catholics are involved in the CEBs. These numbers can vary sharply over short time periods. When I first visited Colina in 1989 I was told that there were more than thirty CEBs, due to a recent mission carried out by two redemptorist friars a few months earlier. When I returned four months later to do my fieldwork, however, most of the newly formed groups had ceased to exist. The popularity of the RCC also fluctuates. My informants told me that there were times when eighty to a hundred people participated in the weekly prayer meeting in the parish church, while I never counted more than about sixty. One of the reasons for the decline or fluctuation might be that most young people go to school in the evening, so they cannot participate in the meetings. Another explanation participants often offered me is the general attitude of people, of not "being interested to hear of God."

For the interested believer, the potential member of a group, it is easier to take a look at the meetings of the RCC than of the CEBs. Since the meetings of the CEBs do not always take place in the same location, it is more difficult to attend without previous appointment. The groups are small and one cannot enter unnoticed. The meetings of the RCC take place in the church, at a fixed time, and the doors are always open. So who are the people who become members of Catholic associations?

In Colina I did not observe a majority of people from the middle class in the prayer meetings of the RCC as is reported for other locations, both in and outside Brazil.[9] The CEBs as well as the RCC attract people from the same layer of society, that is, the poor but not the poorest of the poor.[10] As for the age of the members more difference between the groups can be observed. Whereas the CEBs fail to draw the youth, the RCC in Garanhuns attracts more young people. This corresponds with the image of the RCC in Brazil in general.[11]

The most striking characteristic of the lay participation in local Catholicism is the large number of women involved in it. In the Catholicism of the Colina neighborhood, as in the rest of Brazil, women outnumber men on all fronts except for the altar. In a survey I conducted in the nine CEBs functioning in Colina in the second half of 1990, I found that 90 percent of the participants were women. Countings during the meetings of the RCC in the same period gave an equal impression, though I also attended meetings with only one or two men present.

As to the leadership of the groups, the picture changes slightly. Three out of nine CEBs in Colina are headed by men. Except for two of these men, all the CEB leaders run a group either in their own street or near to their house. The two men who are leaders of CEBs outside their direct surroundings consider themselves "apostles," traveling to spread the word. They start up CEBs in other parts of the parish, accompany these groups for one or two years and try to motivate other people to take over, after which they move on to their next project. The direction of the RCC resembles the strategy of the two CEB "apostles," with the difference that the leaders of the RCC prayer group are from another parish in town, where the prayer meetings have a longer history. The purpose of the group is to bring out leaders from Colina, but until now no suitable candidates have emerged.[12] At the time of my research no men were involved in the leadership of the prayer group in Colina.

So when we speak of the participants in both CEBs and the RCC, we are mainly talking about women. As I have already observed this is often reported as a general feature of Brazilian Catholicism. In the literature on lay activism in Catholicism the most common explanation given is that this is in accordance with gender ideals in the wider society, where religion is considered "women's business" (cf. Drogus 1990, 64; Hewitt 1991, 63). This also means that men active in church activities are distrusted. One quite emancipated female leader of a CEB confided to me that "men who get involved in church matters are half male half female." For women it is appropriate to participate in all kinds of associations and groups related to the Catholic church. For many it is even a duty to spend part of their time on religious matters, as this is part of their responsibility as wives and mothers. It is not only a duty to take care of the religious well-being of the family, often this is also the only culturally approved reason to leave the house.

Another reason given for the disproportional participation of women is more practical. The women involved are mostly married women with children and without a job outside the house. They have spare time (something the poorest of the poor don't have), or at least flexible time. They also feel a need to break the monotony of doing housework and perceive the time spent on religious meetings as time for themselves (cf. Caldeira 1990, 57).

The consequences of the overwhelming participation of women are, however, seldom drawn into the analysis of Catholic lay associations.[13] But people's choice of religion is connected to socio-economic positions, gender, age, education, time available, and so on (cf. Burdick 1993). Furthermore meaning-seekers do not only reproduce what they hear and see, they also adapt, change, pick out parts, and leave aside other aspects of religious systems. By participating in such great number, women give form and content to the groups. If we are to understand the RCC and the CEBs we must pay attention to the meaning-making processes of these actors in the religious realm. It may be clarifying to consider the possibility that their religious participation fulfills specific gendered needs for these women (cf. Caldeira 1990, 48-9). The pre-eminent presence of women in the religious groups under study helps us to understand much of the actual shape and meaning of these associations. It is one of the main explanations for the similarities in the practice of the CEBs and the RCC at the local level, as I will show in the following sections.

Meaning of the Groups

Participation in religious groups, whether in the CEBs or the RCC, is quite different from plain mass attendance because the communication is more direct and people become more involved during the meetings. The tone of the two types of meeting contrasts, with a lot of singing and gesticulation alternating with murmuring prayers in the case of the RCC and a calm atmosphere of prayer and reflection in the case of the CEBs. Despite these different emphases in the groups, there is a resemblance in the "decentering of authority in meaning, discourse, and social form" (Csordas 1995, 6) that takes place in the groups formed by laity. In the CEBs the participants read a text and discuss it. The same occurs during the meetings of the RCC, but in these the testimonies of the acting of the Holy Spirit in the life of individual members are more important. The discussions and personal narratives give meaning and form to both groups. I want to highlight two aspects: first the process of "learning about God" and second the engagement with other women in the group. I will also look at the conversion experience of the women.

Women from both groups told me over and over that the importance of their participation was that they learned more about the Word of God. As well as the readings and explanations during the group meetings there are special Bible courses for the leaders and members of CEBs organized by the parish and the so-called seminaries of the RCC. Illiteracy is an obstacle for many women, but often their eagerness to "learn about God" is a strong motivation to improve their reading ability.[14] In the case of the RCC those who cannot read and write are not allowed to attend the seminary unless they find someone prepared to accompany them during the whole course.

Participants in the groups appreciate that the Gospel is now available to everyone and not only to the priest, recalling that thirty years ago they didn't understand a word of it because it was read in Latin. In an article on neighborhood movements and Catholic discourse in a shanty town in Vitória Banck suggests that access to the Word of God symbolizes "... access to the world of written words, holy, magic or profane, the written codes which are constantly demonstrated to be all important in the modern world" (1990, 75). This meaning may be especially important for women, who are generally more excluded than men from the blessings of this modern world. They appreciate the freedom to talk in the church and interpret the Bible. They state that their self-confidence has increased and that they have the feeling that they now count as real persons.

An important contribution to this is the second aspect. The things they learn are not only of a religious nature. In both groups participants are encouraged to verbalize their views and beliefs and speak in public. If we consider that women in general have few other public cultural spheres in which to speak out, this skill may be especially important for them. They gain self-esteem and feel respected because everybody listens to what they have to say.

Further, the religious meetings are an occasion to meet and to discuss all kinds of topics. The groups serve more than just a religious goal, as Marisa, a CEB leader explained to me: "Most of the time we work with the *roteiro*, but when we don't have one we do it with the Bible itself. And often with ... just us meeting to chat, pray a rosary, and sing—we sing a lot because our group is very enjoyable" (August 1990).

Participation in the CEB is a break from the monotony of daily life. Women come out of their isolation in the home. In the groups the women are among equals, which creates an atmosphere of safety. Marisa explained that her "work for the church" is so important to her because the warmth and kindness she receives in the groups is good compensation for the fact that her husband never showed her any respect or affection. For Marisa the CEB is a kind of refuge. In her opinion that is the motivation for many women who participate in religious groups. At the meetings you talk and hear the everyday problems of the other women and you can establish friendship ties.

Whether the women share a liberationist reflection on a Bible text from the *roteiro* or are exposed to a testifying Charismatic, they connect the Word of God to the lives of ordinary people, of ordinary women, of themselves. They talk about the problems they have to face to keep the household going, like the lack of water in the neighborhood or the purchases that get more expensive every day. But they also talk about their children who are growing up in an environment of violence and their husbands who only criticize the way they run the household or the neighbor who is ill and needs their help. In both groups "women's problems" or at least the female points of view enter the scene in this way. Thus the women give content to the groups that corresponds to their gendered position in Colina. This may be an (extra) reason for men not to become members: what happens in the groups has less to do with their lives and situations.

Seen in this light the traditional role of women of participating in religion serves their gender needs in contemporary society. This is not to say that in the meetings a feminist consciousness arises. That would be a much too far-reaching conclusion. For many women, however, the group has served as an eye-opener; they feel "empowered" by their religious participation. For some it might be an incentive and legitimation for change, as in the case of Socorro who gained the courage to divorce her abusive husband. Her testimony clearly revealed that she had learned to defend herself since she joined the RCC. Her identity changed from that of a dependent housewife to a self-confident woman and mother.

Often the changes are less dramatic, but nevertheless important for the women. They appear most clearly in what I call "conversion stories."[15] In the explanation for their participation the women describe in religious terms how they experienced their move from "passive" Catholics to "active" believers as a profound change in their lives. All the RCC women with whom I had personal conversations related to me an important experience they had had, which convinced them of the power of the Holy Spirit. In most cases this experience was to do with healing, often of an undefined illness. But more important in their perception was that they came to true belief. For Dona Teresa, mother of seven children of whom one is involved in crime, this peace of heart she has found in the RCC keeps her going:

> Before I was a very agitated person, you know. Any trifle and I was annoyed. After I joined the Renewal I think my life changed, because my children often provoke me but I do not get preoccupied the way I used to ... Do you know why? Because we have this very great faith in God at the hour of prayer (Dona Teresa, March 1991).

Although the personal testimonies have a less prominent place in the CEB meetings, in the personal conversations with women involved in these groups they told me stories of a great turning point in their lives, which can be called "conversion stories" too. Marisa for example told me about the first time she went to a meeting of the CEB in the house of a very poor family:

> ... I don't know why, but the people liked me. And I embraced them all. These stinking women, smelling of the entrails of oxes (because they treat them) ... Then I started to like it, seeing this wonderful affection. Their kindness in the way they treated me, it seemed as if I was a goddess. So I liked it. What a beautiful thing isn't it? They treated me so well, with so much love ... And their love enchanted me and that is why I started working [in the community] (August 1990).

For Marisa it was love at first sight. After this first introduction to the CEB she became a very active member and this changed her life. Before she "only lived between the four walls" of her house and felt "nervous" because of her husband who drinks and only criticized her. Now she has learned that other people appreciate the things she does and found the strength to stand up for herself against her husband.

So in the accounts of the women of both groups the personal experience of consolation and peace in the midst of the harsh world they live in, is the main motivation for their participation. They find this consolation not only in the Word of God, but also in the sympathy of other members of the group. This helps them overcome problems in daily life and is in some cases the motor for profound changes in their lives. Within the Catholic universe of Colina the RCC and the CEBs both function as a kind of "women's group" because of the interpretation the women themselves give to these groups. In the next section I will show how this similarity in significance in the personal lives of participants has its counterpart in the religious discourses produced and reproduced in the local groups.

Gendered Interpretation of Symbols

It is not surprising that the RCC and the CEBs are so often depicted as two opposite branches of Catholicism. The ideologies these groups are based upon follow very different lines. According to liberation theology, CEBs set out from a critical reading of Bible texts to make a socio-political analysis of contemporary society. In the RCC the stress is on the personal experience of the Holy Spirit. In general this different emphasis leads observers to contrast the two groups as social (group) versus personal (individual) respectively, in much the same way as the differences between Pentecostal churches and progressive Catholicism are often described (cf. Comblin 1983, 256; Stoll 1993, 5). But how are the principal themes of the discourse of the CEBs and the RCC worked out in the local groups? In this article I will show how two central elements in the rhetoric and symbolism of the RCC and the CEBs, the "Holy Spirit" and "community" respectively, are used in the groups.

In Liberation Theology the idea of community becomes an indispensable stage in the construction of a better world and ultimately the

coming of the Kingdom of God. The poor are especially fit to form
this community because they are the chosen people. In the local
groups the community is, however, not perceived as "all the poor" but
experienced as a congregation of neighbors who pray, worship and
live together. As Dona Olívia, a long time CEB participant, explained:
"Community is the individual united, working together with others,
not wanting to do things alone. It is doing things together, communi-
cating with each other" (October 1990). Less emphasis is given to the
political project implied in the theories of liberation theology. The
religious meaning of the community is in the assembly of equals and
not in the concrete project of fighting for political and social justice.

The use of the concept of community, so central in the jargon of
progressive Catholicism, is not limited to the CEBs. The difference in
the perception of community by members of the RCC is not very
large. The words of Dona Iraci indicate that the idea of community is
a meaningful symbol for Charismatics too: "The only way this world
could become a good world is if everybody lived in a community, if
everybody lived in prayer groups, everybody participated in the
groups, these things, everything would be different" (Dona Irací,
March 1991). For Dona Iraci "community" signifies the group of wor-
shipers praying and praising together. This interpretation of "community" is not necessarily limited to her prayer group. In many cases
the word is used to designate the "community of Catholics" in general.

In the meetings of the RCC the preeminent place is taken by the
Holy Spirit, the core force for religious experience and inspiration. In
song and prayer the participants seek the experience of the Holy
Spirit. You have to "open your heart to let the light of heaven enter"
(289).[16] "You have to be prepared to feel the Holy Spirit of God, to let
him stir your heart" (528). All informants referred to this experience
in one way or another, explaining to me why the RCC is important
for them. Like Valéria, a single woman of twenty-seven, who said: "I
feel him closer to me, through these songs, these words ... we feel his
presence, Christ alive." There is a strong sense of surrender in this. At
the same time, however, it is a source of empowerment: "send your
fire, give us your power" (510). As was discussed in the previous section, this is an important experience for the women, which changes
their lives. This change brought about by the Holy Spirit is not a miracle performed upon the believing person, but a profound change in his

or her worldview and personal involvement achieved through belief and praying. In the RCC group in Colina this aspect receives much more attention than the miraculous healings or exorcism sessions that are emphasized in the media. For the persevering believer the Holy Spirit can bring a spiritual liberation from the hardships of everyday life. As one woman put it during a prayer meeting: "I would want everybody present here to feel the peace of heart that I feel and many others already feel too."

Just as the use of the concept of community is not exclusive to the CEBs, so the Holy Spirit is not an exclusive symbol of the RCC. In the CEBs it is common to ask for the help of the Holy Spirit at the beginning of a meeting or when difficult decisions have to be taken. One CEB meeting started for example as follows: "Let us sing to the "Holy Spirit" to see if it illuminates our hearts, in order to have more courage to talk. Come, come, Holy Spirit, enlighten our meeting. Come, come, Holy Spirit, enlighten our community. Come, come, Holy Spirit, enlighten the bus drivers [followed by many other categories]." Here the emphasis is not on the personal experience of the Holy Spirit, but on the inspiration it gives to the community assembled. In the CEBs it is a more general meaning that is attributed to the Holy Spirit. This interpretation, however, does not contradict its usage in the RCC.

These not-so-different interpretations of the central symbols in the discourse of the groups, can be attributed to various factors. First, both groups ground their beliefs in a common Catholic heritage. The members of the groups were already Catholics before they started participating. They fit the new discourses into their existing beliefs. Second, the influence of the priest should not be overlooked. During mass and his occasional visits to the meetings of the groups, believers are exposed to his liberation theology ideas.

Finally the gender of the members of the groups is important. The progressive discourse contains particular contradictions for women. Drogus (1990; 1992) eloquently showed that the consciousness-raising ideal of liberation theology comprises a double moral standard for women. Women are addressed with regard to their class position and not their gender position. They are encouraged to think and act as conscious citizens but at the same time it is stressed that their role in the struggle for the liberation of the poor is as wives and mothers

(Drogus 1990, 66-7). The progressive church promotes formal equality between men and women from a Christian perspective but the women's role is restricted to the private sphere (Alvarez 1990, 68-69). Women have to reconcile this discrepancy in ideas and end up interpreting the generalized symbols of the liberationist discourse in a "domestic" way. This means, for example, that in practice for the majority of the women involved in CEBs the community is restricted to their neighbors or their CEB.[17] In this way the religious symbolism expresses the tensions in gender roles (cf. Bynum 1986).

This can explain why in Colina the most powerful symbol (cf. Hackett 1993) seems to be yet another one: liberation. In "liberation" the Holy Spirit and the community are linked, it is the community of the people of God who strive for liberation. In the RCC this is explicitly an individual, a personal liberation. After singing the song *Christ pulls down the prisons, He comes to liberate us*, the leader of the prayer meeting asks: "Do you believe Jesus is the only one that liberates? Do you believe Jesus is the only one that cures? Do you believe Jesus is the only one that saves? Say alleluia! Those who believe now ask the Holy Spirit to wash our hearts" (Rosa, prayer meeting, August 1990).

For the CEBs "liberation" applies to the people of God and has the connotation of liberation from injustice. To achieve this goal the formation of a community is the first step and for many participants this already means a liberation from the chains of the household as became I explained above. The gendered interpretation of liberation becomes a personal experience in the first place. In this way, liberation is a powerful symbol to many women involved in both the RCC and the CEBs. The experience of "empowerment" so important in the lives of these women, has a religious counterpart in the symbol of liberation present in the language of both groups. Without discarding the different approaches of the lay associations, this commonality should not be overlooked too easily.

The Politics of Charity

In the discussions on the contrast between the "progressive" CEBs and the "conservative" RCC one of the hottest issues is the question of the social and political involvement of both groups. Generally it is argued that the emphasis on personal spiritual development in the RCC contradicts interest in (communitarian) social issues. Della Cava (1990, 3) called the RCC the antithesis of liberation theology, which stresses political and social consciousness. Comblin (1983, 258) argued that internationally organized movements like the RCC are indifferent to the situation in specific countries, precisely because of their global orientation. In turn, progressive Catholicism calls the laity to participate in social movements and political parties. Through the critical reading of the scripture and reflection on the conditions of life in the neighborhood or hamlet, people should develop a consciousness of social injustice and unite to fight for improvement. In Garanhuns, however, reality does not live up to these expectations. The political discourse of the progressive church has not caught on well with the women of the CEBs, while the charity-centered message of the RCC has found fertile ground in the neighborhood.

The main reason for this must be sought in cultural ideas of the different realms of society. Most members of the lay groups in Colina regard religion and politics as two separate fields that should not be mixed. During my fieldwork I several times observed mocking faces when the priest gave a sermon on the political responsibility of the people. More than once people complained to me about the mixing of politics and religion during mass. They come to mass to hear of God, not to be bothered with the misery they know only too well. This is not only true for members of the RCC but for many participants of CEBs too. As one woman explained to me: "The priest here talks about the whole neighborhood, my God, he starts up on the hill and only ends downtown."

If religion and politics are two separate fields for the ordinary mass attender, this is especially true for women. Religion is the realm for women, and politics, understood as political parties, belongs to men (Caldeira 1990, 54). As Drogus (1990, 64) put it: "She is culturally defined as excluded from the political sphere, limited to the domestic sphere." Caldeira (1990) found that women involved in social movements perceive a strong polarity between "women's talk" and "political things" and the same cultural construction seems to apply to the CEBs. Because the majority of CEB members are women, the political project of liberation theology is especially difficult to put into practice. Few women succeed in overcoming the prejudice of their family and friends towards the involvement of women in politics. More important, however, they themselves do not see a role such as this for women in the liberation of the poor. They are involved in a religious group and that is a good thing to do. Some think their group should develop more activities and feel frustrated. However, they link their failing to practical obstacles such as their husband who does not let them leave their house sufficiently or the priest who does not lend enough support.

In practice social action by the CEBs is mostly restricted to what Brazilians call *assistencialismo*, or charitable works, for example, for someone who needs a mattress or a blanket or food or medicine. In such a case the group arranges provision by everyone giving some money or asking the priest or rich people for help. If the amount of money needed is bigger, they organize a campaign. This is done when for example someone needs surgery. They then go to the radio station and ask for some broadcasting time to announce their campaign and subsequently go from door to door, asking for money. Sometimes they even organize a dance in the community center of the neighborhood.

While for the women involved in the CEBs charitable work is often disguised in a discourse about socio-political action, for the women in the Charismatic prayer group it is the main aim of their activities outside the church. Active members do what they call evangelization work in their neighborhood and often encounter families in trouble when they visit homes. In the prayer meetings participants bring these problems to the group and often it is decided to collect money to help the poor. The discourse surrounding this charitable work is articulated more clearly than in the case of the CEBs: "We seek a growing spirituality, a maturation. When we take the Word of God to homes, this makes the people grow spiritually in the faith ... At the same time we help people who are most in need, we buy them food" (Rosa, March 1991). In this way the quest for a deepening of the personal contact with God does not rule out an eye for the social injustices in society. But it is not only through the door to door evangelization that society appears in the customs of the RCC. As I showed in the preceding sections, testimonies are an important component of the prayer meetings. The testimonies are stories of personal suffering and God's help in overcoming the problem. The personal suffering of most people has a lot to do with the social injustices of Brazilian society, with unemployment, low salaries, and unhealthy conditions being the reasons for most acute experiences of despair. Although the prayer groups do not have as their goal the putting into motion a process of political consciousness-raising, for many people that I knew their involvement in the group had this side effect. The argument referred to above, that the internationality of the RCC leads to indifference to the situation in which it exists, therefore has a counter argument: it could be argued that exactly because the international and national headquarters of the RCC do not pay much attention to social and political issues, this leaves room for local initiatives. Some of the most pronounced militants in the PT (socialist party) in Garanhuns at the time of the presidential elections in 1989 were young Charismatic men.

In the day-to-day reality of the parish we must conclude that the different ideologies of the CEBs and the Charismatic prayer group lead to the same results with regard to their social activism. Both are mainly occupied with charitable works. Sometimes, however, the presumed roles of the RCC and the CEBs even seem to be turned upside down. A few months before I arrived in Garanhuns, there was a strike by the street sweepers. The strikers made a camp in the principal avenue in Garanhuns and wanted to stay there until they received the salary they deserved. In the meantime they had nothing to eat. Since I was told about this only afterwards, it is difficult to reconstruct exactly what happened, but it seems that no syndicate, political party, nor the church supported the street-sweepers, except for the RCC. The women from the prayer groups started a campaign to collect food and clothes for the strikers and, most importantly, accompanied them in the camp. The motivation was charity, but I wonder if it was not understood in political terms as well, at least as a criticism of the policy of the mayor and his staff.

Conclusion

In the literature the CEBs and the RCC are depicted as two parts of Catholicism that are complete opposites. In this article it has become clear that at the local level the difference is not so great. The explanation for this was sought in the characteristics of the members of the local groups: most of them are women. There are no significant sociological differences between the members of both groups. Several women participate in both. By participating in great numbers in the groups the women interpret the discourses and symbols in their own way, thereby giving form and meaning that are different from the significance more commonly attributed to these groups in ideological terms. Both RCC prayer groups and the CEBs become "women's groups" in a sense and the gendered interpretations of symbols and purpose of the groups make them of comparable meaning in the local Catholicism and in the lives of the women who are involved in them. Participation means a break from the daily routine within the cultural approved boundaries of religion, a "liberation" from the enclosed sphere of the household and an empowering re-interpretation of religious ideas. Through acts of charity this personal experience is made useful for the community as a whole.

Notes

1. Therefore it is surprising that in the scientific study of Pentecostalism so little attention is paid to this movement. Recent publications on Latin American Pentecostalism ignore the Catholic branch of it (e.g. the edited volume of Garrard and Stoll 1993). However, for important contributions see Benedetti 1988; Mariz and Machado 1994; Machado 1993; and this volume.
2. 'Progressive' and 'conservative' are the terms mostly used by journalists, scientists and even bishops, priests, and other pastoral agents in discussions on the policy of the (Latin American) Catholic church. Though these terms lack a clear, precise significance I use them here in a general sense, in the absence of better words.
3. The diocese of Garanhuns does not always use the term *Comunidade Eclesial de Base* in the official documents, but the emphasis on evangelization ideally leads to the formation of CEBs.
4. Father Milton was educated at the Regional Seminary of CNBB (Brazilian National Conference of Bishops) in Recife, an initiative of the well-known now retired Dom Hélder Câmara who in the 1960s and 1970s was one of the principal leaders of the Church's "option for the poor" movement. The education at this seminary was based on the ideas formulated in Liberation Theology. In September 1989 this seminary was closed as part of the measurements to gain control over the progressive church by the bishop of the Archdiocese of Olinda and Recife, Dom José Cardoso.
5. This is exactly the subject of much discussion among liberation theologians and others involved in the ideological construction of CEBs. Some would like to see the Catholic Base Communities as "being church," or otherwise re-

placing the traditional parishes. I will not engage in this discussion (see Van der Ploeg 1990; Oliveira 1990; Comblin 1987).

6. As is suggested by Froehle (in Stewart-Gambino 1992, 12) when he suggests that it is dangerous to bet on one horse in a time of declining influence of the church.

7. With reference to CEBs this was also observed by Macedo (1986, 138).

8. That explains the pragmatic attitude of Father Milton as described above. As he confided to me: "By joining them once in a while you can keep an eye on them and try to influence them."

9. In most literature on the topic a close relation between the Catholic Charismatic Renewal Movement and middle-class participation is reported. Probably this has to do with the fact that the origins of the movement are to be found in the world of universities (see Benedetti 1988, 241).

10. This was also observed in other locations. See Mariz 1994, 45.

11. But not with reports on the RCC in other parts of the world, where the movement attracts more middle-aged and older people (see Boudewijnse 1991; McGuire 1982; Roelofs 1990, 107).

12. It seems this is difficult. In 1990-91 my informants assured me that the group had various potential leaders from the neighborhood, who only needed to learn a bit more. On my return in 1994 however the group was still accompanied by women from the other groups.

13. Caldeira (1990, 48-9) made the same observation with reference to the discussions on "new" social movements.

14. Mariz (1994, 135-6) found that the emphasis on knowledge of the Bible stimulated members of religious groups to learn to read which in turn is a tool that can help people to overcome poverty.

15. My use of the word "conversion" is less specific than it would be in theological usage.

16. Numbers refer to songs in the songbook Renovação (1990).

17. Below I will show the consequences for the actions these women undertake.

References

Alvarez, Sonia E., Women's Participation in the Brazilian "People's Church": A Critical Appraisal. *Feminist Studies* 16, no. 2 (1990), 381-408.

Banck, Geert A., "Cultural Dilemmas Behind Strategy: Brazilian Neighbourhood Movements and Catholic Discourse," *The European Journal of Development Research* 2, no. 1 (1990), 65-88.

Benedetti, Luiz R., *Templo, praça, coração. A articulação do campo religioso católico.* (Ph.D. Thesis, Departamento de Sociologia, Universidade de São Paulo), 1988.

Beozzo, José O., "Indícios de uma reação conservadora. Do concílio Vaticano à eleição de João Paulo II," *Comunicações do ISER* 9, no. 39 (1990), 5-16.

Boudewijnse, Barbara, "The Development of the Charismatic Movement within the Catholic Church of Curaçao." In *Popular Power in Latin American Religions*, eds. André F. Droogers, Gerrit Huizer, and Hans Siebers. Saarbrücken/Fort Lauderdale: Breitenbach, 1991.

Bruneau, Thomas C., *The Church in Brazil. The Politics of Religion*. Austin: University of Texas Press, 1982.

Burdick, John, *Looking for God in Brazil. The Progressive Catholic Church in Urban Brazil's Religious Arena*. Berkeley: University of California Press, 1993.

Bynum, Caroline Walker, "Introduction: The Complexity of Symbols." In *Gender and Religion: On the Complexity of Symbols*, eds. Caroline Walker Bynum, Stevan Harrell and Paula Richman. Boston: Beacon Press, 1986.

Caldeira, Teresa Pires do Rio, "Women, Daily Life and Politics." In *Women and Social Change in Latin America*, ed. Elizabeth Jelin. London/Atlantic Highlands, N.J.: Zed Books (UNRISD), 1990.

Castro, Gustavo de Passo, *As Comunidades do Dom. Um estudo de CEB's no Recife*. Recife: Fundação Joaquim Nabuco/Editora Massangana, 1987.

Comblin, José, "Os 'Movimentos' e a Pastoral Latino-americana," *Revista Eclesiástica Brasileira* 43, no. 170 (1983), 227-262.

———, "Os leigos," *Comunicações do ISER* 6, no. 26 (1987), 26-38.

Csordas, Thomas J., "Oxymorons and Short-Circuits in the Re-Enchantment of the World. The Case of the Catholic Charismatic Renewal," *Etnofoor* 8, no. 1 (1995), 5-26.

Della Cava, Ralph, *The Ten-Year Crusade Towards the Third Christian Millenium: An Account of Evangelization 2000 and Lumen 2000*. New York: The Columbia University/New York University Consortium (Conference paper no. 27), 1990.

———, "Vatican Policy, 1978-1990. An Updated Overview," *Social Research* 59, no. 1 (1992), 169-199.

Drogus, Carol A., "Reconstructing the Feminine: Women in São Paulo's CEBs," *Archives de Sciences Sociales des Religiones* 71, (1990), 63-74.

———, "Popular Movements and the Limits of Political Mobilization at the Grassroots in Brazil." In *Conflict and Competition. The Latin American Church in a Changing Environment*, eds. Edward L. Cleary and Hannah Stewart-Gambino. Boulder/London: Lynne Rienner Publishers, 1992.

Garrard-Burnett, Virginia and David Stoll (eds.), *Rethinking Protestantism in Latin America*, Philadelphia, Pa.: Temple University Press, 1993.

Hackett, Rosalind I.J., "The Symbolics of Power Discourse among Contemporary Religious Groups in West Africa." In *Religious Transformations and Socio-Political Change. Eastern Europe and Latin America*, ed. Luther Martin. Berlin/New York: Mouton de Gruyter, 1993.

Hewitt, Warren E., *Base Christian Communities and Social Change in Brazil.* Lincoln/London: University of Nebraska Press, 1991.

Hoogen, Lisette van den, "The Romanization of the Brazilian Church: Women's Participation in a Religious Association in Prados, Minas Gerais," *Sociological Analysis* 51, no. 2 (1990), 171-188.

Istoé, "A nova cruzada. Os carismáticos crescem no País e se firmam como a arma católica contra os pentecostais," *Istoé*, 3 de julho (1991), 28-30.

Lernoux, Penny, *People of God. The Struggle for World Catholicism.* New York: Viking, 1989.

Lesbaupin, Ivo, "O Vaticano e a Igreja no Brasil," *Comunicações do ISER* 9, no. 39 (1990), 17-32.

Libânio, João B., "Inverno da Igreja," *Tempo e presença (Publicação do CEDI)* 12, no. 249 (1990), 29-31.

Macedo, Carmen Cinira de Andrade, *Tempo de gênesis. O povo das Comunidades Eclesiais de Base.* São Paulo: Brasiliense, 1986.

Machado, Maria das Dores Campos, *Charismatics and Pentecostals: A Comparison of Religiousness and Intra-Family Relations within the Brazilian Middle Class.* (Budapest Conference of the International Society for the Sociology of Religion), 1993.

Mariz, Cecília Loreto, *Coping with Poverty. Pentecostals and Christian Base Communities in Brazil.* Philadelphia, Pa.: Temple University Press, 1994.

Mariz, Cecília Loreto, and Maria das Dores C. Machado, "Sincretismo e trânsito religioso: comparando carismáticos e pentecostais," *Comunicações do ISER* 45, (1994), 24-34.

Oliveira, Pedro A. Ribeiro de, "CEBs: estrutura ou movimento?," *Revista Eclesiástica Brasileira* 50, no. 200 (1990), 930-940.

Ploeg, Roberto van der, "A igreja dos pobres no nordeste," *Cadernos de CEAS*, no. 132 (1991), 61-70.

Renovação Carismática Católica, *Louvemos ao Senhor.* (Livro de cânticos). São Paulo/Campinas: Edições Loyola/Distribuidora Louvemos ao Senhor Ltda, 1990.

Roelofs, Gerard, "Pinkstertaal onder rooms-katholieke charismatici: een benadering in termen van genres," *Religieuze bewegingen in Nederland* 20, (1990), 105-118.

Stewart-Gambino, Hannah, "Introduction: New Game, New Rules." In *Conflict and Competition. The Latin American Church in a Changing Environment*, eds. Edward L. Cleary and Hannah Stewart-Gambino. Boulder/London: Lynne Rienner Publishers, 1992.

Stoll, David, "Introduction: Rethinking Protestantism in Latin America." In *Rethinking Protestantism in Latin America*, eds. Virginia Garrard-Burnett and David Stoll. Philadelphia, Pa.: Temple University Press, 1993.

Veja, "Fé em desencanto. O êxode dos católicos de classe média sangra uma Igreja já enfraquecida pelo assédio das seitas evangélicas sobre os pobres," *Veja* (25 de dezembro, 1991), 32-38.

Bibliography on Pentecostalism in Latin America and the Caribbean

(including Charismatic Movements)

André Droogers

1. Only publications in English, French, German, Portuguese, and Spanish have been included.
2. Only publications *on* Pentecostalism, either by Pentecostals or by others, have been included, not Pentecostal *religious* publications.
3. Publications without an author have been included under their title instead.
4. In the case of anthologies, the book and the individual articles (if of interest) have both been included. After the book's title, individual authors are noted.
5. It was not possible to consult all the titles mentioned. Several of them have been taken from secondary sources. In some cases, the data are incomplete.

6. If Spanish or Portuguese authors have double names, the first name has been included alphabetically.
7. If the title does not provide enough information on the region or topic, if possible it has been added between brackets.
8. The present bibliography is based on the one published in "Algo Mas Que Opio" and has been updated till December 1995.
9. Jean-Pierre Bastian, Mark Droogers, Alejandro Frigerio, Manuel J. Gaxiola-Gaxiola, Roswith Gerloff, Bernardo Guerrero, Walter Hollenweger, Cornelis van der Laan, Paul van der Laan, Jorge Laffitte, Daniel Miguez, Luis Samandú, Marjo de Theije, and Jacob Uitermark have contributed in one way or another to the preparation of this bibliography. I am grateful for their help.

A

ABD-EL-JALI, R.P., et al. (eds.), 1956, L'EGLISE, L'OCCIDENT, LE MONDE. Paris: Arthème Fayard. [Cf. Gaete 1956]
ADAMS, Richard N., 1983, CONSERVATIVE EVANGELISM IN LATIN AMERICA. Royal Anthropological Institute News 59, 2-4.
A fé..., 1990, A FÉ QUE MOVE MULTIDÕES AVANÇA NO PAÍS. AS SEITAS EVANGÉLICAS MULTIPLICAM OS FIÉS E ARMAM SEU LANCE MAIS OUSADO: A CONQUISTA DA TELEVISÃO E DO RÁDIO. Veja, 16 de maio, pp. 46-52.
A fé..., 1990, A FÉ NOS MILHÕES. COM UM ESTILO DE ANIMADOR DE AUDITÓRIO, EDIR MACEDO LOTA ESTÁDIOS E SE TORNA O MAIS POPULAR DOS PASTORES. Veja, 17 de outubro, pp. 52-53.
ALBAN ESTRADA, María; MUÑOZ, Juan Pablo, 1987, CON DIOS TODO SE PUEDE, LA INVASION DE LAS SECTAS AL ECUADOR. Quito: Planeta, Colección Espejo del Ecuador 1.
ALBO, Xavier, 1988, ¡OXFADIFA, OFAIFA! UN PENTECOSTES CHIRIGUANO. América Indígena, 48, 1: 63-125. [Mexico]
ALEXANDER, Bobby C., 1989, PENTECOSTAL RITUAL RECONSIDERED: "ANTI-STRUCTURAL" DIMENSIONS OF POSSESSION. Journal of Ritual Studies 3, 1.
ALISEDO, Pedro, et al., 1981, EL INSTITUTO LINGUISTICO DE VERANO. Mexico: Proceso.
ALMEIDA, Abraão de (ed.), 1982, HISTORIA DAS ASSEMBLEIAS DE DEUS NO BRASIL. Rio de Janeiro: CEPAD Casa Publicadora das Assembléias de Deus.
Alternativas..., 1991, ALTERNATIVAS DOS DESESPERADOS: COMO SE PODE LER O PENTECOSTALISMO AUTONOMO. Rio de Janeiro: CEDI.
ALVAREZ, Carmelo, 1985a, EL MOVIMIENTO DE SANTIDAD Y EL SURGIMIENTO DE LOS PENTECOSTALES. In: Sepulveda 1985: 15-19. [Chile]
ALVAREZ, Carmelo, 1985b, DISTINTIVOS TEOLOGICOS PENTECOSTALES. In: Sepulveda 1985: 139-143. [Chile]

ALVAREZ, C.E., 1988, LOS PENTECOSTALES EN AMERICA LATINA ECUM-
ENICOS EVANGELICOS. Pasos 18, 2: 1-4.
ALVAREZ, Carmelo, 1990a, LAS IGLESIAS PROTESTANTES EN LA PRESENTE
COYUNTURA. Pasos no. 29.
ALVAREZ, Carmelo, 1990b, LATIN AMERICAN PENTECOSTALS: ECUMENI-
CAL AND EVANGELICAL. Pneuma (The Journal of the Society for Pentecostal
Studies) 9, 1, 91-95.
ALVAREZ, Carmelo, et al., 1988, IGLESIA PENTECOSTAL DE CHILE: HIS-
TORIA Y PRESENCIA. Version preliminar. Santiago de Chile: Centro Ecume-
nico Diego de Medellin.
ALVAREZ, Carmelo et al., 1990, HISTORIA DE LA IGLESIA PENTECOSTAL DE
CHILE. Santiago: Rehue Ediciones.
ALVAREZ, Carmelo E. (ed.), 1992, PENTECOSTALISMO Y LIBERACION, UNA
EXPERIENCIA LATINOAMERICANA. San José, Costa Rica: CEPLA/DEI.
[Cf. Alvarez 1992, Cabezas 1992, Castillo 1992, Chavarría 1992, Gonzalez 1992,
Lugo, Gamaliel 1992, Pilco 1992, Sepúlveda, Juan 1992, Sepúlveda, Narciso 1992ab,
Silva and Stevannatto 1992, Vaccaro 1992]
ALVAREZ, Carmelo E. 1992, LO POPULAR: CLAVE HERMENEUTICA DEL
MOVIMIENTO PENTECOSTAL. In: Alvarez 1992: 89-100.
ALVES, Rubem A., 1979, PROTESTANTISMO E REPRESSÃO. São Paulo: Editora
Ática. [See also Alves 1985]
ALVES, Rubem A., 1984, A EMPRESA DA CURA DIVINA: UM FENOMENO
RELIGIOSO? In: Valle y Queiróz 1984: 11-117. [Brazil, see also Teixeira Monteiro
1984]
ALVES, Rubem Azevedo, 1985, PROTESTANTISM AND REPRESSION: A BRA-
ZILIAN CASE STUDY. London: SCM Press.
AMAN, Kenneth, 1987, FIGHTING FOR GOD: THE MILITARY AND RELI-
GION IN CHILE. Cross Currents 36: 459-66.
AMATULLI-VALENTE, Flaviano, 1987, EL PROTESTANTISMO EN MEXICO:
HECHOS, INTERROGANTES Y RETOS. México, D.F.: Apóstolos de la Pala-
bra.
AMAGEIRAS, Aldo, 1991, ESTRATEGIAS PROSELITISTAS: PRACTICAS DE
RECLUTAMIENTO Y VIDA COTIDIANO EN ORGANIZACIONES RELI-
GIOSAS DEL CONURBANO BONAERENSE. Sociedad y Religión 8, 24-40.
AMERICAS WATCH, 1982, GUATEMALA: MASSIVE EXTRAJUDICIAL EXE-
CUTIONS IN RURAL AREAS UNDER THE GOVERNMENT OF GEN-
ERAL EFRAIN RIOS-MONTT. New York: Americas Watch.
ANDERSON, Robert Mapes, 1979, VISION OF THE DESINHERITED: THE MAK-
ING OF MODERN PENTECOSTALISM. New York: Oxford University Press.
ANFUSO, Joseph; SCZEPANSKI, David, 1985, RIOS-MONTT: SERVANT OR
DICTATOR. Ventura, Calif.: Regal Books.
ANFUSO, Joseph; SCZEPANSKI, David, 1986, SIERVO O DICTADOR: DIOS
DA... DIOS QUITA. Barcelona: Ediciones Sa-Ber.
ANNIS, Sheldon, 1987, GOD AND PRODUCTION IN A GUATEMALAN
TOWN. Austin: University of Texas Press.
ANTONIAZZI, Alberto, 1994a, A IGREJA CATOLICA FACE A EXPANSãO DO
PENTECOSTALISMO. In: Antoniazzi 1994b: 17-23.

ANTONIAZZI, Alberto et al., 1994b, NEM ANJOS NEM DEMONIOS, INTER-PRETAÇÕES SOCIOLOGICAS DO PENTECOSTALISMO. Petrópolis: Vozes.

ANTONIO, W. d', and PIKE, F. (eds.), 1964, RELIGION, REVOLUTION AND REFORM. New York. [Cf. Willems 1964]

APARICIO, James, 1985, LAS NUEVAS TRIBUS. OTRO INSTITUTO LINGUIST-ICO DE VERANO? Diálogo Social 18, 174: 48-49.

ARAUJO, Véronique Boyer, 1995, "MACUMBEIRAS" E "CRENTES": AS MUL-HERES VEEM OS HOMENS. Horizontes Antropológicos (UFRGS, Porto Alegre, Brazil) 1, 131-140.

ARLT, Augusto E. Fernandez, 1962, THE SIGNIFICANCE OF THE CHILEAN PENTECOSTALS' ADMISSION TO THE WORLD COUNCIL OF CHUR-CHES. The International Review of Missions 51: 480-482.

ARMSTRONG, Robert G., 1983, REPLY TO JONATHAN BENTHALL. Royal Anthropological Institute News 55, 13. [Cf. Benthall 1982, SIL]

ASSERETO, Maria Josefina Amerlinck y, 1970, IXMIQUILPAN: UN ESTUDIO COMPARATIVO DE EVANGELISTAS Y CATOLICOS. Mexico D.F.: Universidad Iberoaméricana, Escuela de Antropologia Social. Thesis.

ASSMANN, Hugo, 1986, A IGREJA ELETRONICA E SEU IMPACTO NA AMER-ICA LATINA, CONVITE A UM ESTUDO. Petrópolis: Vozes & WACC/ALC.

ASSMANN, Hugo, 1987, LA IGLESIA ELECTRONICA Y SU IMPACTO EN AMERICA LATINA. San José, Costa Rica: DEI.

ASSMANN, Hugo, 1989, A IGREJA ELETRôNICA. In: Landim 1989c: 65-73.

AUBREE, Marion, 1984, LES NOUVELLES TRIBUS DE LA CHRETIENTE. Raison Présente 72: 71-87.

AULIE, Henry W., 1979, THE CHRISTIAN MOVEMENT AMONG THE CHOLS OF MEXICO, WITH SPECIAL REFERENCE TO PROBLEMS OF SECOND GENERATION CHRISTIANITY. Pasadena, Calif.: Fuller Theological Seminary. Ph.D.

AUSTIN, Diane J., 1981, BORN AGAIN... AND AGAIN AND AGAIN: COMMU-NITAS AND SOCIAL CHANGE AMONG JAMAICAN PENTECOSTAL-ISTS. Journal of Anthropological Research 37, 3: 226-246.

AVALES DE CAVILLA, Ana María, 1982, SE REABRE DEBATE SOBRE MISION NEW TRIBES EN VENEZUELA. Noticias Aliadas 1, abril: 7,8.

AVILA, M. Buse de, 1985, PARA REFLEXIONAR SOBRE LAS SECTAS. Cajamarca: Publicaciones del Obispado. [Peru]

AVINA, Jeff, 1985, EVANGELICAL REVIVAL SWEEPS BRAZIL. Latinamerica Press 17: 6.

B

BACCHETTA, Vittorio, 1985, BRAZIL'S DIVERSE PROTESTANT GROUPS UNITED IN CONSERVATIVE SOCIAL ROLE. Latinamerica Press 17, 45: 5-6.

BAEZ-CAMARGO, G., 1957-58, PROTESTANTS IN LATIN AMERICA: 2. MEX-ICO. Religion in Life 27: 35-44.

BAIRD, Harry Russell, 1979, AN ANALYTICAL HISTORY OF THE CHURCH OF CHRIST MISSIONS IN BRAZIL. Pasadena, Calif.: Fuller Theological Seminary. Ph.D.

BAKLANOFF, E.N. (ed.), 1966, NEW PERSPECTIVES OF BRAZIL. Nashville, Tenn.: Vanderbilt University Press. [Cf. Willems 1966]

BAMAT, Tomás, 1986, ¿SALVACION O DOMINACION?: LAS SECTAS RELIGI-OSAS EN EL ECUADOR. Quito: Editorial El Conejo.

BAMAT, Tomás, 1986, HISTORIC ECUMENICAL MEETING STUDIES GROWTH OF REGION'S RELIGIOUS SECTS. Latinamerica Press 18, 45: 3,4,8.

BARBOSA, Marcos Aurélio de Souza, 1985, A EXPERIENCIA DO ESPIRITO SANTO: O PENTECOSTALISMO NO BRASIL. In: Imagens... 1985: 60-71.

BARBOSA, Roberto, 1974, BREAD AND GOSPEL: AFFIRMING A TOTAL FAITH—AN INTERVIEW WITH BRAZILIAN PENTECOSTALIST MA-NOEL DE MELLO. The Christian Century, Dec. 25, 1974: 1223-1226. [Igreja Pentecostal O Brasil Para Cristo]

BARRETO, Adalberto, 1990a, O PERIGO DO EXORCISMO. Texto uso interno da Disciplina de Medicina Social do Depto. Saude Comunitária. Fortaleza: Universi-dade Federal de Ceará.

BARRETO, Adalberto, 1990b, SEQUESTRO DE ALMAS. Jornal do Povo (Fortaleza - Ceará), dia 1/10/1990.

BARRETO, Adalberto, n.d., PRONTO SOCORRO DO REINO DE DEUS. Mimeo. Fortaleza: Author's edition.

BARRETO, Adalberto, n.d., O REINO DE SATANAS I. Mimeo. Fortaleza: Author's edition.

BARRETT, David B. (ed.), 1982, WORLD CHRISTIAN ENCYCLOPEDIA: A COMPARATIVE SURVEY OF CHURCHES AND RELIGIONS IN THE MODERN WORLD, A.D. 1900-2000. Oxford etc.: Oxford University Press.

BARRETT, David B., 1988, THE TWENTIETH-CENTURY PENTECOSTAL/ CHARISMATIC RENEWAL IN THE HOLY SPIRIT, WITH ITS GOAL OF WORLD EVANGELIZATION. International Bulletin of Missionary Research 12, 3: 119-129.

BARTOLOME, L., 1971, MILLENARIAN ACTIVITIES AMONG INDIANS OF THE ARGENTINE CHACO FROM 1905 TO 1933. Buenos Aires. [Argentina, unpublished]

BASTIAN, Jean-Pierre, 1978, EL PROTESTANTISMO LATINOAMERICANO EN BUSQUEDA DE SU IDENTIDAD Y FUTURO. Estudios Ecuménicos 34: 35-42.

BASTIAN, Jean-Pierre, 1979, PROTESTANTISMO Y POLITICA EN MEXICO. Taller de Teología, 5: 7-23.

BASTIAN, Jean-Pierre, 1981, GUERRA FRIA, CRISIS DEL PROJECTO LIBERAL Y ATOMIZACION DE LOS PROTESTANTISMOS LATINO-AMERICANOS 1949-1959. Cristianismo y Sociedad, 92, 2: 7-12.

BASTIAN, Jean-Pierre, 1981, PROTESTANTISMO Y POLITICA EN MEXICO. Revista Mexicana de Sociología, 431: 1947-1966.

BASTIAN, Jean-Pierre, 1982, PROTESTANTISMOS MINORITARIOS Y PRESEN-TATARIOS EN MEXICO. Actas del II Simposio sobre religión popular e identi-dad. México D.C.: UNAM.

BASTIAN, Jean-Pierre, 1983, PROTESTANTISMO Y SOCIEDAD EN MEXICO. México: Casa Unida de Publicaciones.

BASTIAN, Jean-Pierre, 1984, PROTESTANTISMOS LATINOAMERICANOS ENTRE LA RESISTENCIA Y LA SUMISION 1961-1983. Cristianismo y Sociedad 82: 49-68.

BASTIAN, Jean-Pierre, 1985, DISIDENCIA RELIGIOSA EN EL CAMPO MEXICANO. In: De la Rosa and Reily, pp. 177-192.

BASTIAN, Jean-Pierre, 1985, DISSIDENCE RELIGIEUSE DANS LE MILIEU RURAL MEXICAIN. Social Compass 32, 2-3: 245-260.

BASTIAN, Jean-Pierre, 1985, PARA UNA APROXIMACION TEORICA DEL FENOMENO RELIGIOSO PROTESTANTE EN AMERICA CENTRAL. Cristianismo y Sociedad 85: 61-68.

BASTIAN, Jean-Pierre, 1986, BREVE HISTORIA DEL PROTESTANTISMO EN AMERICA LATINA. México: Casa Unida de Publicaciones.

BASTIAN, Jean-Pierre, 1986, PROTESTANTISMO POPULAR Y POLITICA EN GUATEMALA Y NICARAGUA. Revista Mexicana de Sociología 48, 3: 181-200.

BASTIAN, Jean-Pierre, 1986, DISIDENCIA RELIGIOSA PROTESTANTE E IMPERIALISMO EN MEXICO. In: Concha Malo, pp. 293-308.

BASTIAN, Jean-Pierre, 1986, RELIGION POPULAR PROTESTANTE Y COMPORTAMIENTO POLITICO EN AMERICA CENTRAL. Cristianismo y Sociedad 88.

BASTIAN, Jean-Pierre, 1987, MODELOS DE MUJER PROTESTANTE: IDEOLOGIA RELIGIOSA Y EDUCACION FEMININA, 1889-1910. In: Presencia ..., pp. 163-180.

BASTIAN, Jean-Pierre, 1988a, EL PARADIGMA DE 1789, SOCIEDADES DE IDEAS Y REVOLUCION MEXICANA. Historia Mexicana 1: 79-110.

BASTIAN, Jean-Pierre, 1988b, LAS SOCIEDADES PROTESTANTES Y LA OPOSICION A PORFIRIO DIAZ 1877-1911. Historia Mexicana 3: 469-512.

BASTIAN, Jean-Pierre, 1988c, PROTESTANTISMO E ESTADO NA NICARAGUA E NA GUATEMALA: RELAÇÃO DE CLIENTELA. Estudos de Religião (São Paulo) 5, 9-23.

BASTIAN, Jean-Pierre, 1989, LOS DISIDENTES, SOCIEDADES PROTESTANTES Y REVOLUCION EN MEXICO 1872-1911. México: El Colegio de México-Fondo de Cultura Económica.

BASTIAN, Jean-Pierre, 1991a, LA MUTACION DEL PROTESTANTISMO LATINOAMERICANO: UNA PERSPECTIVA SOCIO-HISTORICA. Teología en Comunidad (Santiago de Chile), no. 6/7.

BASTIAN, Jean-Pierre, 1991b, LA FRACTURE CONTINUEE: AMERIQUE LATINE—AMERIQUE DU NORD, DEUX VERSIONS DU CHRISTIANISME. Lumière et Vie 208.

BASTIAN, Jean-Pierre, 1992, LES PROTESTANTISMES LATINO-AMERICAINS: UN OBJET A INTERROGER ET A CONSTRUIRE. Social Compass 39, 3: 327-356.

BASTIDE, Roger, 1971, NICHT-KATHOLISCHE RELIGIONEN IN BRASILIEN. Internationales Jahrbuch für Religionssoziologie 1971: 83-98.

BAUTZ, Wolfgang, Noel GONZALEZ, and Javier OROZCO, 1994, POLITICA Y RELIGION: ESTUDIO DE CASE: LOS EVANGELICOS EN NICARAGUA. Managua, Nicaragua: CIEETS.

Behind..., 1985, BEHIND THE HEADLINES, COLOMBIA IS WITNESSING A MAJOR RELIGIOUS REVIVAL. Christianity Today 29, 13: 40.

BELLI, Humberto, n.d., NICARAGUA: CHRISTIANS UNDER FIRE. San José, Costa Rica; Garden City, Mich.: Puebla Institute.

BENTHALL, Jonathan, 1982, THE SUMMER INSTITUTE OF LINGUISTICS. Royal Anthropological Institute News 53: 1-5. [Cf. Armstrong 1983]

BENZ, Ernst, 1970, DER HEILIGE GEIST IN AMERIKA. Düsseldorf, Köln: Eugen Diedericks Verlag. [Puerto Rico]

BERBERIAN, Samuel, 1980, MOVIMIENTO CARISMATICO EN LATINOAMERICA 1960-1980. Mariano Gálvez University. M.A. Thesis.

BERBERIAN, Samuel, 1983, TWO DECADES OF RENEWAL: A STUDY OF THE CHARISMATIC RENEWAL IN LATIN AMERICA, 1960-1980. Guatemala: Ediciones Saber.

BERG, Daniel, 1955, ENVIADO POR DEUS, MEMORIAS DE DANIEL BERG. São Paulo: Assembléias de Deus. [Brazil, Assembléias de Deus]

BERNALES, Andrés Opazo, 1987, LA IGLESIA Y EL PUEBLO COMO SUJETO POLITICO. Polémica (S. José, Costa Rica) 3: 2-14.

BERNALES, Andrés Opazo, 1991, EL MOVIMIENTO PROTESTANTE EN CENTROAMERICA. UNA APROXIMACION CUANTITATIVA. In: Samandu 1991a: 11-65.

BERNARD, H. Russell, 1985, THE POWER OF PRINT: THE ROLE OF LITERACY IN PRESERVING NATIVE CULTURES. Human Organization 44, 1: 88-93. [SIL]

BERRYMAN, Phillip, 1984, THE RELIGIOUS ROOTS OF REBELLION: CHRISTIANS IN CENTRAL AMERICAN REVOLUTIONS. Maryknoll, N.Y.: Orbis.

BIESKE, Sigifredo, n.d., EL EXPLOSIVO CRECIMIENTO DE LA IGLESIA EVANGELICA EN COSTA RICA. San José, Costa Rica: EDUCA.

BIRDWELL-PHEASANT, Donna, 1980, THE POWER OF PENTECOSTALISM IN A BELIZEAN VILLAGE. In: Glazier 1980: 95-109.

BISNAUTH, Dale A., 1988, PENTECOSTAL MOVEMENT VALID. Caribbean Contact, February 1988, 12.

BITTENCOURT, José, 1985, A MEMORIA É SEMPRE SUBVERSIVA: AS ASSEMBLEIAS DE DEUS NO CONTEXTO BRASILEIRO. In: Imagens... 1985: 32-37.

BITTENCOURT, José, 1989, AS SEITAS NO CONTEXTO DO PROTESTANTISMO HISTÓRICO. In: Landim 1989a: 27-32. [Brazil]

BITTENCOURT, José, 1994, REMEDIO AMARGO. In: Antoniazzi 1994b: 24-33.

BLOCH-HOELL, Nils, 1964, THE PENTECOST MOVEMENT: ITS ORIGIN, DEVELOPMENT, AND DISTINCTIVE CHARACTER. Oslo/London: Universitetsforlaget/Allen & Unwin.

BOBSIN, Oneide, 1984, PRODUÇAO RELIGIOSA E SIGNIFICAÇAO SOCIAL DO PENTECOSTALISMO A PARTIR DE SUA PRATICA E REPRESENTAÇAO. São Paulo: Pontífica Universidade Católica de São Paulo. [Brazil, M.A. Thesis]

BOBSIN, Oneide, 1995, TEOLOGIA DA PROSPERIDADE OU ESTRATEGIA DE SOBREVIVENCIA. Estudos Teológicos (São Leopoldo RS) 35, 1, 21-38.

BOMBART, J.P., 1969, LES CULTES PROTESTANTS DANS UNE FAVELA DE RIO DE JANEIRO. América Latina (Rio de Janeiro) 12, 3: 137-156.

BONILLA, P., s.f., CRISIS DEL PROTESTANTISMO COSTARRICENSE ACTUAL. Pastoralia 18: 65-128.

BORGES COSTAS, Esdras, 1968, RELIGIÃO E DESENVOLVIMENTO ECONOMICO NO NORDESTE DO BRASIL (IGREJAS PROTESTANTES). Brussels (The Hague: ISS, Leuven: Feres).

BORGES COSTAS, Esdras , 1969, PROTESTANTISME ET DEVELOPPEMENT AU NORD-EST DU BRESIL. Social Compass 16, 1: 51-61.

BOTTASSO, Juan, 1984, LAS MISIONES PROTESTANTES Y LA ACUL-TURACION DE LOS SHUAR. América Indígena 44, 1: 143-156.

BOUDEWIJNSE, Barbara, André DROOGERS, and Frans KAMSTEEG (eds.), 1991, ALGO MAS QUE OPIO, UNA LECTURA ANTROPOLOGICA DEL PEN-TECOSTALISMO LATINOAMERICANO Y CARIBEÑO. San José, Costa Rica: DEI.

BOURGUIGNON, Erika (ed.), 1973, RELIGION, ALTERED STATES OF CON-SCIOUSNESS AND SOCIAL CHANGE. Columbus: Ohio State University Press. [Goff 1973]

BOYER-ARAÚJO, Véronique, 1995, "MACUMBEIRAS" E "CRENTES": AS MULHERES VÊEM OS HOMENS. Horizontes Antropológicos (UFRGS, Porto Alegre), 1, 1: 131-140.

BRAGA, J. (ed.), 1990, RELIGIAO E CIDADANIA. Salvador: OEA, UFBA, EGBA.

BRANDÃO, Carlos Rodrigues, 1980, OS DEUSES DO POVO, UM ESTUDO SOBRE A RELIGIÃO POPULAR. São Paulo: Brasiliense. [Brazil]

BRANDÃO, Carlos Rodrigues, 1992, CRENÇA E IDENTIDADE, CAMPO RELIGIOSO E MUDANÇA CULTURAL. In: Pierre Sanchis (ed.), CATO-LICISMO: UNIDADE RELIGIOSA E PLURALISMO CULTURAL. Cato-licismo no Brasil atual, vol. 3. Rio de Janeiro / São Paulo: ISER / Edições Loyola, pp.7-74.

BRANDT-BESSIRE, Daniel, 1988, AUX SOURCES DE LA SPIRITUALITÉ PENTE-COTISTE. Paris: Labor et Fides.

BRECKENRIDGE, David C., 1951, PENTECOSTAL PROGRESS IN CHILE. World Dominion 29: 295-298.

BRIDGES, Julian C., 1973, EXPANSION EVANGELICA EN MEXICO. Madrid, Miami: Editorial Mundo Hispano.

BRIDGES, Julian C., 1980, EVANGELICAL EXPANSION IN MEXICO: A STUDY OF THE NUMBER, DISTRIBUTION, AND GROWTH OF THE PROTES-TANT POPULATION, 1957-1970. In: Brown and Cooper 1980: 150-168.

BRINKERHOFF, Merlin B.; BIBBY, Reginald W., 1985, CIRCULATION OF THE SAINTS IN SOUTH AMERICA: A COMPARATIVE STUDY. Journal for the Scientific Study of Religion 24, 1: 39-55.

BROWN, Lyle C.; COOPER, William F. (eds.), 1980, RELIGION IN LATIN AMER-ICAN LIFE AND LITERATURE. Waco, Tex.: Markham Press Fund. [Cf. Bridges 1980]

BROWN, Oral Carl, 1972, HAITIAN VODOU IN RELATION TO NEGRITUDE AND CHRISTIANITY: A STUDY IN ACCULTURATION AND APPLIED ANTHROPOLOGY. Indiana University, Anthropology Department. [Ph.D.]

BRUMBACK, Carl, 1961, SUDDENLY ... FROM HEAVEN: A HISTORY OF THE ASSEMBLIES OF GOD. Springfield, Miss.: Gospel Publishing House.

BRUSCO, Elisabeth, 1986a, THE HOUSEHOLD BASIS OF EVANGELICAL RELI-GION AND THE REFORMATION OF MACHISMO IN COLOMBIA. Ann Arbor, Mich.: University Microfilms. [Ph.D., City University of New York]

BRUSCO, Elizabeth, 1986b, COLOMBIAN EVANGELICALISM AS A STRATE-GIC FORM OF WOMEN'S COLLECTIVE ACTION. Feminist Issues 6, 2: 1-13.

BRUSCO, Elizabeth E., 1993, THE REFORMATION OF MACHISMO: ASCETISM AND MASCULINITY AMONG COLOMBIAN EVANGELICALS. In: Garrard-Burnett and Stoll 1993: 143-158.

BRUSCO, Elizabeth E., 1995, THE REFORMATION OF MACHISMO. EVAN-GELICAL CONVERSION AND GENDER IN COLOMBIA. Austin: University of Texas Press.

BURCHARDT, Gabriele, 1986, "SEKTEN SIND UNBEGLICHENE RECH-NUNGEN DER KIRCHE". ZUM PHAENOMEN "NEUER RELIGIöSER BE-WEGUNGEN" IN LATEINAMERIKA. Herder Korrespondenz 40, 3: 124-128.

BURDICK, John, 1990, GOSSIP AND SECRECY: WOMEN'S ARTICULATION OF DOMESTIC CONFLICT IN THREE RELIGIONS OF URBAN BRAZIL. Sociological Analysis 51: 153-170.

BURDICK, John, 1992, RETHINKING THE STUDY OF SOCIAL MOVEMENTS: THE CASE OF CHRISTIAN BASE COMMUNITIES IN URBAN BRAZIL. In: Escobar and Alvarez 1992: 171-184. [Comparison with Pentecostals]

BURDICK, John, 1993a, LOOKING FOR GOD IN BRAZIL. THE PROGRESSIVE CATHOLIC CHURCH IN URBAN BRAZIL'S RELIGIOUS ARENA. Berkeley: University of California Press. [Chapter 7 on Pentecostals]

BURDICK, John, 1993b, STRUGGLING AGAINST THE DEVIL: PENTECOST-ALISM AND SOCIAL MOVEMENTS IN URBAN BRAZIL. In: Garrard-Burnett and Stoll 1993: 20-44.

BURNETT, Virginia G., 1986, A HISTORY OF PROTESTANTISM IN GUATE-MALA. Tulane University. [Ph.D.]

BUSWELL, James O., 1981, SURVIVAL INTERNATIONAL AND THE MISSION-ARY IMAGE: A CRITIQUE AND EXHORTATION. [Unpublished]

BUTLER FLORA, Cornelia, 1973, SOCIAL DISLOCATION AND PENTE-COSTALISM, A MULTIVARIATE ANALYSIS. Sociological Analysis 34, 4: 296-305.

BUTLER FLORA, Cornelia, 1975, PENTECOSTAL WOMAN IN COLOMBIA RELIGIOUS CHANGE AND THE STATUS OF WORKING-CLASS WOM-AN. Journal of Interamerican Studies and World Affairs 17, 4: 411-425.

BUTLER FLORA, Cornelia , 1976,1978, PENTECOSTALISM IN COLOMBIA: BAPTISM BY FIRE AND SPIRIT. Rutherford N.J.: Fairleigh Dickinson University Press (1976); Cranbury N.J.: Associated University Presses (1978).

BUTLER FLORA, Cornelia 1980, PENTECOSTALISM AND DEVELOPMENT: THE COLOMBIAN CASE. In: Glazier 1980: 81-93.

C

CABESTRERO, Teofilo, 1983, MINISTERS OF GOD, MINISTERS OF THE PEO-PLE: TESTIMONIES OF FAITH FROM NICARAGUA. Maryknoll, N.Y.: Orbis.

CABEZAS, Roger, 1991, THE EXPERIENCE OF THE LATIN AMERICAN PEN-TECOSTAL ENCUENTRO. Pneuma (The Journal of the Society for the Study of Pentecostalism) 13, 2, 175-188.

CABEZAS, Roger, 1992, LOS DONES DEL ESPIRITU SANTO: EDIFICANDO EL CUERPO. In: Alvarez 1992: 155-177.

CABRAL, Joal, 1982, RELIGIONES, SECTAS Y HEREJIAS. Editorial Vida.

CALDERON B., Moisés A., n.d., HISTORIA DE LA IGLESIA EVANGELICA APOSTOLICA DEL NOMBRE DE JESUS EN EL ECUADOR. Quito: Author's edition.

CAMARGO, Cândido Procópio Ferreira de, et al., 1973, CATOLICOS, PROTESTANTES, ESPIRITAS. Petrópolis: Vozes. [Brazil, Cf. Muniz de Sousa 1973]

CAMPBELL, Joseph E., 1951, THE PENTECOSTAL HOLINESS CHURCH 1898-1948. Franklin Springs, Ga.: Pentecostal Holiness Church.

CAMPICHE, Roland J., 1987, SECTAS Y NUEVOS MOVIMIENTOS RELIGIOSOS: DIVERGENCIAS Y CONVERGENCIAS. Cristianismo y Sociedad 93, 3, 9-20.

CAMPOS, Alvaro; RODRIGUEZ, Mario, 1986, RELIGION Y IDEOLOGIA: ANALISIS PSICOSOCIAL DE TRES DENOMINACIONES PENTECOSTALES DEL AREA METROPOLITANA, SAN JOSÉ. [M.A. Thesis, Universidad de Costa Rica]

CAMPOS, Leonildo Silveira, 1982, O MILAGRE NO AR - PERSUASaõ A SERVIÇO DE QUEM? LEVANTAMENTO DE TECNICAS PERSUASIVAS NUM PROGRAMA RADIOFONICO EM SAÕ PAULO. Simpósio (ASTE): 26: 92-114. [Brazil]

CAMPOS, Renato Carneiro, 1967, IGREJA, POLÍTICA E REGIÃO. Recife: Instituto Joaquim Nabuco de Pesquisas Sociais - MEC.

CANALES, Manuel et al., 1987, LA SUBJETIVIDAD POPULAR, LA RELIGION DE LOS SECTORES POPULARES: EL CAMPO PENTECOSTAL. Santiago: SEPADE.

CANALES, Manuel et al., 1991, EN TIERRA EXTRANA II, PARA UNA SOCIOLOGIA DE LA RELIGIOSIDAD POPULAR PROTESTANTE. Santiago: SEPADE, Amerindia. [See also En tierra... 1988]

CARDENAS, Gonzalo Castillo, 1964, EL CRISTIANISMO EVANGELICO EN LA AMERICA LATINA. Cristianismo y Sociedad 2: 61-65.

CARDENAS, Gonzalo Castillo, 1964, PROTESTANT CHRISTIANITY IN LATIN AMERICA: AN INTERPRETATION OF TODAY'S SITUATION. Student World 57, 1: 61-66.

CARDIEL CORONEL, José Cuauhtémoc, 1983, CAMBIO SOCIAL Y DOMINACION IDEOLOGICA: 43 AÑOS DE EVANGELIZCION DEL ILV EN LA ZONA CHOL DE TUMBALA. [M.A.Thesis, Universidad Autónoma Metropolitana-Iztapalapa, México]

CARDOSO, Onésimo de Oliveira, 1984, A IGREJA ELETRONICA - OS PROGRAMAS RELIGIOSOS NA TELEVISÃO BRASILEIRA. Comunicação e Sociedade 6, 12, 5-28.

CARRASCO MALHUE, Pedro , 1982, SACERDOTE, PROFETA Y BRUJO, LA CONFIRMACION DEL CAMPO RELIGIOSO EN UN PUEBLO DEL ESTADO DE OAXACA, MEXICO. Taller de Teología, 10: 19-39.

CARRASCO MALHUE, Pedro, 1983, PROTESTANTISMO Y CAMPO RELIGIOSO EN UN PUEBLO DEL ESTADO DE OAXACA, MEXICO. México D.F.: Instituto Internacional de Estudios Superiores. [M.A. Thesis]

CARRASCO MALHUE, Pedro, 1988, ¿CONVERTIR PARA NO TRANSFORMAR? Cristianismo y Sociedad 95, 1, 7-50.

CARILLO ALDAY, Salvador, 1973, RENOVACION CRISTIANA EN EL ESPIRITU SANTO. México: Instituto de Sagrada Escritura.

CARRILLO ORTIZ, Mario, s.f., LA IGLESIA EVANGELICA EN GUATEMALA. Polémica 9.

CARRION, Mario, 1986, FUGITIVO DE LA TIERRA PROMETIDA. Pueblo Indio (Edición Tawantinsuyu) 2, 8: 28-29.

CAROZZI, María Julia, 1993a, CONTRIBUCIONES DEL ESTUDIO DE LOS NUEVOS MOVIMIENTOS RELIGIOSOS A LA SOCIOLOGIA DE LA RELIGION: UNA EVALUACION CRITICA. In: Frigerio 1993, I: 15-45.

CAROZZI, María Julia, 1993b, TENDENCIAS EN EL ESTUDIO DE LOS NUEVOS MOVIMIENTOS RELIGIOSOS EN LOS MEDIOS DE COMUNICACIóN EN ARGENTINA. Sociedad y Religión, 10/11: 3-23.

CARVALHO SOARES, Mariza de, 1989, GUERRA SANTA NO PAÍS DO SINCRETISMO. In: Landim 1989c: 75-104. [Brazil, Igreja Universal do Reino de Deus]

CASAGRANDE, Joseph B., 1978, RELIGIOUS CONVERSION AND SOCIAL CHANGE IN AN INDIAN COMMUNITY OF HIGHLAND ECUADOR. In: Hartmann y Oberem 1978: 105-111.

CASCO, Miguel Angel, 1982, LAS SECTAS EN NICARAGUA. Ponencia Congreso Nicaragüense de Ciencias Sociales, Associación Nicaragüense de Científicos Sociales.

CASCO, Miguel Angel, 1989, LOS EVANGELICOS DE NICARAGUA A DIEZ ANOS DE REVOLUCION. Amanecer (CAV, Managua) no. 61.

CASTANEDA, Amilcar, 1982, LOS ISRAELITAS DEL NUEVO PACTO UNIVERSAL DE PERU. San José, Costa Rica: Seminário Bíblico Centro-Americano.

CASTILLO, Ramón, 1992, ELEMENTOS PARA UNA HISTORIA DEL PENTECOSTALISMO EN VENEZUELA. In: Alvarez 1992: 59-75.

CASTRO, Emilio, 1972, PENTECOSTALISM AND ECUMENISM IN LATIN AMERICA. Christian Century, September, 955-957.

CATO, Clive Stilson, 1984, PENTECOSTALISM: ITS SOCIAL AND RELIGIOUS IMPLICATIONS FOR JAMAICAN SOCIETY. Mona, Jamaica: University of West Indies. [M.A. Thesis]

CEDOLASI, 1986, BIBLIOGRAFIA SOBRE SECTAS. Estudios Ecuménicos 5, 2: 67-68.

CELAM, 1985, LAS SECTAS EN AMERICA LATINA. Buenos Aires: Claretiana.

CELEP, 1987, EL EVANGELIO Y LA RELIGION ELECTRONICA. Pastoralia 9, 10.

CENTRO DE CAPACITACION SOCIAL, 1983, LAS SECTAS: SALVACION BAJO LAS CARPAS. Diálogo Social 148: 18-22.

CENTRO DE PLANIFICACION Y ESTUDIOS SOCIALES, 1984, VISION MUNDIAL: EVALUACION Y SEGUIMIENTO EN ALGUNAS COMUNIDADES DE LA SIERRA ECUATORIANA. Quito: Ediciones Abya Yala.

CENTRO ECUMENICO ANTONIO VALDIVIESO, 1982, LOS EVANGELICOS EN LOS TRES AÑOS DE REVOLUCION. Amanecer, junio-julio: 24-25.

CENTRO ECUMENICO ANTONIO VALDIVIESO, 1984, CONFLICTO EN LAS ASAMBLEAS DE DIOS. Amanecer, marzo-abril: 9-10.

CENTRO ECUMENICO ANTONIO VALDIVIESO, s.f., LAS SECTAS EN NICARAGUA: HERENCIA DEL PASADO E INSTRUMENTO DEL IMPERIALISMO. III Congresso Nicaragüense de Ciencias Sociales, Managua.

CEPEDA, R. (ed.), 1986, LA IGLESIA MISIONERA EN CUBA. San José, Costa Rica: DEI. [Cf. Gonzalez 1986]

CERI-GUA, 1987, LAS SECTAS FUNDAMENTALISTAS Y LA CONTRAIN-SURGENCIA EN GUATEMALA. Servicio Especial, marzo.

CÉSAR, Waldo A., 1968, SITUAÇÃO SOCIAL E CRESCIMENTO DO PROTES-TANTISMO NA AMERICA LATINA. In: César 1968: 7-36.

CÉSAR, Waldo A., et al., 1968, PROTESTANTISMO E IMPERIALISMO NA AMERICA LATINA. Petrópolis: Vozes, Questões Abertas.

CÉSAR, Waldo A., 1973, PARA UMA SOCIOLOGIA DO PROTESTANTISMO BRASILEIRO. Petrópolis: Vozes, Trilhas 2.

CHACON, Arturo, 1964, THE PENTECOSTAL MOVEMENT IN CHILE. Student World 57, 1: 85-88.

CHACON, Arturo (ed.), 1988, DEMOCRACIA Y EVANGELIO. Santiago: REHUE. [Cf. Sepúlveda 1988]

CHAUNU, P., 1965, POUR UNE SOCIOLOGIE DU PROTESTANTISME LATI-NO-AMERICAIN: PROBLEMES DE METHODE. Cahiers de sociologie économique 12: 5-18.

CHAVARRIA, Adonis Niño, 1992, BREVE HISTORIA DEL MOVIMIENTO PEN-TECOSTAL EN NICARAGUA. In: Alvarez 1992: 47-57.

CHORDAS, Thomas J., 1980, CATHOLIC PENTECOSTALISM: A NEW WORD IN THE NEW WORLD. In: Glazier 1980: 143-175. [Caribbean, México, Chile]

CHRISTIANITY TODAY INSTITUTE, 1992, WHY IS LATIN AMERICA TURN-ING PROTESTANT? Christianity Today, April 6.

Church of God..., 1954, CHURCH OF GOD IN THE AMERICAS. Cleveland, Tenn.: Board of Foreign Missions, Church of God.

CLAWSON, David Leslie, 1976, RELIGION AND CHANGE IN A MEXICAN VILLAGE. [Ph.D., University of Florida]

CLAWSON, David, 1984, RELIGIOUS ALLEGIANCE AND ECONOMIC DE-VELOPMENT IN RURAL LATIN AMERICA. Journal of Interamerican Studies and World Affairs 26, 4: 499-524.

COKE, Hugh M., 1978, AN ETHNOHISTORY OF BIBLE TRANSLATION AMONG THE MAYA. Pasadena, Calif.: Fuller Theological Seminary. [Ph.D.]

COMISIÓN EPISCOPAL DE CHILE, 1989, PENTECOSTALISMO, SECTAS Y PASTORAL. Santiago: CEC. [chile]

Compreendendo..., 1982, COMPREENDENDO A RENOVAÇÃO. Porto Alegre: Renovaçaô. [15 articles from Lutheran Renewal International]

COLEMAN, Kenneth M. et al., 1993, PROTESTANTISM IN EL SALVADOR: CONVENTIONAL WISDOM VERSUS THE SURVEY EVIDENCE. In: Garrard-Burnett and Stoll 1993: 111-142.

CONCEIÇAO, Manuel da, 1980, ESSA TERRA É NOSSA. Petrópolis: Vozes. [Brazil]

CONCHA MALO, Miguel, et al., 1986, LA PARTICIPACION DE LOS CRIST-IANOS EN EL PROCESO POPULAR DE LIBERACION EN MEXICO (1968-1983). México D.C.: Siglo Veintiuno.

CONCILIO NACIONAL EVANGELICO DEL PERU, 1986, DIRECTORIO EVANGELICO 1986, LIMA, CALLAO Y BALNEARIOS. Lima: Departamento de Proyección Misionera, Estadística y Estudios Socio-Religiosos.

CONDE. Emílio, 1960, HISTORIA DAS ASSEMBLEIAS DE DEUS NO BRASIL. Rio de Janeiro: Casa Publicadora Assembléias de Deus.

CONFERENCIA EPISCOPAL PANAMEÑA, 1984, CARTA PASTORAL, EL ECUMENISMO: OBJETIVOS, LOGROS Y FALLAS EN PANAMA. Mimeo, 18 octubre 1984.

CONGREGAÇÃO CRISTÃ NO BRASIL, s.f., BREVE HISTORICA, FÉ, DOUTRINA E ESTATUTOS. Saõ Paulo: Indústrias Reunidas Irmaõs Spina.

CONN, Charles W., 1956, PILLARS OF PENTECOST. Cleveland, Tenn.: Pathway Press. [Iglesia de Dios]

CONN, Charles W., 1959, WHERE THE SAINTS HAVE TROD: A HISTORY OF THE CHURCH OF GOD MISSIONS. Cleveland, Tenn.: Pathway Press.

CONN, Charles W., 1955, LIKE A MIGHTY ARMY MOVES THE CHURCH OF GOD 1886-1955. Cleveland, Tenn.: Church of God Publishing House.

CONSEJO EPISCOPAL LATINOMAERICANA (CELAM), 1982, SECTAS EN AMERICA LATINA. Guatemala: Gutenberg.

Consultation..., 1985, CONSULTATION ON PENTECOSTALISM AND LIBERATION THEOLOGY. Occasional Essays 12, 2: 150-155.

Contemporary..., 1986, CONTEMPORARY RELIGIOUS MOVEMENTS AND THEIR CHALLENGE TO OUR CHURCHES. Consultación Cuenca, 4-10 octubre. [Cf. Gouvea Mendonça 1986]

CONWAY, Frederick James, 1978, PENTECOSTALISM IN THE CONTEXT OF HAITIAN RELIGION AND HEALTH PRACTICE. Ann Arbor, Mich.: University Microfilms. [Ph.D., The American University, Washington D.C.]

CONWAY, Frederick J., 1980, PENTECOSTALISM IN HAITI: HEALING AND HIERARCHY. In: Glazier 1980: 7-26.

COOK, Guilherme Bewick, 1973, ANALISIS SOCIO-TEOLOGICO DEL MOVIMIENTO DE RENOVACION CARISMATICA CON REFERENCIA ESPECIAL AL CASO COSTARRICENSE. San José, Costa Rica: Publicaciones INDEF. [Thesis, Seminario Bíblico Latinoamericano, San José]

COOK, William, 1983, INTERVIEW WITH CHILEAN PENTECOSTALS (WCC, VANCOUVER 1983). International Review of Mission 72: 591-595.

COOK, Scott, 1965, 1971, THE PROPHETS: A REVIVALIST FOLK RELIGIOUS MOVEMENT IN PUERTO RICO. Caribbean Studies 4, 4: 20-35; reprinted in Horowitz 1971: 560-579.

CORPORACIÓN iglesia evangélica pentecostal, 1977, HISTORIA DEL AVIVAMIENTO. ORIGEN Y DESARROLLO DE LA IGLESIA EVANGÉLICA PENTECOSTAL. Santiago, Eben-Ezer.

CORRAL PRIETO, Luis, 1984, LAS IGLESIAS EVANGELICAS DE GUATEMALA. Universidad Francisco Marroquín. [M.A. Thesis]

CORREA M., Pedro, s.f., IGLESIA LOCAL E IDENTIDAD CRISTIANA Y PROTESTANTISMO. ESTUDIO SOBRE CONGREGACIONES EVANGELICOS DE ALGUNOS SECTORES POPULARES DE SANTIAGO. Santiago de Chile: Centro Ecumenico Diego de Medellin, Documento de Trabajo.

CORTEN, André, 1995a, LE PENTECÔTISME AU BRÉSIL. ÉMOTION DU PAUVRE ET ROMANTISME THÉOLOGIQUE. Paris: Karthala. [Brazil]

CORTEN, André, 1995b, LA GLOSSOLALIE DANS LE PENTECÔTISME BRÉSILIEN. UNE ÉNONCIATION PROTOPOLITIQUE. Revue française de science politique 45, 2: 259-281. [Brazil]

CORTES, Benjamin, 1992, LA EVANGELIZACION PROTESTANTE EN LA CULTURA NICARAGUENSE. Misión evangélica hoy (Managua, CIEETS), no. 3.

COX, Harvey, 1995, FIRE FROM HEAVEN: THE RISE OF PENTECOSTAL SPIRITUALITY AND THE RESHAPING OF RELIGION IN THE TWENTY-FIRST CENTURY. Reading, Mass. etc: Addison-Wesley Publishing Company.

COSTA, Neusa Meirelles, 1985, RELATORIO DE PESQUISA: ASSEMBLEIA DE DEUS - OPINIOES E ATITUDES DE SEUS MEMBROS. In: Imagens... 1985: 38-59. [Brazil]

COSTAS, Orlando E., 1975, EL PROTESTANTISMO EN AMERICA LATINA HOY: ENSAYOS DEL CAMINO. San José, Costa Rica: IINDEF Publicaciones.

COSTAS, Orlando E., 1976, THEOLOGY OF THE CROSSROADS IN CONTEMPORARY LATIN AMERICA: MISSIOLOGY IN MAINLINE PROTESTANTISM 1969-1974. Amsterdam: Rodopi. [Ph.D., Vrije Universiteit, Amsterdam]

COSTAS, Orlando E., 1978, CONVERSION AS A COMPLEX EXPERIENCE. Gospel in Context 1: 14-24.

COSTAS, Orlando E., 1984, ORIGEN Y DESARROLLO DEL MOVIMIENTO DE CRECIMIENTO DE LA IGLESIA. Misión 3, 1: 7-13; 3, 2: 56-60.

COSTELLO, Gerald M., 1979, MISSION TO LATIN AMERICA: THE SUCCESSES AND FAILURES OF A TWENTIETH CENTURY CRUSADE. Maryknoll, N.Y.: Orbis.

COTTER, George, 1983, SPIES, STRINGS AND MISSIONARIES. Christian Century: 321-325.

CROUCH, Archie R., 1970, A SHOOT OUT OF THE DRY GROUND: THE MOST RAPIDLY GROWING CHURCH IN MEXICO. New World Outlook (United Methodist Church, New York), N.S., 30, 8: 33-35. [Iglesia Cristiana Independiente Pentecostal]

Cuantos protestantes..., 1955, ¿CUANTOS PROTESTANTES HAY EN CHILE? Mensaje 4, 44: 421.

Cultura y..., 1988, CULTURA Y EVANGELIZACIÓN EN AMÉRICA LATINA. Santiago: Ediciones Paulinas-Ilades. [Poblete 1988]

CURRY, Donald Edward, 1968, LUSIADA: AN ANTHROPOLOGICAL STUDY OF THE GROWTH OF PROTESTANTISM IN BRAZIL. Ann Arbor, Mich.: University Microfilms. [Ph.D., Columbia University]

CURRY, Donald Edward, 1970, MESSIANISM AND PROTESTANTISM IN BRAZIL'S SERTÃO. Journal of Inter-American Studies and World Affairs 13, 3: 416-438.

CURRY, Donald Edward, 1975, PROTESTANTISM. In: Encyclopedia of Latin America, New York: McGraw-Hill.

CURRY, Donald Edward, 1987, UNIDADE E PRATICA DA FE. Rio de Janeiro: CEDI.

CUTLER, Donald R. (ed.), 1969, THE RELIGIOUS SITUATION: 1969. Boston: Beacon Press. [Cf. Lalive d'Epinay 1969]

D

DAMBORIENA, Prudencio, 1957, EL PROTESTANTISMO EN CHILE. Mensaje 6, 59: 145-154.

DAMBORIENA, Prudencio, 1958, A VERY ACTIVE PROTESTANT SECT IN CHILE: THE PENTECOSTALS. Christ to the World 3, 1: 111-122.

DAMBORIENA, Prudencio, 1958, PROTESTANTISME LATINO-AMERICAIN. Nouvelle revue théologique 90, 10: 944-965, 1062-1176.

DAMBORIENA, Prudencio, 1958, UNE SECTE PROTESTANTE TRES ACTIVE AU CHILI: LES PENTECOTISTES. Le Christ au Monde (Roma) 3, 1: 103-115.

DAMBORIENA, Prudencio, 1962, THE PENTECOSTALS IN CHILE. Catholic Mind 60: 27-32.

DAMBORIENA, Prudencio, 1963, EL PROTESTANTISMO EN AMERICA LATINA. Freiburg, Madrid: Oficina Internacional de Investigaciones Sociales de FERES, 2 tomos.

DAMBORIENA, Prudencio, 1969, TONGUES AS OF FIRE, PENTECOSTALISM IN CONTEMPORARY CHRISTIANITY. Washington D.C., Cleveland: Corpus Books.

DAMEN, Franz, 1986, EL PENTECOSTALISMO EN BOLIVIA. Fe y Pueblo 3, 14: 22-23.

DAMEN, Franz, 1986, EL PENTECOSTALISMO: ALGUNOS RASGOS. Fe y Pueblo 3, 14: 31-39.

DAMEN, Franz, 1986, EL PENTECOSTALISMO: RUPTURA Y CONTINUIDAD. Fe y Pueblo 3, 14: 44-49.

DAMEN, Franz, 1988, EL DESAFIO DE LAS SECTAS. Serie Fe y Compromiso: 5; Oruro/La Paz: Secretariado Nacional de Ecumenismo.

DAMEN, Franz; PREISWERK, Matias, 1986, PENTECOSTALISMO Y RELIGIOSIDAD POPULAR: DOS ENFOQUES. Fe y Pueblo 3, 14: 40-43.

DANTAS FILHO, Elias, 1988, O MOVIMENTO PENTECOSTAL BRASILEIRO: SUA HISTORIA E INFLUENCIA SOBRE AS DENOMINAÇÕES TRADICIONAIS NO BRASIL. Ann Arbor, Mich./Godstone, Surrey: University Microfilms International.

DARY, Claudia, 1989, PROTESTANTISMO EN UNA COMUNIDAD TZUTUJIL: EL CASO DE SANTIAGO ATITLAN. In: El Protestantismo ..., pp. 49-85.

DAVIS, J. Merle, 1943, HOW THE CHURCH GROWS IN BRAZIL: A STUDY OF THE ECONOMIC AND SOCIAL BASIS OF THE EVANGELICAL CHURCH IN BRAZIL. International Mission Conference.

DAVIS, Sheldon, 1983, GUATEMALA: THE EVANGELICAL HOLY WAR IN EL QUICHE. Global Reporter, 1, 1: 9-10.

DAYTON, Donald W., 1987, THEOLOGICAL ROOTS OF PENTECOSTALISM. Foreword by Martin E. Marty. Grand Rapids, MI: Francis Asbury Press.

DAYTON, Donald W., 1988a, THE HOLY SPIRIT AND CHRISTIAN EXPANSION IN THE TWENTIETH CENTURY. Missiology 16, 4: 397-407.

DAYTON, Donals W., 1988b, PENTECOSTAL/CHARISMATIC RENEWAL AND SOCIAL CHANGE: A WESTERN PERSPECTIVE. Transformation, 5, 4: 7-13.

DAYTON, Donald W., 1991a, RAICES TEOLOGICAS DEL PENTECOSTALISMO. Buenos Aires: Nueva Creación.

DAYTON, Donald W., 1991b, ALGUNAS REFLEXIONES SOBRE EL PENTECOSTALISMO LATINOAMERICANO Y SUS IMPLICACIONES ECUMENICAS. Cuadernos de Teología, 11, 2: 5-20.

DAYTON, Edward R. (ed.), 1981, MISSION HANDBOOK: NORTH AMERICAN PROTESTANT MINISTRIES OVERSEAS. Monrovia, Calif.: Missions Advanced Research Center (MARC), World Vision.

DAYTON, Edward R.; WILSON, Samuel (eds.), 1983, UNREACHED PEOPLES '83. Monrovia, Calif.: Missions Advanced Research Center.

DAYTON, Edward R.; WILSON, Samuel (eds.), 1984, THE FUTURE OF WORLD EVANGELIZATION: UNREACHED PEOPLES '84. Monrovia, Calif.: Missions Advanced Research Center.

DEIROS, Pablo A. (ed.), 1986, LOS EVANGELICOS Y EL PODER POLITICO EN AMERICA LATINA. Grand Rapids, Mich.: Eerdmans.

DEKKER, James C., 1985, NORTH AMERICAN PROTESTANT THEOLOGY: IMPACT ON CENTRAL AMERICA. Evangelical Review of Theology 9, 3, 226-243.

DI BELLA, M.P.; SIGNORELLI, A., 1983, LE "IMMAGINI" DELL'AMERICA. I GRUPPI PENTECOSTALI DEL MEZZGIORNO IN CULTURA POPULARE E CULTURA DI MASSA. Ricerca Folclorica (La) Milano 7: 79-83.

DIAMOND, Sarah, 1988, HOLY WARRIORS. NACLA, Report on the Americas 22, 5: 28-40.

DIAS, Zwinglio M., 1977, KRISEN UND AUFGABEN IM BRASILIANISCHEN PROTESTANTISMUS, EINE STUDIE ZU DEN SOZIALGESCHICHTLI- CHEN BEDINGUNGEN UND VOLKSPÄDAGOGISCHEN MÖGLICH- KEITEN DER EVANGELISATION. Universität Hamburg. [Ph.D.]

Dinheiro..., 1990, DINHEIRO NO ALTAR. COMO A IGREJA DO REINO DE DEUS ERGUEU UM IMPÉRIO DE EMPRESAS E EMISSORAS DE RÁDIO E TV COM DOAÇÕES DOS FIÉIS. Veja, 25 de abril, pág. 50-51.

Directorio..., 1982, DIRECTORIO EVANGELICO 1981-82. Lima: Ediciones CLAI.

Directorio..., 1983, DIRECTORIO DE IGLESIAS, ORGANIZACIONES Y MINIS- TERIOS DEL MOVIMIENTO PROTESTANTE. San José, Costa Rica: INDEF.

DIRKSEN, Murl Owen, 1984, PENTECOSTAL HEALING: A FACET OF THE PERSONALISTIC HEALTH SYSTEM IN PAKAL-NA, A VILLAGE IN SOUTHERN MEXICO. Ann Arbor, Mich.: University Microfilms. [Ph.D., University of Tennessee]

Documentos..., 1984, DOCUMENTOS DEL CONGRESO PARA EVANGELISTAS DE CENTROAMERICA Y PANAMA. San José, Costa Rica, setiembre 1984. [Cf. Justiniano 1984, Mora 1984, Paninski 1984, Vasquez 1984, Zapata 1984]

DODSON, Michael, 1986, THE POLITICS OF RELIGION IN REVOLUTIONARY NICARAGUA. Annals of the American Society of Political and Social Scientists 483: 36-49.

Dominación ideológica..., 1979, DOMINACION IDEOLOGICA Y CIENCIA SO- CIAL, EL INSTITUTO LINGUISTICO DE VERANO EN MEXICO. México: Nueva Lectura, Colegio de Etnólogos y Antropólogos Sociales A.C., Declaración José Carlos Mariátegui.

DOMINGUEZ, Enrique, 1984, THE GREAT COMMISSION. NACLA, Report on the Americas 18, 1: 12-22.

DOMINGUEZ, Enrique; HUNTINGTON, Deborah (eds.), 1984, THE SALVA- TION BROKERS: CONSERVATIVE EVANGELICALS IN CENTRAL AMERICA. NACLA, Report on the Americas 18, 1: 2-36.

DOMINGUEZ, Enrique; HUNTINGTON, Deborah (eds.), 1984, LOS TRAFI-CANTES DE LA SALVACION: EVANGELICOS CONSERVADORES EN CENTRO AMERICA. NACLA, Report on the Americas 18, 1.

DOMINGUEZ, Roberto, 1971, PIONEROS DE PENTECOSTES EN EL MUNDO DE HABLA HISPANA, VOL. 1: NORTEAMERICA Y LAS ANTILLAS. Miami, Fa.: Literatura Evangélica.

DROGUS, Carol Ann, 1994, RELIGIOUS CHANGE AND WOMEN'S STATUS IN LATIN AMERICA: A COMPARISON OF CATHOLIC BASE COMMUNI-TIES AND PENTECOSTAL CHURCHES. Helen Kellogg Institute for International Studies Working paper no. 206. Notre Dame, Ind.: University of Notre Dame.

DROOGERS, André, 1994, THE NORMALIZATION OF RELIGIOUS EXPERI-ENCE: HEALING, PROPHECY, DREAMS, AND VISIONS. In: Poewe 1994: 33-49.

DUARTE, Carlos, 1995, LAS MIL Y UNA CARAS DE LA RELIGION: SECTAS Y NUEVOS MOVIMIENTOS RELIGIOSOS EN AMERICA LATINA. Quito: CLAI.

E

EARLE, Duncan, 1992, AUTHORITY, SOCIAL CONFLICT, AND THE RISE OF PROTESTANT RELIGIOUS CONVERSION IN A MAYAN VILLAGE. Social Compass, 39, 3: 379-389.

EASTON, William C., 1954, COLOMBIAN CONFLICT. London: Christian Litera-ture Crusade. [World Wide Evangelization Crusade]

ECHEVARRIA, Máximo, 1986, EL NUEVO PACTO Y EL VIEJO INFIERNO EN LA AMAZONIA. Pueblo Indio (Edición Tawantinsuyu) 2, 8: 38-41.

ECKSTEIN, Susan (ed.), 1989a, POWER AND POPULAR PROTEST. LATIN AMERICAN SOCIAL MOVEMENTS. Berkeley: University of California Press.

ECKSTEIN, Susan, 1989b, POWER AND POPULAR PROTEST IN LATIN AME-RICA. In: Eckstein 1989a: 1-60.

EDDY, Norman, 1963, A MOVEMENT OF THE HOLY SPIRIT - PENTECOST-ALISM IN CHILE. Mimeo. [Asambleas de Dios]

EDWARDS, Fred E., 1971, THE ROLE OF THE FAITH MISSION - A BRAZILIAN CASE STUDY. South Pasadena, Calif.: Fuller Theological Seminary.

EGE, Konrad, 1985, ACTUALIDAD DE UN FUNDAMENTALISMO, EL FIN DEL MUNDO. Le Monde Diplomatique 7, 84: 20,21.

EISENSTADT, S. (ed.), 1968, THE PROTESTANT ETHIC AND MODERNIZA-TION: A COMPARATIVE VIEW. New York. [Cf. Willems 1968]

ELDRIDGE, Joseph T., 1991, PENTECOSTALISM AND SOCIAL CHANGE IN CENTRAL AMERICA. Towson State Journal of International Affairs 25, 2: 10-12.

El Frente..., 1986, EL FRENTE PROTESTANTE. Pueblo Indio (Edición Tawan-tinsuyu) 2, 8: 17-21.

ELIZAGA, Julio C., 1990, LAS SECTAS NOS INVADEN I. Boletín Salesiano (Monte-video), 10.

ELIZAGA, Julio C., 1990, LAS SECTAS NOS INVADEN II. Boletín Salesiano (Mon-tevideo), 11.

266   More Than Opium

El Protestantismo..., 1989, EL PROTESTANTISMO EN GUATEMALA. Universi-
dad de San Carlos de Guatemala, Cuadernos de Investigación, no. 2-89. [Cf. Dary
1989, Samandú 1989, Similox 1989, Salazar 1989]
ELLIOTT, William W., s.f., SOCIOCULTURAL CHANGE IN A PENTECOSTAL
GROUP: A CASE STUDY IN EDUCATION AND CULTURE OF THE
CHURCH IN SONORA, MEXICO. Knoxville: University of Tennessee. [Ph.D.]
ENDRUVEIT, Wilson Harle, 1975, PENTECOSTALISM IN BRAZIL: A HISTORI-
CAL AND THEOLOGICAL STUDY OF ITS CHARACTERISTICS. Evanston,
Ill.: Northwestern University. [Ph.D.]
En tierra..., 1988, EN TIERRA EXTRAÑA: ITINERARIO DEL PUEBLO PENTE-
COSTAL DE CHILE. Santiago: Amerindia, SEPADE.
ERICKSON, Leif, 1989, MAS ALLA DE LA AURORA. Lima: Asambleas de Dios.
ERSKINE, Noel Leo, 1978, BLACK RELIGION AND IDENTITY: A JAMAICAN
PERSPECTIVE. Nueva York: Union Theological Seminary. [Ph.D.]
ESCOBAR, Arturo, and Sonia E. Alvarez (eds.), 1992, THE MAKING OF SOCIAL
MOVEMENTS IN LATIN AMERICA: IDENTITY, STRATEGY, AND DE-
MOCRACY. Boulder, Colo.: Westview Press. [Cf. Burdick 1992]
ESPARZA, Graciela, 1991, LET'S QUESTION THE MINISTRY OF WOMEN.
Pneuma (The Journal of the Society for Pentecostal Studies) 13, 2, 157-160.
ESPINOZA, Enrique, 1984, LA SECTA ISRAEL DEL NUEVO PACTO UNIVER-
SAL: UN MOVIMIENTO MESIANICO PERUANO. Revista Teológica Limense
18, 1: 47-81.
Espírito Santo..., 1966, O ESPIRITO SANTO E O MOVIMENTO PENTECOSTAL,
SIMPOSIO DA ASTE. São Paulo: ASTE, mimeo. [Brazil, conference papers, Octo-
ber 4-8, 1965]
Espírito Santo..., 1967, O ESPIRITO SANTO GLORIFICANDO O CRISTO. Rio de
Janeiro: Casa Publicadora das Assembléias de Deus. [Brazil, 8th Pentecostal World
Conference, Rio de Janeiro, July 18-23, 1967]
Evangelical Handbook.., 1939, EVANGELICAL HANDBOOK OF LATIN AMER-
ICA. London: World Dominion Press.
EVANS, Timothy E., RELIGIOUS CONVERSION IN QUETZALTENANGO,
GUATEMALA. Pittsburgh, Pa.: University of Pittsburgh. [Ph.D.]
EZCURRA, Ana María, 1982, LA OFENSIVA NEOCONSERVADORA. LAS IGLE-
SIAS DE U.S.A. Y LA LUCHA IDEOLOGICA HACIA AMERICA LATINA.
Madrid: IEPALA (Instituto de Estudios Políticos para América Latina y Africa).
EZCURRA, Ana María, 1983, THE NEOCONSERVATIVE OFFENSIVE: U.S.
CHURCHES AND THE IDEOLOGICAL STRUGGLE FOR LATIN AMER-
ICA. New York: Circus Publications.
EZCURRA, Ana Maria, 1984, IDEOLOGICAL AGGRESSION AGAINST THE
SANDINISTA REVOLUTION: THE POLITICAL OPPOSITION CHURCH
IN NICARAGUA. New York: Circus Publications.

F

FAJARDO, Andrés, 1987, FROM THE VOLCANO: PROTESTANT CONVER-
SION AMONG THE IXIL MAYA OF HIGHLAND GUATEMALA. [M.A.
Thesis, Harvard College]

Fe cristiana..., 1972, FE CRISTIANA Y CAMBIO SOCIAL EN AMERICA LATINA, ENCUENTRO DE EL ESCURIAL. Salamanca: Ed. Sígueme. [Cf. Miguez Bonino 1972]

FEIRREIRA, J.A., 1966, O ESPIRITO SANTO E A RENOVAÇAO DOS CRISTAOS. In: O espírito... 1966: 14-20.

FELDMAN, Harry, 1983, MORE ON THE ANTAGONISM BETWEEN ANTHROPOLOGISTS AND MISSIONARIES. Current Anthropology: 24, 114-115. [SIL]

FENTON, Jerry, 1969, UNDERSTANDING THE RELIGIOUS BACKGROUND OF THE PUERTO RICAN. Cuernavaca: Centro Intercultural de Documentación.

FERNANDES, Rubem César, 1977, O DEBATE ENTRE SOCIOLOGOS A PROPOSITO DOS PENTECOSTAIS. Cadernos do ISER 6: 49-60.

FERNANDES, Rubem César, 1981, FUNDAMENTALISMO A LA DERECHA Y A LA IZQUIERDA: MISIONES EVANGELICAS Y TENSIONES IDEOLOGICAS. Cristianismo y Sociedad 69-70, 3-4: 21-50.

FERNANDES, Rubem César, 1982, OS CAVALEIROS DO BOM JESUS, UMA INTRODUÇÃO AS RELIGIÕES POPULARES. São Paulo: Brasiliense.

FERNANDES, Rubem César, 1990, BATISMO DE FOGO. Idéias, Jornal do Brasil, 21 de outubro, pp. 4/5.

FERNANDES, Rubem César, 1994, GOVERNO DAS ALMAS, AS DENOMINAÇÕES EVANGELICAS DO GRANDE RIO. In: Antoniazzi 1994b: 163-203. [Also in: Revista de Rio de Janeiro, 1 (1994), 2]

FERNANDEZ, Celestino, 1983, LAS SECTAS: UN EXTRAÑO SUPERMERCADO ESPIRITUAL. Vida Nueva 1381: 23-30. [Colombia]

FERRIS, George, 1981, PROTESTANTISM IN NICARAGUA: ITS HISTORICAL ROOTS AND INFLUENCES AFFECTING ITS GROWTH. Temple University. [Ph.D.]

FONSECA, Claudia, 1991, LA RELIGION DANS LA VIE QUOTIDIENNE D'UN GROUPE POPULAIRE BRESILIEN. Archives de Sciences Sociales des Religions 73, 125-139.

FONSECA, Claudia (ed.), 1993, FRONTEIRAS DA CULTURA: HORIZONTES E TERRITORIOS DA ANTROPOLOGIA NA AMERICA LATINA. Porto Alegre: Editora da Universidade (UFRGS). [Cf. Hugarte 1993]

FONTAINE TALAVARE, Arturo, and Harald BEYER, 1991, RETRATO DEL MOVIMIENTO EVANGELICO A LA LUZ DE LAS ENCUESTAS DE OPINION PUBLICA. Revista de Estudios Publicos (Santiago de Chile), 44, 63-124.

FORNI, Floreal H., 1989, ESTUDIO COMPARATIVO DE LOS GRUPOS ORGANIZADOS PARA LA ACTIVIDAD RELIGIOSA QUE TIENEN IMPACTO POPULAR EN EL GRAN BUENOS AIRES. Sociedad y Religión 7: 72-80.

FORNI, Floreal H., 1991, ESTUDIO COMPARATIVO DE LOS GRUPOS ORGANIZADOS PARA LA ACTIVIDAD RELIGIOSA EN EL GRAN BUENOS AIRES II. Sociedad y Religión 8: 85-103.

FORNI, Floreal H., 1992, EMERGENCIA DE NUEVAS CORRIENTES RELIGIOSAS O "IGLESIAS ALTERNATIVAS" SOBRE FINES DEL SIGLO. Sociedad y Religión 9, 10-48.

FORNI, Floreal H., 1993, NUEVOS MOVIMIENTOS RELIGIOSOS EN ARGENTINA. In: Frigerio 1993, II: 7-23.

FORTUNY, Patricia, 1981, EL PROTESTANTISMO EN YUCATAN, ESTRUC-
TURA Y FUNCION DEL CULTO EN LA SOCIEDAD RELIGIOSA ESTU-
DIADA. Yucatán: Historia y Economía 5: 35-47. [Mexico]

FORTUNY, Patricia, 1982, INSERCION Y DIFUSION DEL SECTARISMO RELI-
GIOSO EN EL CAMPO YUCATECO. Yucatán: Historia y Economía 6: 3-23.
[Mexico]

FORTUNY, Patricia, 1994, ORIGINS, DEVELOPMENT AND PERSPECTIVES
OF LA LUZ DEL MUNDO CHURCH. Religion 25, 2, 147-162.

FOULKES, I.W. de, 1987, ALGUNOS FENOMENOS LINGUISTICOS EN LOS
SERMONES DE UN EVANGELISTA NORTEAMERICANO DIFUNDIDOS
EN AMERICA LATINA. Pastoralia 18: 39-54.

FRANKLIN, Karl J., 1987, CURRENT CONCERNS OF ANTHROPOLOGISTS
AND MISSIONARIES. Dallas, Tex.: The International Museum of Cultures Publication number 22. [SIL, Wycliffe]

FRASE, Ronald, 1975, A SOCIOLOGICAL ANALYSIS OF THE DEVELOPMENT
OF BRAZILIAN PROTESTANTISM: A STUDY IN SOCIAL CHANGE.
Princeton Theological Seminary. [Ph.D.]

FREEMAN, Jo, 1983, SOCIAL MOVEMENTS OF THE SIXTIES AND SEVEN-
TIES. New York: Longman. [Cf. Gerlach 1983]

FRESTON, Paul, 1989, TEOCRATAS, FISIOLÓGICOS, NOVA DIREITA E
PROGRESSISTAS: PROTESTANTES E POLÍTICA NA NOVA REPÚBLICA.
Grupo de Trabalho Religião e Sociedade. Paper read at the XIII Encontro Anual da
ANPOCS, October 24-27, 1989, Caxambu, Minas Gerais.

FRESTON, Paul, 1992, EVANGELICOS NA POLITICA BRASILEIRA. Religião e
Sociedade (ISER) 16, 1/2, 26-44.

FRESTON, Paul, 1993a, BROTHER VOTES FOR BROTHER: THE NEW POLI-
TICS OF PROTESTANTISM IN BRAZIL. In: Garrard-Burnett and Stoll 1993: 66-
110.

FRESTON, Paul, 1993b, PROTESTANTES E POLITICA NO BRASIL: DA
CONSTITUIÇÃO AO IMPEACHMENT. [Ph.D., Campinas: Unicamp]

FRESTON, Paul, 1994a, BREVE HISTORIA DO PENTECOSTALISMO BRASIL-
EIRO. In: Antoniazzi 1994b: 67-159.

FRESTON, Paul, 1994b, PENTECOSTALISM IN BRAZIL: A BRIEF HISTORY.
Religion 25, 2, 119-133.

FRIGERIO, Alejandro, 1993, "LA INVASION DE LAS SECTAS": EL DEBATE
SOBRE NUEVOS MOVIMIENTOS RELIGIOSOS EN LOS MEDIOS DE
COMUNICACION EN ARGENTINA. Sociedad y Religión, 10/11: 24-51.

FRIGERIO, Alejandro, 1994, ESTUDIOS RECIENTES SOBRE EL PENTECOST-
ALISMO EN EL CONO SUR: PROBLEMAS Y PERSPECTIVAS. In: Frigerio
1994: 10-29.

FRIGERIO, Alejandro (ed.), 1993, NUEVOS MOVIMIENTOS RELIGIOSOS Y
CIENCIAS SOCIALES, vol. I & II. Buenos Aires: Centro Editor de América Latina.

FRIGERIO, Alejandro (ed.), 1994, EL PENTECOSTALISMO EN LA ARGENTINA.
Buenos Aires: Centro Editor de América Latina.

FRODSHAM, Stanley Howard, 1946, WITH SIGNS FOLLOWING. THE STORY
OF THE PENTECOSTAL REVIVAL IN THE TWENTIETH CENTURY.
Springfield, Miss.: Gospel Publishing House.

FRY, Peter Henry; HOWE, Gary Nigel, 1975, DUAS RESPOSTAS A AFLIÇÃO: UMBANDA E PENTECOSTALISMO. Debate e Crítica (São Paulo, HUCITEC), 6: 75-94. [Brazil]

G

GAETE, Arturo, 1956, UN CAS D'ADAPTATION: LES 'PENTECOSTALES' AU CHILI. In: Abd-el-Jali 1956: 142-149.

GALILEA, Carmen, 1987, LUGARES DE CULTO RELIGIOSO EN SANTIAGO. DISTRIBUCION, POBLACION Y PERSPECTIVAS. Santiago: Centro Bellarmino, CISOC.

GALILEA, Carmen, 1991, EL PREDICADOR PENTECOSTAL. Santiago: Centro Bellarmino, CISOC.

GALLIANO, Gabriel, 1992, PENTECOSTALISMO, POBREZA URBANA Y RELACIONES SOCIALES EN UN BARRIO DEL GRAN BUENOS AIRES. Paper presented at the II Jornadas Sobre Alternativas Religiosas en los Sectores Populares de Latinoaméric, organized by the journal Sociedad y Religión, 24-25 de agosto de 1992.

GALLIANO, Gabriel, 1994, MILENARISMO PENTECOSTAL, POBREZA URBANA Y INTERACCION SOCIAL EN EL GRAN BUENOS AIRES. In: Frigerio 1994: 95-113.

GARCIA-RUIZ, Jesús, 1985a, LAS SECTAS FUNDAMENTALISTAS EN GUATEMALA. Guatemala: Ciencia y Tecnología para Guatemala, Cuaderno 4.

GARCIA-RUIZ, Jesús, 1985b, LE RELIGIEUX COMME LIEU DE PENETRATION POLITIQUE ET IDEOLOGIQUE AU GUATEMALA. Revue Française d'Études Américaines 10.

GARCIA-RUIZ, Jesús, 1992, PROCESOS SOCIALES Y PROTESTANTISMOS CENTROAMERICANOS: TIPOLOGIA Y PRESENCIA ESPACIAL. Paris: CNRS.

GARMA NAVARRO, Carlos, 1982, EL PROTESTANTISMO EN UNA COMUNIDAD TOTONACA, UN ESTUDIO POLITICO. Cuadernos de Investigación (INAH, Cuicuilco) 2: 113-129. [Mexico, also in RELIGION POPULAR: HEGEMONIA Y RESISTENCIA, México: Cuicuilco]

GARMA NAVARRO, Carlos , 1983, PODER, CONFLICTO Y REELABORACION SIMBOLICA: PROTESTANTISMO EN UNA COMUNIDAD TOTONACA. México: Escuela Nacional de Antropología e Historia. [Mexico, thesis]

GARMA NAVARRO, Carlos, 1984, LIDERAZGO PROTESTANTE EN UNA LUCHA CAMPESINA EN MEXICO. América Indígena 44, 1: 127-141.

GARMA NAVARRO, Carlos, 1987, PROTESTANTISMO EN UNA COMUNIDAD TOTONACA DE PUEBLA, MEXICO. México: Instituto Nacional Indigenista, Serie de Antropología Social, número 76.

GARMA NAVARRO, Carlos, 1988, LIDERAZGO, MENSAJE RELIGIOSO Y CONTEXTO SOCIAL. Cristianismo y Sociedad 95, 1, 89-99.

GARMA NAVARRO, Carlos, 1988, LOS ESTUDIOS ANTROPOLOGICOS SOBRE EL PROTESTANTISMO EN MEXICO. Revista Iztapalapa (Universidad Autónoma de México-Iztapalapa): 8, 15: 53-66.

GARRARD-BURNETT, Virginia, 1986, A HISTORY OF PROTESTANTISM IN GUATEMALA. Tulane University. [Ph.D.]

GARRARD-BURNETT, Virginia, 1989, PROTESTANTISM IN RURAL GUATE-
MALA, 1872-1954. Latin American Research Review 24, 2: 127-142.
GARRARD-BURNETT, Virginia, 1990, POSITIVISMO, LIBERALISMO E IMPUL-
SO MISIONERO: MISSIONES PROTESTANTES EN GUATEMALA, 1880-
1920. Mesoamérica, 19.
GARRARD-BURNETT, Virginia, 1993, CONCLUSION: IS THIS LATIN AMER-
ICA'S REFORMATION? In: Garrard-Burnett and Stoll 1993: 199-210.
GARRARD-BURNETT, Virginia, and David STOLL (eds.), 1993, RETHINKING
PROTESTANTISM IN LATIN AMERICA. Philadelphia, Pa.: Temple University
Press.
GARRISON, Vivian, 1974, SECTARIANISM AND PSYCHOSOCIAL ADJUST-
MENT: A CONTROLLED COMPARISON OF PUERTO RICAN PENTE-
COSTALS AND CATHOLICS. In: Zaretsky and Leone 1974: 298-329.
GATES. Charles Wise, 1982, THE BRAZILIAN REVIVAL OF 1952: ITS ANTECEN-
DENTS AND ITS EFFECTS. Pasadena, Calif.: Fuller Theological Seminary.
[Ph.D.]
GAXIOLA, Adoniram, 1991, POVERTY AS A MEETING AND PARTING
PLACE: SIMILARITIES AND CONTRASTS IN THE EXPERIENCES OF
LATIN AMERICAN PENTECOSTALISM AND ECCLESIAL BASE COM-
MUNITIES. Pneuma (The Journal of the Society for Pentecostal Studies) 13, 2, 167-
174.
GAXIOLA LOPEZ, Malovio, 1964, HISTORIA DE LA IGLESIA APOSTOLICA DE
LA FE EN CRISTO JESUS. México: Librería Latinoamericana. [Mexico]
GAXIOLA-GAXIOLA, Manuel J., 1975, THE SERPENT AND THE DOVE: A
HISTORY OF THE APOSTOLIC CHURCH OF THE FAITH IN CHRIST
JESUS IN MEXICO (1914-1964). Pasadena, Calif.: Fuller Theological Seminary.
[M.A. Thesis]
GAXIOLA-GAXIOLA, Manuel Jesus, 1975, LA SERPENTE Y LA PALOMA,
ANALISIS DEL CRECIMIENTO DE LA IGLESIA APOSTOLICA DE LA FE
EN CRISTO JESUS DE MEXICO. South Pasadena, Calif.: William Carey Library.
GAXIOLA-GAXIOLA, Manuel J., 1977, THE PENTECOSTAL MINISTRY. In: Mi-
nistry with... 1977. Also: International Review of Mission 66, 1.
GAXIOLA-GAXIOLA, Manuel J., 1984, THE SPANISH SPEAKING ONENESS
CHURCHES IN LATIN AMERICA: SEARCH FOR IDENTITY AND POSSI-
BILITIES OF DOCTRINAL RENEWAL. In: Papers...1984: 121-144.
GAXIOLA-GAXIOLA, Manuel J., 1991, LATIN AMERICAN PENTECOSTAL-
ISM: A MOSAIC WITHIN A MOSAIC. Pneuma (The Journal of the Society of
Pentecostal Studies), 13, 2, 107-129.
GEE, Donald, 1967, WIND AND FLAME, INCORPORATING THE FORMER
BOOK "THE PENTECOSTAL MOVEMENT" WITH ADDITIONAL CHAP-
TERS. Croydon: Assemblies of God Publishing House.
GELPI, D., 1973, EL PENTECOSTALISMO AMERICANO. Concilium: 89: 403-410.
GERBERT, Martin, 1970, RELIGIONEN IN BRASILIEN, EINE ANALYSE DER
NICHT-KATHOLISCHEN RELIGIONSFORMEN UND IHRER ENT-
WICKLUNG IM SOZIALEN WANDEL DER BRASILIANISCHEN GESELL-
SCHAFT. Berlin: Colloquium Verlag, Bibliotheca Ibero-Americano, Vol. 13.
GERLACH, Luther P., 1974, PENTECOSTALISM: REVOLUTION OR COUN-
TER-REVOLUTION? In: Zaretsky and Leone 1974: 669-699. [Haiti]

GERLACH, Luther P., 1983, MOVEMENTS OF REVOLUTIONARY CHANGE: SOME STRUCTURAL CHARACTERISTICS. In: Freeman 1983.

GILL, Kenneth D., 1984, A MEXICAN JESUS' NAME EXPERIENCE. In: Papers... 1984: 102-120.

GILL, Lesley, 1988, BOLIVIA: PENTECOSTALS FILL A GAP (WOMEN AND POVERTY IN THE ANDES II). Christianity and Crisis: 395-397.

GILL, Lesley, 1990, "LIKE A VEIL TO COVER THEM": WOMEN AND THE PENTECOSTAL MOVEMENT IN LA PAZ. American Ethnologist, 17, 4: 708-721.

GILL, Lesley, 1993, RELIGIOUS MOBILITY AND THE MANY WORDS OF GOD IN LA PAZ, BOLIVIA. In: Garrard-Burnett and Stoll 1993: 180-198.

GIMENEZ, Gilberto, 1978, CULTURA POPULAR Y RELIGION EN EL ANAHUAC. México: Centro de Estudios Ecuménicos.

GINETTE, Cano; NEUFELDT, Karl; et al., 1981, LOS NUEVOS CONQUISTADORES. Quito: CEDIS.

GLAZIER, Stephen D., 1977, THE ECONOMICS OF TOLERATION: RELIGIOUS PLURALISM IN THE SPIRITUAL BAPTIST CHURCH. Ponencia, Annual Meeting Society for the Scientific Study of Religion, Chicago.

GLAZIER, Stephen D., 1980, PENTECOSTAL EXORCISM AND MODERNIZATION IN TRINIDAD, WEST INDIES. In Glazier (ed.) 1980: 67-80.

GLAZIER, Stephen D., 1980, RELIGION AND CONTEMPORARY RELIGIOUS MOVEMENTS IN THE CARIBBEAN: A REPORT. Sociological Analysis 41, 2, 181-183.

GLAZIER, Stephen D. (ed.), 1980, PERSPECTIVES ON PENTECOSTALISM: CASE STUDIES FROM THE CARIBBEAN AND LATIN AMERICA. Washington, D.C.: University Press of America.

GLAZIER, Stephen D., 1982, AFRICAN CULTS AND CHRISTIAN CHURCHES IN TRINIDAD. Journal of Religious Thought 39, 17-25.

GLAZIER, Stephen D., 1983, CARIBBEAN PILGRIMAGES: A TYPOLOGY. Journal for the Scientific Study of Religion 22, 4: 316-325.

GLAZIER, Stephen D., 1983, MARCHING THE PILGRIMS HOME: LEADERSHIP AND DECISION MAKING IN AN AFRO-CARIBBEAN FAITH. Westport, Conn.: Greenwood.

GLAZIER, Stephen D., s.f., MOURNING AND THE ARTICULATION OF LIFE CRISIS AMONG THE SPIRITUAL BAPTISTS OF TRINIDAD. University of Connecticut: Department of Anthropology.

GODDARD, Burton L. (ed.), 1967, ENCYCLOPEDIA OF MODERN CHRISTIAN MISSIONS: THE AGENCIES. Camden, N.J.: Thomas Nelson.

GÓES, Paulo de, 1988, CONGREGAÇÃO CRISTÃ NO BRASIL: O PODER DO DISCURSO SOBRE A ORGANIZAÇÃO. Estudos de Religião (São Paulo) 5, 25-35.

GOFF, James E., 1965, PROTESTANT PERSECUTION IN COLOMBIA 1948-1958. Cuernavaca, México: CIDOC.

GOFF, James E., 1966, CENSO DE LA OBRA EVANGELICA EN COLOMBIA, PARTE 1 INTRODUCCION Y MEMBRESIA, PARTE 2 ESCUELAS Y OTRAS INSTITUCIONES. Bogotá: Confederación Evangélica de Colombia.

GOFF, James E., 1973, APOSTOLICS OF YUCATAN. In: Bourguignon, 1973: 198-218.

GOICOCHEA, Antonio, 1983, SECTAS PROTESTANTES. Lima: Ediciones TAU. [Perú]

GOLDER, Morris E., 1973, HISTORY OF THE PENTECOSTAL ASSEMBLIES OF THE WORLD. Indianapolis, Ind.: author's edition.

GOLDIN, L.R., and B.METZ, 1991, AN EXPRESSION OF CULTURAL CHANGE: INVISIBLE CONVERTS TO PROTESTANTISM AMONG HIGHLAND GUATEMALA MAYANS. Ethnology 30, 4: 325-338.

GOMES, Geziel N., 1967, PORQUE SOU PENTECOSTAL. Rio de Janeiro: Casa Publicadora das Assembléias de Deus. [Brazil]

GOMES, José Francisco, 1985, RELIGIÃO E POLITICA: OS PENTECOSTAIS NO RECIFE. Recife: Universidade Federal de Pernambuco. [M.A. Thesis]

GOMES, Wilson, 1992, CINCO TESES EQUIVOCADAS SOBRE AS NOVAS SEITAS POPULARES. Cadernos do CEAS, 39-53.

GOMES, Wilson, 1994, NEM ANJOS NEM DEMONIOS. In: Antoniazzi 1994b: 225-270. [Brazil]

GONZALEZ, A., 1986, LA IGLESIA CRISTIANA PENTECOSTAL DE CUBA COMO MISIONERA Y MISIONADA. In: Cepeda 1986.

GONZALEZ, Justo L., 1967, HISTORIA DE LAS MISIONES. New York: TEF. [Chapter 9 Latin America]

GONZALEZ, Justo L., 1969, THE DEVELOPMENT OF CHRISTIANITY IN THE LATIN CARIBBEAN. Grand Rapids, Mich.: Eerdmans.

GONZALEZ, Noel, 1993, EL PROTESTANTISMO NICARAGUENSE. UNA PERSPECTIVE EN TORNO A SU DISTRIBUCION Y CRECIMIENTO. Revista de Historia del Protestantismo Nicaragüense (Managua, CIEETS), no. 3.

GONZALEZ, Rhode, 1992, LA PARTICIPACION DE LA MUJER: UN ENFOQUE PENTECOSTAL BIBLICO TEOLOGICO. In: Alvarez 1992: 179-188.

GONZALEZ ALVARADO, Eloy, 1986, PRESENCIA MISIONERA EN EL NORTE DEL PERU. Lima. [Iglesia Santidad de Peregrinos]

GONZALES MARTINEZ, José Luis; RONZELEN, Teresa María van, 1983, RELIGIOSIDAD POPULAR EN EL PERU. Lima: Centro de Estudios y Publicaciones.

GOODMAN, Felicitas D., 1969, PHONETIC ANALYSIS OF GLOSSOLALIA IN FOUR CULTURAL SETTINGS. Journal for the Scientific Study of Religion 8: 227-239.

GOODMAN, Felicitas D., 1972, SPEAKING IN TONGUES, A CROSS-CULTURAL STUDY OF GLOSSOLALIA. Chicago/London: University of Chicago Press.

GOODMAN, Felicitas D., 1972, UN CULTO DE CRISIS EN YUCATAN. Sociedad Mexicana de Antropología, Religión en Mesoamérica, XXII Mesa Redonda, 617-621. [Mexico]

GOODMAN, Felicitas D., 1973, APOSTOLICS OF YUCATAN, A CASE HISTORY OF A RELIGIOUS MOVEMENT. In: Bourguignon 1973: 178-218. [Mexico]

GOODMAN, Felicitas D., 1974, DISTURBANCES IN THE APOSTOLIC CHURCH, A TRANCE-BASED UPHEAVAL IN YUCATAN. In: Goodman et al. 1974: 227-364.

GOODMAN, Felicitas D., et al., 1974, TRANCE, HEALING AND HALLUCINATION, THREE FIELD STUDIES IN RELIGIOUS EXPERIENCE. New York: John Wiley. [Cf. Goodman 1974, Henney 1974]

GOODMAN, Felicitas D., 1974, PROGNOSIS: A NEW RELIGION? In: Zaretsky and Leone 1974: 244-254. [Mexico]

GOODMAN, Felicitas D., 1975, BELIEF SYSTEM, MILLENARY EXPECTA-
TIONS, AND BEHAVIOR. In: Hill 1975: 130-138.
GOODMAN, Felicitas D., 1988a, HOW ABOUT DEMONS? POSSESSION AND
EXORCISM IN THE MODERN WORLD. Bloomington & Indianapolis: Indiana
University Press. [Mexico, cap. 4]
GOODMAN, Felicitas D., 1988b, ECSTASY, RITUAL, AND ALTERNATE REAL-
ITY: RELIGION IN A PLURALISTIC WORLD. Bloomington & Indianapolis:
Indiana University Press.
GOODMAN, Felicitas D., 1990, WHERE THE SPIRITS RIDE THE WIND:
TRANCE JOURNEYS AND OTHER ECSTATIC EXPERIENCES. Bloom-
ington & Indianapolis: Indiana University Press.
GOSLIN, Tomás S., 1956, LOS EVANGELICOS EN LA AMERICA LATINA:
SIGLO XIX, LOS COMIENZOS. Buenos Aires: La Aurora.
GOUVEA MENDONÇA, Antonio , 1986, DESAFIOS DOS PENTECOSTAIS AS
IGREJAS EVANGELICAS TRADICIONAIS. Tempo e Presença 209: 20,21.
[Brazil]
GOUVEA MENDONÇA, Antonio, 1986, SECTS: SOME THEORETICAL RE-
FLECTIONS. In: Contemporary... 1986.
GOUVEIA, Eliane H., 1987, O SILENCIO QUE DEVE SER OUVIDO: MUL-
HERES PENTECOSTAIS EM SÃO PAULO. São Paulo: Pontífica Universidade
Católica. [M.A. Thesis]
GREEN, Linda, 1993, SHIFTING AFFILIATIONS: MAYAN WIDOWS AND
EVANGELICOS IN GUATEMALA. In: Garrard-Burnett and Stoll 1993: 159-179.
GREEN, Raul, 1983, EL DESAFIO DE LOS PROTESTANTES Y DE LAS SECTAS.
Le Monde Diplomatique 51.
GROSS, Sue Anderson, 1968, RELIGIOUS SECTARIANISM IN THE SERTÃO OF
NORTHEAST BRAZIL, 1815-1966. Journal of Inter-American Studies 10: 369-383.
GRÜNDLER, Johannes, 1961, LEXIKON DER CHRISTLICHEN KIRCHEN UND
SEKTEN. Viena etc.: Herder.
Guatemala..., 1983, GUATEMALA: EL PAIS-EXPERIMENTO DE LAS IGLESIAS
FUNDAMENTALISTAS. Altercom 29.
GUERRERO, Bernardo, 1978, LOS PENTECOSTALES Y EL PROCESSO DE
DESINTEGRACION DE LAS COMUNIDADES DEL NORTE GRANDE
CHILENO. Antofagasta: Universidad del Norte, Facultad de Ciencias Sociales,
Departamento de Sociología. [M.A. Thesis]
GUERRERO, Bernardo, 1980, LA ESTRUCTURA DEL MOVIMIENTO PENTE-
COSTAL EN EL ALTIPLANO CHILENO. Cuaderno de Investigación Social
(CIREN, Iquique), 3: 1-12.
GUERRERO, Bernardo, 1981, LA VIOLENCIA PENTECOSTAL EN EL ALTIPLA-
NO CHILENO. Cuaderno de Investigación Social (CIREN, Iquique), 4: 34-44.
GUERRERO, Bernardo, 1984, MOVIMIENTO PENTECOSTAL Y CORRIENTES
MODERNISTAS EN EL ALTIPLANO CHILENO. Cuaderno de Investigación
Social (CIREN, Iquique), 8.
GUERRERO, Bernardo, 1990, LAS CAMPANAS DEL DOLOR: VIOLENCIA Y
CONFLICTO EN LOS ANDES CHILENOS. Iquique: Ediciones El Jote Errante.
GUERRERO, Bernardo, 1992, CONVERSION Y SALUD EN EL ALTIPLANO
CHILENO. NOTAS SOBRE EL CRECIMIENTO PENTECOSTAL EN LA

COMUNA DE COLCHANE. Revista Ciencia y Tecnología, Serie Ciencias Sociales (Universidad Arturo Prat, Iquique), 1, 19-24.

GUERRERO, Bernardo, 1993, IDENTIDAD AYMARA E IDENTIDAD PENTE-COSTAL: NOTAS PARA LA DISCUSION. Revista Ciencia y Tecnología, Serie Ciencias Sociales (Universidad Arturo Prat, Iquique), 3, 15-24.

GUERRERO, Bernardo, 1994a, ESTUDIOS SOBRE EL MOVIMIENTO PENTE-COSTAL EN AMERICA LATINA. Iquique, Chile: CREAR, Cuaderno de Investigación Social 35.

GUERRERO, Bernardo, 1994b, DE LA INVISIBILIDAD A LA VISIBILIDAD ACADEMICA: ESTUDIOS SOBRE EL MOVIMIENTO PENTECOSTAL EN LA SOCIEDAD ANDINA. Diálogo Andino (Arica, Chile), 13, 39-48.

GUERRERO, Bernardo, 1995, A DIOS ROGANDO...: LOS PENTECOSTALES EN LA SOCIEDAD AYMARA DEL NORTE GRANDE DE CHILE. Amsterdam: Vrije Universiteit, VU University Press. [Ph.D.]

Guia..., 1953, GUIA DE LAS IGLESIAS EVANGELICAS Y OTRAS NO CATO-LICO-ROMANAS. Buenos Aires: La Aurora. [Argentina]

GUIGOU, Nicolás, 1993, EL DINERO EN EL PROCESO DE INTEGRACION Y DESARROLLO DE LAS IGLESIAS PENTECOSTALES BRASILEÑAS EN EL URUGUAY. Sociedad y Religión, 10/11: 96-104.

GUILLÉN, Miguel, 1982, LA HISTORIA DEL CONCILIO LATINO AMERICA-NO DE IGLESIAS CRISTIANAS. Brownsville, Tex.: Latin American Council of Christian Churches. [Mexico, USA, history of a pentecostal church among Mexicans in the USA and Mexico]

GUIMARÃES, J.E., 1992, RAZÃO E RELIGIÃO: PENTECOSTAIS, VISÕES DE MUNDO E CONDUTA. [Master's Thesis, CPDA-UFRRJ, Rio de Janeiro]

GULLICK, Charles, 1971, SHAKERS AND ECSTASY. New Fire (Oxford, Society of St. John the Evangelist), 9: 7-11. [St. Vincent, Spiritual Baptists]

GUTIERREZ, Benjamin F., 1995, EN LA FUERZA DEL ESPÍRITU: LOS PENTE-COSTALES EN AMÉRICA LATINA, UN DESAFÍO A LAS IGLESIAS HISTÓ-RICAS. México: APRAL, Guatemala: CELEP. [general, Chile, Brazil, Cuba, Chiapas, women, relation with historical churches]

H

HADDEN, Jeffrey; SHUPE, Anson (eds.), 1986, PROPHETIC RELIGION AND POLITICS. Nueva York: Paragon. [Cf. Poloma]

HARGRAVE, O.T., 1958, A HISTORY OF THE CHURCH OF GOD IN MEX-ICO. San Antonio, Tex.: Trinity University. [M.A. Thesis]

HARNDEN, Philip, 1977, TODAY'S WYCLIFFE VERSION. The Other Side: mayo, 24-34; 46-48.

HARPER, Gordon P., 1963, THE CHILDREN OF HIPOLITO - A STUDY OF BRAZILIAN PENTECOSTALISM. Harvard University, unpublished research report.

HARTMANN,R; OBEREM, U. (eds.), 1978, AMERIKANISTISCHE STUDIEN. St. Augustin: Anthropos-Institut, Collectanea Instituti Anthropos 20 (1). [Cf. Casagrande 1978]

HASLAM, David, 1987, FAITH IN STRUGGLE: THE PROTESTANT CHURCH-ES IN NICARAGUA AND THEIR RESPONSE TO THE REVOLUTION. London: Epworth Press.

HASSE, Elemer, 1964, LUZ SOBRE O FENOMENO PENTECOSTAL. São Paulo: author's edition. [Brazil]

HAYES, Victor C. (ed.), 1980, RELIGIOUS EXPERIENCE IN WORLD RELI-GIONS. Selected Papers, Number 3. Bedford Park: The Australian Association for the Study of Religions. [Cf. Ireland 1980]

HEATH, S. Brice, 1977, LA POLITICA DEL LENGUAJE EN MEXICO. México: Instituto Nacional Indigenista. [SIL]

HEFLEY, Jame; HEFLEY Martin, 1974, UNCLE CAM. Waco, Tex.: Word Books. [SIL]

HEGY, Pierre, 1971, INTRODUCCION A LA SOCIOLOGIA RELIGIOSA DEL PERU. Lima: Ediciones Libraria "Studium".

HENNEY, Jeannette H., 1967, TRANCE BEHAVIOUR AMONG THE SHAKERS OF ST. VINCENT. Columbus, Ohio: The Ohio State University Cross Cultural Study of Dissociated States, Working Paper no. 8.

HENNEY, Jeannette H., 1968, SPIRIT POSSESSION BELIEF AND TRANCE BE-HAVIOR IN A RELIGIOUS GROUP IN ST.VINCENT, BRITISH WEST IN-DIES. Columbus, Ohio: The Ohio State University. [Ph.D., spiritual baptists]

HENNEY, Jeannette H., 1971, THE SHAKERS OF ST. VINCENT: A STABLE RE-LIGION. In: Bourguignon 1971: 219-263. [Spiritual baptists]

HENNEY, Jeannette H., 1974, SPIRIT-POSSESSION BELIEF AND TRANCE BE-HAVIOR IN TWO FUNDAMENTALIST GROUPS IN ST. VINCENT. In: Goodman 1974: 1-111.

HERNANDEZ, Juan Antonio, 1985, EL FANATISMO DE LOS "CARISMATI-COS". Correo del Sur 1215. [Mexico]

HILL, Carole E. (ed.), 1975, SYMBOLS AND SOCIETY, ESSAYS ON BELIEF SYS-TEMS IN ACTION. Athens: University of Georgia Press. [Cf. Goodman 1975]

HILL, Jonathan D., 1984, LOS MISIONEROS Y LAS FRONTERAS. América Indíge-na 44, 1: 183-190. [Brazil, Venezuela, Colombia, New Tribes]

Historia..., 1977, HISTORIA DEL AVIVAMIENTO ORIGEN Y DESARROLLO DE LA IGLESIA EVANGELICA PENTECOSTAL. Corporación Iglesia Evangé-lica Pentecostal. [Chile]

HODGES, Serena M. (ed.), 1956, LOOK ON THE FIELDS, A MISSIONARY SUR-VEY (DATA SUPPLIED BY ASSEMBLIES OF GOD MISSIONARIES). Spring-field, Miss.: Gospel Publishing House.

HOFF, Paul B., 1984, THE PENTECOSTAL MOVEMENT OF CHILE. World Pentecost 3: 4-6.

HOFFNAGEL, Judith Chambliss, 1978, THE BELIEVERS: PENTECOSTALISM IN A BRAZILIAN CITY. Ann Arbor, Mich.: University Microfilms International. [Ph.D., Indiana University]

HOFFNAGEL, Judith Chambliss, 1980, PENTECOSTALISM: A REVOLUTION-ARY OR CONSERVATIVE MOVEMENT? In: Glazier 1980: 111-123. [Brazil]

HOFMAN, J. Samuel, 1983, OPPOSITION TO SIL IN LATIN AMERICA. Mission-ary Monthly: Junio-Julio, 3-4;8.

HOLLAND, Clifton (ed.), 1981, WORLD CHRISTIANITY: CENTRAL AMERICA AND THE CARIBBEAN. Monrovia, Calif.: MARC (Missions Advanced Research and Communications Center).

HOLLENWEGER, Walter J., 1964, ENTHUSIASTES CHRISTENTUM IN BRASILIEN, Reformatio 13: 484-488, 623-631.

HOLLENWEGER, Walter J., 1965, HANDBUCH DER PFINGSTBEWEGUNG. TEILDRUCK: AUFSTELLUNG UND KLASSIFIZIERUNG DER ORGANISATIONEN DER PFINGSTBEWEGUNG. München: Uni-Druck. [Ph.D., Universität Zürich]

HOLLENWEGER, Walter J., 1965-1967, HANDBUCH DER PFINGSTBEWEGUNG. 10 vols. [Mimeo, vol. 02b on Latin America and the Caribbean, pp. 855-1116]

HOLLENWEGER, Walter J., 1968, EVANGELISM AND BRAZILIAN PENTECOSTALS. Ecumenical Review 20: 163-170.

HOLLENWEGER, Walter J., 1969, O MOVIMENTO PENTECOSTAL NO BRASIL. Simpósio 2, 3: 5-41.

HOLLENWEGER. Walter J., 1969, ENTHUSIASTES CHRISTENTUM IN BRASILIEN. In: Tschuy 1969: 97-106. [Same as Hollenweger 1964]

HOLLENWEGER, Walter J., 1969, ENTHUSIASTES CHRISTENTUM; DIE PFINGSTBEWEGUNG IN GESCHICHTE UND GEGENWART. Wuppertal, Zürich: Brockhaus.

HOLLENWEGER, Walter J., 1970, PENTECOSTALISM AND THE THIRD WORLD. Dialogue 9, 2: 122-129.

HOLLENWEGER, Walter J., 1970, A BLACK PENTECOSTAL CONCEPT: A FORGOTTEN CHAPTER OF BLACK HISTORY - THE PENTECOSTALS' CONTRIBUTION. Concept (Geneva, WCC) 30: 4-5, 18.

HOLLENWEGER, Walter J. (ed.), 1971, DIE PFINGSTKIRCHEN, SELBSTDARSTELLUNGEN, DOKUMENTE, KOMMENTARE. Stuttgart: Evangelisches Verlagswerk.

HOLLENWEGER, Walter J., 1972, THE PENTECOSTALS: THE CHARISMATIC MOVEMENT IN THE CHURCHES. Minneapolis: Augsburg Publishing House.

HOLLENWEGER, Walter J., 1973, PFINGSTLER, KATHOLIKEN UND POLITIK IN LATEINAMERIKA. Reformatio 22, 6: 334-341.

HOLLENWEGER, Walter J., 1974, CHARISMATIC AND PENTECOSTAL MOVEMENTS. In: Kirkpatrick 1974.

HOLLENWEGER, Walter J., 1974, PENTECOST BETWEEN BLACK AND WHITE. Belfast: Christian Journals.

HOLLENWEGER, Walter J., 1976, EL PENTECOSTALISMO, HISTORIA Y DOCTRINAS. Buenos Aires, Argentina: Asociación Editoral La Aurora.

HOLLENWEGER, Walter J., 1977, CHRISTEN OHNE SCHRIFTEN. FÜNF FALLSTUDIEN ZUR SOZIALETHIK MÜNDLICHER RELIGION. Erlangen: Evangelisch-Lutherische Mission.

HOLLENWEGER, Walter J., 1980, ROOTS AND FRUITS OF THE CHARISMATIC RENEWAL IN THE THIRD WORLD: IMPLICATIONS FOR MISSION. Theological Renewal 14.

HOLLENWEGER, Walter J., 1982, METHODISM'S PAST IN PENTECOSTALISM'S PRESENT; A CASE STUDY OF A CULTURAL CLASH IN CHILE. Methodist History 20: 169-182.

HOLLENWEGER, Walter J., 1985, AS ASSEMBLEIAS DE DEUS NO BRASIL. In: Imagens...1985: 22-31.
HOMRIGHAUSEN, E.G., 1970, THE CHURCH IN THE WORLD; PENTECOSTALISM AND THE THIRD WORLD. Theology Today 26, 4: 446-450.
HOOVER, Willis C., 1931, n.d., HISTORIA DEL AVIVAMIENTO PENTECOSTAL EN CHILE. Santiago: Imprensa El Esfuerzo (1931). Santiago: Comunidad Evangelica de Chile, PRESOR (n.d.).
HOOVER, Willis C., 1932, PENTECOST IN CHILE. World Dominion 10: 155-161.
HOOVER, Willis C., HISTORIA DEL AVIVAMIENTO: ORIGEN Y DESARROLLO DE LA IGLESIA EVANGELICA PENTECOSTAL. Santiago: Corporación Iglesia Evangélica Pentecostal.
HOPKIN, John Barton, 1984, MUSIC IN JAMAICAN PENTECOSTAL CHURCHES. Jamaica Journal (Kingston: The Institute of Jamaica).
HOROWITZ, Michael M. (ed.), 1971, PEOPLES AND CULTURES OF THE CARIBBEAN: AN ANTHROPOLOGICAL READER. Garden City, N.Y.: Natural History Press. [Cf. Cook 1965, 1971]
HOWE, Gary Nigel, 1977, REPRESENTAÇÕES RELIGIOSAS E CAPITALISMO: UMA "LEITURA" ESTRUTURALISTA DO PENTECOSTALISMO NO BRASIL. Cadernos do ISER 6: 39-48.
HOWE, Gary Nigel, 1980, CAPITALISM AND RELIGION AT THE PERIPHERY: PENTECOSTALISM AND UMBANDA IN BRAZIL. In: Glazier 1980: 125-141.
HUAMAN P., Santiago A., 1982, LA PRIMERA HISTORIA DEL MOVIMIENTO PENTECOSTAL DEL PERU. Lima: El gallo de oro.
HUCK, Eugene, and Edward MOSELEY, 1970, MILITANTS, MERCHANTS AND MISSIONARIES: U.S. EXPANSION IN MIDDLE AMERICA. Bloomington Ala.: University of Alabama Press.
HUGARTE, Renzo Pi, 1992a, CULTOS DE POSESION Y EMPRESAS DE CURA DIVINA EN EL URUGUAY: DESAROLLO Y ESTUDIOS. Sociedad y Religión 9, 26-39.
HUGARTE, Renzo Pi, 1992b, LA IGLESIA PENTECOSTAL "DIOS ES AMOR" EN EL URUGUAY. Cadernos de Antropologia (UFRGS, Porto Alegre) 9, 63-96.
HUGARTE, Renzo Pi, 1993, PERMEABILIDAD Y DINAMICA DE LAS FRONTEIRAS CULTURALES: UMBANDA Y PENTECOSTALISMO EN EL URUGUAY. In: Fonseca 1993: 122-131.
HUNKA, Jack W., 1967, THE HISTORY/PHILOSOPHY OF ASSEMBLIES OF GOD IN LATIN AMERICA. Western Evangelical Seminary.
HUNTINGTON, Deborah, 1984, GOD'S SAVING PLAN. NACLA, Report on the Americas 18, 1: 23-33.
HUNTINGTON, Deborah, 1984, THE PROPHET MOTIVE. NACLA, Report on the Americas 18, 1: 2-11.
HURBON, Laënnec, 1987, LOS NUEVOS MOVIMIENTOS RELIGIOSOS EN EL CARIBE. Cristianismo y Sociedad 93, 3, 37-64.
HUTCHINSON, William R., 1987, ERRAND TO THE WORLD: AMERICAN PROTESTANT THOUGHT AND FOREIGN MISSION. Chicago etc.: University of Chicago Press.
HUTTEN, Kurt, 1963, DIE STÄRKSTE PROTESTANTISCHE KONFESSION LATEINAMERIKAS. Materialdienst (Stuttgart) 26: 118.

HVALKOF, Soren; AABY, Peter, 1981, IS GOD AN AMERICAN? AN ANTHRO-POLOGICAL PERSPECTIVE ON THE MISSIONARY WORK OF THE SUMMER INSTITUTE OF LINGUISTICS. Copenhagen/London: International Workgroup for Indigenous Affairs/Survival International. [SIL]

HVALKOF, Soren; STOLL, David, 1984, ON THE SUMMER INSTITUTE OF LINGUISTICS AND ITS CRITICS. Current Anthropology: 25, 124-125.

I

IBARRA, Adoniram, 1991, A PROTEST MUSIC BORN FROM CHRISTIAN FAITH. Pneuma (The Journal of the Society for Pentecostal Studies) 13, 2, 151-156.

IBARRA BELLON, Araceli; REISE L., Alisa Lanczyner, 1972, LA HERMOSA PRO-VINCIA, NACIMIENTO Y VIDA DE UNA SECTA CRISTIANA EN GUA-DALAJARA. Guadalajara: Universidad de Guadalajara. [Mexico, M.A. Thesis]

IGLESIAS, Maria, 1995, PENTECOSTALISMOS II: UN MOVIMIENTO ME-SIANICO EN LA PROVINCIA DEL CHACO: NAPALPI, 1924. In: Religiosidad Popular: 78-96. [See also Santamaria 1995]

Imagens..., 1985, IMAGENS DA ASSEMBLEIA DE DEUS. Rudge Ramos, São Bernar-do do Campo SP: IMES, Cadernos de Pós-graduação Ciências da Religião 4. [Brazil, Assembléias de Deus]

IMMERMAN, Richard H., 1982, THE CIA IN GUATEMALA. Austin: University of Texas Press.

INSTITUTO DE RELACIONES ECUMENCIAS, s.f., EL USO DE LAS SECTAS RELIGIOSAS EN AMERICA LATINA. Documentos de circulación interna no. 3. [Argentina]

Intelligence..., s.f., INTELLIGENCE INFILTRATION INTO RELIGIOUS ORGA-NIZATIONS. Socio Pastoral Institute, Special Issue 3, Year Two, Mimeo.

Invasión..., s.f., INVASION DE SECTAS PROTESTANTES. Asunción: Vicariato Castrense. [Paraguay]

IRELAND, Rowan, 1980, GETTING IT RIGHT: THE EVERYDAY EXPERIENCE OF PENTECOSTALISM AND SPIRITUALISM IN A NORTHEAST BRAZIL-IAN TOWN. In: Hayes 1980: 145-159.

IRELAND, Rowan, 1987, THE POLITICS OF BRAZILIAN PENTECOSTALS. Bundoora: La Trobe University. [Paper SAANZ Conference, University of South Wales, July 1987]

IRELAND, Rowan, 1991, KINGDOMS COME: RELIGION AND POLITICS IN BRAZIL. Pittsburgh, Pa.: University of Pittsburgh Press.

IRELAND, Rowan, 1993, THE CRENTES OF CAMPO ALEGRE AND THE RELI-GIOUS CONSTRUCTION OF BRAZILIAN POLITICS. In: Garrard-Burnett and Stoll 1993: 45-65.

IRELAND, Rowan, 1994, PENTECOSTALISM, CONVERSION, AND POLITICS IN BRAZIL. Religion 25, 2, 135-145.

J

JACKSON, Jean E., 1984, TRADUCCIONES COMPETITIVAS DES EVANGELIO EN EL VAUPES, COLOMBIA. América Indígena 44, 1: 49-94. [SIL, Nuevas Tribus]

JIMENEZ, Julio, 1985, LA IGLESIA DENUNCIA EL NARCOTRAFICO Y LA UTILIZACION DE LAS SECTAS. Vida Nueva 1484.

JOHNSON, Norbert E., 1970, THE HISTORY, DYNAMIC, AND PROBLEMS OF THE PENTECOSTAL MOVEMENT IN CHILE. Richmond, Va.: Union Theological Seminary.

JOHNSON, Robert Edward, 1984, AN HISTORICAL ANALYSIS OF THE SOURCES OF RELIGIOUS ABERTURA IN BRAZIL. Southwestern Baptist Theological Seminary. [Ph.D.]

JONES, Charles E., 1974, A GUIDE TO THE STUDY OF THE HOLINESS MOVEMENT. Metuchen, N.J.: Scarecrow Press/American Theological Library, ATLA Bibliography Series no. 1.

JONES, Charles E., 1983, A GUIDE TO THE STUDY OF THE PENTECOSTAL MOVEMENT. Metuchen, N.J.: Scarecrow Press/American Theological Library Association, ATLA Bibliography Series no. 6, 2 Vols.

JONHSON, Norbert E., s.f., THE HISTORY, DYNAMICS AND PROBLEMS OF THE PENTECOSTAL MOVEMENT IN CHILE. Richmond, Va.: Union Theological Seminary. [M.A. Thesis]

JORDAN, W.F., 1926, CENTRAL AMERICAN INDIANS AND THE BIBLE. Nueva York: Fleming H. Revell.

JUNGKUNTZ, Theodore, 1981, UM CATECISMO LUTERANO CARISMATICO. Porto Alegre: Renovação. [Brazil]

Junta..., 1979, JUNTA CURBS RELIGIOUS LIBERTY OF SECTS IN ARGENTINA. Latinamerica Press 11, 43: 5-7.

JUSTINIANO, Rolando, 1984, COMO FINANCIAR LAS CAMPAÑAS. In: Documentos... 1984.

K

KAMI, Peter, 1975, REVOLUTIONARY CUBAN PENTECOSTALS. Bristol: Pentecost and Politics.

KAMI, Peter, n.d., THE CHURCH IN REVOLUTIONARY CUBA. In: Cuba now...

KAMSTEEG, Frans, 1990a, CURACIÓN PENTECOSTAL Y PODER: UN CASO PERUANO. Anthropológica, 8: 247-273.

KAMSTEEG, Frans, 1990b, LÍDERES Y LAICOS ENTRE LOS GRUPOS PENTECOSTALES DE AREQUIPA, PERÚ. Cristianismo y Sociedad, 106: 59-75.

KAMSTEEG, Frans, 1991a, PENTECOSTAL HEALING AND POWER: A PERUVIAN CASE. In: Droogers, A.F., G. Huizer and H. Siebers (eds), Popular Power in Latin American Religions. Saarbrücken, Fort Lauderdale: Verlag Breitenbach Publishers, pp. 196-218.

KAMSTEEG, Frans, 1991b, PASTOR Y DISCÍPULO. EL ROL DE LOS LÍDERES Y LAICOS EN EL CRECIMIENTO DE LAS IGLESIAS PENTECOSTALES DE AREQUIPA, PERÚ. In: Boudewijnse, Barbara; André Droogers and Frans Kam-

280   More Than Opium

steeg (eds), *Algo más que opio. Una lectura antropológica del pentecostalismo latino-americano y caribeño.* San José: DEI, pp. 95-113.

KAMSTEEG, Frans, 1993, THE MESSAGE AND THE PEOPLE - THE DIFFER-ENT MEANINGS OF A PENTECOSTAL EVANGELISTIC CAMPAIGN. A CASE FROM SOUTHERN PERU. In: Rostas, Susanna and André Droogers (eds), *The Popular Use of Popular Religion in Latin America.* Amsterdam: CEDLA, pp. 127-144.

KAMSTEEG, Frans, 1995, PROPHETIC PENTECOSTALISM IN CHILE: A CASE STUDY ON RELIGION AND DEVELOPMENT POLICY. Amsterdam: Vrije Universiteit. [Ph.D.]

KATOLLA-SCHÄFER, K., 1987, DIE ROLLE DER PFINGSTKIRCHLICHEN MISSION IN SOZIOKULTURELLEN VERÄNDERUNGEN IM HOCH-LAND GUATEMALAS. Tübingen: Eberhardt-Karls-Universität.

KEMPER, W., 1965, ARCHISCH-EKSTATISCHE MASSENBEWEGUNGEN IM HEUTIGEN BRASILIEN. In: Bitter 1965:133-150.

KENDRICK, Klaude, 1961, THE PROMISE FULFILLED: A HISTORY OF THE MODERN PENTECOSTAL MOVEMENT. Springfield, Miss.: Gospel Publishing House. [Thesis, University of Texas, Austin 1959]

KESSEL, Juan van; GUERRERO J., Bernardo, 1987, "SANIDAD Y SALVACION" EN EL ALTIPLANO CHILENO: DEL YATIRI AL PASTOR. Iquique: CIREN, Cuaderno de Investigación Social no. 21.

KESSLER, J.B., 1967, A STUDY OF THE OLDER PROTESTANT MISSIONS AND CHURCHES IN PERU AND CHILE, WITH SPECIAL REFERENCE TO PROBLEMS OF DIVISION, NATIONALISM AND NATIVE MINISTRY. Goes: Oosterbaan & Le Cointre. [Ph.D., University of Utrecht]

KESSLER, Jean B., 1989, A SUMMARY OF THE COSTA RICAN EVANGELICAL CRISIS: AUGUST, 1989. Pasadena, Calif.: IDEAS/Church Growth Studies Program. (Mimeo)

KEYES, Lawrence E., 1983, THE LAST AGE OF MISSIONS: A STUDY OF THIRD WORLD MISSION SOCIETIES. Pasadena, Calif.: William Carey Library.

KIRKPATRICK, D. (ed.), 1974, THE HOLY SPIRIT. Tydings: World Methodist Council.

KLIEWER, Gerd Uwe, 1975, DAS NEUE VOLK DER PFINGSTLER; RELIGION, UNTERENTWICKLUNG UND SOZIALER WANDEL IN LATEINAME-RIKA. Bern: Herbert Lang, Studien zur interkulturellen Geschichte des Christentums no. 3.

KLIEWER, Gerd Uwe, 1976, DOUTRINA PENTECOSTAL E AMBIENTE SO-CIAL. Estudos Teológicos (São Leopoldo) 16, 3: 37-44. [Brazil]

KLIEWER, Gerd Uwe, 1982, ASSEMBLÉIA DE DEUS E ELEIÇÕES NUM MUNICÍPIO DE MATO GROSSO. Comunicações do ISER, 3: 12-15.

KLOPPENBURG, Boaventura, 1975, REFLEXIONES PSICOLOGICO-TEOLO-GICAS SOBRE LA FENOMENOLOGIA PENTECOSTAL. Medellin, Teología y Pastoral para América Latina 1, 3: 297-314.

KNOWLTON, David, 1988, SEARCHING MINDS AND QUESTING HEARTS: PROTESTANTISM AND SOCIAL CONTEXT IN BOLIVIA. Austin: University of Texas. [Ph.D.]

KUHL, Paul E., 1982, PROTESTANT MISSIONARY ACTIVITY AND FREEDOM OF RELIGION IN ECUADOR, PERU AND BOLIVIA. [Ph.D., Southern Illinois University, Carbondale]

KUNKEL, Heimberto, 1987, CONTEMPORARY RELIGIOUS MOVEMENTS CHALLENGE LATIN AMERICAN CHURCHES. LW Information 2, 10.

L

La penetración..., 1982, LA PENETRACION PROTESTANTE EN HONDURAS. Boletín Informativo de Honduras 18.

La Penetración..., 1983, LA PENETRACION PROTESTANTE EN HONDURAS. Boletín Informativo de Honduras 23.

La santa..., 1984, LA SANTA CONTRAINSURGENCIA: SECTAS PROTESTANTES EN CENTRO-AMERICA. Diálogo Social 17, 169, 47-49.

LAGOS SCHUFFENEGER, Humberto, 1978, LA LIBERTAD RELIGIOSA EN CHILE, LOS EVANGELICOS Y EL GOBIERNO MILITAR. Santiago de Chile: Edición UNELAM/Vicaria de la Solidaridad.

LAGOS SCHUFFENEGER, Humberto, 1983, LA FUNCION DE LAS MINORIAS RELIGIOSAS: LAS TRANSACCIONES DEL PROTESTANTISMO CHILENO EN EL PERIODO 1973-1981 DEL GOBIERNO MILITAR. Louvain-la-Neuve: Ed. Cabay. [Ph.D.]

LAGOS SCHUFFENEGER, Humberto, 1983, LA LIBERTAD RELIGIOSA Y LAS CORPORACIONES DE DERECHO PROTESTANTES, CHILE 1973-1981. Madrid: Universidad Complutense. [M.A. Thesis]

LAGOS SCHUFFENEGER, Humberto, 1984, LA FUNCION DE LA RELIGION EN EL GOBIERNO MILITAR, EN EL MODELO POLITICO AUTORITARIO Y EN LAS FUERZAS ARMADAS Y DE ORDEN DE CHILE. Primer Congreso Chileno de Sociología: 1984. Also in: Revista Andes 1985, 34-42.

LAGOS SCHUFFENEGER, Humberto, 1985, SECTAS RELIGIOSAS EN CHILE: ¿OPRESION O LIBERACION? Santiago de Chile: Ediciones PRESOR.

LAGOS SCHUFFENEGER, Humberto, 1987, SECTAS RELIGIOSAS EN CHILE: ¿FE O IDEOLOGIA? Santiago: Ediciones Lar y Presor.

LAGOS SCHUFFENEGER, Humberto, 1988, CRISIS DE LA ESPERANZA. RELIGIÓN Y AUTORITARISMO EN CHILE. Santiago: Presor/Lar

LAGOS SCHUFFENEGER, Humberto, s.f., LA CRISIS DE HEGEMIONIA EN CHILE Y LA FUNCION DE LAS IGLESIAS EVANGELICAS. Santiago de Chile: PRESOR (Programa Evangélico de Estudios Socio-religiosos).

LAGOS SCHUFFENEGER, Humberto, and Arturo CHACON HERRERA, 1986, LA FUNCION DE LA RELIGION EN LAS FUERZAS ARMADAS Y DE ORDEN. Santiago de Chile: Ed. Rehue, PRESOR. [Chile]

LAGOS SCHUFFENEGER, Humberto, and Arturo CHACON HERRERA, 1987, LOS EVANGELICOS EN CHILE: UNA LECTURA SOCIOLOGICA. Santiago: Ediciones Lar y Presor.

LALIVE D'EPINAY, Christian, 1967, CHANGEMENTS SOCIAUX ET DEVELOPPEMENT D'UNE SECTE: LE PENTECOTISME AU CHILI. Archives de Sociologie des Religions 12, 23: 65-90.

LALIVE D'EPINAY, Christian, 1967, LE PENTECOTISME DANS LA SOCIETE CHILIENNE, ESSAI D'APPROCHE SOCIOLOGIQUE. Geneva: Université de Genève, 2 Vols. [M.A. Thesis]

LALIVE D'EPINAY, Christian, 1967, PASTORES CHILENOS Y ABERTURA HACIA EL ECUMENISMO. Mensaje 163.

LALIVE D'EPINAY, Christian, 1967, THE TRAINING OF PASTORS AND THEOLOGICAL EDUCATION: THE CASE OF CHILE. International Review of Missions 56: 185-192.

LALIVE D'EPINAY, Christian, 1968, TOWARD A TYPOLOGY OF LATIN AMERICAN PROTESTANTISM. Review of Religious Research 10: 4-11. LALIVE D'EPINAY, Christian, 1968, EL REFUGIO DE LAS MASAS, ESTUDIO SOCIOLOGICO DEL PROTESTANTISMO CHILENO. Santiago de Chile: Editorial del Pacífico.

LALIVE D'EPINAY, Christian, 1968, THE PENTECOSTAL 'CONQUISTA' IN CHILE. Ecumenical Review 20, 1: 16-32.

LALIVE D'EPINAY, Christian, 1969, HAVEN OF THE MASSES. A STUDY OF THE PENTECOSTAL MOVEMENT IN CHILE. London: Lutterworth Press.

LALIVE D'EPINAY, Christian, 1969, THE PENTECOSTAL 'CONQUEST' OF CHILE: RUDIMENTS OF A BETTER UNDERSTANDING. In: Cutler 1969: 179-193.

LALIVE D'EPINAY, Christian, 1970, LES PROTESTANTISMES LATINO-AME-RICAINS, UN MODELE TYPOLOGIQUE. Archives de Sociologie des Religions 30: 33-57.

LALIVE D'EPINAY, Christian, 1970, O REFUGIO DAS MASSAS, ESTUDO SO-CIOLOGICO DO PROTESTANTISMO CHILENO. Rio de Janeiro: Paz e Terra.

LALIVE D'EPINAY, Christian, 1974, LES RELIGIONS AU CHILE ENTRE L'ALIENATION ET LA PRISE DE CONSCIENCE. Social Compass 21: 85-100.

LALIVE D'EPINAY, Christian, 1975, RÉLIGION, DYNAMIQUE SOCIALE ET DÉPENDANCE. LES MOUVEMENTS PROTESTANTS EN ARGENTINE ET AU CHILI. Paris/La Haye: Mouton.

LALIVE D'EPINAY, Christian, 1976, LE ROLE PARTICULIER DES MOUVE-MENTS PROTESTANTS POPULAIRES. Le Monde Diplomatique, 16 mai 1976.

LALIVE D'EPINAY, Christian, 1977, RELIGIAO, ESPIRITUALIDADE E SOCIE-DADE, ESTUDO SOCIOLOGICO DO PENTECOSTALISMO LATINO-AMERICANO. Cadernos do Iser, 6: 5-10.

LALIVE D'EPINAY, Christian, 1978, CONFORMISME PASSIF, CONFORMISMO ACTIF ET SOLIDARITE DE CLASSE. COMMENTAIRE A L'ARTICLE DE J. TENNEKES. Social Compass 25, 1: 80-84.

LALIVE D'EPINAY, Christian, 1981, DEPENDANCE SOCIALE ET RELIGION, PASTEURS ET PROTESTANTISMES LATINO-AMERICAINS. Archives de Sciences Sociales des Religions 52, 1: 85-98.

LALIVE D'EPINAY, Christian, 1983, POLITICAL REGIMES AND MILLE-NARIANISM IN A DEPENDENT SOCIETY: REFLECTIONS ON PENTE-COSTALISM IN CHILE. Concilium 161: 42-54.

LANDIM, Leilah, 1989, QUEM SÃO AS "SEITAS"? In: Landim 1989a: 11-21. [Brazil]

LANDIM, Leilah (ed.), 1989a, SINAIS DOS TEMPOS. IGREJAS E SEITAS NO BRASIL. Rio de Janeiro: ISER.

LANDIM, Leilah (ed.), 1989b, SINAIS DOS TEMPOS. TRADIÇÕES RELIGIOSAS NO BRASIL. Rio de Janeiro: ISER. [Cf. Mendonça 1989]

LANDIM, Leilah (ed.), 1989c, SINAIS DOS TEMPOS. DIVERSIDADE RELIGIOSA NO BRASIL. Rio de Janeiro: ISER.

LANCASTER, Roger N., 1988, THANKS TO GOD AND THE REVOLUTION. POPULAR RELIGION AND CLASS CONSCIOUSNESS IN THE NEW NICARAGUA. New York: Columbia University Press.

LARSON, Peter Alden, 1973, MIGRATION AND CHURCH GROWTH IN ARGENTINA. Pasadena, Calif.: Fuller Theological Seminary. [Thesis]

LARUFFA, Anthony L, 1966, PENTECOSTALISM IN A PUERTO RICAN COMMUNITY. [Ph.D., Columbia University, New York]

LARUFFA, Anthony, 1969, CULTURE CHANGE AND PENTECOSTALISM IN PUERTO RICO. Social and Economic Studies 18: 273-281.

LARUFFA, Anthony L., 1972, SAN CIPRIANO: LIFE IN A PUERTO RICAN COMMUNITY. New York: Gordon and Breach.

LARUFFA, Anthony L., 1980, PENTECOSTALISM IN PUERTO RICAN SOCIETY. In: Glazier 1980: 49-65.

Las nuevas..., 1983, LAS "NUEVAS RELIGIONES". Amigo del hogar 442. [Dominican Republic]

Las sectas..., 1982, LAS SECTAS EN PANAMA, Diálogo Social 148. Las sectas..., 1983, LAS SECTAS PROTESTANTES. Orientación 432. [Ecuador]

Las sectas..., 1984, LAS SECTAS EN EL PERU. Misión sin fronteras 58.

LAURENTIN, René, 1982, MIRACLES IN EL PASO? Ann Arbor, Mich.: Servant Books. [Mexico]

LAWSON, David L., 1979, RELIGIOUS AFFILIATION AND AGRICULTURAL INNOVATION IN A HIGHLAND MEXICAN VILLAGE. [Paper Annual Meeting Association of American Geographers, April 9-12, 1979]

LEHMANN, David, 1993, WOMEN AND PENTECOSTAL PROTESTANTISM IN BAHIA. Paper read during a workshop on Religion and Gender in Latin America, Annual Conference Society for Latin American Studies, Manchester, April 2-4, 1993.

LEON, Victor de, 1979, THE SILENT PENTECOSTALS, A BIOGRAPHICAL HISTORY OF THE PENTECOSTAL MOVEMENT AMONG THE HISPANICS IN THE TWENTIETH CENTURY. La Habra: author's edition.

LÉONARD, Émile G., 1953, L'ILLUMINISME DANS UN PROTESTANTISME DE CONSTITUTION RÉCENTE (BRÉSIL). Paris: P.U.F., Bibliothèque de l'École des Hautes Études, Section des Sciences Religieuses, vol. LXV. [Also in: Revue de l'Histoire des Religions 1952]

LÉONARD, Émile G., 1963, O PROTESTANTISMO BRASILEIRO, ESTUDO DE ECLESIOLOGIA E HISTORIA SOCIAL. São Paulo: ASTE. [Also in: Revista de História, Rio de Janeiro]

LÉONARD, Émile G., 1952, L'ÉVANGILE AU BRÉSIL. Revue d'Évangelisation 7, 38: 208-235.

LERNOUX, Penny, 1980, CRY OF THE PEOPLE: UNITED STATES INVOLVEMENT IN THE RISE OF FASCISM, TORTURE AND MURDER AND THE PERSECUTION OF THE CATHOLIC CHURCH IN LATIN AMERICA. Garden City, N.Y.: Doubleday.

284   More Than Opium

LEVINE, Daniel (ed.), 1979, CHURCHES AND POLITICS IN LATIN AMERICA.
Beverley Hills, Calif.: Sage.
LEVINE, Daniel H., 1981, RELIGION, SOCIETY AND POLITICS: STATES OF
ART. Latin American Research Review: 16, 185-209.
LEVINE, Daniel H., 1985, RELIGION AND POLITICS: DRAWING LINES, UN-
DERSTANDING CHANGE. Latin American Research Review: 20, 185-201.
LEVINE. Daniel (ed.), 1986, RELIGION AND POLITICAL CONFLICT IN LATIN
AMERICA. Chapel Hill & London: The University of North Carolina Press.
LEWIS, Norman, 1988, THE MISSIONARIES. London: Secker and Wartburg. [SIL,
New Tribes Mission]
LINS, Paulo, and Maria de Lourdes da SILVA, 1990, BANDIDOS E EVANGELICOS:
EXTREMOS QUE SE TOCAM. Religião e Sociedade 15, 1, 166-173.
LOEWEN, Jacob A.; BUCKWALTER, Albert; KRATZ, James, 1965, SHAMANISM,
ILLNESS, AND POWER IN TOBA CHURCH LIFE. Practical Anthropology 12:
250-280. [Argentina]
LOPEZ, Mauricio, 1960, THE CHURCH AND THE LAY MOVEMENT IN LATIN
AMERICA. Geneva: CMI Publicación, Documento no. IX.
LOYOLA, Maria Andréa, 1983, L'ESPRIT ET LE CORPS, DES THERAPEUTI-
QUES POPULAIRES DANS LA BANLIEUE DE RIO. Paris: Éd. de la Maison
des Sciences de l'Homme. [Brazil]
LOYOLA, Maria Andréa, 1984, MEDICOS E CURANDEIROS, CONFLITO SO-
CIAL E SAUDE. São Paulo: DIFEL. [Brazil, healing]
LUGO, Gamaliel, 1992, ETICA SOCIAL PENTECOSTAL: SANTIDAD COM-
PROMETIDA. In: Alvarez 1992: 101-122.
LUGO, Juan L., 1951, PENTECOSTES EN PUERTO RICO O LA VIDA DE UN
MISIONERO. San Juan: Puerto Rico Gospel Press. [Iglesia de Diós Pentecostal]
Luis..., 1983, LUIS PALAU, RIOS MONTT, REAGAN O LA CRUZADA RELI-
GIOSA ANTISANDINISTA. La Religión en los Periódicos, febrero 11-18, 1983.
[Nicaragua]
LYRA, Jorge Buarque, s.f., ORIENTAÇAO EVANGELICA (INTERDENOMINA-
CIONAL) PARA SALVAR O BRASIL. Niteroi: author's edition. [O Brasil Para
Cristo]
LYRA, Jorge Buarque, s.f. (1964), O MOVIMENTO PENTECOSTAL NO BRASIL,
PROFILAXIA CRISTA DESSE MOVIMENTO EM DEFESA DE "O BRASIL
PARA CRISTO." Niteroi: author's edition. [O Brasil Para Cristo]

M

MACHADO, Maria das Dores Campos, 1994, ADESÃO RELIGIOSA E SEUS EFEI-
TOS NA ESFERA PRIVADA: UM ESTUDO COMPARATIVO DOS CARIS-
MATICOS E PENTECOSTAIS DO RIO DE JANEIRO. Ph.D. Instituto Univer-
sitário de Pesquisa, Rio de Janeiro.
MALLIMACI, Fortunato, 1993, CATOLICISMO INTEGRAL, IDENTIDAD
NACIONAL Y NUEVOS MOVIMIENTOS RELIGIOSOS. In: Frigerio 1993, II:
24-48.
MANNING, Frank E., 1980, PENTECOSTALISM: CHRISTIANITY AND REPU-
TATION. In: Glazier 1980: 177-187.

MARASCHIN, Jaci Correia, 1985, IMAGENS DA ASSEMBLEIA DE DEUS. In: Imagens... 1985: 6-21. [Brazil]
MARGOLIES, Luise, 1980, THE PARADOXICAL GROWTH OF PENTE-COSTALISM. In: Glazier 1980: 1-5.
MARIZ, Cecília L., 1988, RELIGIÃO E POBREZA: UMA COMPARAÇÃO ENTRE CEBS E IGREJAS PENTECOSTAIS. Comunicações do ISER 7, 30: 10-19.
MARIZ, Cecília L., 1989, RELIGION AND COPING WITH POVERTY IN BRA-ZIL. Ann Arbor, Mich.: University Microfilms. [Ph.D.]
MARIZ, Cecília L., 1990, IGREJAS PENTECOSTAIS E ESTRATEGIAS DE SOBRE-VIVENCIA. In: Braga 1990: 89-112.
MARIZ, Cecília L., 1991, POVERTY AND MOTIVATION TO JOIN A RELIGI-OUS GROUP: COMPARING PENTECOSTALISM AND BASE COMMUNI-TIES IN BRAZIL. Paper presented at the XXI Conference of the ISSR, Maynooth, Ireland, August 19-23, 1991.
MARIZ, Cecília Loreto, 1994a, LIBERTAÇAO E ETICA, UMA ANALISE DO DISCURSO DE PENTECOSTAIS QUE SE RECUPERAM DO ALCOOLIS-MO. In: Antoniazzi 1994b: 204-224. [Brazil]
MARIZ, Cecília Loreto, 1994b, COPING WITH POVERTY: PENTECOSTALS AND CHRISTIAN BASE COMMUNITIES IN BRAZIL. Philadelphia, Pa.: Temple University Press.
MARIZ, Cecília L., 1995, EL DEBATE EN TORNO DEL PENTECOSTALISMO AUTONOMO EN BRASIL. Sociedad y Religión 13: 21-32
MARIZ, Cecília L., and Maria das Dores C. Machado, 1994, SINCRETISMO E TRÂNSITO RELIGIOSO: COMPARANDO CARISMÁTICOS E PENTECOS-TAIS. Comunicações do ISER 45: 24-34.
MAROSTICA, Mat, 1994, LA IGLESIA EVANGELICA COMO MOVIMIENTO SOCIAL. Sociedad y Religión 12: 3-17.
MARQUINA, Brigido, 1980, LAS NUEVAS TRIBUS. Caracas: Comité evangélico venezolano por la justicia. [Venezuela]
MARTIN, Bernice, 1994, NEW MUTATIONS OF THE PROTESTANT ETHIC AMONG LATIN AMERICAN PENTECOSTALS. Religion 25, 2, 101-117.
MARTIN, David, 1990, TONGUES OF FIRE: THE EXPLOSION OF PROTES-TANTISM IN LATIN AMERICA. Oxford: Blackwell.
MARTIN, David, 1991, EL PROTESTANTISMO RADICAL AN AMERICA LATI-NA. Revista de Estudios Públicos (Santiago), 44, 39-62.
MARTIN, David, 1992, EVANGELICALS AND ECONOMIC CULTURE IN LATIN AMERICA: AN INTERIM COMMENT ON RESEARCH IN PRO-GRESS. Social Compass, 39, 1: 9-14.
MARTIN, David, 1994, EVANGELICAL AND CHARISMATIC CHRISTIANITY IN LATIN AMERICA. In: Poewe 1994: 73-86.
MARTIN, David, and David LEE, 1989, AFTER CATHOLICISM: THE NEW PRO-TESTANTS AND THE RISE OF CAPITALISM IN LATIN AMERICA. Na-tional Review, Sept. 29, pp. 30-35.
MARTIN, Nieves San, 1985, LA CIA SE VISTE DE SECTAS RELIGIOSAS PARA ESPIAR. Vida Nueva 1478.
MARTIN-BARO, Ignacio, 1989, 'SOLO DIOS SALVA': SENTIDO POLITICO DE LA CONVERSION RELIGIOSA. Revista Chilena de Psicologia, 1, 13-20.

MARTINEZ, A., 1989, LAS SECTAS EN NICARAGUA. OFERTA Y DEMANDA DE SALVACION. San José, Managua: DEI, CAV.

MARTINEZ, Abelino, 1991, COMPORTAMIENTOS SOCIALES EN EL PROTES-TANTISMO Y EN EL PENTECOSTALISMO POPULAR NICARAGUENSE. In: Samandú 1991a: 183-227.

MARTINS, Jos Pedro S., 1987, PHENOMENAL GROWTH OF SECTS, ELEC-TRONIC CHURCH RELATED TO CONTINENT'S POVERTY. Latinamerica Press 19, 16: 5-6.

MARTINS, Syr O.E., 1958, SEJA CURADO AGORA! São Paulo: Los Angeles Editora. [Brazil]

MARZAL, Manuel, 1983, LA TRANSFORMACION RELIGIOSA PERUANA. Lima: Pontificia Universidad Católica del Perú.

MARZAL. Manuel, 1988, IGLESIA CULTURAL Y NUEVAS IGLESIAS. América Indígena 48, 1, 139-164.

MARZAL. Manuel, 1988, LOS CAMINOS RELIGIOSOS DE LOS INMIGRANTES EN LA GRAN LIMA, EL CASO DE EL AUGUSTINO. Lima: Pontificia Universidad Católica del Perú.

MATURANA, Manuel, 1985, DIOS QUIERE QUE TODOS VIVAMOS EN CONDICIONES DIGNAS. ENTREVISTA A MANUEL MATURANA, LAI-CO PENTECOSTAL, PRESIDENTE DEL CAMPAMENTO J.F. FRESNO. Evangelio y Sociedad 1: 40-46.

MATZAT, Donald G. (ed.), 1981, SERVINDO A RENOVAÇAO, AS HISTORIAS DOS HOMENS DO SERVIÇO LUTERANO DE RENOVAÇAO CARISMA-TICA. Porto Alegre: Renovação. [Brazil]

MAUST, John, 1984, CITIES OF CHANGE: URBAN GROWTH AND GOD'S PEOPLE IN TEN LATIN AMERICAN CITIES. Latin America Mission.

MAYNARD, Kent, 1977, CHRISTIANITY AND RELIGION: EVANGELICAL IDENTITY AND SOCIOCULTURAL ORGANIZATION IN URBAN ECUA-DOR. Indiana University. [Ph.D.]

MAYNARD, Kent, 1988, ON PROTESTANTS AND PASTORALISTS: THE SEGMENTARY NATURE OF SOCIO-CULTURAL ORGANISATION. Man 23, 1: 101-117.

MCDONNEL, Kilian, 1980, PRESENCE, POWER, PRAISE: DOCUMENTS ON CHARISMATIC RENEWAL. Collegeville, Minn.: The Liturgical Press, 3 Vols. Panamá, México. [Vol. 2 on Latin America]

MCGEE, Gary Blair, 1984, "THIS GOSPEL ... SHALL BE PREACHED": A HIS-TORY AND THEOLOGY OF ASSEMBLIES OF GOD FOREIGN MISSIONS: 1914-1959. Saint Louis: Saint Louis University. [Thesis]

MEDELLIN LOZANO, Fernando, 1984, EXPERIENCIA SECTARIA EN UNA COMUNIDAD PENTECOSTAL DE BOGOTA. Bogotá: Universidad Nacional de Colombia, Departamento de Antropología.

MEDELLIN LOZANO, Fernando, 1985, RELIGIONES POPULARES CONTRA LA EMANCIPACION. América Indígena 45, 4: 625-646. [Colombia]

MELENDEZ, Albino, 1987, LOS EVANGELICOS EN NICARAGUA. APRO-XIMACION EVANGELISTICA. Managua: CEPAD.

MELLO, Manoel de, 1971, PARTICIPATION IS EVERYTHING; EVANGELISM FROM THE POINT OF VIEW OF A BRAZILIAN PENTECOSTAL. International Review of Mission 60, 238: 245-248. [O Brasil Para Cristo]

MELLO, Manoel de, 1974, THE GOSPEL WITH BREAD - AN INTERVIEW WITH MANUEL DE MELLO SILVA, FOUNDER OF THE BRAZIL FOR CHRIST MOVEMENT. Monthly Letter About Evangelism 7. [O Brasil Para Cristo] Memoria..., s.f., MEMORIA DE LA CONSULTA SOBRE LA RENOVACION DE LA IGLESIA QUE NECESITAMOS, MONTERREY. México: Federación Evangélica de México.

MENDIZABAL, Antonio Goicoechea, 1980, EVANGELICOS, EVANGELISTAS, IGLESIAS EVANGELICAS. TAU 3, 15: 6-11.

MENDONÇA, Antonio Gouvêa, 1988, SEITAS E IGREJAS. Estudos de Religião (São Paulo) 5, 79-89.

MENDONÇA, Antonio Gouvêa, 1989, UM PANORAMA DO PROTESTANTISMO BRASILEIRO ATUAL. In: Landim 1989a: 37-86.

MENDONÇA, A.G., and P. VELASQUES Filho, 1990, INTRODUÇÃO AO PROTESTANTISMO NO BRASIL. São Paulo: Ed. Loyola.

MENDOZA, Lázara, 1982, EVANGELICOS OTOMIES DE IXMIQUILPAN, HGO. Patzcuaro: Programa de Etnolingüística. [Thesis]

MENZIES, William, 1971, ANOINTED TO SERVE: THE STORY OF THE ASSEMBLIES OF GOD. Springfield, Miss.: Gospel Publishing House.

MERGIER, Anne-Marie, 1983, HONDURAS, LABORATORIO DE REPRESION ESTADOUNIDENSE, EL PAIS ES SOCOVADO POR SECTAS RELIGIOSAS. Proceso, 4 abril 1983: 41-42.

MEYER, Harding, 1968, "DIE PFINGSTBEWEGUNG IN BRASILIEN". Die Evangelische Diaspora, Jahrbuch des Gustav-Adolf-Vereins 39: 9-50.

MIGUEZ BONINO, José 1972, VISION DEL CAMBIO SOCIAL Y SUS TAREAS DESDE LAS IGLESIAS CRISTIANAS NO-CATOLICAS. In: Fe cristiana... 1972: 179-202.

MIGUEZ BONINO, José, 1985, PRESENCIA Y AUSENCIA PROTESTANTE EN EL ARGENTINA DEL PROCESO MILITAR. Cristianismo y Sociedad 83: 81-85.

MILLER, Elmer S., 1967, PENTECOSTALISM AMONG THE ARGENTINE TOBA: ANALYSIS OF A RELIGIOUSLY ORIENTATED SOCIAL MOVEMENT. [Ph.D., University of Pittsburgh, Pa.]

MILLER, Elmer S., 1970, THE CHRISTIAN MISSIONARY, AGENT OF SECULARIZATION. Anthropological Quarterly 43, 1: 14-22. [Argentina]

MILLER, Elmer S., 1971, THE ARGENTINE TOBA EVANGELICAL RELIGIOUS SERVICE. Ethnology 10, 2: 149-159.

MILLER, Elmer S., 1973, LOS TOBAS Y EL MILENARISMO. Actualidad Antropológica 11: 17-20. [Argentina]

MILLER, Elmer S., 1974, THE IMPACT OF PENTECOSTAL SYMBOLISM ON ARGENTINE TOBA CONCEPTS OF POWER. Buenos Aires.

MILLER, Elmer S., 1975, SHAMANS, POWER SYMBOLS, AND CHANGE IN ARGENTINE TOBA CULTURE. American Ethnologist 10.

MILLER, Elmer S., 1979, LOS TOBAS ARGENTINOS, ARMONIA Y DISONANCIA EN UNA SOCIEDAD. México etc.: Siglo Veintiuno.

MILLER, Elmer S., 1980, HARMONY AND DISSONANCE IN ARGENTINE TOBA SOCIETY. New Haven, Conn.: HRAF.

MILLER, John Melvin, 1976, A STUDY OF MISSIOLOGICAL PROBLEMS OF CULTURAL ADAPTATION AND ITS MANIFESTATION IN CERTAIN

EVANGELICAL CHURCHES IN SINALOA, MEXICO. Dallas, Tex.: Southern Methodist University. [Thesis]

MILLER, Richard L., 1980, THE PERILS OF SUCCESS: POST-WORLD WAR II LATIN AMERICAN PROTESTANTISM. In: Brown and Cooper 1980: 52-66.

MILLS, Watson E., 1985, CHARISMATIC RELIGION IN MODERN RESEARCH: A BIBLIOGRAPHY. Macon, Ga.: Mercer University Press, NABPR (National Association of Baptist Professors of Religion), Bibliographic Series, Number 1.

Ministry with..., 1977, MINISTRY WITH THE POOR: A WORLD CONSULTATION IN LATIN AMERICA. Geneva: TEF, WCC. [Cf. Gaxiola-Gaxiola 1977]

MINNERY, Tom, 1983, WHY THE GOSPEL GROWS IN SOCIALIST NICARAGUA: THE REVOLUTION TURNED AGAINST CAPITALISM BUT NOT CHRISTIANITY. Christianity Today 27, 34-42.

MINTZ, S., 1960, WORKER IN THE CANE. New Haven, Conn.: Yale University Press. [Case study of a person converted to a revival movement]

MISCHEL, Frances, 1959, FAITH HEALING AND MEDICAL PRACTICE IN THE SOUTHERN CARIBBEAN. Southwestern Journal of Anthropology 15, 4: 407-417.

MIP (Misión Iglesia Pentecostal), 1984, BREVE RESEÑA HISTÓRICA SOBRE LA MISIÓN 'IGLESIA PENTECOSTAL'. Santiago, SEPADE. [internal document]

Missionary..., s.f., THE MISSIONARY MANUAL. Springfield, Miss.: Assemblies of God, Foreign Missions Department.

MIZUKI, John, 1977, THE GROWTH OF JAPANESE CHURCHES IN BRAZIL- Pasadena, Calif.: Fuller Theological Seminary. [Thesis]

MOLINA E., Rojas A., 1985, LA ESTRUCTURACION DE LA VISION DEL MUNDO DE LOS PENTECOSTALISTAS (LOS CASOS DE LA IGLESIA. ASAMBLEAS DE DIOS DE HATILLO Y LA IGLESIA SANTIDAD PENTECOSTAL DE HATILLO 8). Ciudad Universitaria Rodrigo Facio.

MONTEIRO DE LIMA, Délcio, 1986, OS DEMONIOS DESCEM DO NORTE. Rio de Janeiro: Francisco Alves.

MONTERROSO-REYES, Victor M., 1976, EVANGELISM-IN-DEPTH IN PARAGUAY. Pasadena, Calif.: Fuller Theological Seminary. [Thesis]

MONTOYA, Daniel, 1988, SEITAS: ORIGEM E EXPANSÃO. Estudos de Religião (São Paulo) 5, 71-77.

MOORE, Joseph G., 1953, RELIGION OF JAMAICAN NEGROES: A STUDY OF AFRO-AMERICAN ACCULTURATION. Evanston, Ill.: Northwestern University, Department of Anthropology. [Thesis]

MOORE, Thomas R., 1984, EL ILV Y UNA "TRIBU RECIEN ENCONTRADA": LA EXPERIENCIA AMARAKAERI. América Indígena 44, 1: 25-48. [Perú, SIL]

MORA, Alvaro Muñoz, 1984, LA EVANGELIZACION Y LOS MEDIOS SOCIALES DE COMUNICACION. In: Documentos... 1984.

MORACHO, Félix, 1975, EL PENTECOSTALISMO CATOLICO EN VENEZUELA. SIC (Centro Gumilla) 372; also in: Perspectivas de Diálogo (Montevideo) 10, 94: 114.

MORRISH, Ivor, 1982, OBEAH, CHRIST, AND RASTAMAN: JAMAICA AND ITS RELIGION. Cambridge: James Clarke.

MOSONYI, Esteban E. et al., 1981, EL CASO NUEVAS TRIBUS. Caracas: Editorial Ateneo de Caracas, Colección Testimonios.

MOTHE, Devonson la, s.f., "NEW WAVE" MISSIONARIES INVADE GRENADA. Caribbean Contact (Caribbean Council of Churches) 15, 12:7. [Youth with a Mission]

MOURA, Abdalaziz de, 1968/69, L'EGLISE CATHOLIQUE ET L'EGLISE PENTECOTISTE AU BRESIL ET LES POINTS DE RENCONTRE ENTRE ELLES. Bossey: Ecumenical Institute, Graduate School of Ecumenical Studies. [Unpublished paper]

MOURA, Abdalaziz de, 1971, O PENTECOSTALISMO COMO FENOMENO RELIGIOSO POPULAR NO BRASIL. Revista Eclesiástica Brasileira 31, 121: 78-94.

MOURA, Abdalaziz de, 1972, PENTECOSTALISM AND BRAZILIAN RELIGION. Theology Digest 20: 44-48.

MOURA, Abdalaziz de, s.f., IMPORTANCIA DAS IGREJAS PENTECOSTAIS PARA A IGREJA CATOLICA. Recife: Boa Vista, mimeo. [Brazil, Paper CNBB (Bishops' Conference of Brazil), Recife 1969]

MOURA, Abdalaziz de, 1976, O PENTECOSTALISMO COMO FENOMENO RELIGIOSO POPULAR NO BRASIL. Revista Eclesiástica Brasileira 36, 141: 202-205.

MULRAIN, George M., 1984, THEOLOGY IN FOLK CULTURE: THE THEOLOGICAL SIGNIFICANCE OF HAITIAN FOLK RELIGION. Bern etc.: Peter Lang.

MULRAIN, George M., 1986, TOOLS FOR MISSION IN THE CARIBBEAN CULTURE. International Review of Mission 85, 297: 51-58.

MUNIZ DE SOUZA, Beatriz, 1966, FUNÇOES SOCIAIS E PSICOLOGICAS DO PROTESTANTISMO PENTECOSTAL DE SãO PAULO. In: O espírito... 1966: 71-75. [Brazil]

MUNIZ DE SOUZA, Beatriz, 1967, PENTECOSTALISMO EM SãO PAULO. Rio Claro: Universidade de Campinas, Faculdade de Filosofia, Ciências e Letras de Rio Claro. [Brazil, Ph.D.]

MUNIZ DE SOUZA, Beatriz, 1968, ASPECTOS DO PROTESTANTISMO PENTECOSTAL EM SãO PAULO. In: César et al. 1968: 100-114. [Brazil]

MUNIZ DE SOUZA, Beatriz, 1969, A EXPERIENCIA DA SALVAÇÃO, PENTECOSTAIS EM SÃO PAULO. São Paulo: Duas Cidades. [Brazil]

MUNIZ DE SOUSA, Beatriz, 1973, PROTESTANTISMO NO BRASIL. In: Camargo 1973.

MUNIZ DE SOUZA, Beatriz, 1974, IMAGENS DE JESUS CRISTO NO PENTECOSTALISMO. In: Quem é... 1974: 143. [Brazil]

MUÑOZ RAMIREZ, Humberto, 1956, ¿HACIA DONDE VA EL PROTESTANTISMO? Mensaje 5, 54: 408-410. [Chile]

MUÑOZ RAMIREZ, Humberto, 1957, SOCIOLOGIA RELIGIOSA DE CHILE. Santiago: Ediciones Paulinas.

MUÑOZ RAMIREZ, Humberto, 1960, VISION GENERAL DEL PROTESTANTISMO EN LATINOAMERICA. Anales de la Facultad de Teología (Universidad Católica de Chile) 11.

MUÑOZ RAMIREZ, Humberto, 1974, NUESTROS HERMANOS EVANGELICOS. Santiago: Ediciones Nueva Universidad Católica de Chile. [Chile]

MUÑOZ RAMIREZ, Humberto, 1985, LOS PENTECOSTALES. In Equipe de reflexion 1985: 149-163.

MUÑOZ RAMIREZ, Humberto, 1989, LOS PENTECOSTALES. In: Santagada D., Osvaldo et al., Sectas en América Latina. Lima: Ediciones Paulinas/CELAM, pp. 139-155.

MURATORIO, Blanca, 1980, PROTESTANTISM AND CAPITALISM REVIS-ITED, IN THE RURAL HIGHLANDS OF ECUADOR. Journal of Peasant Studies 8, 1: 37-60.

MURATORIO, Blanca, 1981, PROTESTANTISM, ETHNICITY, AND CLASS·IN CHIMBORAZO. In: Whitten 1981: 506-534. [Ecuador]

N

NASH, June, 1960, PROTESTANTISM IN AN INDIAN VILLAGE IN THE WEST-ERN HIGHLANDS OF GUATEMALA. Alpha Kappa Delta 30, Special Issue: 49-58.

Nas ondas..., 1991, NAS ONDAS DE DEUS. IGREJAS TRADICIONAIS DIS-CUTEM REAÇÃO À CONCORRÊNCIA DOS PREGADORES ELETRÔ-NICOS. Istoé Senhor, 6 de fevreiro, pp. 47-49.

NELSON, Reed Elliot, 1984, ANALISE ORGANIZACIONAL DE UMA IGREJA BRASILEIRA: A CONGREGAÇAO CRISTA NO BRASIL. Revista Eclesiástica Brasileira 44, 176: 544-558.

NELSON, Reed Elliot, 1985, FUNÇOES ORGANIZACIONAIS DO CULTO NUMA IGREJA ANARQUISTA. Religião e Sociedade 12, 1: 112-126. [Brazil, Congregação Cristã no Brasil]

NELSON, Reed Elliot, 1988, ORGANIZATIONAL HOMOGENEITY, GROWTH, AND CONFLICT IN BRAZILIAN PROTESTANTISM. Sociological Analysis 48, 4: 319-327.

NELSON, Wilton N., 1957, A HISTORY OF PROTESTANTISM IN COSTA RICA. Princeton, N.J.: Princeton Theological Seminary. [Thesis]

NELSON, Wilton N., 1963, EVANGELICAL SURGE IN LATIN AMERICA-Christianity Today 7: 1009-1010.

NELSON, Wilton N., 1982, EL PROTESTANTISMO EN CENTRO AMERICA: UNA HISTORIA DEL INICIO Y DESARROLLO DE LA OBRA EVANGELI-CA EN EL ISTMO CENTROAMERICANO. Miami: Editorial Caribe.

NELSON, Wilton N., 1983, HISTORIA DEL PROTESTANTISMO EN COSTA RICA. San José, Costa Rica: IINDEF.

NELSON, Wilton N., 1984, CLASIFICACION TEOLOGICA DE LAS IGLESIAS PROTESTANTES EN COSTA RICA O LAS RAICES DEL PROTESTANTIS-MO COSTARRICENSE. Senderos (Instituto Teológico de América Central) 20: 29-40.

NELSON, Wilton N., 1984, PROTESTANTISM IN CENTRAL AMERICA. Grand Rapids, Mich: Eerdmans.

New..., 1986, NEW TESTAMENT CHURCH OF GOD 50TH ANNIVERSARY, BARBADOS W.I. 1936-1986. Barbados: Sunshine Publications Barbados.

NIDA, Eugene A., 1958, THE RELATIONSHIP OF SOCIAL STRUCTURE TO THE PROBLEMS OF EVANGELISM IN LATIN AMERICA. Practical Anthro-pology 5, 3: 101-123.

NIDA, Eugene A., 1961, THE INDIGENOUS CHURCHES OF LATIN AMERICA. Practical Anthropology 8: 97-105, 110.

NIDA, Eugene A., 1961, COMMUNICATION OF THE GOSPEL TO LATIN AMERICA. Practical Anthropology 8: 145-156.

NIDA, Eugene A., 1969, DIE PFINGSTKIRCHEN IN LATEINAMERIKA. In: Tschuy 1969: 90-96.

NIDA, Eugene A., s.f., THE INDIGENOUS CHURCHES IN LATIN AMERICA. New York: The Committee on Cooperation in Latin America, Division of Foreign Missions, National Council of the Churches of Christ in the U.S.A.

NIKLAUS, Robert, 1983, LATIN AMERICA: COUNTER-EVANGELISM. Evengelical Mission Quarterly 19, 3, 259-260.

NOLASCO, Margarita, 1980, EL INSTITUTO LINGUISTICO DE VERANO. In: Lingüística e Indigenismo. Mexico: UNAM.

NOUWEN, Henri, 1967, THE PENTECOSTAL MOVEMENT: THREE PERSPEC-TIVES. Scholastic 109: 15-17.

NOVAES, Regina R., 1980, OS PENTECOSTAIS E A ORGANIZAÇãO DOS TRA-BALHADORES. Religião e Sociedade 5, 65-89. [Brazil]

NOVAES, Regina R., 1985, OS ESCOLHIDOS DE DEUS: PENTECOSTAIS, TRABALHADORES E CIDADANIA. Rio de Janeiro/São Paulo: ISER/Ed. Marco Zero, Cadernos do ISER no. 19. [Brazil]

NYSTROM, Samuel, 1944, MIRACLES WROUGHT IN BRAZIL. Pentecost Evangel 32: 6-7.

O

O avanço..., 1981, O AVANÇO DOS CRENTES. PENTECOSTAIS: O MILAGRE DA MULTIPLICAÇAO. Veja, October 7, pp. 56-64. [Brazil]

O céu..., 1990, O CÉU NA TERRA. EDIR MACEDO JURA QUE NA IGREJA UNI-VERSAL DO REINO DE DEUS NÃO HÁ DESEMPREGO, AIDS, CÂNCER. Istoé Senhor, 20 de junho, pp. 3-6.

O'CONNOR, Mary, 1979, TWO KINDS OF RELIGIOUS MOVEMENTS AMONG THE MAYO INDIANS OF SONORA, MEXICO. Journal for the Scientific Study of Religion 18, 3: 260-268.

OCHAGAVIA, Juan, 1967, EL ECUMENISMO, CAMINO HACIA LA UNIDAD. Mensaje 16, 164: 554-560. [Chile]

OLIVA, Enrique López, 1983, LAS SECTAS CONTRAINSURGENCIA RELI-GIOSA? OCLAE 10. [Cuba]

OLSON, Lawrence, 1960, ENFASES NO MOVIMENTO PENTECOSTAL. Rio de Janeiro: Livros Evangélicos. [Brazil]

OLSON, Lawrence, 1961, A HALF CENTURY OF PENTECOST IN BRAZIL. Pentecostal Evangel 2472: 6-7.

OOSTERWAL, Gottfried, 1973, MODERN MESSIANIC MOVEMENTS. Elkart, Ind.: Herald Press.

OPAZO BERNALES, Andrés, 1990, EL MOVIMIENTO PROTESTANTE CEN-TROAMERICANA: UNA APROXIMACION CUANTITATIVA. In: Sawande 1990.

ORELLANA U., Luis, 1989, BREVE HISTORIA DEL MOVIMIENTO PENTE-COSTAL CHILENO EN SU PRIMER ESTADIO (1909-1932). Santiago, CTE. [thesis]

ORO, Ari Pedro, 1990, RELIGIÕES PENTECOSTAIS E MEIOS DE COMU-
NICAÇÃO DE MASSA NO SUL DO BRASIL. Revista Eclesiástica Brasileira 50,
198, 304-334.

ORO, Ari Pedro, 1991, O DISCURSO DOS PREGADORES ELETRÔNICOS.
Cadernos de Antropologia (UFRGS, Porto Alegre), 2: 23-38.

ORO, Ari Pedro, 1993a, RELIGIONES POPULARES Y MODERNIDAD EN BRA-
SIL. Sociedad y Religión, 10/11: 52-61.

ORO, Ari Pedro, 1993b, PODEM PASSAR A SACOLINHA: UM ESTUDO SOBRE
AS REPRESENTAÇÕES DO DINHEIRO NO NEOPENTECOSTALISMO
BRASILEIRO. Cadernos de Antropologia (UFRGS, Porto Alegre) 10. [Also in:
Revista Eclesiástica Brasileira 53 (1993), 301-323]

ORO, Ari Pedro, 1994a, O "EXPANSIONISMO" RELIGIOSO BRASILEIRO PARA
OS PAISES DO PRATA. Revista Eclesiástica Brasileira 216, 875-895.

ORO, Ari Pedro, 1994b, EVALUATION DE L'EMERGENCE DES ESCTES EN
AMERIQUE LATINE. Studies in Religion / Sciences Religieuses 23, 2, 211-225.

ORR, J. Edwin, 1978, EVANGELICAL AWAKENINGS IN LATIN AMERICA.
Minneapolis, Minn.: Bethany Fellowship. [Also Medellin: Tipografia Union]

ORTEGA, Hugo, 1986, LAS SECTAS. SU OBJETIVO ES EL CONTROL IDEOLO-
GICO Y RELIGIOSO. Dialogo Social 19, 189: 45-46.

ORTEGA-AGUILAR (ed.), 1966, HISTORIA DE LA ASAMBLEA APOSTOLICA
DE LA FE EN CRISTO JESUS: 1916-1966. Los Angeles, Calif.: Apostolic Assembly.

ORTIZ, Juan, 1993, PRESENCIA DE LAS IGLESIAS EVANGÉLICAS EN CHILE
EN EL SIGLO XIX. Evangelio y Sociedad, 18, I-VIII.

OSPINA, A., 1954, THE PROTESTANT DENOMINATION IN COLOMBIA.
Bogota: National Press.

OSSA, Manuel, 1989, ESPIRITUALIDAD POPULAR Y ACCIÓN POLÍTICA. EL
PASTOR VÍCTOR MORA Y LA MISIÓN WESLEYANA NACIONAL. 40
AÑOS DE HISTORIA RELIGIOSA Y SOCIAL (1928-1969). Santiago: Rehue.

OSSA, Manuel, 1991, LO AJENO Y LO PROPIO: IDENTIDAD PENTECOSTAL Y
TRABAJO. Santiago: Rehue.

P

P'AXI R., C. QUISPE, N. ESCOBAR, R. CONDE, 1986, RELIGION AYMARA Y
CRISTIANISMO. Fe y Pueblo: 3, agosto: 6-13.

PACHECO, Antonio Cruz, 1970, LA RELIGIOSIDAD POPULAR CHILENA,
ESTUDIO SOCIOLOGICO. Santiago: CISOC, Centro Bellarmino.

PAGE, John Joseph, 1984, BRASIL PARA CRISTO: THE CULTURAL CON-
STRUCTION OF PENTECOSTAL NETWORKS IN BRAZIL. Ann Arbor,
Mich.: University Microfilms International. [Ph.D., New York University]

PALAU, Luis, 1983, LUIS PALAU: CALLING THE NATIONS TO CHRIST. Chicago: Moody Press.

PALMA, Daniel, 1969, SEISCIENTOS MIL EN CHILE. Cuadernos de Marcha (Mon-
tevideo) 29: 43-47. [Interview on Pentecostals]

PALMA, Irma (ed.), 1988, EN TIERRA EXTRAÑA. ITINERARIO DEL PUEBLO
PENTECOSTAL CHILENO. Santiago: Amerinda.

PALMA, Marta, 1985, A PENTECOSTAL CHURCH IN THE ECUMENICAL MOVEMENT. Ecumenical Review, 37: 223-229. [Chile]

PALMA, Samuel, and Hugo Villela, 1991, EL PENTECOSTALISMO: UNA RELIGION POPULAR DEL PROTESTANTISMO LATINOAMERICANO. Cristianismo y Sociedad 109, 87-95.

PALMER, Donald C., 1974, AN EXPLOSION OF PEOPLE EVANGELISM: AN ANALYSIS OF PENTECOSTAL GROWTH IN COLOMBIA. Chicago: Moody Press.

PALOMA, Margaret M., 1989, THE ASSEMBLIES OF GOD AT THE CROSSROADS: CHARISMA AND INSTITUTIONAL DILEMMAS. Knoxville: University of Tennessee Press.

PANINSKI, Alberto Barrientos, 1984, EL EVANGELISTA Y LA RESPONSABILIDAD SOCIAL. In: Documentos... 1984.

PANINSKI, Alberto Barrientos, 1984, EL EVANGELISTA Y LA TEOLOGIA DE LA LIBERACION. In: Documentos... 1984.

PANTOJAS GARCIA, Emilio, 1976, LA IGLESIA PROTESTANTE Y LA AMERICANIZACION DE PUERTO RICO 1898-1917. Bayamón PR: Prisa.

PAPE, Carlos, 1967, LOS EVANGELICOS SOMOS ASI... REFLEXIONES SOBRE EL 1ER CICLO DE CONFERENCIAS DE LA COMUNIDAD TEOLOGICA EVANGELICA DE SANTIAGO. Mensaje 16, 156: 35-39. [Chile]

Papers..., 1984, PAPERS PRESENTED TO THE FIRST OCCASIONAL SYMPOSIUM ON ASPECTS OF THE ONENESS PENTECOSTAL MOVEMENT, HELD AT HARVARD DIVINITY SCHOOL, JULY 5-7, 1984. [Unpublished, Cf. Gaxiola-Gaxiola 1984, Gill 1984]

Para una historia..., 1984, PARA UNA HISTORIA DE LOS CRISTIANISMOS EN AMERICA LATINA. Cristianismo y Sociedad 82. [Cf. Bastian 1984, Dussel 1984]

PAREDES-ALFARO, Rubén Elías, 1980, THE PROTESTANT MOVEMENT IN ECUADOR AND PERU: A COMPARATIVE SOCIO-ANTHROPOLOGICAL STUDY OF THE ESTABLISHMENT AND DIFFUSION OF PROTESTANTISM IN TWO CENTRAL HIGHLAND REGIONS. Los Angeles: University of California. [Thesis]

PAREDES-ALFARO, Rubén Elías, 1984, LA NUEVA PRESENCIA EVANGELICA INDIGENA. Misión 3, 3.

PAUL, Irven, 1946, ACCULTURATION IN CHILE: A STUDY OF THE RELATION OF EVANGELICAL CHRISTIANITY TO CHRISTIAN CULTURE WITH A VIEW TO THE FORMATION OF EFFECTIVE MISSIONARY PRINCIPLES AND PRACTICES. Hartford, Conn.: Hartford Seminary Foundation. [Thesis]

PAULY, Evaldo Luis, 1987, E OS CRENTES? CONVERSA COM A FE DOS PENTECOSTAIS. São Leopoldo: Sinodal. [Brazil]

PECK, Jane C., 1984, REFLECTIONS FROM COSTA RICA ON PROTESTANTISM'S DEPENDENCE AND NONLIBERATIVE SOCIAL FUNCTION. Journal of Ecumenical Studies 21, 181-189.

Penetración..., 1983, PENETRACION DE SECTAS EN HONDURAS. Correo del Sur (México) 1131.

Penetración..., 1985, PENETRACION IDEOLOGICA NORTEAMERICANA Y ANTI-YANQUISMO, PERSPECTIVA HISTORICA. Cristianismo y Sociedad 86.

294 More Than Opium

Penetración..., 1986, PENETRACION DE LOS 'PROTESTANTISMOS'. Pensamiento propio 36: 26-40. [Cuba]

Pentecost..., 1975, PENTECOST AND POLITICS: THE CHARISMATIC CHURCH OF THE WORLD'S POOR. Wick: SCM Publications.

Pentecostalismo..., 1977, O PENTECOSTALISMO. Cadernos do ISER 6.

Pentecostalismo..., 1985, PENTECOSTALISMO Y TEOLOGIA DE LA LIBERACION. Pastoralia (CELEP) 7, 7.

Pentecostalismo..., 1989, PENTECOSTALISMO, SECTAS Y PASTORAL. Santiago: Comisión Episcopal de Chile.

PENTON, Marvin James, 1965, MEXICO'S REFORMATION: A HISTORY OF MEXICAN PROTESTANTISM FROM ITS INCEPTION TO THE PRESENT. Ann Arbor, Mich.: University Microfilms. [Ph.D., State University of Iowa]

PEREIRA RAMALHO, Jether, 1977, ALGUMAS NOTAS SOBRE DUAS PERSPECTIVAS DE PASTORAL POPULAR: A DAS COMUNIDADES ECLESIAIS DE BASE E A DOS GRUPOS EVANGELICOS PENTECOSTAIS. Cadernos do ISER 6: 31-39. [Brazil]

PEREIRA RAMALHO, Jether, 1977, BASIC POPULAR COMMUNITIES IN BRAZIL: SOME NOTES ON PASTORAL ACTIVITY IN TWO TYPES. Ecumenical Review 29, 4: 394-401.

PEREIRA RAMOS, Jovelino, 1968, PROTESTANTISMO BRASILEIRO: VISAO PANORAMICA. Paz e Terra 2, 6: 73-94.

PEREZ TORRES, Rubén, 1979, THE PASTOR'S ROLE IN EDUCATIONAL MINISTRY IN THE PENTECOSTAL CHURCH OF GOD IN PUERTO RICO. Claremont School of Theology. [Ph.D.]

PERKIN, Noel; GARLOCK, John, 1963, OUR WORLD WITNESS, A SURVEY OF ASSEMBLIES OF GOD FOREIGN MISSIONS. Springfield, Mass.: Gospel Publishing House.

PETRELLA, Vaccaro de; SUSANA, Lidia, 1986, THE TENSION BETWEEN EVANGELISM AND SOCIAL ACTION IN THE PENTECOSTAL MOVEMENT. International Review of Mission 75, 297: 34-38. [Argentina]

PIEDRA S., Arturo, 1984, ORIGENES Y AFECTOS DEL PROTESTANTISMO EN COSTA RICA. Senderos (Instituto Teológico de América Central) 20: 3-28.

PIEDRA, Arturo, 1991, PROTESTANTISMO Y SOCIEDAD EN CENTROAMERICA. In: Samandú 1991a: 267-297.

PILCO, Senia, 1992, MOVIMIENTO PENTECOSTAL, MOVIMIENTO CARISMATICO Y MOVIMIENTOS RELIGIOSOS CONTEMPORANEOS. In: Alvarez 1992: 235-246.

PIXLEY, J., 1982, LA CAPTURA DEL MOVIMIENTO EVANGELICO EN GUATEMALA: LA LUCHA IDEOLOGICA EN LAS IGLESIAS. Cristianismo y Sociedad: no. 74.

PIXLEY, Jorge, 1983, ALGUNAS LECCIONES DE LA EXPERIENCIA DE RIOS MONTT. Cristianismo y Sociedad 76: 7-12. [Guatemala]

PIXLEY, Jorge, 1985, EL FUNDAMENTALISMO. Estudios Ecuménicos 3.

POBLETE, Renato, 1960, CONSIDERACION SOCIOLOGICA DE LAS SECTAS CHILENAS. Anales de la Facultad de Teología (Universidad Católica de Chile) 11.

POBLETE, Renato, 1960, SOCIOLOGICAL APPROACH TO THE SECTS. Social Compass 7, 5-6: 383-406.

POBLETE, Renato, 1988, EVANGELIZACION DE LA CULTURA, RELIGIO-SIDAD POPULAR Y RELIGIOSIDAD PENTECOSTAL. In: Cultura y... 1988: 151-161.

POBLETE, Renato; GALILEA, Carmen, 1984, MOVIMIENTO PENTECOSTAL E IGLESIA CATOLICA EN MEDIOS POPULARES. Santiago de Chile: Centro Bellarmino, Departamento de Investigaciones Sociológicas. [Chile]

POEWE, Karla (ed.), 1994, CHARISMATIC CHRISTIANITY AS A GLOBAL CUL-TURE. Columbia: University of South Carolina Press. [Cf. Droogers 1994, Martin 1994]

POLLAK-ELTZ, Angelina, 1970, SHANGO-KULT UND SHOUTERKIRCHE AUF TRINIDAD UND GRANADA. Anthropos 65, 5/6: 814-833.

POLLAK-ELTZ, Angelina, 1976, EL PENTECOSTALISMO CATOLICO EN VENEZUELA. Sic (Caracas) 384: 172-177.

POLLAK-ELTZ, Angelina, 1978, PENTECOSTALISM IN VENEZUELA. Anthropos 73: 461-482.

POLLAK-ELTZ, Angelina, 1992, LA RELIGIOSIDAD POPULAR EN VENE-ZUELA. Sociedad y Religión 9, 15-25.

POLOMA, Margaret M., 1986, PENTECOSTALS AND POLITICS IN NORTH AND CENTRAL AMERICA. In: Hadden y Shupe, pp. 329-352.

PONCE, Marcelo, 1983, LA MANIPULACION DE LA RELIGION EN GUATE-MALA. Ulaje Comparte 30.

PRANDI, Reginaldo, 1992, CONSTRUCCIONES DE ESPACIOS PUBLICOS DE EXPRESION EN RELIGIONES POPULARES. Sociedad y Religión 9, 4-14.

Presencia..., 1987, PRESENCIA Y TRANSPARENCIA: LA MUJER EN LA HISTO-RIA DE MEXICO. Mexico: El Colegio de México. [Cf. Bastian 1987]

PRIEN, Hans-Jürgen, 1978, DIE GESCHICHTE DES CHRISTENTUMS IN LA-TEINAMERIKA. Göttingen: Vandenhoeck & Ruprecht.

PRIEN, Hans-Jürgen (ed.), 1981, LATEINAMERIKA: GESELLSCHAFT, KIRCHE, THEOLOGIE. Göttingen: Vandenhoeck & Ruprecht, 2 Vols.

PRIETO, Luis C., 1980, LAS IGLESIAS EVANGELICAS DE GUATEMALA. Universidad Francisco Marroquim, Departamento de Teologia.

Protestantes..., 1968, PROTESTANTES E IMPERIALISMO NA AMERICA LATI-NA. Petrópolis: Vozes.

Protestantes..., 1969, PROTESTANTES EN AMERICA LATINA. Cuadernos de Marcha 29.

Protestantes..., 1983, PROTESTANTISMOS Y SOCIEDADES LATINOAME-RICANAS. Cristianismo y Sociedad 76.

PUSCHEL, Joh., 1974, GESUNDHEITSDIENSTE BRASILIANISCHER KIR-CHEN. Nachrichten a.d. Ärtzlichen Mission 25, 1: 4-7.

Q

QUARRACINO A., Bravo E.; y otros, 1981, SECTAS EN AMERICA LATINA. Bogotá: CELAM.

QUEIROZ, Marcos de Souza, 1985, POLITICA, RELIGIÃO E CURA RELIGIOSA NUMA SITUAÇÃO DE MUDANÇA. Ciência e Cultura 37, 4: 541-553. [Brazil]

Quem é..., 1974, QUEM É JESUS CRISTO NO BRASIL? São Paulo: ASTE. [Cf. Muniz de Souza 1974]

R

RAFFERTY, Kate, 1984, GOSPEL AIR POWER IN CENTRAL AMERICA. Religious Broadcasting, abril, 22-23.

RAMIREZ, Raymundo, 1972, LIBRO HISTORICO, MOVIMIENTO DE LA IGLESIA CRISTIANA INDENDIENTE PENTECOSTES (BODAS DE OURO). Pachuca, Hgo., México.

RAMIREZ, Raymundo (ed.), 1972, BODAS DE OURO: MOVIMIENTO DE LA IGLESIA CRISTIANA INDEPENDIENTE PENTECOSTES (MEXICO). Pachuca.

RAMOS, Marcos Antonio, 1986, PANORAMA DEL PROTESTANTISMO EN CUBA, LA PRESENCIA DE LOS PROTESTANTES O EVANGELICOS EN LA HISTORIA DE CUBA DESDE LA COLONIZACION ESPAÑOLA HASTA LA REVOLUCION. San José, Costa Rica/Miami: Editorial Caribe.

RANCE, Susanna, 1987, BOLIVIA: POLITICAL, CHURCH LEADERS FEAR SPREAD OF NEW RELIGIOUS GROUPS. Latinamerica Press 19, 18: 3-4.

RANDALL, Donna M., 1983, THE BELIEFS AND PRACTICES OF THE PENTECOSTAL (ONENESS) APOSTOLIC PEOPLE OF JAMAICA. University of West Indies. [M.A. Thesis]

RAPHAEL, Alison, 1975, MIRACLES IN BRAZIL: A STUDY OF THE PENTECOSTAL MOVEMENT 'O BRASIL PARA CRISTO'. Columbia University, Department of History. [M.A. Thesis]

RAPPAPORT, Joanne, 1984, LAS MISIONES PROTESTANTES Y LA RESISTENCIA INDIGENA EN EL SUR DE COLOMBIA. América Indígena 44, 1: 111-126. [SIL]

READ, William R., 1965, NEW PATTERNS OF CHURCH GROWTH IN BRAZIL. Grand Rapids, Mich.: Eerdmans.

READ, William R., 1967, FERMENTO RELIGIOSO NAS MASSAS DO BRASIL. Campinas SP: Livraria Cristã Unida.

READ, William R.; MONTERROSO Victor M.; JOHNSON, Harmon A., 1970, LATIN AMERICAN CHURCH GROWTH. Grand Rapids Mich.: Eerdmans.

READ, W., V. MONTERROSO, and H. JOHNSON, 1971, AVANCE EVANGELICO EN LA AMERICA LATINA. Buenos Aires: Casa Bautista de Publicaciones.

READ, William, Victor MONTERROSO, and Hamon JOHNSON, 1972, O CRESCIMENTO DA IGREJA NA AMÉRICA LATINA. São Paulo: Editora Mundo Cristão.

READ, William R.; INESON, Frank A., 1973, BRAZIL 1980: THE PROTESTANT HANDBOOK. THE DYNAMICS OF CHURCH GROWTH IN THE 1950'S AND 60'S AND THE TREMENDOUS POTENTIAL FOR THE 70'S. Monrovia, Calif.: MARC.

Reglamento..., 1944, REGLAMENTO LOCAL DE LA IGLESIA EVANGELICA DE LAS ASEMBLEAS DE DIOS EN LA REPUBLICA DOMINICANA. Ciudad Trujillo: Tip. Prensa Bíblica.

REINA, Rubén; SCHWARTZ, Norman, 1974, THE STRUCTURAL CONTEXT OF RELIGIOUS CONVERSION IN PETEN, GUATEMALA: STATUS, COMMUNITY AND MULTI-COMMUNITY. American Ethnologist 9, 1: 157-192.

Religião..., 1978, A RELIGIÃO DO POVO. São Paulo: Edições Paulinas. [Cf. Rolim 1978]

Religiosidad..., 1995, RELIGIOSIDAD POPULAR EN LA ARGENTINA. Buenos Aires: Centro Editor de América Latina CEAL. [Cf. Iglesias 1995, Santamaria 1995]

REMBAO, Alberto, 1957, PROTESTANT LATIN AMERICA: SIGHT AND IN-SIGHT. International Review of Missions 46: 30-36.

REYBURN, W., 1954, THE TOBA INDIANS OF THE ARGENTINE CHACO: AN INTERPRETIVE REPORT. Elkhart, Ind.: Mennonite Board of Missions and Charities.

REYBURN, William D.; REYBURN, Mary F., 1956, TOBA CACIQUESHIP AND THE GOSPEL. International Review of Missions 45: 194-205. [Argentina]

REYES, Alberto, 1982, LA INVASION DE LAS SECTAS. La Religión en los Periódicos, marzo 1-17, 1982. [Nicaragua]

RIBEIRO DE OLIVEIRA, Pedro A., 1977, A RENOVAÇAO CARISMATICA CATOLICA, NOTAS DE PESQUISAS. Cadernos do ISER 6: 25-30. [Brazil]

RIBEIRO DE OLIVEIRA, Pedro A., 1978, LE RENOUVEAU CHARISMATIQUE AU BRÉSIL. Social Compass 25, 1: 43-54.

RIBEIRO, René, 1966, O PENTECOSTALISMO NO BRASIL. Revista Vozes 63, 2: 125-136.

RIBEIRO, René, 1982, ANTROPOLOGIA DE RELIGIAO E OUTROS ESTUDOS. Recife: Ed. Massangana/Fundação Joaquim Nabuco. [Brazil, 289-299, reprint of Ribeiro 1966]

RICHARD, Pablo, 1982, LA IGLESIA DE LOS POBRES EN AMERICA CENTRAL. San José, Costa Rica: DEI.

RICHARD, Pablo, 1985, SECTAS USAN TECNICAS DE MARKETING, DOLARES, PARA "VENDER" EVANGELIO. Noticias Aliadas 17: 5,6,8.

RICO, Jose M., 1967, EL CRISTIANISMO EVANGELICO Y EL CONCILIO VATICANO II. Miami, Fla.: Editorial Vida.

RIVAS-RIVAS, Saul, 1986, EL ILV Y "LAS NUEVAS TRIBUS". Pueblo Indio (Edición Tawantinsuyu) 2, 8: 26-27.

RIVERA, Cecilia, 1984, LA RELIGION EN EL PERU 1900-1983. Lima: Celadec. [Bibliography]

RIVIERE, Gilles, 1986, CAMBIOS SOCIALES Y PENTECOSTALISMO EN UNA COMUNIDAD AYMARA. Fe y Pueblo (Centro de Teología Popular, La Paz) 3, 14: 24-30. [Bolivia]

ROBERTS, Bryan, 1967, EL PROTESTANTISMO EN DOS BARRIOS MARGINALES DE GUATEMALA. Guatemala: Cuadernos de Estudios Centroamericanos no. 2.

ROBERTS, Bryan R., 1968, PROTESTANT GROUPS AND COPING WITH URBAN LIFE IN GUATEMALA CITY. American Journal of Sociology 73: 753-767.

ROBERTSON, Roland (ed.), 1969, SOCIOLOGY OF RELIGION, SELECTED READINGS. Harmondsworth: Penguin. [Cf. Willems 1969]

ROBINSON, John L., 1980, SOURCES OF BRAZILIAN PROTESTANTISM: HISTORICAL OR CONTEMPORARY? In: Brown & Cooper 1980: 385-393.

ROBLES, Armando, 1983, MOVIMIENTOS ECLESIALES DE LA IGLESIA CATOLICA EN COSTA RICA. El Mensajero del Clero (Ediciones CECOR, San José, Costa Rica), Numero extraordinario, pp. 3-66.

ROCHA, Abelino Martínez, 1991, LOS PROTESTANTISMOS EN LA CRISIS SALVADORENA. In: Samandú 1991a: 111-149.

RODRIGUEZ DIAZ, Daniel R., 1979, IDEOLOGIAS PROTESTANTES Y MISIO-NES: EL CASO DE PUERTO RICO 1898-1930. México: UNAM.

RODRIGUEZ, Pepe, 1985, LAS SECTAS HOY Y AQUI. Ediciones Tribidabo.

ROEBLING, Karl, 1978, PENTECOSTALS AROUND THE WORLD. Hicksville: Exposition Press.

ROHR, Elisabeth, 1987, "GOTT LIEBT UNS EBENSO WIE DIE WEISSEN", DIE SANFTEN VERFüHRER NUTZEN DIE FEHLER DER HERRSCHENDEN AUS. Die Zeit 40 (25 Sept. 1987), 49-51.

ROHR, Elisabeth, 1987, "JESUS WIRD NUR HELFEN...", EIN INTERVIEW MIT DEM INDIANISCHEN BAUERN FABIAN AUS ECUADOR. Die Zeit 40 (25 Sept. 1987), 51,52.

ROHR, Elisabeth, 1987, EUKALYPTUS UND SEKTEN RAUS! EIN RELI-GIONSKRIEG IN DER ECUADORIANISCHEN PROVINZ. Die Zeit 40 (25 Sept. 1987), 52, 54.

ROLIM, F.C., 1973, EXPANSÃO PROTESTANTE EM NOVA IGUAÇU. Revista Eclesiástica Brasileira 33, 131: 660-675. [Brazil]

ROLIM, F.C., 1973, PENTECOSTALISMO. Revista Eclesiástica Brasileira 33, 132: 950-964. [Brazil]

ROLIM, F.C., 1976, PENTECOSTALISMO, GENESE, ESTRUTURA E FUN-ÇOES. Rio de Janeiro, mimeo. [Brazil, Thesis Universidade de São Paulo]

ROLIM, F.C., 1977, A PROPOSITO DO PENTECOSTALISMO DE FORMA PROTESTANTE. Cadernos do ISER 6: 11-20. [Brazil]

ROLIM, F.C., 1978, PENTECOSTALISMO DE FORMA PROTESTANTE. In: Religião...1978: 81-91. [Brazil]

ROLIM, F.C., 1979, PENTECOTISME ET SOCIETE AU BRESIL. Social Compass 26, 2-3: 345-372.

ROLIM, F.C., 1980, RELIGIÃO E CLASSES POPULARES. Petrópolis: Vozes. [Brazil]

ROLIM, F.C., 1981, GENESE DO PENTECOSTALISMO NO BRASIL. Revista Eclesiástica Brasileira 41, 161: 119-140.

ROLIM, F.C., 1982, IGREJAS PENTECOSTAIS. Revista Eclesiástica Brazileira 42, 165: 29-60. [Brazil]

ROLIM, F.C., 1985, PENTECOSTAIS NO BRASIL, UMA INTERPRETAÇÃO SOCIO-RELIGIOSA. Petrópolis: Vozes.

ROLIM, F.C., 1986, O AVANÇO DAS SEITAS. Revista Eclesiástica Brasileira 46: 843-847. [Brazil]

ROLIM, F.C., 1987, O QUE É PENTECOSTALISMO. São Paulo: Brasiliense, Cole-ção Primeiros Passos no. 188. [Brazil]

ROLIM, F.C., 1988, EL PENTECOSTALISMO A PARTIR DEL POBRE. Crist-ianismo y Sociedad 95, 1: 51-69.

ROLIM, F.C., 1989a, ASSEMBLÉIA DE DEUS. In: Landim 1989c: 47-52. [Brazil]

ROLIM, F.C., 1989b, CONGREGAÇÃO CRISTÃ NO BRASIL. In: Landim 1989c: 53-57.

ROLIM, F.C., 1989c, IGREJA PENTECOSTAL DEUS É AMOR. In: Landim 1989c: 59-63. [Brazil]

ROLIM, F.C., 1992, PENTECOTISME ET VISIONS DU MONDE. Social Compass, 39, 3, 401-422.

ROLIM, F.C., 1995, PENTECOSTALISMO: BRASIL E AMÉRICA LATINA. Petrópolis: Vozes, Coleção Teologia e Libertação.

RÖMER, René, 1980, RELIGIOUS SYNCRETISM IN THE CARIBBEAN. In: Wilkerson 1980: 247-268.

ROOY, Sidney H., 1986, SOCIAL REVOLUTION AND THE FUTURE OF THE CHURCH. (A TYPOLOGY OF THE FOUR LARGEST GROUPINGS OF THE CHRISTIAN CHURCH IN LATIN AMERICA: A BRIEF CHARACTERIZATION OF THEIR ATTITUDES TO THE REVOLUTIONARY SITUATION). Occasional Essays 13, 1-2: 60-89.

ROSA, Martin de la; Reily, A. (eds.), 1985, RELIGION Y POLITICA EN MEXICO. Mexico: Siglo XXI. [Cf. Bastian 1985]

ROSIER, I., 1960, ESTUDIO DEL PROTESTANTISMO EN CHILE. Anales de la Faculdad de Teología (Universidad Católica de Chile) 11.

ROSSI, Agnelo, 1938, DIRETORIO PROTESTANTE NO BRASIL. Campinas: Tipografia Paulista.

ROSSI, Agnelo, 1945, O PROTESTANTISMO NO MOMENTO ATUAL BRASILEIRO. Revista Eclesiástica Brasileira 5: 26-99.

ROSSI, Agnelo, 1946, POR QUE MISSOES PROTESTANTES NA AMERICA LATINA? Revista Eclesiástica Brasileira 6: 610-622.

ROSSI, Agnelo, 1952, O PENTECOSTISMO NO BRASIL. Revista Eclesiástica Brasileira 12: 767-792.

ROTBERG, S.; KILSON, M. (eds.), 1976, AFRICAN DIASPORA: INTERPRETIVE ESSAYS. Cambridge, Mass.: Harvard University Press. [Cf. Simpson 1976]

RUIZ C., Alfredo; SMITH, D., 1987, IMPACTO DE LA PROGRAMACION RELIGIOSA DIFUNDIDA POR LOS MEDIOS ELECTRONICOS EN LA POBLACION CRISTIANA ACTIVA DE AMERICA CENTRAL. Pastoralia: 9, 18: 129-161.

RUMBLE, L., 1959, AS ASSEMBLEIAS DE DEUS E OUTRAS IGREJAS PENTECOSTAIS. Petrópolis: Vozes, Vozes em defesa da fé, Caderno 23. [Brazil]

RUNDELL, Merton R., 1957, THE MISSION OF THE PILGRIM HOLINESS CHURCH IN PERU. Indianapolis, Ind.: Butler University.

RUUTH, Anders, 1995, IGREJA UNIVERSAL DO REINO DE DEUS, GUDSRIKET UNIVERSELLA KYRKA - EN BRASILIANSK KYRKOBILDNING. Stockholm: Almqvist and Wiksell International. With a summary in Spanish: IGLESIA UNIVERSAL DEL REINO DE DIOS (pp. 261-299).

RYCROFT. W. Stanley, 1958, RELIGION AND FAITH IN LATIN AMERICA. Philadelphia, Pa.: The Westminster Press.

RYCROFT, Stanley W., 1955, THE CONTRIBUTION OF PROTESTANTISM IN THE CARIBBEAN. In: Wilgus 1955: 159-...

RYCROFT, W. Stanley, 1962, RELIGION Y FE EN LA AMERICA LATINA. Mexico D.F.

RYCROFT, W. Stanley; CLEMMER, Myrtle M., 1961, A STATISTICAL STUDY OF LATIN AMERICA. New York: United Presbyterian Church in the USA.

RYCROFT, W. Stanley; CLEMMER, Myrtle M., 1963, A FACTUAL STUDY OF LATIN AMERICA. New York: United Presbyterian Church in the USA.

S

SABORIO, Arturo Molina, 1984, LA RELIGION: ATACADA POR UNOS Y DEFENDIDA POR OTROS. Apotes (San José, Costa Rica) 4, 19: 19-21.

SAEZ, José Luis, 1984, A QUE VIENEN TANTAS SECTAS? Amigo del Hogar 455-456. [Dominican Republic]

SAEZ, José Luis, 1985, RELIGION, ALIENACION Y COMERCIO EN UN PAIS SUBDESARROLLADO. Amigo del Hogar 457. [Dominican Republic]

SAEZ, José Luis, 1985, A QUE VIENEN TANTAS SECTAS? Amigo del Hogar 458. [Dominican Republic]

SALAZAR, Haydée Canelos de, 1985, FACTORES EXTERNOS, IDEOLOGIA Y DESCOMPOSICION CAMPESINA. Universidad Central del Ecuador, Escuela de Sociología. [M.A. Thesis]

SALESMAN, P. Eliecer, 1982, CUIDADO: LLEGARON LOS PROTESTANTES. Bogotá: Librería Salesiana.

SALDAÑA Z., Angel, 1986, DIEZ TESIS SOBRE LA ACCION DE LAS SECTAS RELIGIOSAS EN MEXICO. Iglesias 3, 29: 6-8.

SALINAS, Maximiliano (ed.), 1987, HISTORIA DEL PEUBLO DE DIOS EN CHILE. LA EVOLUCION DEL CRISTIANISMO DESDE LA PERSPECTIVA DE LOS POBRES. Santiago: CEHILA/REHUE. [Cf. Sepúlveda 1987]

SALLET, Isidro; BINS, Cláudio Luiz (eds.), 1973, MISSãO DA IGREJA NO BRASIL. 5a SEMANA DE REFLEXAO TEOLOGICA. São Paulo/São Leopoldo: Faculdade de Teologia Cristo Rei.

SALVATIERRA, Angel, 1986, CONTEMPORARY MOVEMENTS IN LATIN AMERICA AND THE CARIBBEAN, SOCIOLOGICAL ASPECT. In: Contemporary... 1986. [Paper]

SAMANDU, Luis, 1988, EL PENTECOSTALISMO EN NICARAGUA Y SUS RAICES RELIGIOSAS POPULARES. Pasos: 17, 2: 1-9.

SAMANDU, Luis, 1989, BREVE RESEÑA HISTORICA DEL PROTESTANTISMO EN GUATEMALA. In: El protestantismo...1989, pp. 7-16.

SAMANDU, Luis, 1989, LA IGLESIA DEL NAZARENO EN ALTA VERAPAZ. In: El Protestantismo...1989, pp. 17-47.

SAMANDU, Luis, 1989, EL UNIVERSO RELIGIOSO POPULAR EN CENTRO-AMERICA. Estudios Sociales Centroamericanos (CSUCA) 51: 81-95.

SAMANDU, L.; NIEUWENHOVE, J. van; SIEBERS, H.; GOLDEWIJK, B. K., 1986, LIFE AND DEATH IN CENTRAL AMERICA - A SOCIOLOGICAL, THEOLOGICAL AND POLITICAL INTERPRETATION OF THE IRRUPTION OF THE NEW SUBJECT. Exchange (Leiden) 15, 43-44: 1-98.

SAMANDU, Luis E. (ed.), 1991a, PROTESTANTISMOS Y PROCESOS SOCIALES EN CENTROAMERICA. San José, Costa Rica: EDUCA. (Cf. Martinez 1991, Opazo 1991, Piedra 1991, Samandú 1991b, Valverde 1991ab).

SAMANDU, Luis E., 1991b, ESTRATEGIAS EVANGELICAS HACIA LA POBLACION INDIGENA DE GUATEMALA. In: Samandú 1991a: 67-110.

SANCHIS, Pierre, 1994, O REPTO PENTECOSTAL A CULTURA CATOLICO-BRASILEIRA. In: Antoniazzi 1994b: 34-63.

SANTAGADA, Osvaldo D. (ed.), 1984, LAS SECTAS EN AMERICA LATINA. Buenos Aires: Claretiana.

SANTAGADA, Osvaldo D., 1985, CARACTERIZACION Y SITUACION DE LAS SECTAS EN AMERICA LATINA. Equipo de reflexión, 3-36.

SANTAGADA, Osvaldo D. (ed.), 1984, LAS SECTAS EN AMERICA LATINA. Buenos Aires: Editorial Claretiana. [141-155 on pentecostals]

SANTAGADA, Osvaldo D. (ed.), 1989a, SECTAS EN AMERICA LATINA. Lima: Ediciones Paulinas/CELAM.

SANTAGADA, Osvaldo D., 1989b, CARACTERIZACION Y CONTENIDO DE LAS SECTAS EN AMERICA LATINA. In: Sanatagada 1989a: 9-38.

SANTAMARIA, Daniel, 1995, PENTECOSTALISMOS I: PENTECOSTALISMOS E IDENTIDAD ETNICA, FORMAS DE EDUCACION RELIGIOSA ENTRE LOS ORIGINARIOS DEL CHACO Y SUS MIGRANTES A LOS CENTROS INDUSTRIALES ARGENTINOS. In: Religiosidad Popular 1995: 68-77. [See also Iglesias 1995]

SANTIAGO G., Iván, 1986, PENTECOSTALES GANAN FIELES HONDUREÑOS CON APOYO EE.UU.. Noticias Aliadas, Abril 17, 1986: 6,7.

SANTOS, Aureo Bispo dos, 1977, PENTECOSTALIZAÇAO DO PROTESTANTISMO HISTóRICO. Cadernos do ISER 6: 21-24. [Brazil]

SARACCO, J. Norberto, 1977, TYPE OF MINISTRY ADOPTED BY LATIN AMERICAN PENTECOSTAL CHURCHES. International Review of Mission 261: 64-70.

SARACCO, Norberto José, 1992, PERONISMO Y PENTECOSTALISMO: SUSTITUCION DEL LIDERAZGO CARISMATICO DURANTE LA CAIDA DE PERON (1954). Religión y Sociedad en Sudamérica, 1, 1: 45-53.

SAWANDE, Luis E., 1990, PROTESTANTISMOS Y PROCESOS SOCIALES EN CENTROAMERICA. San José, Costa Rica: EDUCA. [Cf. Opazo Bernales 1990]

SCHÄFER, Heinrich, 1988, BEFREIUNG VOM FUNDAMENTALISMUS: ENTSTEHUNG EINER NEUEN KIRCHLICHEN PRAXIS IM PROTESTANTISMUS GUATEMALAS. Münster: Edition Liberación.

SCHÄFER, Heinrich, 1988, RELIGION DUALISTA CAUSADA POR ANTAGONISMOS SOCIALES. TRASFONDOS SOCIALES DEL PROTESTANTISMO EN CENTROAMERICA. Boletín de Estudios Latinoamericanos y del Caribe 45: 69-90.

SCHÄFER, Heinrich, 1989, UNA TIPOLOGIA DEL PROTESTANTISMO EN CENTROAMERICA. Pasos 24: 10-19.

SCHÄFER, Heinrich, 1990, EL REINO DE LA LIBERTAD. ALGUNAS CONSIDERACIONES ACERCA DE LA FUNCION DE LA ESCATOLOGIA MILENARISTA EN LOS CONFLICTOS SOCIALES DE CENTRO AMERICA. Pasos (DEI), no. 31.

SCHÄFER, Heinrich, 1992, PROTESTANTISMO Y CRISIS SOCIAL EN AMERICA CENTRAL. San José, Costa Rica: DEI.

SCHULZE, Heinz, 1974, WYCLIFFE-INSTITUTE. BIBELVERKüNDIGUNG ODER AUSBEUTUNG? Pogrom 5, 27: 21-22.

SCOPES, Wilfred (ed.), 1962, THE CHRISTIAN MINISTRY IN LATIN AMERICA AND THE CARIBBEAN. Geneva etc.: World Council of Churches, Commission on World Mission and Evangelism, Report of a Survey Commission.

SCOTT, Kenneth D., 1981, ISRAELITES OF THE NEW UNIVERSAL COVENANT, PERU. Aberdeen: University of Aberdeen. [M.A. Thesis]

SCOTT, Kenneth D., 1985, LATIN AMERICA: PERUVIAN NEW RELIGIOUS MOVEMENTS. Missiology 13, 1: 45-59. [Israelitas del Nuevo Pacto Universal]

Sectas y religiosidad..., 1984, SECTAS Y RELIGIOSIDAD EN AMERICA LATINA ¿QUE REPRESENTAN? ¿QUE BUSCAN? ¿COMO ACTUAN? Altercom (Instituto Latinoamericano de Estudios Transnacionales) 44.

Sectas..., 1982, SECTAS SON FANATICAS. La Religión en los Periódicos, julio 12-15, 1982. [Nicaragua]

Sectas..., 1982, SECTAS: PROBLEMA RELIGIOSO Y POLITICO? Corresponsalía Popular 11-12.

Sectas..., 1983, SECTAS. Sucede en la Iglesia 35-36. [Ecuador]

Sectas..., 1983, SECTAS Y COCA COLA. Vida Nueva 1372-1373.

Sectas..., 1983, SECTAS Y CONTRAINSURGENCIA. Informador Guerrillero 25. [Guatemala]

Sectas..., 1984, SECTAS PROTESTANTES EN CENTROAMERICA: LA SANTA CONTRAINSURGENCIA. El Parcial 12.

Sectas..., 1985, SECTAS PROTESTANTES Y EL ECUMENISMO EN MEXICO. Estudios Ecuménicos 4.

Sectas..., 1986, SECTAS O NUEVOS MOVIMENTOS RELIGIOSOS. DESAFIOS PASTORALLES. Iglesias 3, 31: 27-34.

Sects..., 1986, SECTS OR NEW RELIGIOUS MOVEMENTS, PASTORAL CHALLENGE. Ateísmo y Diálogo 21, 2: 117-135.

SEGATO, Rita Laura, 1991, ALGUNAS PROPUESTAS PARA EL ESTUDIO DEL CAMBIO RELIGIOSO: LA EXPANSION EVANGELICA EN LA PUNA JUJEÑA. Sociedad y Religión 8, 41-59.

SEGATO, Rita Laura, 1993, CAMBIO RELIGIOSO Y DESETNIFICACION: LA EXPANSION EVANGELICA EN LOS ANDES CENTRALES. Etnia (Olavarría, Argentina) 38/39, 85-124.

SEIBERT, Ute, and Pedro CORREA, 1989, HISTORIA DEL PROTESTANTISMO EN CHILE. Santiago: REHUE.

Selected..., 1978, SELECTED BIBLIOGRAPHY ON ESTABLISHED RELIGIONS AND POPULAR CULTS IN THE CARIBBEAN. Barbados: CADEC Documentation Service.

SEMÁN, Pablo, 1994, IDENTIDAD DE LOS JOVENES PENTECOSTALES. In: Frigerio 1994: 80-95.

SEPADE (equipo evangelio y sociedad), 1990, SEPADE: 15 AÑOS ACOMPAÑANDO EL DESPERTAR SOLIDARIO DE LAS IGLESIAS PENTECOSTALES, evangelio y sociedad 6: 22-29.

SEPULVEDA, Juan, 1981a, PENTECOSTALISMO Y RELIGIOSIDAD POPULAR. Pastoral Popular (Bogotá) 22, 1: 16-25.

SEPULVEDA, Juan, 1981b, PENTECOSTALISMO Y RELIGIOSIDAD POPULAR. Pastoral Popular (Bogotá) 32, 1: 178-187.

SEPULVEDA, Juan, 1987, EL NACIMIENTO Y DESAROLLO DE LAS IGLESIAS EVANGELICAS. In: Salinas 1987: 247-289.

SEPULVEDA, Juan, 1988, PENTECOSTALISMO Y DEMOCRACIA: UNA INTERPRETACION DE SUS RELACIONES. In: Chacon 1988: 229-250.

SEPULVEDA, Juan, 1989, PENTECOSTALISM AS POPULAR RELIGIOSITY. International Review of Mission 78, 309, 80-88.

Bibliography 303

SEPULVEDA, Juan, 1992, EL CRECIMIENTO DEL MOVIMIENTO PENTECOS-
TAL EN AMERICA LATINA. In: Alvarez 1992: 77-88.
SEPULVEDA, Juan, 1994, THE PERSPECTIVE OF CHILEAN PENTECOSTAL-
ISM. Journal of Pentecostal Theology 4, 41-49.
SEPULVEDA, Juan (ed.), 1984, ANTOLOGIA SOBRE EL PENTECOSTALISMO.
Santiago de Chile: Comunidad Teológica Evangélica. [Chile]
SEPULVEDA, Narciso, 1992a, BREVE SINTESIS HISTORICA DEL MOVIMIEN-
TO PENTECOSTAL EN CHILE. In: Alvarez 1992: 37-45.
SEPULVEDA, Narciso, 1992b, LA PASTORAL PENTECOSTAL: UN CASO DE
MINISTERIO AUTOCTONO. In: Alvarez 1992: 147-153.
SEXTON, James D., 1987, PROTESTANTISM AND MODERNIZATION IN TWO
GUATEMALAN TOWNS. American Ethnologist 5: 280-302.
SHALLY, H., 1966, O DOM DA CURA. In: O espírito... 1966: 86-88.
SHAPIRO, Samuel (ed.), 1967, INTEGRATION OF MAN AND SOCIETY IN LA-
TIN AMERICA. Notre Dame, Ind.: University of Notre Dame Press. [Cf. Yuasa
1967]
SHAULL, Richard M., 1957-58, PROTESTANTISM IN LATIN AMERICA, 1. BRA-
ZIL. Religion in Life 27: 5-14.
SHUSTER, Robert, 1985, DOCUMENTARY SOURCES IN THE UNITED
STATES FOR FOREIGN MISSIONS RESEARCH: A SELECT BIBLIOGRA-
PHY AND CHECKLIST. International Bulletin of Missionary Research 9, 1: 19-
29.
SIEBENEICHLER, Flávio, 1976, CATOLICISMO POPULAR, PENTECOSTISMO,
KIRCHE: RELIGION IN LATEINAMERIKA. Bern: Lang, Regensburger Studien
zur Theologie no. 3.
SIEPIERSKI, Paulo, 1987, EVANGELIZAÇÃO NO BRASIL: UM PERFIL DO
PROTESTANTISMO BRASILEIRO; O CASO PERNAMBUCO. São Paulo:
Sepal.
SILLETA, Alfredo, 1986, LAS SECTAS INVADEN LA ARGENTINA. Buenos Aires:
Contrapunto. (1991, 7a. edición ampliada)
SILLETA, Alfredo, 1989, MULTINACIONALES DE LA FE: RELIGION, SECTAS
E IGLESIA ELECTRONICA. Buenos Aires: Contrapunto.
SILLETA, Alfredo, 1990, TU ERES EL AMOR DE DIOS. Buenos Aires: Puntosur.
SILLETA, Alfredo, 1992, SECTAS: CUANDO EL PARAISO ES UN INFIERNO.
Buenos Aires: Meridion.
SILVA, Manuel, 1991, A BRAZILIAN CHURCH COMES TO NEW YORK. Pneuma
(The Journal of the Society for Pentecostal Studies) 13, 2, 161-165. [Igreja Universal
do Reino de Deus]
SILVA, Orlando, and Joel STEVANNATTO, 1992, EL PENTECOSTALISMO EN
BRASIL. In: Alvarez 1992: 17-35.
SILVA FILHO, Osmar Luiz da, 1991, NOVAS IGREJAS EM FORTALEZA: O
AVANÇO PENTECOSTAL. Comunicações do ISER 10, 40: 48-57.
SIMILOX SALAZAR, Vitalino, 1989, EVANGELIZACION Y TEOLOGIA, DESDE
UNA PERSPECTIVA MAYA-GUATEMALTECA. In: El Protestantismo..., pp.
87-99.
SIMONS, Marlise, 1982, LATIN AMERICA'S NEW GOSPEL. New York Times
Magazine, Nov. 7, 1982, 45.

SIMONS, Marlise, 1986, PROTESTANT SECTS, FORMERLY SCORNED, NOW FIND EL SALVADOR IS FERTILE GROUND. New York Times, 20 enero.

SIMPSON, George Eaton, 1956, JAMAICAN REVIVALIST CULTS. Social and Economic Studies (Kingston) 5: 321-414.

SIMPSON, George Eaton, 1970, RELIGIOUS CULTS OF THE CARIBBEAN: TRINIDAD, JAMAICA AND HAITI. Río Piedras, Puerto Rico: University of Puerto Rico Press, Institute of Caribbean Studies.

SIMPSON, George Eaton, 1976, RELIGIONS OF THE CARIBBEAN. In: Rotberg & Kilson 1976.

SIMPSON, George Eaton, 1978, BLACK RELIGIONS IN THE NEW WORLD. New York: Columbia University Press.

SINCLAIR, John H. (ed.), 1967, 1976, PROTESTANTISM IN LATIN AMERICA: A BIBLIOGRAPHICAL GUIDE. Austin, Tex.: The Hispanic American Institute; 2nd edition, South Pasadena, Calif.: William Carey Library.

SIVAN, Emmanuel, and Gabriel Almond (eds.), 1994, ACCOUNTING FOR FUNDAMENTALISM. Chicago: University of Chicago Press. [Cf. Stoll 1994]

SKAR, Harald O., 1987, QUEST FOR A NEW COVENANT: THE ISRAELITA MOVEMENT IN PERU. In: Skar y Salomon 1987: 233-266.

SKAR, Harald O.; SALOMON, Frank (eds.), 1987, NATIVES AND NEIGHBORS IN SOUTH AMERICA. ANTHROPOLOGICAL ESSAYS. Göteborg: Göteborgs Etnografisk Museum. [Cf. Skar 1987]

SLAY, James L., 1969, THE CHURCH OF GOD IN SOUTH AMERICA. Church of God Evangel 58: 4-7.

SLOCUM, Marianna; HOLMES, Sam (eds.), 1963, WHO BROUGHT THE WORD. Santa Ana, Calif.: Wycliffe Bible Translators, Summer Institute of Linguistics.

SMITH, Ashley, s.f.,1975, PENTECOSTALISM IN JAMAICA. Kingston: Mark Lane. [The William Hammett Lecture 1975, Methodist Book Centre]

SMITH. Ashley, 1982, REAL ROOTS AND POTTED PLANTS: REFLECTIONS ON THE CARIBBEAN CHURCH. Kingston: Mandeville.

SMITH, Dennis A., 1991, COMING OF AGE: A REFLECTION ON PENTECOSTALS, POLITICS AND POPULAR RELIGION IN GUATEMALA. Pneuma (The Journal of the Society for Pentecostal Studies), 13, 2, 131-139.

SMITH, W. Douglas, 1976, TOWARD CONTINUOUS MISSION: STRATEGIZING FOR THE EVANGELIZATION OF BOLIVIA. South Pasadena, Calif.: William Carey Library.

SOARES, Luiz Eduardo, 1993, A GUERRA DOS PENTECOSTAIS CONTRA O AFRO-BRASILEIRO: DIMENSÕES DEMOCRÁTICAS DO CONFLITO RELIGIOSO NO BRASIL. Comunicações do ISER 12, 44: 43-50.

SOBERAL, José Dimas, 1981, QUANTAS SECTAS HAY EN PUERTO RICO.El Visitante 3.

SONEIRA, Jorge, 1991, LOS ESTUDIOS SOCIOLOGICOS SOBRE EL PENTECOSTALISMO EN AMERICA LATINA. Sociedad y Religión 8, 60-68.

SONEIRA, Jorge, 1994, BIOGRAFIA Y RELIGIOSIDAD PENTECOSTAL: UNA APROXIMACION AL ESTUDIO DE LAS CARACTERISTICAS SOCIO-BIO-GRAFICAS DEL CREYENTE PENTECOSTAL. In: Frigerio 1994: 44-60.

SORIA FLORES, Abraham, 1984, EL PROBLEMA DE LAS SECTAS. Senderos 19: 81-91.

SPADAFORA, Ana, 1994, CREENCIAS MILENARISTAS E IDENTIDAD RELI-
GIOSA PENTECOSTAL: EL MINISTERIO ONDAS DE AMOR Y PAZ. In:
Frigerio 1994: 113-127.

SPITTLER, Russell, 1975, WORLD'S LARGEST CONGREGATION: A CATHE-
DRAL IN CHILE. Christianity Today, Jan. 17, 33-39.

SPOERER, Sergio, 1984, LAS TRANSFORMACIONES DEL CAMPO RELIGIOSO
EN AMERICA LATINA: UN ENSAYO DE INTERPRETACION. Primer Congreso Chileno de Sociólogos: 1984.

SPOERER, Sergio, 1986, PENTECOTISME ET RELIGIOSITE POPULAIRE AU
CHILI. Notes et Études Documentaires 4815: 97-110.

SPOERER, Sergio, 1986, RELIGIOSIDAD POPULAR Y CULTURA DEMOCRA-
TICA. Santiago de Chile: Instituto Latinoamericana de Estudios Transnacionales.
Ponencia Segundo Congreso Chileno de Sociología, 12-14 Agosto 1986.

SPRING, Beth, 1985, NICARAGUA–THE GOVERNMENT'S HEAVY HAND
FALLS ON BELIEVERS: SANDINISTAS CRACK DOWN ON PROTES-
TANT ACTIVITY. Christianity Today 29, 18: 51-52.

STAHEL, Tomás, 1985, LAS SECTAS EN EL PARAGUAY, ENTREVISTA A
MONS. CUQUEJO. Acción, Revista Paraguaya de Reflexión y Diálogo 70 (17, 3):
20-24.

STAM, Juan B., 1984, PROYECTO EVANGELIZADOR DE LAS IGLESIAS
PROTESTANTES EN COSTA RICA. Senderos (Instituto Teológico de América
Central) 20: 41-57.

STEVENS-ARROYO, Antonio M., 1981, THE INDIGENOUS ELEMENTS IN THE
POPULAR RELIGION OF THE PUERTO RICANS. New York: Fordham
University. [Ph.D.]

STIPE, Claude, 1980, ANTHROPOLOGISTS VERSUS MISSIONARIES: THE
INFLUENCE OF PRESUPPOSITIONS. Current Anthropology: 21,165-179.

STIPE, Claude, 1983, THE ANTHROPOLOGICAL PERSPECTIVE IN "IS GOD
AN AMERICAN?". Anthropologists and Missionaries: Part II: 26,117-138.

STOKES, Louie W., s.f., HISTORIA DEL MOVIMIENTO PENTECOSTAL EN LA
ARGENTINA. Buenos Aires: author's edition.

STOLL, David, 1982, FISHERS OF MEN OR FOUNDERS OF EMPIRE?: THE WY-
CLIFFE BIBLE TRANSLATORS IN LATIN AMERICA. London: Zed Press.

STOLL, David, 1983, WYCLIFFE BIBLE TRANSLATORS: NOT TELLING THE
WHOLE STORY. The Other Side: February, 20-25; 38-39.

STOLL, David, 1984, "¿CON QUE DERECHO ADOCTRINAN USTEDES A
NUESTROS INDIGENAS?": LA POLEMICA EN TORNO AL INSTITUTO
LINGUISTICO DE VERANO. América Indígena 44, 1: 9-23.

STOLL, David, 1985, PESCADORES DE HOMBRES O FUNDADORES DE IMPE-
RIO. Quito: Abya-yala, Centro de Estudios y Promocion del Desarrollo. [Wycliffe,
SIL]

STOLL, David, 1985, LA IGLESIA DEL VERBO EN EL TRIANGULO IXIL DE
GUATEMALA, 1982. Civilización 3: 83-109.

STOLL, David, 1986, WHAT SHOULD WYCLIFFE DO? Missiology: 14, 37-45.

STOLL, David, 1990, A PROTESTANT REFORMATION IN LATIN AMERICA?
The Christian Century: Jan. 17, 44-48.

STOLL, David, 1990, IS LATIN AMERICA TURNING PROTESTANT? THE POLITICS OF EVANGELICAL GROWTH. Berkeley etc.: University of California Press.

STOLL, David, 1993, INTRODUCTION: RETHINKING PROTESTANTISM IN LATIN AMERICA. In: Garrard-Burnett and Stoll 1993: 1-19.

STOLL, David, 1994, 'JESUS IS LORD OF GUATEMALA': THE PROSPECTS FOR EVANGELICAL REFORM IN A DEATH SQUAD STATE. In: Sivan and Almond 1994.

STOLL, Sandra J., 1983, EMBU, ELEIÇÕES DE 1982: A MOBILIZAÇãO POLITICA DE CEBS E PENTECOSTAIS, UM ESTUDO DE CASO. Comunicações do ISER, 6: 22-43.

STOLL, Sandra J., 1986, PULPITO E PALANQUE: RELIGIÃO E POLITICA NAS ELEIÇÕES DA GRANDE SÃO PAULO. Campinas SP: Unicamp. [M.A. Thesis]

SUENENS, Cardinal Léon-Joseph; CAMARA, Dom Helder, 1980, CHARISMATIC RENEWAL AND SOCIAL ACTION: A DIALOGUE. London: Darton, Longman & Todd, Malines Document 3.

SUENENS, L.-J.; CAMARA, Helder, 1979, RENOUVEAU DANS L'ESPRIT ET SERVICE DE L'HOMME. Bruxelles: Lumen Vitae.

SWEENEY, Ernest S., 1970, FOREIGN MISSIONARIES IN ARGENTINA, 1938-1962: A STUDY OF DEPENDENCE. Cuernavaca, México: Centro Intercultural de Documentación, Sondeos 68.

SYLVESTRE, J., 1986, IRMÃO VOTA EM IRMÃO. Brasília: Pergaminho. [Brazil]

SYLVESTRE, J., 1988, OS EVANGELICOS, A CONSTITUINTE E AS ELEIÇÕES MUNICIPAIS. Brasília: Papiro. [Brazil]

SYMES, A. Patrick, 1955, ACTION STATIONS COLOMBIA. London: Christian Literature Crusade. World Wide Evangelization Crusade.

SYNAN, Vinson, 1973, THE OLD-TIME POWER. A HISTORY OF THE PENTECOSTAL HOLINESS CHURCH. Franklin Springs, Ga.: Advocate Press.

SYNDER, Howard A., 1976, METODISMO E PENTECOSTISMO. DESENVOLVIMENTO HISTORICO. Simpósio (São Paulo) 14: 18-24. [Brazil]

T

TALAVERA, Carlos, 1976, THE CHARISMATIC RENEWAL AND CHRISTIAN SOCIAL COMMITMENT IN LATIN AMERICA. New Covenant 6: 2,3.

TARDUCCI, Monica, 1993, PENTECOSTALISMO Y RELACIONES DE GENERO: UNA REVISION. In: Frigerio 1993, I: 81-96.

TARDUCCI, Monica, 1994, ¿LAS MUJERES EN EL MOVIMIENTO PENTECOSTAL: SUMISION O LIBERACION? In: Frigerio 1994: 60-80.

TAVARES, L., 1966, A MENSAGEM PENTECOTISTA E A REALIDADE BRASILEIRA. In: O espírito... 1966: 33-36.

TAVARES, Levy G., s.f., MINHA PATRIA PARA CRISTO. São Paulo/Brasília: author's edition. [Brazil, O Brasil Para Cristo]

TAYLOR, Clyde W.; GOGGINS, Wade T. (eds.), 1961, PROTESTANT MISSIONS IN LATIN AMERICA, A STATISTICAL SURVEY. Washington, D.C.: Evangelical Foreign Missions Association.

TAYLOR, Jack E., 1962, GOD'S MESSENGERS TO MEXICO'S MASSES. Eugene, Ore.: Institute of Church Growth.

TAYLOR, Robert B., 1983, THE SUMMER INSTITUTE OF LINGUISTICS/WY-CLIFFE BIBLE TRANSLATORS IN ANTHROPOLOGICAL PERSPECTIVE. Anthropologists and Missionaries: Part II: 26, 93-116.

TEIXEIRA MONTEIRO, Douglas, 1984, IGREJAS, SEITAS E AGENCIAS: ASPEC-TOS DE UM ECUMENICISMO POPULAR. In: Valle y Queiróz 1984: 81-111. [Brazil, see also Alves 1984]

TENNEKES, Juan, 1973, LA NUEVA VIDA, EL MOVIMIENTO PENTECOSTAL EN LA SOCIEDAD CHILENA. Amsterdam: Vrije Universiteit, mimeo.

TENNEKES, J., 1978, LE MOUVEMENT PENTECOTISTE CHILIEN ET LA PO-LITIQUE. Social Compass 25, 1: 55-80. [See als Lalive d'Épinay 1978]

TENNEKES, Hans, 1985, EL MOVIMIENTO PENTECOSTAL EN LA SOCIEDAD CHILENA. Amsterdam/Iquique: Universidad Libre/CIREN, Publicaciones Oca-sionales no. 1.

Teologia de..., 1994, TEOLOGIA DE RESULTADOS. COMO FUNCIONA A IGREJA UNIVERSAL, UMA MULTINACIONAL QUE CRESCE EM 32 PAÍ-SES E VANÇA SOBRE ESPAÇOS CATÓLICOS NA ÁREA ASSISTENCIAL. Istoé Senhor, 14 de dezembro.

The Church..., 1982, THE CHURCH IN EL SALVADOR. Bruselas: Pro Mundi Vita Dossiers.

The New Missionary..., 1982, THE NEW MISSIONARY, PROCLAIMING CHRIST'S MESSAGE IN DARING AND DISPUTED WAYS. Time, Dec. 27, pp. 38-44.

The Rise..., 1987, THE RISE OF THE RELIGIOUS RIGHT IN CENTRAL AMER-ICA. Resource Center Bulletin (Albuquerque, New Mexico), 10.

The Rockefeller..., THE ROCKEFELLER REPORT ON THE AMERICAS. New York: Quadrangle Paperback.

THIESSEN, John C., 1961, A SURVEY OF WORLD MISSIONS. Chicago: Moody

THORNTON, W. Philip, 1984, RESOCIALIZATION: ROMAN CATHOLICS BECOMING PROTESTANT IN COLOMBIA. Anthropological Quarterly 57, 1: 28-37.

TOOP, Walter R., 1972, ORGANIZED RELIGIOUS GROUPS IN A VILLAGE OF NORTHEASTERN BRAZIL. Luso-Brazilian Review 9, 2: 58-77. [Assembléia de Deus]

TORT, Maria Isabel; PESSINA, Leonor; SONEIRA, A. Jorge, 1992, EL PENTE-COSTALISMO EN LA ARGENTINA. UN ESTUDIO DE CASO: EL MINIS-TERIO ONDAS DE AMOR Y PAZ DEL PASTOR HECTOR A. GIMENEZ. Buenos Aires: IDICSO/Universidad del Salvador.

TORT, Maria Isabel; PESSINA, Leonor; SONEIRA, A. Jorge, 1993, EL MINISTERIO "ONDAS DE AMOR Y PAZ" DEL PASTOR HECTOR ANIBAL GIMENEZ. In: Frigerio 1993, II: 49-79.

TOWNSEND, William Cameron, 1952, LAZARO CARDENAS. MEXICAN DEM-OCRAT. Ann Arbor, Mich. [Wycliffe]

TOWNSEND, William Cameron, 1972, THEY FOUND A COMMON LAN-GUAGE. New York. [Wycliffe]

TOWNSEND, William Cameron, 1974, HALLARON UNA LENGUA COMUN. COMUNIDAD A TRAVES DE LA EDUCACION BILINGUE. México: Septentenas 131. [Wycliffe]
TOWNSEND, William Cameron, 1975, LAZARO CARDENAS. DEMOCRATA MEXICANO. Barcelona. [Wycliffe]
Traficando..., 1983, TRAFICANDO CON LA FE DEL PUEBLO. Signo 61.
TRIGO, Pedro, 1975, EL PENTECOSTALISMO CATOLICO EN VENEZUELA. SU MARCO HISTORICO. SIC (Caracas) 372; also in: Perspectivas de Diálogo (Montevideo) 10, 94: 113.
TROUTMAN, Charles H., 1971, EVANGELICALS AND THE MIDDLE CLASSES IN LATIN AMERICA. Evangelical Missions Quarterly 7, 2-3: 31-79, 154-163.
TRUJILLO, Jorge, 1981, LOS OSCUROS DISEÑIOS DE DIOS Y DEL IMPERIO, EL INSTITUTO LINGUISTICO DE VERANO EN EL ECUADOR. Quito: Centro de Investigaciones y Estudios Económicos.
TSCHUY, Theo (ed.), 1969, EXPLOSIVES LATEINAMERIKA, DER PROTESTANTISMUS INMITTEN DER SOZIALEN REVOLUTION. Berlin: Lettner Verlag.
TURNER, Frederick C., 1970, EL PROTESTANTISMO Y EL CAMBIO SOCIAL EN LATINOAMERICA. Revista Paraguaya de Sociología 7, 17: 5-27.
TURNER, Frederick C., 1970, PROTESTANTISM AND POLITICS IN CHILE AND BRAZIL (REVIEW ARTICLE). Comparative Studies in Society and History 12, 2: 213-229.
TURNER, Paul R., 1979, RELIGIOUS CONVERSION AND COMMUNITY DEVELOPMENT. Journal for the Scientific Study of Religion 18, 3: 252-260. [Mexico, Wycliffe]
TURON, Simeón Jiménez, 1984, MUERTE CULTURAL CON ANESTESIA. América Indígena 44, 1: 95-99. [Venezuela, Wycliffe]

U

UNDIKS LABARCA, Andrés, 1985, EL CULTO PENTECOSTAL, UNA APROXIMACION SEMIOLOGICA. [Chile, M.A. Thesis, Universidad de Concepción]
URREA, Juan Carlos, 1992, LOS NUEVOS MOVIMIENTOS RELIGIOSOS EN AMERICA LATINA. Santiago: Ediciones Paulinas.

V

VACCARO, Gabriel Osvaldo, 1982, ¡ASI VEO AL SEÑOR!: EN LA IGLESIA, EN LAS LUCHAS ECLESIASTICAS, EN EL GOBIERNO Y RENOVACION DE LA IGLESIA ETC. Buenos Aires: author's edition.
VACCARO, Gabriel Osvaldo, 1988, IDENTIDAD PENTECOSTAL. Quito: CLAI.
VACARRO, Gabriel, 1992, APORTES DEL PENTECOSTALISMO AL MOVIMIENTO ECUMENICO. In: Alvarez 1992: 227-233.
VALDERREY, José, 1985, LAS SECTAS EN CENTROAMERICA. Bruselas: Pro Mundi Vita Boletin no. 100.
VALDERREY, José, 1985, SECTS IN CENTRAL AMERICA. Bruselas: Pro Mundi Vita Bulletin no. 100.

VALENCIA, Eduardo et al., 1988, EN TIERRA EXTRAÑA. ITINERARIO DEL PUEBLO PENTECOSTAL CHILENO. Santiago: Editorial Amerinda.

VALLE, Edênio, and José J. QUEIROZ, (eds.), 1984, A CULTURA DO POVO. São Paulo: Cortez. [Cf. Alves 1984, Monteiro 1984]

VALLE, Rogerio, and Ingrid SARTI, 1994, O RISCO DAS COMPARAÇÕES APRESSADAS. In: Antoniazzi 1994b: 7-13.

VALPUESTA, José, 1985, ANTE LA INVASION DE LAS SECTAS. Acción, Revista Paraguaya de Reflexión y Diálogo 70 (17, 3): 27-31.

VALVERDE, J., 1987, SECTARISMO RELIGIOSO Y CONFLICTO SOCIAL. Polémica 3, 2: 15-25.

VALVERDE, J., 1989, SECTARISMO RELIGIOSO Y DESMOVILIZACION SOCIAL. San José: DEI.

VALVERDE, Jaime, 1991a, PENTECOSTALIZACION Y CAMBIO SOCIAL (EL CASO DE HONDURAS). In: Samandu 1991a: 151-181.

VALVERDE, Jaime, 1991b, EFECTOS SOCIALES E IDEOLOGICOS DE LAS SECTAS DE ORIGEN PROTESTANTE EN COSTA RICA. In: Samandú 1991a: 229-266.

VARGAS, Cristobal, 1983, GUATEMALA NUEVO JERUSALEN? Noticias Aliadas 43.

VASQUEZ, Galo E., 1984, EL EVANGELISTA Y LA PREPARACION DE SUS CAMPAÑAS. In: Documentos... 1984.

VALASCO PEREZ, Carlos, 1982, LA CONQUISTA ARMADA Y ESPIRITUAL DE LA NUEVA ANTEGUERRA. Oaxaca, México: Progreso Bellini.

VELOSO, M., 1960, VISION GENERAL DE LOS PENTECOSTALES CHILENOS. Anales de la Facultad de Teología, (Universidad Católica de Chile) 11.

VERGARA, Ignacio, 1955, AVANCE DE LOS "EVANGELICOS" EN CHILE. Mensaje 3, 41: 257-262.

VERGARA, Ignacio, 1962, EL PROTESTANTISMO EN CHILE. Santiago: Ediciones del Pacífico.

VERTOVEC, Steven A., 1984, THE EAST INDIANS OF TRINIDAD - THEIR SOCIAL, CULTURAL AND RELIGIOUS CONTEXT. Oxford: University of Oxford, Faculty of Anthropology and Geography, Nuffield College. Ponencia. [Chapter 3 Religious Pluralism in Trinidad]

VICENCIO, Ernesto Guerra, 1984, LA ETICA SOCIAL EN LA MISION WESLEYANA NACIONAL. Santiago: CTE.

VIDAL M., Ana M., 1986, EL PENTECOSTAL Y "SU ACTITUD SOCIOPOLOTICA EN EL CHILE DE HOY". Concepción: CEMURI, Estudio Socio-Religioso no. 1.

VINGREN, Gunner, 1917, DIE VERKÜNDIGUNG DES EVANGELIUMS INMITTEN VON LÄRMENDEN PöBEL. DAS AUSGIESSEN DES HEILIGEN GEISTES IN BRASILIEN. Verheissung des Vaters 10, 1: 13-18.

Visión Mundial..., 1984, VISION MUNDIAL EN EL ECUADOR. Quito: CEPLAES, Serie Educación Popular, Cuaderno no. 2.

W

WAGNER, Pedro, 1968, CUIDADO QUE AHI VIENEN LOS PENTECOSTALES. Miami, Fla.: Editorial Vida.

WAGNER, C. Peter, 1970, LATIN AMERICAN THEOLOGY: RADICAL OR EVANGELICAL? Grand Rapids, Mich.: Eerdmans.

WAGNER, C. Peter, 1970, THE PROTESTANT MOVEMENT IN BOLIVIA. South Pasadena, Calif.: William Carey Library.

WAGNER, C. Peter, 1973, LOOK OUT! THE PENTECOSTALS ARE COMING. Carol Stream, Ill.: Creation House.

WAYMIRE, Bob; WAGNER, C. Peter, n.d., THE CHURCH GROWTH SURVEY HANDBOOK. Global Church Growth Survey Handbook.

WEATON, Felipe, 1991, LAS IGLESIAS PENTECOSTALES EN LA BUSQUEDA DE SU MISION ANTE LA CRISE NACIONAL. Amanecer (CAV, Managua), no. 71.

WEBER, Wilfried, 1978, CHARISMATISCHE BEWEGUNG UND THEOLOGIE DER BEFREIUNG. Zeitschrift für Missionswissenschaft und Religionswissenschaft 62, 1: 40-45.

WEBSTER, Douglas, 1964, PATTERNS OF PART-TIME MINISTRY IN SOME CHURCHES IN SOUTH AMERICA. London: World Dominion Press.

WEDEMANN, Walter, 1977, HISTORY OF PROTESTANT MISSIONS TO BRAZIL, 1850-1914. Louisville, Ky.: Southern Baptist Theological Seminary. [Ph.D.]

WEDENOJA, William, 1978, RELIGION AND ADAPTATION IN RURAL JAMAICA. San Diego: University of California. [Ph.D.]

WEDENOJA, William, 1980, MODERNIZATION AND THE PENTECOSTAL MOVEMENT IN JAMAICA. In: Glazier 1980: 27-48.

WESTMEIER, Karl-Wilhelm, 1986, THE ENTHUSIASTIC PROTESTANTS OF BOGOTA, COLOMBIA: REFLECTIONS ON THE GROWTH OF A MOVEMENT. International Review of Mission 85, 297: 13-24.

WESTMEIER, Karl-Wilhelm, 1987, RECONCILING HEAVEN AND EARTH: THE TRANSCENDENTAL ENTHUSIASM AND GROWTH OF AN URBAN PROTESTANT COMMUNITY, BOGOTA, COLOMBIA. Bern: Lang.

WHITTEN, Norman E., 1981, CULTURAL TRANSFORMATIONS AND ETHNICITY IN MODERN ECUADOR. Urbana: University of Illinois Press. [Cf. Muratorio 1981]

WIETESKA, Mike; WIETESKA, Lorna, 1985, BILL EL PENTECOSTAL: UN HOMBRE CON UNA VISION (BIOGRAFIA DE BILL DROST, MISIONERO PENTECOSTAL EN COLOMBIA). Barcelona: CLIE.

WILGUS, A. Curtis (ed.), 1955, THE CARIBBEAN: ITS CULTURE. Gainesville, Fla. [Cf. Rycroft 1955]

WILHELMSEN, Jean, s.f., TRAILS THROUGH TRINIDAD. Des Moines, Iowa: Open Bible Standard Missions.

WILKERSON, J.K., 1980, CULTURAL TRADITION AND CARIBBEAN IDENTITY. Gainesville: University of Florida, Center for Latin American Studies. [Cf. Römer 1980]

WILLEMS, Emílio, 1960, PROTESTANTISMUS UND KLASSENSTRUKTUR IN CHILE. Kölner Zeitschrift für Soziologie und Sozialpsychologie 12: 632-671.

WILLEMS, Emílio, 1963, PROTESTANTISMUS UND KULTURWANDEL IN BRASILIEN UND CHILE. Kölner Zeitschrift für Soziologie und Sozialpschologie 15, 7: 307-333.

WILLEMS, Emílio, 1964, PROTESTANTISM AND CULTURE CHANGE IN BRAZIL AND CHILE. In: d'Antonio y Pike 1964: 91-108.

WILLEMS, Emílio, 1965, RELIGIöSER PLURALISMUS UND KLASSENSTRUK-TUR IN BRASILIEN UND CHILE. Internationales Jahrbuch für Religionssoziologie 1.

WILLEMS, Emílio, 1966, RELIGIOUS MASS MOVEMENTS AND SOCIAL CHANGE IN BRAZIL. In: Baklanoff 1966: 205-232.

WILLEMS, Emílio, 1967, FOLLOWERS OF THE NEW FAITH, CULTURE CHANGE AND THE RISE OF PROTESTANTISM IN BRAZIL AND CHILE. Nashville, Tenn.: Vanderbilt University Press.

WILLEMS, Emílio, 1967, VALIDATION OF AUTHORITY IN PENTECOSTAL SECTS OF CHILE AND BRAZIL. Journal for the Scientific Study of Religion 6: 253-258.

WILLEMS, Emílio, 1967, EL PROTESTANTISMO Y LOS CAMBIOS CULTU-RALES EN BRASIL Y CHILE. Barcelona: Herder.

WILLEMS, Emílio, 1968, CULTURE CHANGE AND THE RISE OF PROTES-TANTISM IN BRAZIL AND CHILE. In: Eisenstadt 1968: 184-210.

WILLEMS, Emílio, 1969, RELIGIOUS PLURALISM AND CLASS-STRUCTURE: BRAZIL AND CHILE. In: Robertson 1969: 361-383.

WILLEMS, Emílio, 1972, EL PROTESTANTISMO Y LOS CAMBIOS CULTU-RALES EN BRASIL Y CHILE. Barcelona: Herder.

WILSON, Everett A., 1983, SANGUINE SAINTS: PENTECOSTALISM IN EL SALVADOR. Church History 52, 2: 186-198.

WILSON, Everett A., 1988, THE CENTRAL AMERICAN EVANGELICALS: FROM PROTEST TO PRAGMATISM. International Review of Mission 77, 305: 94-106.

WILSON, Samuel (ed.), 1979, MISSION HANDBOOK: NORTH AMERICAN PROTESTANT MINISTRIES OVERSEAS. Monrovia, Calif.: MARC (Missions Advanced Research and Communication Center).

WIRPSA, Leslie G., 1985, EVANGELICOS Y PENTECOSTALES ASUMEN FE ANCLADA EN EL PASADO. Noticias Aliadas, 14 noviembre 1985: 3,4.

WRIGHT, Pablo G., 1992, TOBA PENTECOSTALISM REVISITED. Social Compass 39, 3.

WULFHORST, Ingo, 1995, O PENTECOSTALISMO NO BRASIL. Estudos Teológicos (São Leopoldo RS) 35, 1, 7-20.

WYNARCZYK, Hilario H., 1989, TRES EVANGELISTAS CARISMATICOS: OMAR CABRERA, ANNACONDIA, GIMENEZ. Buenos Aires, Author's edition.

WYNARCZYK, Hilario H., 1993, CARLOS ANNACONDIA: UN ESTUDIO DE CASO EN NEOPENTECOSTALISMO. In: Frigerio 1993, II: 80-97.

WYNARCZYK, Hilario, 1995, LA GUERRA ESPIRITUAL EN EL CAMPO EVANGELICO. Sociedad y Religión 13: 111-126.

WYNARCZYK, Hilario H., 1993, CARLOS ANNACONDIA: UN ESTUDIO DE CASO EN NEOPENTECOSTALISMO. In: Frigerio 1993, II: 80-97.

WYNARCZYK, Hilario, and Pablo SEMÁN, 1994, CAMPO EVANGELICO Y PENTECOSTALISM EN LA ARGENTINA. In: Frigerio 1994: 10-29.

WYNARCZYK, Hilario, Pablo SEMÁN, and Mercedes de MAJO, 1995, PANORA-MA ACTUAL DEL MUNDO EVANGELICO. Buenos Aires: Facultad Internacional de Educación Teológica.

Y

YAMILETH, Guido, 1984, PROLIFERACION DE GRUPOS RELIGIOSOS. ¿INOVACION EN LAS IGLESIAS O DESPERTAR NEO-CONSERVADOR? Aportes (San José, Costa Rica) 4, 18: 26-32.

YUASA, Key, 1966, A STUDY OF THE PENTECOSTAL MOVEMENT IN BRAZIL: ITS IMPORTANCE. The Reformed and Presbyterian World 29: 63-72.

YUASA, Key, 1967, INDIGENOUS EXPRESSIONS OF PROTESTANTISM. In Shapiro 1967: 202-208. [Brazil]

Z

ZANUSO, Hermenegildo, 1986, IGLESIAS Y SECTAS EN AMERICA LATINA. México, D.F.: Librería Parroquial de Clavéria.

ZAPATA ARCEYUZ, Virgilio, 1981, HISTORIA DE LA IGLESIA EVANGELICA GUATEMALTECA. Guatemala: Serviprensa.

ZAPATA ARECYUZ, Virgilio, 1982, HISTORIA DE LA IGLESIA EVANGELICA EN GUATEMALA. Guatemala: Génesis Publicidad.

ZAPATA ARCEYUZ, Virgilio, 1984, EL EVANGELISTA Y EL ARTE DE LA COMUNICACION. In: Documentos... 1984.

ZARETSKY, Irving, I.; LEONE, Mark P. (eds.), 1974, RELIGIOUS MOVEMENTS IN CONTEMPORARY AMERICA. Princeton, N.J.: Princeton University Press. [Cf. Garrison 1974, Gerlach 1974, Goodman 1974]

ZAVALA HIDALGO, Rubén, 1989, HISTORIA DE LAS ASAMBLEAS DE DIOS DEL PERU. Lima: Ediciones Dios es Amor.

ZENTENO C., Edmundo (ed.), 1990, 1909-1989. 80 AÑOS DE LA IGLESIA METODISTA PENTECOSTAL EN CHILE. La Voz Pentecostal, 24: 1-80.

ZUB, Roberto, 1993, PROTESTANTISMO Y ELECCIONES EN NICARAGUA. ESTUDIO SOBRE LA ESTRATIFICACION SOCIO-RELIGIOSA Y LAS ACTITUDES POLITICO-ELECTORALES DE LOS PROTESTANTES EN NICARAGUA. Managua: Nicarao/CIEETS.

Author Index

Subject Index

About the Contributors

Henriëtte Barbara Boudewijnse
studied cultural anthropology at the Vrije Universiteit, Amsterdam,
and specialized in religious studies at the State University of Gro-
ningen, the Netherlands. She has published several articles on the
subjects of ritual and ritual studies, on fieldwork methodology, and
on the Catholic Charismatic Movement on Curaçao N.A. and in the
Netherlands. She is preparing a Ph.D. thesis on ritual theory.

André F. Droogers
is professor in the anthropology of religion at the Department of Cultural Anthropology and Sociology of Development of the Vrije Universiteit, Amsterdam, the Netherlands. He lectured and did fieldwork in Zaire and Brasil.

Angela Hoekstra
studied Cultural Anthropology at the Universtity of Utrecht, the
Netherlands. She did research on conservative protestantism in the
northern part of the Netherlands, and then turned to Pentecostalism
in Pernambuco, Brazil. Afterwards, she carried out research in the
field of Medical Anthropology among Yanomami and Ticuna groups
in Brazil, contributing to projects of a Dutch medical assistance organization.

Frans H. Kamsteeg

did anthropological fieldwork in Peru and Chile. His Ph.D. thesis deals with Chilean Pentecostalism and development policy. He has also published on the growth of Peruvian Pentecostal churches. At present he is lecturer at the Department of Culture, Organization and Management of the Vrije Universiteit, Amsterdam, and doing research on culture and identity processes in organizations.

Maria das Dores Campos Machado

is a sociologist holding a Ph.D. from the Instituto Universitário de Pesquisa do Rio de Janeiro. Her dissertation received recognition as the best of 1994 by Brazil's National Association of Graduate Studies and Research in the Social Sciences (ANPOCS). She is currently professor at the Universidade Federal Rural do Rio de Janeiro and MacArthur Foundation fellow. Publications include *Carismáticos e Pentecostais: Adesão Religiosa na Esfera Familiar.* Campinas: Editora Autores Associados, 1996.

Cecilia Mariz

is from Recife, Brazil. She holds a Ph.D. in Sociology of Culture and Religion from Boston University (1989) and presently teaches at the Universidade do Estado do Rio de Janeiro in Rio de Janeiro City . Her book *Coping with Poverty; Pentecostal and Base Communities in Brazil* was published by Temple University Press in 1994.

Daniel Miguez

is an Argentinean sociologist, who studied at the University of Buenos Aires. He now teaches sociology of religion at the University of the Center of the State of Buenos Aires. His Ph.D. studies at the Vrije Universiteit, Amsterdam, were on urban popular sectors and religion in Argentina, and especially on the growth of Pentecostalism during the 1980s.

Hanneke Slootweg

studied anthropology at the State University of Utrecht, the Netherlands, and did fieldwork on women and Pentecostalism in Chile. She currently works for the Chilean non-governmental organization TER in Iquique.

Marjo E.M. de Theije
is an anthropologist. She teaches at the Vrije Universiteit Amsterdam and did research in Brazil on religious brotherhoods in Minas Gerais and on pilgrimage and base communities in Pernambuco (with Cecília Mariz). She has published various articles on these topics. Currently she is finishing a book on Catholic lay groups in Garanhuns.

Allard Willemier Westra
is lecturer at the Department of Culture, Organization and Management of the Vrije Universiteit, the Netherlands. His Ph.D. research was on the Afro-Brazilian Candomblé religion.